enigma
books

ALEXANDER FEKLISOV

and

SERGEI KOSTIN

The Man
Behind the Rosenbergs

By the KGB Spymaster
who was the case officer of
Julius Rosenberg, Klaus Fuchs,
and helped resolve the
Cuban Missile Crisis

Introduction by Ronald Radosh

enigma books

Originally published in French under the title: *Confession d'un agent soviétique*
Translated by Catherine Dop

© enigma books 2001
Introduction copyright © Ronald Radosh 2001
© Éditions du Rocher, 1999

Printed in Canada

Library of Congress Cataloging-in-Publication Data

Feklisov, Aleksandr, 1914-
 [Confession d'un agent soviétique]
The man behind the Rosenbergs : by the KGB spymaster who was
the case officer of Julius Rosenberg, Klaus Fuchs, and helped resolve
the Cuban Missile Crisis / Alexander Feklisov and Sergei Kostin ;
introduction by Ronald Radosh.

 p. cm.

Includes bibliographical references and index.
ISBN: 1-929631-08-1
Translated from the French by Catherine Dop.

1. Feklisov, Alexander, 1914- 2. Rosenberg, Julius, 1918-1953.
3. Rosenberg, Ethel, 1915-1953. 4. Espionage, Soviet—United States.
5. Spies—Soviet Union—Biography. 6. Cuban Missile Crisis, 1962.
7. Soviet Unioin—Relations——United States. 8. United States—
Relations—Soviet Union. I. Kostin, Sergei. II. Radosh, Ronald.
III. Dop, Catherine, 1948- IV. Title. V. Title: Confession d'un agent
soviétique.

UB271.R92 F4513
327.1/2/0947 B

The Man Behind the Rosenbergs

Contents

Abbreviations

Abwher	German military intelligence, 1933-1945
Amtorg	Soviet trade organization based in New York City
Cheka	First Soviet Secret Police 1917-1922
CI	Committee of Information, Soviet intelligence coordination committee 1947-1952, also spelled KI
CIA	Central Intelligence Agency, U.S. foreign espionage
Comintern	Communist International 1919-1943, dissolved by Stalin
CPSU	Communist Party of the Soviet Union
CPUSA	Communist Part of the United States of America
DST	Direction de la Surveillance du Territoire, French counterintelligence
FBI	Federal Bureau of Investigation, U.S. counterespionage
FSB	*Federalnaya Sluzhba Bezopasnosti* – Federal Security Service – new name of the Russian internal security police; formerly the KGB
GDR	German Democratic Republic: East Germany from 1949-1989
GE	General Electric Corporation
Gestapo	Nazi Germany's secret police 1933-1945
GPU	Soviet Secret Police 1922-1934
GRU	Soviet military intelligence
INO	Soviet Foreign Intelligence 1920-1934 initials also used when referring to the PGU
KGB	Committee for State Security – included all the secret services of the USSR
MI5	British counterintelligence
MI6	British foreign intelligence
MID	Soviet foreign ministry
MGB	Ministry of State Security, 1946-1954
NKVD	People's Commissariat for Internal Affairs 1923-1943
NSA	National Security Agency – U.S. signals intelligence unit
OSS	Office of Strategic Services – American foreign espionage during the Second World War (predecessor of the CIA)

PGU   Soviet foreign intelligence from 1934 to 1991 also known as the First Chief Directorate of the KGB

SED   East German Socialist Unity Party 1949-1989

SIS   U.S. Army Signal Intelligence Service, predecessor of the NSA

Stasi   *Staatssicherheits* East German secret police and information service

SVR   *Sluzhba Vneshney Razvedki* foreign intelligence service of Russia since 1991 when it replaced the PGU department of the KGB.

Introduction

By *Ronald Radosh*

A lexander Feklisov, aka Alexander Fomin, aka Kalistrat, was
one of the KGB's top agents in the United States. As a KGB
Rezident in Washington, DC from 1960 to 1964, when he was known
as "Fomin," Feklisov was the KGB's intermediary with ABC News
reporter John Scali during the Cuban Missile Crisis; it was his message to the Kennedy administration from the USSR, that the
United States accept Soviet removal of its missiles in Cuba, in
exchange for a pledge that the island would never be invaded by the
USA, that formed the basis for the peaceful resolution of the crisis.
Indeed, if most Americans now are familiar with Feklisov's name, it
is from the portrayal of him in the recent Hollywood film "Thirteen
Days."

But Feklisov's role in America's past goes back much further
than the 1960s. From 1941 to 1946, Feklisov was a KGB officer
working at the Russian Consulate in New York City. It was in this
capacity that his superior, Anatoly Yatskov (alias Yakovlev), assigned
Feklisov the important task of recruiting personnel to engage in
military and industrial espionage against the United States. His most
famous agent, who had already been recruited by his predecessors
at the NKVD, whom he came to know as a cherished and intimate
friend, was Julius Rosenberg. Feklisov first made known his role as
Rosenberg's control officer in a television documentary aired on

the Discovery Channel in 1997. Readers of his own memoir will note immediately that the small amount of time allotted to him in a one hour TV special could only scratch the surface of his own amazing story.

For the first time, in a riveting narrative, Feklisov tells us of his impoverished childhood, his recruitment into the Soviet espionage apparatus, and how he came to be assigned to work first in the United States and later in Britain, where he was assigned to retrieve material from Klaus Fuchs. His story is important, however, not only for the fascinating details he provides about the life of a KGB agent working in the West. Rather, it provides major historical evidence that fills in the holes in the story of the spy ring put together by Julius Rosenberg, as well as confirms what most everyone now acknowledges, that Rosenberg was a major agent for the Soviets.

In effect, Feklisov was the man behind Julius Rosenberg. In espionage, the work conducted by a volunteer spy, acting for ideological reasons, depends on the establishment of a good working relationship with his spymaster. What Julius Rosenberg did not want, as do our contemporary spies, was money. Indeed, the few times when he did accept funds, it was to help expedite the planned escape of members of his ring, and he took the money very reluctantly. What Julius Rosenberg did want was acceptance, understanding that the Soviet Union appreciated his work and the risks he took, and that he be acknowledged as a fellow partisan fighting for the Communist future. It was all of this that Alexander Feklisov provided. Once Rosenberg was turned over to him, after a previous KGB operative had recruited him, Feklisov became his control, his father figure, his friend, and his comrade in arms. When Rosenberg was arrested and his fate sealed, Feklisov sunk into deep despair. Now, so many decades later, as he nears the end of his own life, he speaks for the first time about his treasured relationship with Rosenberg, which undoubtedly became the proudest episode in his long career with the KGB.

Since July 1995, when the National Security Agency and the CIA released the first batch of its so-called Venona files—the transcripts of double-encrypted Soviet codes sent and received by Soviet diplomatic missions in the United States—we have known, as

David Kahn, then scholar in residence at the NSA put it, that "the Venona intercepts show one thing beyond doubt, that the Rosenbergs spied for the Soviet Union against the United States." It also showed that two of Julius Rosenberg's friends, Al Sarant and Joel Barr, were part of his network, and that both men supplied top-secret material to him for transmission to the Soviets. At the time of Rosenberg's arrest, Barr and Sarant both fled the country, and spent the next few decades developing the military technology of the Soviet Union.

Despite the power of the Venona transcripts, the ardent defenders of the Rosenbergs' innocence persisted in arguing that they were deeply flawed. Robert Meeropol, the youngest son of Ethel and Julius Rosenberg, immediately told Associated Press that "the documents themselves don't tell you anything…You don't know whether the documents are made up out of nothing." Later, Robert and his brother Michael released a lengthy statement arguing that the NSA and CIA had "cooked" the information to justify the original prosecution of their parents, and that the code names for Julius in Venona, "Liberal" and "Antenna," were said to be Julius only by these agencies, and nothing in the documents themselves were proof that the Soviets had given these code names to their father.

For many on the Left, who are suspicious of any documents released by American national security agencies, especially by the CIA, FBI or NSA, the Venona transcripts proved very little. Now, in this memoir, Feklisov notes strongly that the transcripts are accurate, down to every detail, including the identification of the code names. Indeed, after praising the expertise of the American code breaker Meredith Gardner, Feklisov writes that he does not "know how it was possible, starting from pseudonyms and code names in our correspondence, to really identify so many Soviet secret agents, projects and locations," and he speculates that the American agencies were helped by "traitors or turncoats." But he stresses, "apart from a few errors, the decrypted messages are genuine." On the question of Venona, then, Feklisov's testimony should end the protest of the few remaining skeptics.

It is both the strength and the weakness of Alexander Feklisov's account, however, that he remains a true believer in the cause of

Soviet Communism. The American left-wing defenders of the Rosenbergs, from the time of their arrest to the present, waged their campaign on the grounds that the FBI, in order to create a war scare and to stifle growing opposition to the Truman Cold War policies, framed the couple. Feklisov's motive for telling their story is entirely different. He provides the details of Rosenberg's espionage, and that of the members of his ring, in order to give them their day in history—in order to allow the world to learn of their proud service to the international Communist movement, and therefore in his eyes, to world humanity.

Feklisov obviously feels, at this late stage in history, especially since the collapse of what he still views as the noble cause, that those who sacrificed so much on its behalf should now be publicly honored. Julius Rosenberg, who went to his death swearing that he was innocent, is therefore in Feklisov's eyes a hero. Harry Gold, the prosecution's chief witness, who to Feklisov "gave away the store" to the FBI and who testified against the Rosenbergs, is a villain. He calls Julius Rosenberg "an unreconstructed idealist," a "New York partisan" who like all soldiers, "did not want to betray his Russian comrades." He went to his death willingly because he was sure that he thought that having "helped the USSR fight the Nazis he had built a peaceful future for his children and for generations to come."

Indeed, Feklisov is chagrined that the current directors of the SVR, the re-named successor to the KGB, still do not want to publicly admit that Rosenberg was his agent, and that others he recruited, particularly Joel Barr, Alfred Sarant and William Perl, were key parts of his operation. As a friend and the main associate of Rosenberg in espionage, Feklisov does not want to leave this earth without restoring to history the honor he is sure Julius Rosenberg would have appreciated and desired had he lived. He writes that sitting in Moscow observing the trial, he wished that Julius had confessed, and had explained to his countrymen the noble motives that prompted him to spy for the Soviet Union. After all, he writes, Julius was like any solider who "brought our common victory closer to becoming reality." Rosenberg was so enamored with the Soviets, that when Feklisov's predecessor, Semyonov, recruited him, Julius told him: "I find it unfair that you should be fighting the common enemy alone. If I can do anything to help, you can count on me." His recruitment was that simple. It was the failure of his own agency, the KGB, Feklisov asserts, and the Soviet leadership, to not do all in its power to save their agent, either by instructing him to confess and be spared a death sentence, or to acknowledge his job and trade him for an American agent whom the KGB had caught. Feklisov even thinks that the KGB should have arranged for a better defense team, rather than leave the Rosenbergs in the hands of the inexperienced but well-meaning American Communist lawyer, Emanuel Bloch.

Here, where Feklisov engages in theorizing and speculation, his memoir takes on the cast of fantasy, and approaches a 1940s style apologia of the type common to old Bolshevik apparatchiks. He thinks honesty as to Julius Rosenberg's espionage would have allowed the USSR, whose international prestige he mistakenly believes "at that time was very high," to convince Americans that the Rosenbergs and their spy ring were not "Communist spies but anti-fascist activists." But of course they were Communist spies, and Feklisov's apologia is valuable not because it is convincing, since it is not, but because it allows us to see where he is coming from and therefore to understand that his accounts of what these spies actually did is true.

Feklisov's testimony about Rosenberg, Barr and Sarant, William Perl and finally, the co-defendant in the trial, Morton Sobell, is of great importance. As their case agent, we have for the first time an account of the extent of their espionage, and of the damage they did to American national security. Some have argued that because Barr and Sarant had not been indicted, and managed to flee the United States before the government had enough hard data to indict them—since the Venona files could not be used—their guilt is only a hypothesis. Hence they claim that the "industrial" secrets they gave to the Soviets did not amount to much. Feklisov's damning account ends those claims.

Ironically, Feklisov seems to understand that his decision to tell the truth will not comfort the remaining ideologues, who persist against all available evidence to regard the Rosenbergs and their spy ring as simply innocent victims of the Cold War. Thus he writes that he knows his account "will distress …the two Rosenberg sons and Morton Sobell," but he proceeds anyway under the belief that "to hear the truth is better than uncertainty and dark suspicion." Undoubtedly, they will not appreciate his concern for the truth. Morton Sobell, the Rosenberg's co-defendant, condemned the Venona revelations as fraudulent, and has insisted that both he and the Rosenbergs were completely innocent. Now Feklisov reveals that he personally met Sobell many times to retrieve information he was supplying, and that the material he passed on included valuable military secrets pertaining to sonar, infrared rays and the aiming devices for artillery pieces, as well as the very first data on missile guidance systems that would be used for the atomic bomb. They represented thousands of pages of both text and drawings. Among the data were secret reports of the Coordinating Committee for Radio Technology, which Feklisov calls "priceless documents." In addition, he recounts how upon Sobell's eventual release from prison, the KGB received him royally in Moscow, supplying him with a maid, chauffeur and cook, as well as a fur coat for his wife. Ironically, Sobell was put up in a private suite belonging to Armand Hammer, who for a long time secretly assisted the KGB.

Towards the end of his account, Feklisov again returns to a discussion of Morton Sobell. Once again, he writes that Sobell still says "he never had anything to do with Soviet intelligence," and that, in fact, he pretends not to "know who I am." Feklisov is adamant. He explains, in effect begging Sobell's forgiveness and understanding, that his aim was only "to rehabilitate the name of the Rosenbergs as well as his own," and that this goal cannot be accomplished without "telling the truth." As an anti-fascist, he tells Sobell that he "has nothing to be ashamed of." He, like Julius Rosenberg, is a hero for having spied for the Soviet Union, as were "so many other agents of mine." And then, the final *coup de grace*, he tells Sobell that "it is to him, among others, that this book is dedicated." Feklisov does not seem to understand the American psyche, despite all the years he spent in this nation. Like Alger Hiss, who went to his death pretending innocence, Morton Sobell has spent his entire life honoring the lie, waging a defense on the grounds that he and Julius Rosenberg were framed and that they were victims of a political witch-hunt meant to stifle dissent against Truman's Cold War policies. At this late date, to change his story and admit the truth would be to sully the honor of all those innocent fellow travelers who believed them, and who followed their lead in a political campaign based on a lie. That Morton Sobell is obviously not about to do, and while a slim chance exists that Feklisov's words in this book might prompt him to change his mind, the chances are, indeed, very slight.

When I was writing *The Rosenberg File*, I called Morton Sobell and asked for his comment. I cited what he told me in the prologue to the book, but since I had spoken to him on the phone, and did not have a tape of the conversation, I did not identify him by name. I knew at the time he would simply deny speaking to me. Now, so many years later, and after Feklisov's account, I want to make public what Morton Sobell told me. After requesting a personal meeting, Sobell asked what more there could be to write about the case, since so much had already been said. I responded with many unanswered questions that troubled me. Sobell asked, quite curtly, "Are you interested in the historical truth?" I replied that as a historian, this was one of my principal concerns. Then Sobell retorted, to my amazement: "At this time and juncture we're living in, do you think this is helpful? How will the historical truth hurt the Establishment?" He then explained that he was a radical, and not a liberal, and that at the present moment it was best that the historical truth not come out. That time has arrived, and perhaps, now that Feklisov has added his account, even Morton Sobell might decide that before he leaves this life, it no longer makes sense to remain silent.

Together, Julius Rosenberg's ring provided much valuable data to the Soviets. Feklisov tells us that he met Rosenberg at least fifty different times, to obtain documents gathered from Barr and Perl, as well as technical drawings, manuals and other important electronic devices. He tells us the amazing story of what was perhaps Rosenberg's most important piece of information—an actual proximity fuse detonator—— the device that allowed a shell to explode at a short distance from its airborne target, thereby guaranteeing a hit, in addition to correcting the path of an explosive charge towards a plane, a precursor of missile homing devices. It was this device that the Soviets would eventually use to shoot down Major Francis Gary Powers' U-2 plane in 1960, thereby derailing the scheduled Eisenhower-Khrushchev summit.

As for Joel Barr, Al Sarant and William Perl—the three most important members of Julius Rosenberg's spy ring—what they provided was invaluable. Those who assert that whatever Rosenberg's crime, because it was not "the secret" of the A-bomb, but meaningless and trivial information that he gave the Soviets, can no longer make that argument after reading Feklisov. We already know from the Venona files how extensive their espionage was. Feklisov confirms Venona, and adds more detail. We learn, for example, that they were able to give the Soviets the data for the SCR584, a device that determined the speed and trajectory of V-2 rockets and that set the firing of antiaircraft batteries. The data comprised 600 pages of text and drawings, which Barr and Sarant photographed in one evening! In total, we learn that the two gave the Soviet Union over 9,000 pages of secret documents, relating to one hundred different programs in planning stages.

As for Perl, a major American aeronautics engineer working for the predecessor agency that became NASA, his information was of the highest level. We learn for the first time that Feklisov himself met with Perl, and that since his job was designing fighter planes, his recruitment was a priority. Perl did not fail the KGB. He regularly came from Cleveland and carried a briefcase filled with top-secret material, which Feklisov terms an "explosive lode." He also confirms one of the charges made by the prosecution and regularly denied by the Rosenberg's defenders, that friends of theirs named Michael and Ann Sidorovich were used by the KGB as a liaison with Perl. Michael Sidorovich's job was to receive documents from Perl in Cleveland, photograph them, and then hand them back and give the film to the KGB. Over the years, Perl gave them 98 studies, comprising over five thousand pages, half of which the KGB termed "very valuable." As John Earl Haynes and Harvey Klehr conclude in their definitive study, *Venona: Decoding Soviet Espionage in America,* "Perl's position allowed him to deliver to the Soviets some of the most advanced aeronautical research undertaken by the United States, particularly in the development of high-performance military jet aircraft."

Finally, Feklisov tells us about the decision to have Julius recruit his brother-in-law, David Greenglass, a young Army sergeant who because of his engineering background had been assigned to work on the Manhattan Project at Los Alamos. Feklisov says his boss in Moscow was overjoyed, and subsequently he tells us how David's wife, Ruth, traveled to Albuquerque to visit her husband to ask whether he would be willing to provide information.

Feklisov's details about the Rosenberg ring are written with the clear intent to smoke out the SVR—the successor agency to the KGB—to come forth and publicly admit what everyone already knows—that Julius Rosenberg was their agent. He bemoans the reality that the SVR still persists "in not recognizing the very existence of the Rosenberg network," a fact which he attributes to the network's eventual collapse, which he calls one of "Soviet espionage's greatest failures." Feklisov tells us how the KGB was planning to arrange Greenglass's escape to Moscow, in the manner of that carried out by Barr and Sarant. He tells us how Morton Sobell, panicking, fled to Mexico before notifying Rosenberg or Feklisov's successor at the New York KGB, and that he failed to get Soviet intelligence to successfully come to his aid. We learn that Sobell actually went to the Soviet Embassy in Mexico City for help—a foolish step given its constant surveillance—and that they had no advance knowledge of his appearance by the KGB Residence in New York, and hence would not help him. Again, Sobell—who has steadfastly maintained he had only gone on a simple family vacation and was illegally kidnapped by the FBI and returned to the US—will not be happy with Feklisov's account. He concludes by stating that "the main task from the Center's point of view was to get the key members of the network out, mainly Julius Rosenberg and his family." The actual instructions to do so came too late, and Rosenberg would not leave after being instructed by his new case officer, because Ruth had been injured in an accident, and he felt that he could not abandon her at that moment. The only two they were "able to secure the escape" of turned out to be Joel Barr and Alfred Sarant—a fact which Barr himself even denied upon his return to the United States in the 1990s.

After 1946, Feklisov returned home, only to be assigned to London and the KGB's British section. It was there that he became the agent handling Klaus Fuchs, the German born physicist who worked at Los Alamos at the top level, and who gave the major A-bomb secrets to the Soviets. As expected, Feklisov argues that Fuchs was really "innocent of any crime," since Churchill had promised to give the USSR all the technical and economic assistance it desired, including information concerning weapons to be used against the common enemy. Noting that Britain did not plan to share its work on the A-bomb with them, Feklisov simply argues that "Fuchs took it upon himself to correct this sleight of hand." As he notes, all Soviet nuclear weapons "were closely based on American prototypes"; not only the first A-bomb, which has been widely reported, but also the second and third. When Fuchs returned to Britain in 1946, Feklisov was assigned to him, and he recounts in riveting detail his secret meetings and conversations, at which Fuchs regularly handed over material on the latest bomb research carried out at Harwell, the British main research facility. Among other things, we learn how Kurchatov, the scientist in charge of the Russian A-bomb project, worked with Fuchs. Kurchatov would give Feklisov concrete questions to relay to Fuchs, and Fuchs would then give him written answers, as well additional calculations on the plutonium and hydrogen bombs.

Readers will turn as well to Feklisov's fascinating discussion of why Fuchs confessed so readily to the British authorities. Here, the author attempts to reconstruct what he suspects was the scientist's mindset at the time of his arrest. Taking off from interviews Fuchs gave after his release from prison and his move to Communist East Germany, Feklisov argues that despite his belief that the West should not hold a monopoly on atomic weapons, and that passing nuclear secrets to the Soviets was the only guarantee of a better world, Fuchs was no longer the staunch Stalinist he had been in his youth. Feklisov, perhaps revealing his own view of the world as much as that of Fuchs', writes that Fuchs would look askance at the "ideological intolerance, bloody repression of the opposition, [the] personality cult" and the "political trials" that swept through Eastern

Europe and affected those Communists who had fought in Spain or had taken refuge in the West. Thus, he surmises that Fuchs must have wondered whether, upon returning to the Soviet bloc, he too would have found himself prosecuted as an imperialist spy. Moreover, while he lived in the West, Fuchs separated himself from open and ideological Communists, and could not help but have been influenced by what Feklisov terms "anti-Soviet propaganda and the liberal views" of the atmosphere in which he lived.

At this point in his narrative, Feklisov makes a claim that is not supported by the documentary evidence. He believes—his own words are "I think"—that the Americans warned the British of a leak in the British scientific mission sometime between 1944 and 1946, and that MI5 asked the FBI for proof. Here he turns to speculation concerning the FBI record on Harry Gold, Fuchs' courier, who had also retrieved data from David Greenglass in Albuquerque, New Mexico. The FBI files examined by this author for *The Rosenberg File* shows that when the Bureau searched Gold's apartment on May 22, 1950, they found a map of Santa Fe, which was offered as proof that the courier had been to that area to gather data from his contacts. Feklisov, without evidence, asserts that actually Gold must have given this map to the FBI during the summer of 1949; that the map had Fuchs' fingerprints on it, and that MI5 got Fuchs to confess because they told the scientist they had proof from Gold of his espionage, and that Gold had turned him in. It is important to stress that no material in the FBI files, or interviews I have conducted with Robert Lamphere, the FBI liaison to the Venona project and the man who was sent to interrogate Fuchs after his arrest in Britain, confirms this speculation.

Indeed, Feklisov's memoir suffers from those times at which he turns to speculation, and moves away from his own concrete account of his espionage activity, and recollections of events in which he has personal knowledge of what happened. Thus, readers can almost discount entirely his secondary retelling of the trial of Ethel and Julius Rosenberg, and his dependence for his assessment on the discredited work of Walter and Miriam Schneir, whose early study, *Invitation to an Inquest*, posited the Rosenbergs' innocence and developed a well-worn conspiracy theory declaring that Harry Gold was a phony who had made up his story and never was an espionage courier. Strangely, Feklisov seems unaware that after the release of the Venona files in 1995, the Schneirs in effect themselves disowned their own book, and wrote an article for *The Nation* magazine in which they acknowledged the validity of the Venona files as establishing Julius Rosenberg's activity as a Soviet agent. Instead, he repeats the charges made in their book, that "Gold had been manipulated during the trial."

Feklisov had to follow the Rosenberg trial from his vantage point in Moscow. Having already in his own text established Julius Rosenberg's extensive espionage, which he supervised, Feklisov returns to the case at the book's end, only to proclaim their arrest and trial "a tragic farce" in which only a "handful of incriminating witnesses" appeared, all of them "broken by the FBI or testifying with the promise of immunity." The problem with Feklisov's account is that much of what he himself reveals actually confirms the testimony and account of the key witnesses against the Rosenbergs. Of course, as Joyce Milton and I showed in our own account of the case, *The Rosenberg File*, there was perjury committed on the stand, exaggerations of evidence, and even *ex parte communication* between the prosecution and the judge. Moreover, the US Government could not use any of the information they had obtained from the Venona files, because they could not let the Soviets know that they had begun to break the code. But the essential story as told by the prosecution at the trial is validated by Feklisov's own revelations. Some may indeed argue, as he claims, that Max Elitcher, an old friend of Morton Sobell and the only witness against him, was a weak and unconvincing witness. But Feklisov himself validates Elitcher's story, and as we have seen, says that Sobell was guilty of extensive spying and of providing valuable military data to the USSR. Feklisov complains that Elitcher's and the Greenglass' lawyer, O. John Rogge, was negotiating with the prosecution for a deal for his clients. In exchange for their cooperation, they would receive either no sentence or a lighter sentence. This standard procedure is hardly something worthy of condemnation. Instead of dealing with the issues, Feklisov makes a statement that is bizarre and truly amazing. Rogge had been a left-wing lawyer, prominent in Communist and fellow-traveling circles. But he sided with Tito and Yugoslavia in the Tito-Stalin split, and from that moment on, stopped supporting Stalinist causes in the United States. Indeed, Greenglass turned to him for legal aid because he was aware of Rogge's stature as a civil liberties lawyer and a recent anti-Stalinist. In an effort to cast doubt on Rogge's credibility, Feklisov calls him an obstructionist who sought to overturn the approved agenda at a meeting of the World Peace Council, a leading pro-Soviet international front group, in Europe. At that meeting, Rogge shocked delegates by speaking up on behalf of Tito's break with Stalin, which Feklisov never gets around to mentioning. Instead, he makes the uncorroborated and ridiculous charge that Rogge "was a penetration agent of the CIA that ran a special section for international organizations under Tom Braden." Anything is possible, of course. But when he writes something of this nature, we are hearing the words of a 1940s Communist apparatchik, and not that of an intelligence agent telling about what he definitively knows. His conclusion, that the trial of the Rosenbergs was a case of "McCarthyism...out for blood," reeks of the kind of propaganda spread at the time by the international Communist apparatus—the kind of logic that, by now, one hopes Feklisov himself would have abandoned. He may believe, as he writes, that Rosenberg and Sobell were two men "who had helped us out of idealism at a difficult time," but he is wrong that their guilt "was never really proven." The jury was correct to believe the testimony of Harry Gold. If any jurors in the case are still alive, they can be content in knowing that they were right to credit Gold's testimony as believable.

Feklisov writes that Rosenberg and Sobell were simply "two anti-fascists who had helped Russia break the Nazi military machine," and had his country claimed them as their own, praising them for ideological spying, America would not have been able to make them "appear as criminals set against the US government." Here, one must turn to the recent evaluation offered by one of the most astute analysts of the world of intelligence, the writer Thomas Powers. Writing in *The New York Review of Books*, Powers explains that Soviet spies "were of the left generally, they supported liberal causes, they defended the Soviet Union in all circumstances, they were often secret members of the Communist Party, they were uniformly suspicious of American initiatives throughout the world, they could be contemptuous of American democracy, society and culture, and above all, their offenses were often minimized or explained away by apologists who felt that no man should be called traitor who did what he did for the cause of humanity."

This, of course, is precisely the apologia offered to us by Alexander Feklisov. The Soviets were in fact, as he amply demonstrates, running major spy networks in the United States, infiltrating the highest ranks of the US government, and Americans until very late in the game did not face the implications of this. As Powers writes, the Soviets "recruited [spies] from ranks of the left...ran them to steal secrets, and when they got caught at it they went to ground and waited for a better day." To Feklisov, whose mental world is that of the Communist monolith of the 40s and 50s, Rosenberg, Sobell, Barr and the rest might be anti-fascist partisans. But to most Americans, they were, and are, to be considered as traitors to their own land, individuals who betrayed the trust they had been given out of a misguided loyalty to a criminal political system.

There is, of course, much more to Feklisov's memoir, although the Rosenberg case is at its heart. But I must close by calling attention to his fascinating account of the Cuban Missile Crisis, and his recounting of his secret meetings with the ABC News correspondent John Scali, with whom he stood as a go-between for the Soviet government and the Kennedy administration. First, Feklisov confirms—undoubtedly to the dismay of American Cold War revisionist historians who have argued that the Soviet missiles in Cuba were only defensive in nature—that his country indeed had shipped SS4 "missiles with offensive nuclear capability to the island." These had a range of 1200 miles and could easily hit major East Coast cities.

Most revealing in Feklisov's memoir is his account of the various meetings with Scali. Here, we find that with time of the essence, Feklisov took things into his own hands, acting without having the opportunity to consult with Nikita Khrushchev. Hence, he tells Scali that if Kennedy sent troops into Cuba, it would untie Khrushchev's hands, and he would then be free to retaliate, probably in West Berlin. In his own words, he had gone beyond his mission, speaking on behalf of his country without authorization. He would meet with Scali again, negotiating directly and sending reports directly to the Politburo, bypassing the Ministry of Foreign Affairs and Andrei Gromyko. His detailed recollection, told with the requisite tension that allows readers to relive the urgency and seriousness of the moment, adds to the historical record and will have to be taken into account by future historians.

Alexander Feklisov has spoken. His account now stands to be examined, discussed and debated between Cold War historians, students of espionage between the great powers, as well as by historians of Communism. We are fortunate that he has chosen to candidly give us this long-awaited account.

This book is dedicated to my American and British friends who helped the Soviet people crush Nazi Germany and later prevent a nuclear conflict.

—*Alexander Feklisov*

The Crossroads
of History

1962 was the year the Third World War almost broke out. In a speech broadcast on October 22, President John F. Kennedy told the American people that Cuba had become an outpost of the Soviet Union in its struggle against the free world. Moscow was setting up missile sites with nuclear warheads able to strike any target in the United States from the island ruled by Fidel Castro for the past three years.

Nuclear annihilation was only minutes away from Washington and New York, a time frame much too short for any kind of counterattack.

Faced with this direct threat, the White House decided to blockade the island.

The U.S. Navy was ordered to inspect any ship en route to Cuba, regardless of its nationality, and to turn back all those transporting weapons.

At the same time, the President ordered the Pentagon to create a special invasion force of 250,000 ground troops and 90,000 Marines, with air squadrons capable of carrying out two thousand flights per day. B52 bombers of the Strategic Air Command carrying thermonuclear bombs were stationed in south Florida. To maintain nonstop presence in the air, each patrol took off before the preceding one landed.

The threat to the security of the United States was very real and certainly not the figment of someone's imagination!

Despite the colossal Bay of Pigs fiasco in April 1961, the attempted invasion of Cuba by anti-Castro militants with American support, the new Socialist regime felt constantly threatened. To deter any further threat of intervention, the Soviet Union, Cuba's powerful ally, stationed 42,000 officers and soldiers on the island in addition to the usual military counselors.

But Nikita Khrushchev, who was First Secretary of the Central Committee of the Communist Party and President of the Council of Ministers of the USSR, went much further to defend the lone beacon of the revolution in the Western Hemisphere. When the crisis began, in October 1962, there were already 42 nuclear missiles in Cuba and 36 others on their way aboard a Soviet military vessel. The first missiles were being quickly deployed on their launching pads and could be operational within a few hours. Fidel Castro had mobilized an army of one million men and guerrillas and, as shown in correspondence published after the break-up of the Soviet Union, was demanding that Khrushchev immediately launch a nuclear attack on the United States.

During those days when the future of the world lay in the balance, the Soviet First Secretary and the American President established a channel to maintain permanent contact. The telephone lines were so congested, and their messages so urgent, that Khrushchev and Kennedy communicated on an open line without a scrambler.

These were, however, only additional threats rather than attempts to reach political solutions and the slightest incident could bring about a conflagration that would destroy humanity. Many Americans fled the big cities. The world had never come closer to nuclear holocaust...

At that time, under diplomatic cover, I headed the "Rezidentura," in other words the KGB station in Washington. This meant that I was responsible for Soviet intelligence operations in the United States.

When the crisis began on October 21, 1962, all embassy personnel were placed on war footing, working twenty-four hours around the clock. The Americans were doing exactly the same thing. My officers reported to me that the windows at the White House, the Pentagon, the State Department, the FBI and the CIA all had their lights blazing and their parking lots full to capacity every night. Even more than any American or Soviet ordinary citizen, we fully realized that peace was hanging only by a thread. I was acutely aware of the crucial importance of intelligence at those moments when everything was in play; I desperately attempted to find reliable sources to discover the true intentions of the Kennedy administration.

One of my best official contacts was John Scali, a well-known television personality I had been meeting with regularly for the past eighteen months. Scali had a keen mind and moderated an ABC television talk show called *Questions and Answers*, which included politicians, cabinet members and congressmen. He was close to Secretary of State Dean Rusk and often traveled with him. Since he was from Boston, he was intimately connected to the Kennedy clan, including the President himself. We would meet for lunch where both of us played an identical game of cat and mouse, attempting to ferret out information, casually letting drop, as if by mistake, what we really wanted to communicate, while attempting to extract secrets that we each jealously protected.

Obviously, Scali was also after real intelligence—the Americans knew that I was the KGB Rezident. Since he had invited me to lunch the previous Monday, it was my turn to reciprocate and invite him to the Occidental restaurant on Friday, October 26th.

I couldn't imagine that as soon as I dialed the number, Scali would immediately inform Dean Rusk that I had called, and that Rusk, in turn, would tell the President of the United States. Nor could I fathom that Kennedy would take this opportunity to pressure Khrushchev one more time through me—that is, the KGB—and deliver what amounted to an ultimatum: the Soviet Union would announce that it agreed to dismantle its missiles in Cuba.

In the middle of that Washington restaurant, I was accidentally placed at the crossroads of history and I felt a weight on my shoulders that my rather long and colorful career as a Soviet intelligence officer had certainly not prepared me for....

PART ONE

From Worker's Alley to 61st Street

1

I can imagine what my parents felt in their hearts during that summer of 1939.

My parents were, as they say, "poor but honest." My father, the son of a peasant from the Tula region, was a railroad switchman, and my mother a housewife. They barely knew how to read and write, having attended only two years of parochial school each. Ours was a large peasant family. I was born on March 9, 1914, the oldest of five children. My maternal grandparents lived with us.

Home was an old one floor wooden shack in the Rogozhsky section in Moscow, near the "Weavers Gate." Our address was typical of the times: the 12th Worker's Alley. It ended on Worker's Street, a main thoroughfare with a whole web of other tiny streets with similar names, and was one of the most "working class" sections in the capital. Our house had none of the usual urban comforts. Electricity, for example, came only in 1929. Until the early 1930s we even had a cow grazing quietly between the railroad tracks, and we can certainly thank her for our good health and, possibly, the fact that we survived the famine of the 1920s.

At that time our entire life was just one long struggle to survive. My father made 55 rubles per month. To understand what this meant,

I can remember that my first pair of pants cost 15 rubles. Often to make some extra money, my parents, my grandfather and I did maintenance work at the railroad freight yard nearby. Working non-stop for ten hours, the four of us could unload two boxcars of bricks weighing sixteen tons each. After dinner I still had to do my homework before falling asleep like a rock. Like my father, I was well built. When he slapped me, my head would spin and I saw stars all over. As I grew up I learned how to throw a right hook that was quite famous. It was a rough neighborhood and fighting was our favorite sport. One day one street would be fighting against another street and the next day we'd become allies against yet another neighborhood. We'd get to school one hour before class started just to beat up the kids in another class. There was a whole honor code built into our brawls: we never beat anyone on the ground or who simply chose to kneel on one knee, and whoever didn't abide by this code was immediately beaten up by their own gang.

You had to try to stay in one piece. One day, four tough guys grabbed me by the arms and legs and flung me into a six-foot deep ditch where a water main was being installed. I fell in the wrong way and, without my father rushing in to the rescue, I never would have been able to climb out because I was so bruised and battered. Another time I went to a doctor because I thought I had a broken rib. Since his office was on the second floor the doctor laughed heartily: "With a broken rib you'd never climb up one flight of stairs!" However, one month later he had to admit that it was true: the bone had healed by itself but remained crooked. That's the way it stayed and I never did anything to straighten it. My adolescent brawling was a good lesson for me throughout my life. In every circumstance I was always very sure of myself. Obviously this could also be a handicap at times, but it worked mostly to my advantage: if you're scared you are dead before you even start.

Once, with four of my friends, I ran away from home. Some movies at the time told the story of the "besprizorniki," those children who had been abandoned during the Civil War. To live alone in the wilderness was the greatest adventure we could dream of. We ran to a forest not too far from Moscow and spent our first—and last—night outdoors. It was at the end of December and the temperature at night plunged to minus 20°C. We built a fire and huddled around it to sleep, which was none too smart: we only kept warm on one side while the other side of the body stayed frozen, and we all became so chilled that the next morning we could barely make it back to the railroad station. One of my friends died. I only got a serious ear infection that caused me to be deaf in my left ear.

In some ways I was really a "good for nothing." One evening in school I was helping the art teacher set up the scenery for an amateur play. I mixed the colors while he painted. I heard some noise outside and, looking out the window, I saw two lovers just below me and I poured the paint right over their heads. The outraged victims began yelling and cursing! I turned off the light and went to hide on the ground floor. My teacher, seeing what I had done, was forced to follow my lead and hide with me under the stage in the main hall. The couple came back with a policeman who searched the premises but was unable to find us. We had to stay there until morning with the teacher cursing me all night.

It may appear strange that the son of a proletarian worker would love the theater. I had a part in several school plays and this would serve me well on more than one occasion. Since I was failing grammar miserably, it was very possible that I would flunk the final exams. Fortunately, I took the part of a street urchin in the school play, a little hero who eventually dies, not on the barricades of 1832 Gavroche, but rather on those of the Paris Commune of 1871. My Russian teacher was so impressed with my acting that he decided to close his eyes to my spelling mistakes. My theatrical career did not stop there and I played two title roles in other shows.

I went to a school for railroad workers' children and was destined to become a railroad worker, or so it appeared. At fifteen I became an apprentice in a repair shop and today, over sixty years later, I can still remember the serial number of the first dilapidated locomotive that I refurbished, — S189. The "top job" in this line of work was to become an engineer, if you could reach such heights, but this required a special school and I decided to apply, forging my birth date to appear two years older. Unfortunately, one of my comrades betrayed me and told the authorities. My dream came to an end, but the snitch felt my anger all over his body.

Another stroke of bad luck prevented me from becoming a railroad switchman and changed the course of my life. During the summer of 1933 a fire broke out in our neighborhood. Our house did not burn down completely but it was no longer fit to live in. While we waited for the house to be repaired we had to share a small movie theater with six other families in the same situation. The limits of the "rooms" of each family, as well as a central hallway, were traced with chalk. We slept on the ground within our imaginary four walls, among the few miserable possessions the flames had not destroyed.

The fire had two positive consequences for me; first, I was estranged from my gang of street fighters and their brawls; and second, across the street from our temporary lodgings was a bookstore where I often went to browse. One day I bought a book entitled *Equations in Higher Mathematics* and attempted, with some measure of optimism, to try to solve the problems during my free time. To my amazement, none of the results I found matched those given at the back of the book. An engineer I knew smiled when I explained what was happening, showing that he found me somewhat conceited as to my ability. He suggested that I matriculate at a worker's college, the gateway to higher education for the working class, and that's what I did.

One year later I passed the entrance examination for the Moscow School of Communications. My parents, to my great surprise, displayed no happiness when they heard the good news. Instead they lowered their heads in silence. Finally my father spoke up:

"Studies are well and good. But how are we going to live?"

I hadn't thought of that. With my 150 rubles per month I was carrying half the family budget, and my younger brother Gennadi would only reach working age a year later. My grandparents rose to my defense: they shamed my father and even offered him the money they had set aside for their funeral. One of my uncles also joined in and my parents finally surrendered. This doesn't mean that I harbor any bitterness toward them. It's just a kind of sadness, and a reminder of the harshness of those times.

Those were hard but magnificent years and the lack of just about everything could not stop us from bursting with happiness. I remained very much enthralled by the stage and never missed a performance at the Maly Theater extension in Taganka Square. I would go there straight from the locomotive depot, sometimes with one or two friends. One day we sat in the front row and, very hungry right after work, we shared a whole rye bread that we finished as we were watching the play. At intermission, one of the ushers told us not to eat in the theater: the actors could not perform well for an enthusiastic crowd that kept on chewing throughout the performance.

Sports was my second youthful passion. At the university I played all the ball games, I skied and came in second at grenade-throwing[1] at the Federal Student Games. I was tall, muscular, and full of life. Sometimes in February I would go with my friends on a ten kilometer cross-country run in shorts when it was minus 10°C! Those were the days!

A big change in my life occurred in the summer of 1939 after I had finished my training as a radio technician. I was a good student, a good athlete, and an active member of the Communist Party. We sensed that a new war was coming and military school recruiters, looking for potential candidates, were combing our university. Since I was in charge of military and physical education within the Komsomol, the Committee of Communist Youth, I made the recommendations.

Then I was also called upon and it was a great honor. I was summoned to the Central Committee of the Party to be offered an important task, although the man who spoke to me refused to discuss what it was about. To his vague offers I said:

"If you think I fit your requirements, it's fine with me."

In those days we didn't ask too many questions.

I passed my final exams at the end of May and left for a vacation at Gelendzhik, a resort on the Black Sea. This was the first holiday in my entire life and I wanted to enjoy it to the fullest. I had been vacationing for about two weeks when a stranger approached me in the park. He showed me his NKVD[2] card and said I was to leave immediately for Moscow. Naturally, I told him this was my first rest in five years and asked him to tell Moscow that I intended to stay until the end of my holiday.

Two days later I was summoned to the office of the director of the resort. Sitting at his desk was a Georgian in military uniform, the head of the local NKVD. He didn't mince any words; how could I have the audacity to disobey an order coming from Moscow? I asked him for the address I was supposed to go to. He immediately reacted, how dare I set conditions? Perhaps just the name and phone number of the person I was supposed to meet? The Georgian's eyes opened wide, he was crimson with rage. To me the whole thing appeared to be a bad joke; I calmly told him I couldn't go back to Moscow without knowing where I was to go and why. The NKVD officer promised to make a whole lot of trouble for me and left, giving me a dirty look.

I spent twelve more days at the beach without worrying about it too much. I wasn't impressed by the threats of the political police that frightened the entire country. Subconsciously I was convinced that in my world politics played no part: our neighbors in Worker's Alley were all railroad workers, switchmen, and engineers on locomotives. We had no books at home and I spent my free time playing ball when I wasn't getting into a brawl with a rival gang. At the university I had to catch up in just about every major subject, I was involved in sports and even my activity at the Komsomol had failed to open my eyes to some of the realities of those days.

But I was really convinced that my credentials would back me up, since I was a radio technician, equivalent to what high technology is today. The worse that could happen was that I'd be sent back to the depot as a simple mechanic. Since childhood I always gave everything I could to what I was doing. I still loved my locomotives and my worker's tools: the hammer, the file and the vice. If everything went wrong I could always be happy back there!

I returned to Moscow on the last Sunday in June, around 5 p.m., and as soon as I walked in the door with my suitcase I was petrified. My parents both looked as though they were in anguish:

"Well my boy! What happened?" asked my father, his voice hoarse with emotion.

They said that a few days before a stranger had come to the door to ask when I was coming back. Since then a black sedan came regularly to the street and the passenger asked the neighbors if Alexander Feklisov had returned. The entire neighborhood was talking about it. My parents feared for the worse, but they had no fear concerning politics. For everyone in our workers' neighborhood, the purges were something taking place far away that concerned only the powerful and the intelligentsia. The only problem any one of us could have would be considered petty crime and although I swore that I had done nothing wrong, my parents were not convinced. As I repeated my denials my little sisters ran into the apartment, crying out in unison:

"The man in the black car is back! He's looking for Sasha!"[3]

I can still see him now, a big fellow in his forties, with curly hair and hard eyes behind his pince-nez. He asked who I was and told me to follow him into the courtyard. I went without any hesitation, since I was simply intrigued. Could it be related to my visit to the Party Central Committee and the mysterious job they had offered me? It could also be what the Georgian at Gelendzhik had promised would happen to me; either way, I was ready.

The first possibility was the right one. The man's name was Shmatko and he told me that I was admitted to a special school he was in charge of—where I would also be boarding. We had to leave immediately. I only had time to grab my toiletries and a change of underclothes. I would be free to leave every weekend, from Saturday afternoon until 8 a.m. Monday morning for roll call.

My family watched me pack a bar of soap, my toothbrush and toothpaste, a swimsuit and underpants in deadly silence. They were all convinced I was being hauled off to prison. I told my parents I was going to work at a radio station, as Shmatko suggested, but they didn't believe it because I was putting together those very items that prisoners were allowed to take.

The trip to Balashikha lasted about one hour. We took the road to Vladimir, the same one those deported to Siberian exile were taking. Our leaders, with their wry sense of humor, called it the "road of the enthusiasts." The words "NKVD school" must conjure up images of a sort of bunker on a military base, surrounded by barbed wire, sentries, howling attack dogs and strict identity controls at the gate. Actually, nothing could be farther from the truth.

7

The car stopped at a locked gate within a high wooden fence and the driver had to get out to open it himself. Beyond the gates stood a large house among the trees. A welcoming light filtered through the draperies in the windows and the air smelled of lilacs. A dog was barking in the distance. This house, located inward from the road, was no different from the others in the neighborhood.

There were only four full-time Rezidents at the school: Shmatko, his chauffeur, and their wives who did the cooking, served at the table and took care of the laundry. The place had two large study halls and a dining room on the ground floor; five rooms, a living room and a shower on the second floor. Each bedroom had two large beds with thick blankets, two closets, and two desks. At home in the winter I slept on a small chest behind the oven and in the summer on the heating wood that was kept in a shed.

From time to time the director looked at me to see my reaction, and once the visit was over, he frowned at me and said:

"Well, what's wrong?"

I decided to explain how frightened my family was and how I wanted to go back home to spend the night, reassure my parents and return the next morning.

"Okay," he agreed.

One hour later I was back home and repeated the story: I had been hired as an engineer at a secret radio station. Then I went to play soccer with my buddies who also thought I'd been arrested. My family and friends were reassured once I returned, but only for a short time.

The following Saturday, when I came back home, I was a different person. During my entire time as a student I had worn only the exercise suit and ski shoes the university had given me free of charge because I was on the school team, since the centuries old coat I wore ordinarily was completely threadbare. My family was quite surprised to see a real dandy appear on their doorstep. It was one of those hot July months so typical of Moscow's sizzling summers, and in spite of the heat I sported a brand new suit, a white shirt and even a tie, which was as elegant as anyone could be. God knows how uncomfortable I was, but I intended to make an impression. I nonchalantly took off my fedora in front of my family, who kept on staring at me in amazement. That was probably the first hat to have ever entered our house.

Even though the situation was as novel to me as it was for my relatives, I tried to behave as if it were perfectly natural, and pulled out a wad of cash as if I'd done it many times before. Since my mother, who managed the family budget, never took money from someone else's hands, I left the banknotes on the dresser as usual, and my mother, as always, asked me without counting it:

"Do you have enough for yourself?"

I nodded. My scholarship at school was 500 rubles; I kept 100 for myself and gave the balance to my family, which was three times more than my usual contribution. I stayed only a very short time at home that day because I wanted to go to a new show at the theater. When I came back home my parents were already asleep. The next morning at breakfast my mother and father were glum and silent. They listened to everything I said and winced from time to time. I didn't dare ask them why, but fortunately my father decided to break the silence:

"Listen son, your mother and I are very worried. All this money, these fancy clothes… And your disappearance for a whole week. We think you're part of some criminal gang…"

I laughed at first, but during the following visit I no longer felt like laughing at all. I tried to tell my parents that I was an engineer at a secret research center outside Moscow and that I had to sleep there, but they didn't believe me. They were convinced that their son had gone bad until I had the bright idea of showing them my Party card: they saw the amounts relating to the payments I made for my dues. This official document, which was much more important than any identity card, was enough to convince them that the source of my income was perfectly legitimate.

Yet I was only telling my parents a half-truth. Many years later my mother was told that I was part of the intelligence services. My father died without ever knowing.

2

M y studies at the special school lasted one year. There were only ten of us, all of peasant or worker stock, all graduates of technical universities. I would later find out that Pavel Fitin, head of Soviet espionage, had set these guidelines. He was convinced that those fitting such criteria would have more endurance, be more determined and creative than the children of intellectuals who had graduated in the humanities and, according to his view, could only chatter and study.

We took six courses a day: information gathering and counter-espionage techniques, radio transmissions, foreign languages (for me it was English), study of the country where we would be stationed and, obviously, the history of the Communist Party. Naturally, tradecraft, the training as secret agents, was the most important subject. We learned the techniques of making contact, recruitment and management of sources of information; in other words, how to create a "stable" of foreign informants, as well as the countless ways of discovering whether we were under surveillance and, when necessary, how to break a "tail." By the time I completed my courses I could also take apart and assemble a radio transmitter-receiver and communicate in Morse code.

The school's director, Vladimir Shamarnazashvili, worked mostly at his office in the Lubyanka, the headquarters of the NKVD. Vladimir Konyayev, the secretary of our Group—a student just like us—was handling the day-to-day business of the school. Konyayev was a former cavalry officer who had joined the intelligence service out of "revolutionary consciousness," and in so doing, had passed up a well-paid and very important job as director of a printing company. He was some fifteen years older than the others and was therefore nicknamed "Pops." His attitude toward us was that of a mother hen.

I remember a story about him. At school no one was referred to by his real name, and Konyayev, who was a bit absentminded, could never remember his own pseudonym. I can still see him breaking into the lounge where we would listen to music, a registration book in his hand with his glasses over his head:

"It's happening again!" he cried out to all of us. "That blasted Kolpakov is late in paying his dues. Does he expect me to go and beg on my knees?"

We looked at him in stunned silence, then we looked at each other and everyone started to laugh.

"There's nothing to laugh about!" he said, annoyed at our merriment.

After a while one of us could finally say a few coherent words. "But Pops, you're Kolpakov!"

Despite his forgetfulness, Konyayev became an excellent intelligence officer, and he left the service at the end of the 1960s, long past retirement age.

At the school I became friends with a man who would be with me throughout my life. Since I will refer to him very often in this book, I must introduce him in greater detail. Anatoly Yatskov was one year older than I was. He had come from Ackerman (known today as Belgorod-Dniestrovski), in Ukraine, to the capital at the age of seventeen with his mother and two brothers. He had worked as an unskilled laborer while completing his university studies, and in 1937 graduated from the Moscow Polygraphic School. One day I visited him at home in Khimki, in the suburbs of Moscow. I remember him sitting on the porch of the wooden house as he played the mandolin; Anatoly was just as gifted for music as he was for languages. He was also, beside myself, one of the best chess players in our group, but I would beat him at skiing. Our friendship was not without a kind of rivalry.

In many ways Anatoly was the opposite of me. He was exuberant and loved to wage bets on just about anything. If two sparrows, a brown male and a gray female, were sitting together on the branch of a tree he'd call me right away:

"I bet the brown bird will fly away first..."

"That's also exactly what I think," I would answer, teasing him.

But Anatoly didn't give up so easily.

"So I bet the gray one will fly away first!"

At the end of our course of study we took exams in front of a commission headed by Pavel Sudoplatov.[4] Out of ten candidates only six were admitted to the INO,[5] the foreign intelligence section: four as lieutenants, and Yatskov and myself as captains; both of us were sent to the American section. At that time, including typists, the entire Center had no more than one hundred and twenty people. Pavel Fitin, who headed the Center, was a quiet, fair-haired, imposing man who spoke very little and preferred to ask questions. As a young beginner I had little contact with him. My immediate boss, Fyodor Budkov, was about forty-five, and also a perfect example of the shadowy world of espionage. He spoke in such a low whisper that you had to strain to hear him.

There was only one older officer in our section and he was not a young recruit who had just passed his exams like myself. My outspoken amazement on the first day created such uneasiness that I never mentioned it again. I later learned that the Stalinist purges had not spared the intelligence services. The leadership of the INO had been decimated just as much as the Red Army by the end of the 1930s. In Europe, some of our best officers who had been in place in different countries for years, with real foreign passports and reputations as honest citizens of Switzerland, Germany, France, or America, had been called back to Moscow to either be executed or hauled off to the camps of the Gulag. Around 1938 all the covert stations had been shut down, while the "legals" working under diplomatic cover generally had only one or two mostly young and inexperienced agents.

I often wonder why I was chosen for the intelligence service. Of course I had been a good student at the intelligence school; I was very strong and had the stamina of a young buck, but besides my broken rib, I was also completely deaf in my left ear because of my running away from home. I also had only fifty percent vision in my left eye, which had been wounded by a shard of burning metal while I was operating a planing machine as a shop apprentice. Basically I was operational only on the right side of my body.

But there was an even bigger problem than my health. In January 1940 toward the middle of my studies, we were ordered to get married. The motive was quite simple, bachelors were almost never sent on a mission to the West. In the world of espionage, a beautiful woman is one of the most tempting ways to turn an agent. It's strange that the "honey trap" should still work even though it has been used since the dawn of history, but that's human nature. When I was appointed to work for the Center at the end of August, I was still not married. When Budkov, my boss, found out he gave a long whistle as a comment on my chances of being stationed overseas. Being a bachelor was a severe handicap to my future as an intelligence officer.

"How can you recruit any agents if you can't even recruit a wife?" he asked "As far as I'm concerned I have my doubts as to your ability to do so. Tomorrow we shall discuss this with comrade Fitin."

I spent the night tossing and turning on the hard chest behind the oven blaming myself while I was visiting with my parents. "Congratulations! You enjoyed yourself and now it's time to pay for it."

In the meantime I did have a fling with a young woman, Lydia, who taught us English at the school. She was six years older than I was and about to marry a divorced university professor. She had only one problem: she was a virgin, and was convinced that any potential husband could only be suspicious of a woman of thirty-two whom no other man had wanted. She was probably wrong, but that was the way she saw things, and decided to have an affair with me, behaving very nicely, as any cultured woman would. We would attend the famous Morozov lectures on Shakespeare together and all the plays in the Moscow theaters. She spoke only in English to me, which was very useful. It was she who decided that we should break up.

"I know I would not be the right wife for you," she told me "but I do hope that you did not lose anything because of our affair."

Then she told me something that sounded childish and a bit overly romantic.

"Whenever you're faced with a difficult choice, just remember me. I won't give you bad advice."

I nodded my assent, far from imagining that six years later her words would come to pass exactly as she had said.

We broke up as good friends but this was no help to me at all.

The next day Budkov and the head of personnel went to discuss the matter with Fitin. They asked me to come along but kept me waiting in the anteroom. Later I found out that the head of personnel had saved the day for me, praising me to the sky before giving them his most persuasive argument in my favor:

"If you want my opinion, it's rather good that he didn't get married on command. It goes to prove that he's a serious sort of fellow."

That's how my future in intelligence was decided. On the same day I had a long briefing with Maxim Prudnikov, the assistant head of intelligence. First he had me speak about myself, then he described the situation to me. Before the war in Europe began, the United States was on the fringe of international politics, but from now on their part in world affairs was bound to increase. The stations—or "Rezidenturi"—of the NKVD in the United States were short of people, especially smart people, and we had to fill the empty slots.

I therefore had two missions: first, to organize a clandestine radio link between America and the Center; second, to learn operational work as fast as possible. Obviously I lacked experience, but the more I could learn in Moscow the faster I would be productive in New York, where I was being stationed very shortly. Since I am stolid by nature, I don't get excited easily and I am not inclined to show my emotions nor harbor any wild dreams. I am someone who is so fearless and sure of myself that no one will ever see jumping for joy. My country wanted to send me to New York? Fine, I would do my best to be useful, yet for someone living in a Moscow suburb New York is as far away as the moon, just a dot on a map. No one I knew could swear that that city actually existed other than on paper.

Fortunately a witness soon appeared, an *illegal*,[6] who was coming home after a long period in the West. Originally from Baku, he was a tall man in his forties with dark hair, a handsome oriental face and sharp, intelligent eyes. His name was Iskhak Akhmerov.[7] Always very affable and well dressed, he had a special disarming charisma, and spoke English better than Russian, which he had not used for many years. Since his wife was American, even in Moscow he did not have much opportunity to speak Russian. As far as I was concerned he was a walking encyclopedia. No matter what question I had on the United States or intelligence work, he would give me an immediate answer in English, or if I had trouble understanding him, in Russian. Every morning to familiarize myself with my future assignment he would have me translate intelligence reports from English to Russian, which I then would type out with two fingers.

The afternoons were spent on radio practice and obviously all messages were coded; make one mistake in a single digit and the entire message would become unintelligible. To learn all these techniques quickly, I was soon assigned to contact sessions with covert operators in neighboring countries, whose signals were easy to recognize. Yet, to my great shame, at the beginning of a transmission I often heard the conventional code "change operators," and I would then let a more experienced operator take over, because they could communicate at tremendous speed with barely audible signals.

Yet my trainers were very patient. Every day I had to be in contact with a real illegal and I knew that a simple mistake on my part could lead to the failure of the entire operation. I was quite tense in front of my radio transmitter, but this shock treatment was very effective. After twenty days the "change operator" code—my nemesis during this entire period—disappeared completely from my correspondents' vocabulary.

In October 1940, while I was in training, I began a two-month practice period at the People's Commissariat of Foreign Affairs, the NKID, whose headquarters were directly across from the NKVD. The employees of the two ministries were in the habit of referring to their counterparts across the street as the "neighbors," and the term was so well entrenched in our vocabulary that it remained long after the diplomats left for their new Stalin-style architecture "skyscraper" in Smolensk Square. Intelligence old-timers still use the term. I spent part of my time with the "neighbors" reading TASS agency dispatches, reports from the various sections of our Washington embassy and from the Consulate General in New York, as well as American newspapers.

My day at the NKID began at 9 a.m. After 6 p.m., when most of the Foreign Affairs ministry offices were empty, I would walk across the square back to my section at the INO or at the radio communications center. In early December I was given a radio receiver and transmitter built especially for me. It was very powerful and could maintain stable communications between New York and Moscow. First I tested it at headquarters, establishing contacts with colleagues at Minsk, Kiev, and finally at Ashkhabad, in Turkmenia, some 2,500 kilometers from the capital. Then I went for a few days to Batum, in Georgia, to prove that I could start a transmission on my own. While I was gone, Anatoly Yatskov was sent to the United States.

When I returned on January 3, 1941, Budkov gave me the big news: I was to leave as fast as possible.

It took me two weeks to get ready. In those days there were so few Soviet citizens going abroad that each one would receive instructions in person from the People's Commissar for Foreign Affairs. I went to the anteroom of Vyacheslav Molotov's office with two colleagues who were to be stationed in Great Britain. To reach their destination they had to travel around the world, that is, because of the war in Europe, they had to go via Japan and the United States. Molotov was short, energetic and full of vigor, wearing a dark purple three-piece suit of a fabric I immediately recognized as the Soviet "Metro" type. He made vigorous gestures while pacing his office and speaking very concisely and passionately at the same time. When he was finished with an idea he would pause a little. I thought that—consciously or not—he was imitating Lenin, at least the Lenin I was used to seeing in Soviet films.[8]

But at that time Molotov was not just a top leader in the government, he was also the highest-level official that I had ever met. At the beginning of our conversation he told us that for three months

Japan had consistently refused to issue us transit visas. Fortunately a Japanese general and his entourage had crossed the USSR to reach Germany and the Japanese embassy in Moscow was compelled to issue the authorizations we requested. Molotov then asked each one of us questions on our background. When it was my turn, I had to admit that I was not married.

"Why is that, my little comrade?" asked the People's Commissar. "You know that we never send bachelors overseas, especially to the United States. The Americans will slip a blonde or a brunette into your bed very quickly and you'll be in quite a mess!"

He seemed to enjoy his choice of words and I thought I was finished. Fortunately, Andrei Vlasov, head of NKID, was present.

"Comrade Feklisov is very much aware, Vyacheslav Mikhailovich," he interrupted. "His superiors have every confidence in him both politically and morally. What's more," he added, grinning salaciously, "there are quite a few pretty girls within the Soviet colony in New York. He will have the luxury of a choice to get married over there."

"All right, all right." said Molotov in a conciliatory tone "Go ahead, Comrade Feklisov, do your best and don't betray the confidence we have placed in you."

The basic instructions were very simple; the Soviet government was doing its best to avoid being dragged into a war that was now spreading, and all Soviets living abroad must also work toward this goal. Further, it was very important to discover any secret initiatives by Great Britain and the United States to seek a separate agreement with Nazi Germany, and for them all to turn against the Soviet Union. One of the priorities was to discover any contacts between the Nazis and the Western powers.

Molotov's words would have sounded surprising to my compatriots, who were informed only through the newspapers. I could already see the difference between what was printed in the papers and the reality that only the professionals knew. The Soviet attitude toward the Third Reich was changing very quickly. For the past few weeks even *Pravda* was publishing reports of the barbaric way the Luftwaffe was bombing England. The articles gave details concerning the damage done and the number of victims in increasingly compassionate tones. Behind the scenes, Nazi Germany, tied to the USSR by a non-aggression pact, was viewed increasingly as a threat. Nevertheless, simple people could see all this very clearly. I will never forget my last conversation with my father.

"The pact is a piece of paper," he told me. "The Germans are two-faced; I know them well. I fought against them in one war and soon we shall have to do it again."

At that time I would get home around midnight and saw my parents only at breakfast. I could not tell them I was about to work in the United States. According to the story my superiors had approved, I was to be stationed at Vladivostok in the Soviet Far East. My mother made me an orange colored satin shirt she was very proud of, and when I was ready to leave all my possessions could fit in a tiny suitcase.

On my last day I spent the morning at home. The train to Vladivostok was leaving the Yaroslavl station at four in the afternoon. My entire family was huddled close to me, ready to indulge any of my wishes. My grandfather repeated to me several times:

"Don't you realize you're going to the edge of the world? Take me with you!"

Had he only known the truth!

During our farewell dinner there was a long silence. Everyone was sad and my mother's eyes were full of tears. Our neighbors were coming to bid me farewell. My father insisted on accompanying me to the tramway stop. We looked like quite a pair; me, all dressed up in a black coat, gray hat, good shiny shoes, black leather gloves, and him, dressed in an old colorless coat and a worn *shapka*. The passersby noticed how strangely we looked.

"You should buy yourself some new winter clothes," I said reproachfully.

"Who cares! My clothes will last me one or two more years!" he answered. The tram arrived and we embraced each other heartily.

"Work hard, Sasha! Don't dishonor your parents! Behave yourself! Maybe we will not see each other again! And don't trust the Germans, I know them only too well!"

From the back of the tram I watched him disappear at the end of the street, stooped over, waving good bye with his old *shapka*.

He was right. Six months later Germany attacked us. And he died in September 1942.

There is nothing like the train to set your ideas straight, especially the Transsiberian! During the ten-day trip from Moscow to Vladivostok, on the shores of the Pacific Ocean, I had time to organize my thoughts following the past eighteen eventful months, which, for me, had been without any kind of peace and quiet. It was January 1941, half the planet was already at war, and the Atlantic was off limits to passenger ships, which meant the only way to go from Europe to America was through the Soviet Union and Japan. The train was full of passengers on their way to the New World. I shared my compartment with three Soviet officers. In the compartment next to mine were two code clerks on their way to Washington with their wives, while I was going to New York and my first overseas assignment at the far end of the world, in what the newspapers called the "cradle of capitalism."

The travelers killed time by talking, playing chess or dominos, eating and sleeping, and I did just like everybody else, but most of all I imagined what I would find in America and thought about what I was leaving behind in Russia. The train stopped often to load water or coal or to change locomotives. It was hot inside the cabin and I took advantage of every stop to breathe some fresh air. I shall always remember the little station stop at Erofey Pavlovich, in the heart of Siberia, where I went jogging a bit faster than usual. The temperature was minus 55°C, but the air was pure and dry and you could breathe easily.

At Vladivostok, the last stop in the homeland, we waited for five days for the ship that was to take us across the Sea of Japan.

3

As I tossed and turned in my bunk in the train compartment, I tried to imagine my initial impressions as I first encountered the forbidden land that was mysteriously called "foreign." Was everything there—nature, cities, people—different from where we came from? Well, there were to be no first impressions! We reached Tsuruga on the coast of Honshu in the middle of a dark night and a thick snowstorm. The Soviet vice consul took us to the Consulate where he was living. I spent the whole night shivering in an enormous and very cold room, and woke up at dawn, happy not to have to try to sleep anymore. I went outside and was amazed at the incredible scene in front of me: flat-top pine trees that looked like umbrellas surrounded the area; the snow capping the trees sparkled in the morning sunshine that grew warmer by the minute and the flakes fell as they melted into droplets. It looked as if it were raining diamonds! I was bewitched by it all for several minutes. As I came to my senses, the snow had melted completely and the trees were now crowned in their usual green.

Japan was not a disappointment. From that first morning until we left its shores, this exotic country continued to surprise me. The vice consul, after offering us tea, took our little group back to the railroad station where we boarded the train to Yokohama. Inside the train, the seats were not set in rows but along the sides. In the middle of this wide passage was a round opening in the floor, about twelve inches in diameter, circled by a brass ring, where people threw out their refuse. Passengers walked about the car. At one point two military men went by and saluted each other, stopping to bow while their faces didn't show the faintest kind of emotion. Then they bowed even lower and for a few seconds they saluted each other with deeper and deeper bows, before going their separate ways, poker-faced, without having exchanged a single word.

At Yokohama we stayed at the Imperial Hotel and quickly came under very tight surveillance. Every time we went out—and we did so generally in a group, the two code clerks, their wives, and myself—a man, either on foot, on a bicycle, or by car would shadow us. They made no attempt to hide and were always impeccably courteous. Once, during a stroll, our "guardian angel" came up to say we should go no further because there was a military area just ahead. We turned around and the man took off his hat and bowed repeatedly to thank us. Another time, the wind blew off the hat of one of our code clerks and our shadow caught it and handed it back to its owner with a happy smile.

We waited in Yokohama for an entire week. Around the middle of our stay I decided to visit our embassy in nearby Tokyo and get the latest news. Japanese counterespionage did not expect to see me leave the hotel by myself and since the surveillance team had not planned for such an occurrence, I drove them all into a panic. At first, inside the lobby, the doorman tried to gain some time by blocking my way while repeating politely the few Russian words he knew: "Hello! Nice weather! Hello! Nice weather!" I walked around him and got into one of the cabs parked in front of the entrance. "To the railroad station!" I told the driver.

The doorman caught up with us and said something in Japanese to the driver, who understood the situation immediately and turned toward me with a long thread of words in his native tongue. Despite my repeated requests the car didn't move and now the whole thing was beginning to look funny to me.
"Very well," I said.

I got out and took the taxi right behind it. As the car was about to move a Japanese man, completely out of breath, opened the door, took the seat next to the driver and, when he turned to speak to me, I saw it was the same man who had caught my colleague's hat.

"Mister," he said in English, "I will pay for half the ride, okay?"

How could I refuse an old acquaintance who was being so courteous? The man took the train with me to Tokyo, then the bus all the way to the embassy. He was waiting for me when I came out and didn't leave my side until I was back at the Imperial Hotel at Yokohama.

Surveillance was not always so easygoing. The embassy told me we could send news to our families through the diplomatic pouch, due to leave a few days later. Back at the hotel I told my little group, and that evening I gathered a nice little pile of letters, placing them all in the top drawer of the desk near the window, which I locked before going to sleep. A strange noise woke me in the middle of the night. I opened my eyes and listened carefully in the darkness and I soon heard a scratching sound and saw the curtain moving. I jumped up and ran to the window. Through the opening a man's face was smiling at me. This professional "hotel thief" quickly slid down a ladder held by his two confederates and they all disappeared into the night. Their mission, apparently, was to steal our letters.

A much more serious incident took place on the day we were supposed to leave. At breakfast in the hotel restaurant, Misha, one of the code clerks, remembered that he had forgotten his and his wife's passports under the pillow. The couple immediately went upstairs, but a few minutes later his wife returned looking distraught: their passports were gone! We all immediately went up to their room. Misha was in front of the bed tossing up the blankets, the pillows, and the sheets for the hundredth time. A young maid dressed in a kimono looked at him impassively. I asked her in English if by chance she had found the passports, but the only answers I got were a series of "No Sirs!"— even when I asked her if she spoke English! This was a serious situation. Not only were Misha and his wife prevented from continuing their trip to the United States, but also— and this was a real disaster—authentic Soviet passports were now in the hands of an ally of Nazi Germany. The maid was about to leave when Nikolai, the other code clerk, stopped her.

"She's the only one who could have taken them," he said. "We must frisk her!" The Japanese woman was easily convinced of the seriousness of our intentions; she put her hand in her pocket and extracted the two passports. Then in excellent English she begged us not to tell anyone in the hotel manager's office, or she would lose her job and had a child to care for. Japanese counterespionage was forcing her to lift documents belonging to foreigners. The tension and our anger quickly abated, and we returned downstairs to finish our breakfast. The week in Japan was a good lesson for us all: our enemies were not asleep, and we had to remain alert to avoid falling into their traps.

We left Yokohama aboard a Japanese ship, the *Yawata Maru*, to San Francisco via Honolulu. Both couples had a double cabin each and I was sharing mine with two young Dutch travelers. At first they didn't say much, but after some time we broke the ice. The Wehrmacht already occupied the Netherlands, and my two traveling companions were going to Canada where the British were setting up units to fight the Nazis. They were convinced that the European countries by themselves could not overcome Germany and its allies, and their dream was to see the United States and the Soviet Union enter the war as soon as possible.

The stopover at Honolulu lasted about thirty hours, during which time we visited pineapple plantations, palm forests and the huge beaches all over the island. It was quite a change from the vast snow-covered spaces of Russia. From a high point in the mountains we could see every detail of the Pearl Harbor naval base. Ten months later, on December 7, 1941, a Japanese surprise attack would hand the U.S. Navy its most crushing defeat, prompting President Roosevelt to declare war on Japan.

But this was all still far away and I took advantage of our leisure time during the Pacific Ocean crossing by swimming in the pool before every meal and staying on deck as much as possible to breathe in the salty air. But it would have been hard to describe the habits of my Dutch friends as healthy. After their sleepless nights they would get up for breakfast with huge hangovers and quickly have a drink. After dinner they were back in the bar for a good time with the Russian hostesses whom the Japanese had hired in Manchuria for the pleasure of the passengers. Three days before arriving at San Francisco they were robbed of their passports. Seconded by some Americans they had befriended, the Dutch went several times to demand that the Japanese captain hand back their passports and each time they ended up in a fistfight. The nightclub was shut down. The Americans threatened to have the *Yawata Maru* impounded at San Francisco if their friends were not given their passports back. I don't know how the story ended but it reminded our little group of what had happened to us at the Imperial Hotel at Yokohama.

At noon, leaning against the handrail, we saw the entrance to San Francisco Bay and the skyscrapers in the city. I must say that we didn't expect the welcome we were given in America. As soon as the gangplank was set up so many reporters assailed us that we couldn't get off the ship. For a few minutes we were jostled around amid the flashes of the news photographers and a series of aggressive and insulting questions:

"So, have you Bolsheviks caught up with the capitalist countries? Or perhaps you have passed them by now?"

We looked around in amazement, trying to get out of this situation. Help came from a group of men dressed in overalls, who came on board and yelled at us in Russian:

"Comrades, don't talk to these scabs!"

The longshoremen pushed the newsmen aside, took our bags and escorted us to the entrance where a Soviet vice consul was waiting. They strongly refused the tip we offered them and wished us a pleasant stay in the United States.

It was the first demonstration of the class struggle I had ever seen, and it felt good to know that our country had friends, even in America. We then crossed America from coast to coast, four thousand miles for five whole days of mountains, deserts, prairies, forests, and lakes that slipped by the windows of our train compartment.

My trip lasted a total of forty days; I had left Moscow on January 17, 1941 and arrived in New York on February 27. By the end of the journey I had stopped gazing eagerly and being surprised at everything I was discovering. Naturally there would be more surprises to come, but I was now ready to take on my new job.

4

Before getting acquainted with the city in which I was to spend the next five years, I had to learn my own identity better. To everyone, including my superiors, I was Alexander Fomin. That was the name on my passport, and it was standard practice that if for any reason I was identified as an intelligence agent, I ran fewer risks of being unmasked in another country using a different name.

For security reasons, even within coded messages between the New York station and the Center in Moscow, almost all the operatives and many politicians, cities, organizations, plans, and documents were identified by a code name. Mine was "Kalistrat." For most of my Soviet colleagues I was an ordinary trainee at the Consulate of the Soviet Union in New York, which was a rather thin cover. One day, while answering a question from a Soviet diplomat, Yatskov said jokingly:

"It is an important job, but during the entire history of the trainees not a single one ever reached diplomatic status."

Yatskov, my eternal friend and rival, was suddenly and unexpectedly named vice consul just before leaving. When I left the United States five years later, I was still a trainee with an ordinary passport, a large sheet folded into four parts, and therefore not covered by diplomatic immunity. For the sake of historical trivia, since the NKVD checked all passports, Pavel Fitin, the director of the INO, actually signed mine. Without compromising me, the name of the big boss did not help me at all. Had I been caught, U.S. authorities had every legal right—at least in theory, since the war was to make this even more of a moot point—to arrest, prosecute and sentence me to any kind of punishment. Only NKVD men knew this; the "clean" diplomats, meaning those who had nothing to do with the secret services, were convinced that trainees didn't need diplomatic passports.

Moreover, my intelligence activities and the fact that I was an NKVD officer were to be kept secret from everyone outside the Rezidentura. I shall always remember my detailed interrogation by Consul General Viktor Fedyushin upon arrival. Tactfully but insistently he asked many pointed questions about the different branches of the Foreign Ministry and asked me to name scores of department heads to be sure that I belonged to Foreign Affairs and not to the Big House. My many months of training with the "neighbors" suddenly became extremely useful.

This game was constantly kept up by our services and, strange as it may appear, I had absolutely no contact with my true employers for over two months! The only persons I communicated with were Consul Fedyushin and Konstantin Fedoseyev, whom I was replacing at the Consulate. I didn't even know where the Rezidentura was located. Had Anatoly Yatskov, who had arrived some months ahead of me, not been there, I would certainly have come to the conclusion that the Service had written me off. In spite of my phlegmatic temperament, had it not been for Anatoly's presence, I must admit I came close to feeling wronged. A few days after my arrival I told him how puzzled I felt.

"Don't worry," he answered reassuringly. "It's standard procedure here; I just went through the same thing myself. In any case you must first thoroughly learn your work at the Consulate. You will not have much time once you're up there." He pointed vaguely toward the ceiling. "Right now they're observing you. Don't think about it anymore!"

I quickly concluded that the decision to let newcomers learn their new cover jobs thoroughly and therefore be able to fulfill them completely later on was a reasonable one. I learned how to do my job as well as any other government functionary. This not only allowed Moscow to save on one job function but I derived, as an intelligence officer, immeasurable benefits from the experience. My cover brought me into contact with many people, allowing me to broaden my horizons, gather valuable information, and make new recruits. Most of all, as far as the FBI was concerned, I appeared to fit the profile of the perfect administrative employee.

I took advantage of my free time to study the city, exploring a different part of New York by bus, subway, or on foot every evening. I would "learn" about Gotham one neighborhood at a time. Toward the end of my stay I knew the city like the back of my hand. Its deserted streets and parks offered ideal places for secret meetings, since it was so easy to see if anyone was following. The main thoroughfares were clogged with traffic while the side streets were perfect for shaking any "tail." There were subway stations where one could easily change direction, jump into or out of a subway car at the last minute.

Those quiet moments in what was my normal activity also allowed me to improve my English. I had difficulty understanding American English. Reading the newspapers every day was not enough, so I spent hours listening to the radio and went to the movies very often. At first I barely understood the film's story line and would walk out with a tremendous headache from the effort I was making to concentrate. But I told myself that I was in America to serve my country and couldn't waste a single hour neglecting to improve my work.

My job at the Consulate was to receive those Soviet citizens who resided in New York or other states that were our responsibility and solve their administrative problems. I examined visa requests and took care of Soviet sailors calling at ports in the northeast. In 1941 there were some 120,000 persons who had "rights to Soviet citizenship." These were Russians living in America prior to the First World War, a few White refugees who had left after the civil war and some people who had escaped the famine and hard times (the borders of the Soviet Union had remained open until the beginning of the 1930s). They had refused to renounce their Russian nationality once it became Soviet and were bearers of an *ad hoc* identity document. The difference between a regular passport like my own and someone with a right to citizenship was that they had to register at the Consulate every year and could only return to the USSR with a special entry visa. Every day I would see six or seven persons in this category.

Yatskov's desk faced mine in the same room. He took care of the documents, affidavits, and civil identity documents which we had to request from the USSR. After asking him more than once when I would start my real work I did not belabor the issue further. To avoid asking useless questions is part of the job. Everything is compartmentalized in intelligence work and each one knows only what he needs to know.

Two months later, on a beautiful morning in May 1941, Anatoly said:

"Come on, we're going upstairs!"

He took me to the third floor for the first time and ushered me into a large room that was the office of the entire Rezidentura personnel. A man I didn't know, since I had never seen him at the Consulate, welcomed me and yet Pavel Klarin, whose real name was Pastelnyak, was officially a vice consul. His real function was the number two Rezident of the INO branch in New York.

He was an imposing man about fifty-five years old, with a slightly pocked face and a hard look in his eyes. As a career army man Pastelnyak had served in the border guards.[9] In 1938 he was placed in charge of security at the Soviet exhibit at the New York World's Fair. At that time the United States was vastly increasing its role in international affairs. At the end of the fair, Pastelnyak was ordered to stay behind. In April 1941, Gaik Ovakimyan, the NKVD Rezident, was ensnared in an FBI trap and ordered out of the country, so Pastelnyak was filling in. He knew only a few words of English and mostly did administrative work. A military man to the core, he loved discipline and his favorite word was "subordination."

That day, Pastelnyak was holding my orders, which had arrived through the diplomatic pouch. He read me some parts of them. My mission was to maintain a clandestine radio link between the

Rezidentura and the Center, as well as fulfill the tasks given to me by the Rezident. Before I could be entrusted with "managing" agents, my boss wanted to check my skills by giving me the job of translating intelligence reports and official FBI and OSS[10] documents, identify meeting points for secret encounters and other such work. I was also to try to make useful contacts among Americans through my cover job, where I would spend the mornings, but in the afternoons I'd be working at the Rezidentura. None of the regular consular employees, however, was to see me enter the room! Then he showed me my living quarters where I was also to operate the radio transmitter.

"Three days to move. Daily report on the work done! You are dismissed!"

For the last two months I had been living in a small room in the Soviet school on East 87th Street. The building was not extraterritorial and didn't even have any guards. The Consulate General and the adjoining building, housing the dining room, the English classes for consular personnel and a few apartments, however, were Soviet State property, and off limits to U.S. authorities. The Consulate was located at 7 East 61st Street, between Madison and Fifth Avenues, and was sandwiched between two other buildings. Its narrow facade—two windows on either side of the main door— had three floors with an attic under the roof, which was to be my room. My new quarters were made up of a small room with a drop ceiling, a closet where I set up my radio transmitter and a small repair shop.

My radio, as big as two VCR's on top of one another, had arrived through the "pouch." Despite its powerful configuration, it was still too limited for transatlantic communications. It also required an enormous amount of electric power and since the New York voltage was only 120v, whenever I was transmitting the lights dimmed within the entire building. I had to quickly find a solution to prevent the FBI from finding out what was happening!

One of our American "correspondents" was an electrician who was able to pass a heavy industrial electric line to the basement of the Consulate, but we couldn't allow him to work in the secret areas. I therefore had to install the line and place the huge armored cables in the elevator, which turned out to be easy, but things became more complicated when we had to connect the lines, since I obviously couldn't ask the power authority to cut the electricity! So I decided to work with "live" wires. I only asked a colleague for back up: in case of electrocution he was to separate me from the wires with a wooden pole. The work was even more dangerous due to the excessive humidity in the basement and my heavy perspiration during the operation, but fortunately everything went without a hitch.

I also had a second technical problem. During the first transmissions I realized that the internal antenna was useless and since very tall buildings surrounded the Consulate, even an external antenna did not improve things that much. I found a warehouse in New Jersey that sold very long bamboo poles and I personally built casings with the assistance of a few friends, setting up a good horizontal antenna ten feet above the rooftop. Transmission quality became excellent during the daytime and at night, and just in time too: the international situation was deteriorating daily and the Rezidentura had to communicate with the Center more and more frequently.

At the time relations between the USSR and the United States were quite tense. Since the signing, in August 1939, of the German-Soviet Non-Aggression Pact, Washington considered the USSR friendly to Nazi Germany. American newspapers constantly mentioned Soviet shipments of oil, wheat or precious metals that were helping Hitler conquer Europe. Congress passed new laws ending economic and commercial relations between America and the Soviet Union, and many contracts to ship equipment that could end up in the Third Reich were canceled. The U.S. administration even requested that the Russian government recall all of its commercial delegates, thereby reducing the size of the New York Soviet colony by the day.

U.S. counterespionage became more focused in its surveillance of the remaining Soviet citizens who were being followed constantly and had wiretaps on their telephones. This would last until the United States entered the war in December 1941. The FBI had several

operations directed at INO personnel. In February 1941 an undercover agent entrapped an officer of the Soviet naval attaché and
two months later it would be Ovakimyan's turn.

Each side had its own set of truths: American officials thought
of the USSR practically as an ally of the Nazis while our superiors gave us a different view. During assemblies of Consulate personnel, they made the point that the USSR had been forced to
sign the Non-Aggression Pact with Germany because of the attitude of the Western powers, which were inciting the Nazis to attack our country. We also learned that these intrigues were almost
succeeding, as our ambassador, Konstantin Umansky, told us in
April 1941:

"Hitler is drunk with his military successes and is preparing to
attack the USSR. It's obvious we will not be able to avoid a war with
Germany."

Like everyone else I hoped that this dire prediction would not
come to pass, so much so that the outbreak of the war caught me
entirely by surprise. I went to sleep at midnight, New York time, on
June 21, 1941, while hostilities had already begun six hours earlier.
It was only around seven the next morning that the consular officer
on duty that Sunday woke me up:

"Hitler has attacked us!"

I didn't immediately grasp what was happening. I turned on the
radio. On every station there was news of harsh fighting on Soviet
soil and I remembered my father's admonition the day I left Moscow. When I came down from the attic my colleagues were already
at their stations and none of us was in the mood to talk. We were
stunned. The phones were ringing constantly with American newsmen requesting comments from us. We had nothing to say. Consul
General Fedyushin called a meeting that morning. Just like our country, we were to consider ourselves at war and the most severe form
of discipline would be enforced.

The announcement of the Nazi attack on the USSR revealed
the different attitudes toward my country within American society.
Some people, like Henry Ford, the founder of the motor company,
Joseph P. Kennedy, father of the future President, and other busi-

nessmen with industrial and financial interests in Germany, welcomed the aggression. Others, simple people for the most part, expressed their sympathy with our cause. At public meetings held by left-wing organizations, many Americans demanded that their country get involved in the war. Two viewpoints could be found within these extremes: one egotistical and cynical, the other more realistic and constructive.

Harry Truman, the future President of the United States, and an influential Senator at the time, held the first point of view, which can be summarized as follows: if Germany was winning, we must help Russia; if Russia was winning, the help should go to Germany. The first prize for bluntness would go to the New York *Daily News,* which published a cartoon depicting the USSR and Germany as two snakes fighting each other. The caption read, "Let's let them eat each other!" On the other hand, President Roosevelt represented the moderate wing of the American establishment. He would often say that he was not all-powerful and that his policies were only the sum total of all American political forces. He was, however, very much aware of the danger the Third Reich represented and the need for a great anti-fascist alliance. His attitude toward the USSR in general, now that it was bearing the brunt of the war effort, was favorable.

From the end of 1941 until September 1945 the United States shipped airplanes, tanks, cannon, all kinds of vehicles, food, clothing and other goods to the USSR, a considerable help to our country during the deadliest war in its history. Yet despite this truce and in the face of a common danger, America was careful not to bolster the Soviet regime too much. The total war supplies shipped to the Soviet Union did not exceed 10 billion dollars, while the other allies of the United States were to receive over 36 billion dollars. The total help given from 1941 to 1945 by the United States, Great Britain, and Canada amounted to 4% of Soviet industrial production during the war.[11]

The secret documents we were able to read proved that American and British leaders agreed only to provide defensive weapons to the USSR. Under various pretenses they always delayed deliveries of long-range bombers, tractors for long-range cannon, radio

technical equipment and a good many other offensive or vei͟
vanced weapons. I personally witnessed this at the pier where a
shipment of 12-ton trucks was due to be loaded on a Soviet cargo
ship. At the last minute an American military representative
stopped the loading operation, saying that the trucks had been
brought by mistake. At the end of 1942 a group of Soviet pilots
under the command of one of our aces, Mikhail Gromov, arrived
in the United States via the Bering Straits to fly an agreed-upon
shipment of twenty strategic bombers back to the USSR. They
were not to be delivered: here as well a mistake was the pretense
we were given.

Parallel to official American assistance, a private foundation,
Russian War Relief, was created to help the war effort of the USSR.
Its aims were only charitable and government representatives within
its management were careful to avoid it taking a political position.
Russian War Relief organized fundraising to purchase medical supplies, food and clothing for Soviet citizens. This humanitarian aid
came to over 1.5 billion dollars, about one-sixth of the govern-
ment-sponsored supplies.

I was asked, long after the war, if my stay in America hadn't
troubled my conscience. After all, I was spying on the country that
was helping my homeland survive and win one of the cruelest of
all wars. I answered with "Which America are you referring to?"

I was on the side of the simple Americans, those who came to
the rallies and the fundraisers, who were anti-fascists like we were.
They were also outraged by the attitude of their leaders, just like we
were. Every day our secret agents—but also the newspapers—told
the story of Washington's double standard. The long-promised second front didn't come in 1942 nor in 1943 but only during the
summer of 1944 when the Red Army's victory was no longer in
doubt. The time saved and paid in the blood of millions of my
compatriots and other fighters in Europe, was doubly useful to the
United States. First, the weaker the Soviet Union would be at the
end of the war, the easier it would be for America to mold the
world to suit its purpose. On the other hand, and this was even
more sordid, every day of fighting that passed produced immense
profits for American industrialists.[12]

Leonid Kvasnikov, my boss at the time, had to handle the same question. Long after the war he wrote that the secret intelligence operations of that period should be considered as ways of modifying American policy in the interest of the security, not just of the United States, but also of the entire world. He may certainly be right. However, my version of the facts was far simpler: when you know you are being taken advantage of you have every right to be clever.

5

We were some five thousand miles removed from the fighting but we felt the impact of the war just like all our fellow citizens. I had a map hanging in my room where I traced the Red Army's retreat and then its victorious advance everyday. I regret that I didn't take it with me when I left New York, for once I was back in Moscow I realized that I had abandoned part of myself when I left that map behind. A few days after the war began, Consulate employees decided to donate part of their salary to the defense fund. Those who had families gave twenty to twenty-five percent; since I was bachelor I was able to go as high as forty percent. At that time I was paid a little more than ninety dollars a month. As for the cost of living, my first American suit cost me nineteen dollars, breakfast used to cost twenty cents, and dinner one dollar. Since the living standards of the Soviet people were rapidly deteriorating, we could send a care package to our relatives each month. They were all the same—flour, oatmeal, oil, sugar—and they cost twelve dollars each. That was how my family found out I was in America. These shipments were of considerable help to them, even though sometimes a brick of the same weight replaced the long-expected goods! The fifty-five dollars I had left over was the strict minimum allowing me to survive. This austerity lasted for about two years, and at the end I carefully hid my collars and shirt cuffs because they were so frayed.

We worked 16 to 18 hours a day until the end of the war, which meant our lives were reduced to sleeping and working, but nobody complained. Everyone had a close relative at the front. My brother Gennadi lost a leg; Boris, the youngest in the family, who was a driver, came back unscathed; my sisters were digging ditches at Bryansk; and my mother worked in the rear, in the Urals. All of us understood that the few hours of sleep we were missing were only a small contribution to the common struggle. We all felt guilty for not being on the front lines facing enemy fire.

My days usually began at 4:30 a.m. By 5 a.m. I was wide awake in front of my transmitter key. The Moscow transmitter was very powerful and I had no trouble hearing the messages. After my identifying signal, my first coded message was "I read you loud and clear." "Do you have any messages to send?" the coded answer replied. Even though I couldn't see who was transmitting to me, I could easily imagine him in that same room at the Lubyanka where I had learned the ropes as a telegraph operator. Perhaps he was a jumpy novice just as I had been when I started out. I sent off my encrypted cables in series of numbers and took down the incoming messages. Originally my radio was intended to be a backup in case the regular telegraph office refused to send coded messages to Moscow. The connection was excellent and with the beginning of the war, the flow of communications had increased so much in both directions that my radio communications became a daily event. I also sent some short messages from the Consulate, allowing us to save on foreign currency, since we had to pay Western Union in dollars, which were in short supply, and I would even hook up twice a day, early in the morning and early in the afternoon. The Rezident also ordered me to listen in on Moscow radio news broadcasts and report to him every morning.

My duties as a radio operator lasted two years. During the summer of 1943 the *Journal American* ran a story about the FBI intercepting radio transmissions originating from the Soviet Consulate in New York. The Center, once informed, told us to stop transmitting. However, the State Department issued no official protest about this matter, as no doubt the American embassy in Moscow was also using a radio transmitter. From then on we used the official telegraph service to send even our secret cables, as we had done before the war. The Consulate subscribed to Western Union and all we had to do was press a call button for a runner to come and pick up our coded messages very quickly for transmission to Moscow. Obviously the FBI was making copies of all these secret communications. I have been told that these copies, in the end, filled several rented warehouses, which had to be kept under guard, and our secret correspondence with the Center was probably more expensive for the Americans than it was for us.

Following my morning radio session, I'd go downstairs for breakfast. During my entire life as a bachelor I never cooked for myself. I would walk to the coffee shop around the corner, which opened at six in the morning, to have a hot dog and a cup of coffee. I then returned to the Consulate to handle the mail and read American and Soviet newspapers. My first visitors started around 9 a.m. At the beginning of the war, when Soviet-American exchanges had practically stopped, these were for the most part economic émigrés from before the Revolution, who had fled our country seeking a better life and for whom the right to Soviet citizenship was only a source of problems. The Americans looked upon them as foreigners and there was no chance they could get a job either with the government or with any of the large companies. They were rather old and most of them wanted to return home, but in spite of their repeated requests the Soviet authorities systematically refused to grant them the right to repatriation. They were suspects to both sides.

At that time there were so many citizens of the various republics that made up the USSR in the United States that their fraternal associations funded more than one hundred newspapers in Russian, Ukrainian, Armenian, Lithuanian, etc. Almost all of them were anti-Soviet, but there were some exceptions. The Ukrainian and Lithuanian minorities were the best organized. At the Consulate Pastelnyak and Pavelas Ratomskis, the future head of the diplomatic service of Soviet Lithuania, were in charge of keeping an eye on them.[13] The Russians living in New York included all kinds of people and had three newspapers and two clubs. The ordinary folk mostly read *Russky Golos* (The Voice of Russia), which had positions close to those of the USSR. The intellectuals—writers, actors and painters who had emigrated in the 1920s and 30s—favored *Novoye Russkoye Slovo* (The New Russian Word).

It was the most popular Russian-language newspaper, and had a markedly anti-Soviet stance that did not prevent it from publishing articles on history, art and Russian literature that I read with great interest. After the war began its editorial comments became increasingly patriotic and supportive of the people fighting, even going so far as to reprint articles from the Soviet press. Only Rybakov's monarchists and the Vonsyatzky's Russian Fascists, the "silver shirts," openly called for the defeat of the Soviet Union.

Obviously this very mixed society did not visit the Soviet Consulate. Only the economic émigrés came regularly to renew their rights to Soviet citizenship every year—which required payment of a tax—and to make their donation to the Red Army fund. The official receipt was for them the symbol of their patriotism, which they displayed proudly to their friends and family. Often some of them or their children would volunteer to fight the enemy. These requests were systematically denied, with the exception of three men who were practically NKVD agents. Most of these people felt cut off from their roots. Their children had become one hundred percent American and, because of xenophobia or a kind of rudimentary anti-Communism, their neighbors often showed hostility. The Red Army's retreat became more painful when someone's native city or village fell into the hands of the Nazis. We had the hardest time to comfort everyone, since we were also suffering from the same situation and did not know what to say, other than to repeat our confidence in final victory.

I vividly remember one of those visitors, around mid-October 1941, when the Nazis were near the outskirts of Moscow. A rather aging man had come by to offer a few dollars for the fund. He was unable to control the emotion in his voice and wiped the tears that he couldn't prevent from flowing. Was Moscow about to fall? Why wasn't America doing anything to help the Russians? I did my best to comfort him. After about a half an hour he finally decided to leave.

"I feel better now," he said. "It has been two days that I have been trying to go to work, but I can't. Tomorrow I'll go."

Before leaving my office he looked up at Stalin's portrait hang-ing on the wall.

"Hang in there, Joseph!" he cried out.

In the face of such an overwhelming challenge, the disputes of years past with the liberal Russian intelligentsia seemed to have faded away. The new consul general, Evgeny Kiselev, was a passionate lover of music, and he quickly established excellent relations with the top European émigrés. At our modest receptions one could rub elbows with great orchestra conductors such as Bruno Walter and Arturo Toscanini, Toscanini's son-in-law, Vladimir Horowitz, the famous pianist who had studied at the Kiev conservatory, and the black singer Paul Robeson. Russian composer Alexander Grechaninov was also a frequent visitor. He was seventy-seven years old and quite frequently would breakdown in tears before his daugh-ter took him into the hall to calm him down.

One of the most faithful guests at our receptions was Nikolai Malko, whose story was as instructive as it was incomprehensible. This great conductor was the director of the Marie Theater in Leningrad, which would later become the Kirov Theater. It was a job everyone wanted and probably the reason he had been asked to give a series of lectures overseas in 1928 to defend Soviet music. Before leaving he was received by Anatoly Lunacharsky, the People's Commissar for Education. For years Malko sent regular reports back to Moscow without ever receiving an answer. He explained it by the first political trials of the 1930s. His status was ambiguous: without being an émigré he resided overseas. Possibly Soviet music leaders were afraid of being associated with such a dubious charac-ter. Malko, however, did have a Soviet passport that he would vali-date regularly at the Consulate.

Among the best-known personalities among Russian émigrés was the pianist Sergei Rachmaninov, who had left right after the October Revolution and had been living in the United States since 1918 but had never set foot in our Consulate. Malko knew him well: they had given concerts together in Russia and overseas and continued to see each other in America. He said Rachmaninov suf-fered very much because of the break with his homeland and felt abandoned. The leadership of Soviet music had never contacted him nor invited him to come to Moscow. A rather secretive man, Rachmaninov avoided any political conversations, especially regarding the Soviet Union. However, since the beginning of the war he had sent, through third parties, large contributions to our Consul General, with the assurances of his sincere love for his homeland.

An Estonian pianist, Vladimir Padva, who had come to renew his right to Soviet citizenship and make a contribution to the relief fund, suggested that I attend a concert by the great composer at Carnegie Hall. I can still remember the date: November 1, 1941. I can also remember that the ticket, in the third row of the stalls, cost me a good portion of my salary. During the first part Rachmaninov played Mozart, Beethoven, Schumann, and Bach. After the intermission he played his own compositions. I can still see him coming onto the stage and walking toward the piano in long strides. He bowed with dignity at the audience and sat upon his stool, remaining motionless for a few seconds, eyes closed, his head leaning forward and his long arms hanging down practically to the floor. Then, as if waking up, his fingers touched the keys and he played without any display of emotion, barely moving his upper body. His long ashen face looked tired and serious. One could sense him being ill or depressed and it fit exactly with what Malko said about his frame of mind. I left Carnegie Hall feeling very nostalgic and unfulfilled.

About two months later I went to the Russian baths at Second Street and Second Avenue. I had barely walked in when I heard a song being sung by a powerful choir. In the resting room after the hot steam bath were thirty naked men with towels around their waists, sitting on the benches and singing in Russian. An old man with his back to me accompanied them on a guitar. They were singing so well that I forgot why I had come and went to the bar to order a beer.

"Who are these people?" I asked the bartender.

"You mean you don't know them?" He looked puzzled. "It's the choir of the Don Cossacks! They're famous all over the world. Their leader is Serge Jarov. There he is!"

He pointed to a little man sitting next to the guitar player whose face I could now see. It was Rachmaninov.

The Cossacks started singing the *Angelus*, a song that makes every Russian heart beat faster, and suddenly Rachmaninov changed completely. He put his guitar on the bench and stood up to direct the choir. From time to time he would stop the singers to change the tempo or tell them to sing louder or lower. So now I had seen the great composer not only in formal dress and starched shirt but also wearing only a towel as he made music. Once he was satisfied with the result, he asked the singers to sing the *Angelus* without stopping, which was the greatest musical experience of my life.

The *Angelus* in the evening, how many thoughts come to mind? My youth in my homeland, where I was in love, where my father's house was. When I left it forever is when I heard the bells ringing for the last time.

This émigré choir, directed by one of the great musicians of this century, was full of pure nostalgia that moved the old people at the Consulate, and I felt it deeply too. Rachmaninov died in California in March 1943. He wanted to be buried in his homeland near Novgorod, a wish our Consulate in San Francisco was ready to help fulfill, but his wife and daughters were surrounded by people who were not favorable towards the Soviet Union and convinced them otherwise. He is buried at Kensico Cemetery near New York City.

After the Japanese attack on Pearl Harbor on December 7, 1941, the United States went to war with Nazi Germany and the number of Soviet specialists who were sent in to ferry war supplies, equipment, and much needed consumer products grew very quickly. These were often the same employees who had left New York just six months before when commercial relations had been interrupted. In 1944 Amtorg[13] had about 2,500 Soviet employees, in addition to those of the intergovernmental commission, located in Washington.

My work at the Consulate suddenly multiplied two- or three-fold. I saw between fifteen and twenty people every day. On top of that I went to the pier every two to three days where, from 1942 to 1945, between five and twenty Soviet ships were anchored on the east coast of the United States. I spent many an afternoon on the waterfront. Every time a ship arrived I checked that no one on board was sick, and gave instructions to the crew on how they should behave in America. The seamen were impatient to have news of the war. During the Atlantic crossing they were under orders not to use the radio, in order to avoid attracting German submarines. The ocean trip between America or England and Murmansk, the only port in the Soviet far north that could be used all year, was just as dangerous as being in the front lines. The Germans had an armada of submarines, surface ships and planes precisely to interdict allied shipping and supplies on Norwegian ports and airfields, yet the convoys kept on sailing relentlessly to support the efforts of the Soviet soldiers.

I shall only relate two stories among the many tragic or heroic actions that Soviet sailors told me. The cargo *Stary Bolshevik* ("Old Bolshevik") was under the command of Ivan Afanasyev, a veteran seafarer who looked the part: he was about sixty years old, lean, muscular, heavily tanned, with a deep but firm voice everyone could hear.

The ship was packed to the gills, the cargo hold was full of artillery shells and other ordnance, while pieces of airplane fuselage were wrapped in tarpaulin on deck and tightly fastened to the bulwark, leaving very narrow pathways around the cannon.

"It's not a ship, it's a powder keg!" Afanasyev told me as I was getting off the deck in April 1942. "If one shell hits us we won't have time for a prayer."

I knew about the heavy fighting taking place in the seas off Norway and the Barents and I just nodded, wondering whether I would see the brave captain and his crew again. The bad premonitions—or simply stark realism—took shape near Bears Island, where the convoy, some eighty ships under British escort, was attacked by Nazi naval and air forces. The *Stary Bolshevik* was hit by a bomb that started a fire on board. The entire crew fought the flames that could, at any moment, reach the oil tanks. A British destroyer came alongside to rescue the sailors but they refused to leave. To make matters worse, the *Stary Bolshevik* had boiler room problems and was unable to follow the rest of the convoy. The destroyer came alongside once again, at least to save the men. Afanasyev told the British to keep on going without them. The convoy resumed its journey because to stay would have endangered the other ships.

No one in the convoy—except perhaps for their families who knew nothing of all this—held out any hope of seeing those sailors again, yet they were able to put out the fire and repair their engines enough to reach Murmansk with their deadly cargo at a snail's pace without being detected by the Nazis. It was as if a ghost ship had entered the Bay of Kola. All the sailors were decorated; three of them, including Afanasyev, received the title of Hero of the Soviet Union. The British also wished to reward them for their heroic behavior, which is how I got to see Afanasyev once again. It was on a ship under his command—also named the *Stary Bolshevik*, but a different ship—that I returned to the USSR with my wife in September 1946.

I also can't forget some other heroes who were out-and-out daredevils. The United States was providing us with PT boats, which were small, just like the ones used by the Coast Guard, only about twenty feet long with a crew of four or five and we didn't quite know how to get them across the Atlantic.

"But we can sail on our own!" answered our sailors.

The Americans couldn't believe it. Traveling five thousand nautical miles across the ocean in such tiny boats! Even at the pier they pitched so much that the crew looked like a group of acrobats on the tiny deck.

"No problem!" answered the sailors. "But you'll have to give us additional fuel tanks and more machine guns."

They started out in groups of six or eight motorboats, like fast seagulls, barely hitting the waves and following the coast along Newfoundland, Greenland, and Iceland. Sometimes they linked up with the convoys headed for Murmansk and finally reached the Soviet Union. The U.S. Navy representatives couldn't believe their eyes when they saw the boats disappear on the horizon.

"Crazy! None of our men would do such a thing!"

I should mention, with respect to my official duties, the rallies and other support events I had to attend. Our purpose was to promote the idea that a second front had to be opened. Several times a week in New York, Philadelphia, Boston, or other cities that depended upon our Consulate, I attended rallies organized by American associations or by Russian émigrés where I gave a speech. I also spoke on the radio or at a press conference. Sometimes representatives of large American Groups—Rockefeller, Du Pont, Mellon—came to these meetings and would hand us, on behalf of their companies, checks for fifty or one hundred thousand dollars.

At one of these events I met Andrei Andreievich Gromyko, who was to become the Foreign Minister of the USSR, and later President of the Supreme Soviet under Mikhail Gorbachev. At that time he was a counselor at our Washington embassy. I remember a rally at Madison Square Garden, filled to its 22,000-seat capacity. Gromyko had come from Washington expressly to speak and he wished to speak in English, which he didn't know too well in those days. He pronounced words exactly as they were written. For example, in speaking about the perfidious Nazi aggression, he would say "perrr-fi-di-o-ous." "Why don't you speak in Russian!" people would cry out to him from the crowd. But Gromyko was so sure of himself and so stubborn that he went on with his barely comprehensible speech in written rather than spoken English, leaving the rostrum only when he had finished.

The American attitude toward the deadly struggle between the Red Army and the Wehrmacht had undergone a spectacular change. An anecdote will illustrate this transformation.

On Fifth Avenue, between 59th and 60th Streets, was an antique store called "Old Russia," owned by a Russian émigré named Zolotnitzky. The antique dealer would purchase valuable objects, jewelry, antique furniture, and paintings from the heirs of rich industrialists, Russian nobility and even from the imperial family, and sell them in his shop. There were always people stopped outside his storefront admiring the Fabergé eggs, old jewels, porcelain objects and clocks. Around September 1941, three or four months after the Nazi attack on the USSR, Zolotnitzky placed a small painting in his window *The Cossacks in Berlin, 1814*, with a large card next to it that read: "Shall history repeat itself?" with a big question mark. Our Consulate was just up the avenue and I walked past the window every day. It was a real show for me to watch the reactions of the passersby.

At the beginning, during the fall of 1941 and the winter of 1942, most people only smiled skeptically. The Red Army continued to retreat and was suffering heavy losses. Yet against all odds, the advance of the Wehrmacht was stopped and little by little the passersby lost their skeptical looks. In the fall of 1942 *The New York Times* wrote a short item regarding Zolotnitzky's display, which was truly an act of faith, and "Old Russia" became a real symbol. During the dramatic winter of 1943, as the outcome of the war was being decided at Stalingrad, lively discussions took place on the sidewalk in front of the store. About half of New Yorkers believed that the Cossacks would return to Berlin, not on horseback but in their tanks.

During the summer of 1943, after the battle of Kursk, the comments were unanimous:

"The man is right. History is repeating itself!"

I remember a man saying that history would repeat itself only when the Allies opened a second front in Europe and there was laughter all around.

"The Allies had better get cracking, otherwise the Cossacks will go all the way to Paris as they did in the past!" answered a bearded man, who looked like a student or a hobo.

During the final days of the war, when it became clear that Berlin was about to be taken by Soviet troops, the passersby stopped only rarely in front of the window. Their faces told the story of their disappointment of not having the American army crush the enemy in his lair, as the saying went at the time. On May 9, 1945, the day after the Nazi surrender, the window was rearranged and the painting disappeared. Zolotnitzky had the good taste not to display an exclamation point.

Before getting into the adventures of my professional life as an intelligence officer, I should mention a great change that took place in my private life: as Andrei Vlasov, the head of personnel at NKID had predicted, I got married.

Zina Osipova had come to New York with a group of ten students sent to Columbia University to improve their English, study accounting, and shorthand. The flow of war supplies shipped from the United States to the USSR was growing immeasurably and the documentation for shipping and receiving had to be standardized. Normally, trainees remained in America for one year. This group was the second to arrive in New York, having traveled on a Russian ship, which was not accustomed to transporting pretty young girls. I had my informers everywhere and I knew that not all the girls had been able to resist the young sailors, who had not seen any women in several months. Only Zina and her best friend were frightened of leaving their cabin, running downstairs to the dining room and coming back up to lock themselves in.

When the visitors arrived and came to see me at the Consulate, I was very well disposed toward Zina. The trainees lived two by two in rented studios and I often called on my girlfriend to go to the movies, to a reception, or a rally where I was to speak. Zina was talented and serious, and after her university training period she was offered a job at Amtorg as secretary to Gusev, its President.[14] It was an important job that everyone wanted at the time when the company had reached 2,500 employees. We were married in March 1944 in the basement of the Consulate, which was used as the official office for marriages and other functions. I had so many friends in the Soviet colony that the doormen at the Pierre Hotel, our neighbors, asked the arriving guests "What's the occasion for your reception tonight?" At the banquet all the guests could barely fit at the tables in the large room. Gusev had been invited but did not appear. I later found out through my informants that he was unhappy his secretary was being whisked away from him and he kept on asking questions about me. As far as he was concerned, I was only an obscure trainee at the Consulate. Zina was better informed as to my main mission, and she helped me in my intelligence work, but that is for another chapter.

PART TWO

Foul Play
or Gentlemen's Profession?

6

I have described in detail my legal activities at the Soviet Consulate. Now I must lift the veil on my secret occupations. However, before discussing my agents, who are the real heroes of this story, I must introduce some of my colleagues who will appear throughout this book.

In 1941 the New York Rezidentura of the NKVD had a staff of thirteen, three of whom were technicians. During the war it was very difficult to rotate operational personnel in a normal fashion between the Center and the Rezidenturas overseas, and officers had to stay in place for four or five years straight without any leave. Actually, in New York, only the Rezidents changed frequently. At that time, and contrary to later practice, the heads of Rezidenturas were engaged in recruiting, in addition to being the case officers of the best agents. It was the most effective way to train younger officers on the job. For us the Rezident was neither an inaccessible boss, a bureaucrat, nor a technician. He was more of a "street man," close to us but with more experience. The respect we felt for him was not because of his higher position within the hierarchy but rather due to his professional know-how. It was because our leaders were very dynamic agent runners that they were quickly identified by the FBI and forced to leave the United States. This is why I served under five different commanders during my first tour of duty.

The first commander was someone I did not even know was my real boss. Gaik Badalovich Ovakimyan was expelled from New York before I completed my observation period, while I had not yet been allowed into the secret rooms, and was simply working at my cover jobs. Born in Armenia in 1898, Ovakimyan was trained as a scientist with a doctorate in chemistry and spoke perfect English. A member of the INO since 1931, he had been assigned to the United States two years later, officially as a consulting engineer with Amtorg. In 1940 he was awarded a scholarship at the New York Chemical Institute. His secret specialty was scientific and technical espionage, which he had directed very energetically since 1939.[15]

The FBI was extremely interested in this active member of the Soviet community and a trap was expertly set to catch him. A promising source of information whom we thought could be recruited was in reality a U.S. counterespionage agent. Clever as Ovakimyan was—the FBI had nicknamed him "the foxy Armenian"—he took the bait and in April 1941 was caught during a secret rendezvous. Ovakimyan was not covered by diplomatic immunity and had to appear before a judge, who set bail at $25,000, while he continued to live in New York City awaiting trial. The Nazi aggression against the USSR saved him from prison. At the end of June 1941 President Roosevelt ordered that the charges be dropped, and in July Ovakimyan was able to leave America without any problems. The sources he had recruited remained in place and would stay operational for many years to come. He must be credited with one important discovery: he very quickly pointed out to his superiors in Moscow the new studies on the military uses of uranium, which was to become a major topic of interest of the New York Rezidentura.

After Ovakimyan left, the post was temporarily filled by Pavel Pastelnyak ("Klarin" to the Americans and "Luka" in our coded correspondence), whom I have already mentioned, but he obviously lacked the stature to direct what was becoming one of the

INO's most important stations. The fact that Vasily Mikhailovich Zarubin was named as Rezident confirmed the Center's great interest in our work. Zarubin obviously did not work under his real name. American authorities knew him as Zubilin and within our coded messages with Moscow he was identified as either "Cooper" or "Maxim." Even though we did not know much about him at that time, he was already a legendary character.

Born in 1894 and a member of the Bolshevik Party since 1918, he fought in the civil war and entered the secret services in 1920. In 1925 he was stationed in China, then in Finland in 1926, where he became Rezident. He became an illegal in 1927 and was in charge of our underground post in Berlin, where he married Elizaveta Gorskaya, a refined and communicative woman who had an irresistible power of attraction and whose adventures during the secret war could easily be the subject of another book. The Zarubins set up an illegal network in Germany before operating in France from 1929 to 1933, and then returned to Germany after Hitler's rise to power, remaining there until 1937.

After 1937 Zarubin went to work at the Lubyanka. At the beginning of 1940, when the purges that had already affected the party, the army, and the population, were now in full swing within the NKVD itself where the purgers were being purged, and inside the information service, he was accused of collaborating with the Gestapo. Zarubin was able to avoid the repression and even keep his job because of his firmness and courage. Before being assigned to the United States in the fall of 1941, he went to China to handle none other than an agent, a German, who was the key advisor to Chiang Kai-shek. Zarubin received his orders from Stalin himself before leaving for Washington in October. In practical terms, the Rezident and his men were to make sure that the Anglo-Americans did not sign a separate peace with Hitler to then gang up on the USSR. The mission was to find out the Allies' war plans and secret war objectives and uncover any information on the aims of the Third Reich that Washington or London could possibly have. A key element was all the information regarding the opening of a second front. Finally, Soviet networks in the United States were to concentrate their efforts on securing secrets of cutting-edge war technology being researched by American, British, or Canadian engineers and scientists, which was precisely my area of expertise.

Whether they operated together or separately the Zarubins were just as active in the United States as they had been elsewhere. Officially they resided in Washington where Vasily Mikhailovich was second secretary to the embassy of the USSR, but they practically lived in New York where the Rezidentura was much larger. They had an apartment in Manhattan and their son Petia[16] attended the Soviet school.

I knew Vasily Mikhailovich and had seen him at the Lubyanka just one week after I began working there in the fall of 1940. He captured my imagination at that very first meeting even though he didn't realize it. As I entered Budkov's office, I was speaking as usual in a loud voice (my deafness in one ear made it impossible for me to control my voice level). I had only spoken two words when my boss said "shh!" He pushed me back into the corridor but before the door closed I caught a glimpse of a man sleeping on the couch.

"Let's talk here," said Budkov. "Let him sleep."

"Who is that?"

"Zarubin."

I understood from his voice that I was supposed to know that name.

"But why is he sleeping here?"

"He has just recruited a foreigner and in three hours he's going to recruit another one. He's got to be fresh."

I couldn't believe my ears. Even though I was a novice I knew full well that recruitment represents the end result of a long campaign of seduction, requiring unlimited attention to detail and patience. Furthermore, it was the culmination of the job, an operation that only the top aces were allowed to undertake with the specific approval of their superiors, who would evaluate the pros and cons before giving their authorization. So here was someone who was recruiting people left and right!

Later in New York I understood why Zarubin needed to sleep between operations. When he gave instructions to newly minted agents like myself at the time, he would always repeat:

"When you are about to recruit, never go at it aggressively! Never be in a hurry! You have to set up an atmosphere of calm, of confidence. Invite your friend to the restaurant, have a good meal with excellent wine. Drink as much as he drinks. Your friend must feel at ease, happy to be in your presence. When the moment to order coffee comes is when you can go ahead. You make your recruitment at the end of the meal, while you're having coffee."

Even though his wife, Elizaveta Yulyevna, worked for political intelligence, I saw her quite often because she belonged to our Rezidentura. Her eyesight was rather bad, and Zarubin asked me to cover her several times during her illegal meetings. She always reminded me of the very first beautiful and cultured revolutionary women who had dedicated their lives to the service of their cause. When they had a mission to accomplish, no obstacle could stop them. And she was incredibly brave. In April 1941, with Europe torn apart by war and the aggression against the USSR about to take place, she traveled to Berlin disguised as a German, even though she was actually Jewish, to renew a secret contact.

Zarubin was forty-seven when he arrived in New York. He was of medium height, powerfully built but beginning to gain weight, which didn't prevent him from being an excellent tennis player. His thinning blond hair was plastered back. His gray eyes, always bloodshot from reading and writing innumerable documents, stared at you intensely from behind his steel-rimmed glasses. He knew how to listen and spoke quickly with a metallic voice. Zarubin had a great sense of humor and loved to joke. He really was the life of the party in his work and his private life: he loved to sing and played several instruments. Obviously we operational officers saw him for the most part at the Rezidentura. Despite the enormous amount of work he had to accomplish as manager of many agents and station head, he always found time to give advice to the novices. He was easy to approach, despite his high rank, and we could speak to him informally.

Of all the superiors I was to have, Zarubin came closest to what I imagined to be the ideal leader; he made his own decisions and took responsibility for his choices and mistakes. His favorite saying was "nothing is impossible to a willing heart." Zarubin was reckless and liked men of similar character. He beamed whenever he discovered, while reading a report or listening to an operational description, bold behavior on the part of a young operations man, facing unforeseen circumstances. On the other hand, if someone simply followed the pre-established plan when the situation demanded another course, he would sulk. Mediocre and fearful operations men, who used their brains only to find excuses for their failures, would drive him into a rage. Sometimes after only six months he would send back to Moscow operations men he deemed too frightened or cutting corners, despite the problems we had in bringing in replacements.

He was constantly recruiting and directing an entire stable of men of the highest level, mostly French and Austrians. Under his supervision our Rezidentura became one of the most productive of the entire NKVD. Zarubin was eventually expelled from the United States because he resided in New York while his official posting was Washington. The FBI set its very best agents up against him. One day he was caught during a secret rendezvous, arrested and deported. The Rezidentura was suddenly leaderless and would be headed for one year by Stepan Apresyan, code named Mai.

He was thirty-five years old when he came to New York and had already served in the INO for about ten years. Stepan was a very gifted linguist, having mastered about fifteen languages, even such difficult ones as Finnish, Arabic, and Turkish. With a mind like a computer, he would learn a new language in three or four months. Apresyan's reports were impeccably written for the logic of his argumentation, the style, or the form he used to write them. Even though he was scholarly, he still remained a good fellow, clever at smoothing things over if there were any rough edges, never playing at being the boss.

In 1938 his older brother, who was People's Commissar for the Interior in a Central Asian Soviet Republic, had been arrested and shot during a wave of purges instigated by Nikolai Yezhov. Because of his ties to an "enemy of the people," Stepan, who happened to be working at the Lubyanka, went from his own office directly to the internal prison in the middle wing that cuts across the rectangle formed by the four buildings within the complex. Some of my older comrades told me that they took advantage of his walks in the prison courtyard to throw him cigarettes attached to a little stone through the window, to make sure they landed in the right place. Fortunately for him the "bloody dwarf,"[17] Yezhov, was himself cut down by the hatchet he had wielded so energetically and Lavrenti Beria, the new boss of the organs of repression, decided to rehabilitate the commissar who had been executed. That NKVD decree in effect brought Stepan Apresyan back to life. Not only was he liberated, but allowed back into the intelligence service. Our Rezident had been so deeply traumatized by his own experience as a prisoner that the secret meetings with the agents he handled were absolute torture for him. Several days before a rendezvous he would turn into a withdrawn bundle of nerves, barely listening to what was being said and incapable of making any decisions. At the crucial moment he became frantic and would almost run to the meeting place, anxiously looking behind his back and constantly in fear of being followed. Apresyan was recalled to Moscow in 1945 and worked at the Center until retirement age, spending quiet days using his talent as a linguist in the publishing world.

During the three years I was managing agents in New York, my immediate boss was Leonid Romanovich Kvasnikov—known as Anton. We had a lot in common, having followed identical career paths in more than one instance. Kvasnikov was nine years older than I was, and the son of a railroad worker, like myself. He had become a railroad engineer and studied mechanics, obtaining a degree in engineering and completing the third cycle of graduate studies. When he entered our services in 1938, he became one of the pioneers of scientific and technical intelligence—identified by the code name "XY line." From 1939 to 1942 he was deputy head, then head of that section. He arrived in New York in January 1943, as deputy Rezident for the XY line. Kvasnikov was a rather dry, aloof person who remained a mystery to everyone who met him, which makes it all the more difficult to describe him. It was impossible to have an informal conversation with him, or exchange points of view, not to mention tell any jokes. Furthermore, since he spoke no foreign languages, he did not handle any informants. Yatskov and I gave him a Czech who spoke Russian so that he'd have an agent. However, Kvasnikov was constantly losing contact with his him and we would then have to intervene to reestablish it.

Another reason it was difficult to work with him is that he belonged to Amtorg personnel and therefore could not appear often at the Consulate without arousing the suspicion of the FBI. He came to the Rezidentura, where he was one of the big bosses, only every two to three days. In these circumstances it was impossible for Yatskov and myself to ask for instructions or suggestions when we needed to. Kvasnikov's one strong point was his way of handling "konspiratsya,"[18] he was completely obsessed with secrecy. Within the Rezidentura, officers could only speak in whispers, and we were not allowed to pronounce the names, pseudonyms or any other characteristics that would identify our agents; instead we had to write these on a small piece of paper and show it to the other officer. Despite his rigidity, Yatskov and I managed to get along with him we also happened to be his main field officers and he trusted us. His reputation as a great specialist he owed to his New York team as much as his own talent as an administrator. From 1948 to 1963 he directed scientific and technical intelligence within the KGB. He died in 1993.

I learned a lot from a man who was three years my senior. Semyon Markovich Semyonov had joined the intelligence service in 1937 and had been sent one year later for a two-year course of study at the Massachusetts Institute of Technology. After getting his degree in 1940, he stayed on in the United States as an engineer at Amtorg in New York. He actually was part of scientific and technical intelligence under the code-name "Twain" (Tven, in Russian transliteration). A Jew from Odessa, he was very lively, sensitive and had excellent business acumen, so much so that he often passed for an American businessman. Small and rather frail, he was mild-mannered and smiled easily. When he looked at you his big eyes didn't stop rotating, as if they were two antennas. Extremely outgoing, he knew America, its language and its people very well. Semyonov was perfect at the delicate art of luring and trapping his prey, keeping it in his web, no matter what happened.

I knew some of his agents because I often helped him out. As an Amtorg employee like Kvasnikov, he was closely watched by

American counterespionage and did not always have an excuse to come to the Consulate. I was his partner when he made a pick-up at a secret meeting. On first contact he would take the material from the agent by brush pass.[19] Then he kept on walking and would give it to me in the same manner a few city blocks later. Relieved of the compromising documents, he quietly went to meet his source in a restaurant where he would ask questions about his work and environment, and give him instructions. Meantime, I would hurry back to the Rezidentura to microfilm the documents in time to hand them back to Semyonov by the end of the meal. The next day I would develop the film, carefully study all its contents, and write a detailed report. Semyonov would then come by to add my work into his report and relate useful or noteworthy details about his meeting of the day before. We were both satisfied: he was relieved of a routine task and was less at risk of being caught carrying secret documents, and I was learning on the job, which is really the only way to learn.

Among Semyonov's agents, whom he managed with great energy, were some incredible personalities. The toughest was code named Khvat ("the Vulture"). Contrary to most of our sources, Khvat was not motivated—as his code name indicated—by any ideological or political reasons.

"As far as I'm concerned, the Republicans, the Democrats, the Communists or the Fascists all belong in the same bag," he would say proudly. "If I'm dealing with you it's because I need money! I have to finish building my house, pay for my daughter's college education, and her wardrobe so she will find a decent husband. I couldn't care less about anything else!"

Khvat worked at the Du Pont chemical plant and was passing us information on nylon and the latest varieties of gunpowder. He would hand over a large envelope full of documents to Semyonov during his meetings and would say straightaway:

"One thousand dollars and not a penny less!"

Semyonov, like any good businessman, answered that he couldn't hand over such a large amount sight unseen. The experts had to examine the material first.

"Oh no! That's not at all the way I see it," Khvat would answer. "Come on, it could be completely worthless!"

They would haggle excitedly for a good fifteen minutes. Semyonov would end up handing him a two hundred dollar advance with a promise to give more once the documents had been examined, according to their value. Khvat moaned and ended up accepting. However, once Semyonov handed back the documents— which had been filmed while they had dinner—Khvat would only find another two to three hundred dollars in the envelope, at the most. Once he realized he had been given half of what he had hoped for, he became violently angry:

"Bastards! Crooks! You are nothing but bandits! Highwaymen of the worse kind! This is it! You won't see me again!"

He would stalk away as Semyonov, close behind, tried to calm him down. But Khvat wouldn't listen and seemed not to hear any of his instructions for the next meeting. Semyonov would go home completely depressed and unable to sleep. Though he would spend the entire month until the next meeting worrying about whether or not his agent would appear, he really had nothing to fear. On the scheduled day the greedy man was there, and everything started all over again.

"Why don't you give him what he wants?" I asked him one day. "Your relationship would improve and you could sleep nights."

His answer was a lesson in itself.

"First of all, Khvat is much too greedy and I hate that," answered Semyon with a smile. "And then Kvasnikov and I feel that if we paid him what he wants he would soon finish his house and marry off his daughter. Then we could kiss him good-bye!"

The Center approved this way of handling the agent.

Among all the officers in the Rezidentura, Anatoly Yatskov, also known as Yakovlev (or Alexey in coded messages), was my closest friend. At the NKVD school he had learned French and yet he mastered English in less than one year, thanks to hard work and perseverance. His mission had originally been to create a series of documents for illegals, meaning all the necessary identification papers—passport, identity card, drivers license, insurance policy, birth certificate, etc.—that any regular citizen is expected to have and that are necessary for our agents to appear above suspicion in case they are stopped for questioning. But our station had so many agents who required handling that Yatskov gradually turned in that direction.

In intelligence work, where everything is compartmentalized, no useless questions are asked, even to one's best friends. I had no time to spare from my own job and I was to find out only much later that Anatoly, together with Kvasnikov, were in charge of gathering information on the atom bomb. I was always there when he needed me, and vice versa. We often tailed each other on our way to secret meetings to make sure we were not being followed.

Yatskov, as I mentioned earlier, was an inveterate gambler. He even bet on the Nazis. The day before the aggression, on June 21, 1941, he had become the father of twin girls. For one of them he chose the name Victoria, rare in those days. It was Anatoly's way of telling the Germans who would win in the end: "Since my daughter's name is Victoria, victory will be ours!"

We teased each other constantly like many close friends. Since Anatoly was from Ukraine, I called him khokhol.[20] In turn he'd call me katsap.[21] At the beginning of the war I often told him:

"The khokhols will soon give up Belgorod-Dniestrovky to the Germans!"

And the city promptly fell.

"We shall see how the katsaps will do at Tula!" (My father came from that region.)

"Tula will hold," I said, "because, besides my origins, it is a city that produced weapons."

It so happened that the Nazis were stopped and pushed back near Tula.

"So? What did I tell you?" I nudged him gleefully.

Anatoly frowned. Finally he said:

"Tula held fast only because you weren't there!"

It was our way of commenting on serious matters by joking about them, but it didn't mean we felt like laughing at all.

7

In those days it was both easy and difficult to operate in the United States. It was difficult because we always felt we were under FBI surveillance. From the moment I arrived in New York I was always shadowed as soon as I stepped outside the Consulate. However, at the time apart from my secret radio sessions, I was doing nothing illegal. In December 1941, with America's entry into the war against the Axis, surveillance of the Soviets dwindled spectacularly. The main reason for this was that Germany, Japan, and Italy had about fifty Consulates, innumerable companies and associations and millions of emigrants in the United States. In the 1940s there were more Italians in New York—1.2 million, than in Rome—1 million. The priority for the FBI was to locate and destroy enemy espionage networks, and in a few short months the Americans arrested hundreds of spies and sent many foreign nationals into internment camps. It was my good fortune to begin working as an intelligence officer during this relaxed period.

At the time of the battle of Stalingrad the FBI once again became interested in us. American counterespionage had no doubt noticed how active we were. I remember the words uttered during the winter of 1943 by one of the leaders of the OSS: "We haven't even finished with one enemy and another one sprouts up on the horizon!" I was just beginning to manage my own agents and while I had started with simple operations rather quietly, I was now getting down to serious business just as things were beginning to heat up with Washington's secret agencies.

At the beginning of my meetings with Kvasnikov (he was a dedicated "konspiratsya" theorist, as I said earlier), he always asked whether I had been shadowed in the street. When I answered yes, he would fire off many questions about every detail and would tell me to behave naturally, never showing that I had discovered the tail. He also suggested that I find excuses to leave during the day and evening, to meet American friends, go to the stores or the movies. This would allow me to examine surveillance methods while I had nothing to fear.

During the final years of the war those who followed us were all somewhat inexperienced men, whom the FBI was obviously recruiting from small towns and putting to work after a very short training period. They wore flashy clothes, like black or navy blue raincoats and overcoats in winter; or walked around in shirtsleeves and without a tie in the summer. Once I was followed by a team of at least four agents, one of whom was wearing a soldier's uniform, which allowed me to single him out on three separate occasions: on a subway escalator, at the ticket office of a steamship company where I was buying tickets for my fellow citizens, and in a cafeteria where I was having lunch that day.

It was a good test to enter a bar or a store because one of the agents had to run inside to make sure no rendezvous was in progress. When the target took a bus, someone had to get on board while the others would try to follow unobtrusively by car. It was funny to watch them in the subway. Since they feared I would get into a train that was about to leave the agents following me rushed down the steps as fast as they could. On the platform I kept out of sight behind a column, near the wall or next to another group of travelers. Sometimes, in a deserted subway station, I would end up face to face with the agents following me. At such times I would start thinking happy thoughts and, smiling broadly, walk around humming an American tune. That was supposed to mean that I didn't even see them and had no reason to feel that I was being followed.

Sometimes I couldn't resist the urge to have some fun with these fellows. Once, in a busy street, I noticed that I was being shadowed. The FBI man, on the opposite side of the street, was not doing a good job of appearing natural. I crossed the street and innocently walked straight up to him. He suddenly looked like a pickpocket caught in the act, which was the trademark of these newly trained agents, jumping into the first doorway he could find. Unfortunately the door was locked and in a panic he simply ran away from me.

In all fairness, I eventually received the same kind of treatment. I was on my way back to the Consulate with a thick roll of film, about twenty rolls of ultrasecret documents on microfilm that my agent had rolled one into another, when suddenly a car stopped in front of me and two men got out. That was when the Russian expression "to have one's heart in his heels" has some meaning. Ordinarily I'm no slouch. On the contrary, while I'm very nervous before an important operation I become very calm once it is underway. In this case, however, my body reacted first. A fraction of a second later, as soon as my heart stopped racing, I realized that I would never be able to hide the twenty rolls of film before these characters handcuffed me. I decided to throw my package as hard as I could onto the roof, remembering how well I threw hand grenades in training. Obviously they'd eventually find the film, but the point was to gain as much time as possible. With all these thoughts racing through my mind I didn't even slow down.

The two guys went into a building and didn't even look at me. I arrived in front of the Consulate and rang the doorbell. The door didn't open. I tried again but there was no response. Finally, after the third time I heard the keys turning in the lock and was safe once again. The guard on duty looked at me inquisitively: "What's going on, Alexander Semyonovich? I barely had time to arrive and you were ready to ring the bell again?" On second thought, those two men were probably just two passersby. However, had they been with the FBI, that would have been the way to test me to see if I was going to turn and run. In any case, it was good training for me to feel what it was like to be the hunted prey.

Increased surveillance turned out being very useful and I wound up knowing New York like the back of my hand. I had identified several alleyways or buildings in each neighborhood that had two entrances to shake off any tails, but I never had to use any of them. The best rule is to never show that you know you're being followed, or try to lose the agents following you. Rather than trying to play James Bond in such cases, it is much better to simply cancel the meeting. The FBI was not just following us, it also had fixed observation posts. The Consulate faced the luxurious Pierre Hotel, which was about fifty stories high. We were so positive that one or more rooms were rented by counterespionage all year round that we never even bothered finding out which ones they were. We were very active, however, in weeding out the hidden microphones in our offices.

One day, at the beginning of my tour, as I was taking my Consulate telephone apart, I noticed that the wires were shunted to a condenser, allowing for the adjustment of a high-frequency modulator, which could be read on some other part of the phone line. Thanks to this gadget, the FBI could listen in on everything that was being said in the room! I showed the trick to Yatskov, whose desk was directly opposite my own. Without a second's hesitation Anatoly grabbed the condenser and ripped it out, then immediately dialed the number: the phone was working! I took his phone apart as well and found the same system. The second condenser was also thrown into the wastepaper basket.

That afternoon an American electrician appeared at the Consulate.

"I'm from the telephone company. You're having problems with some of your phones?"

Yatskov answered pointedly:

"You are the ones with the problems. Our phones work very well."

Since then we always unplugged our telephones before any serious conversation. As for the Rezidentura, not only was it completely soundproof, it had no phones at all.

My apartment was also being watched. After we were married, Zina and I rented a large studio at 64 West 89th Street. It took us less than one month to notice a neighbor across the street, a skinny woman who appeared to be the building manager. We often saw her standing at the corner or sitting on a park bench. Was it a coincidence? I had a little plan to find out. Late one afternoon I called Zina at Amtorg to tell her I'd be home at about 7 p.m., since I was sure one or even both phones were bugged. My wife was therefore not far from the house around six-thirty. From a distance she saw the skinny woman leave her apartment and sit at her favorite park bench looking in the direction I was supposed to come from. She was not waiting long and I appeared at the right time. Zina saw the woman get up immediately and disappear into the entrance where a pay phone was hooked into the wall. She saw her dial a number, say a few words and hang up. To be certain, we repeated this little scene twice later. There was no question the woman was working for the FBI. Even though I have fun recalling all these anecdotes, one shouldn't get the impression that they were part of some game; it's always useful to know the opposition's set-up.

I must say that American counterespionage had few reasons to suspect me, and this explains the "amateurishness" with which the surveillance was conducted. First of all, I had replaced an "above-board" member of the Consular staff, Konstantin Fedoseyev. In spite of all the tricks commonly used, it often happens—all over the world, I may add—that secret agents using official cover end up filling the same jobs: those that the diplomats reserve for their intelligence colleagues. Secondly, I was handling my job at the Consulate receiving visitors, processing visas and tickets, and going to the pier when ships arrived. I even had an American assistant, a Doctor Feinstein, who worked at Amtorg and helped me when we had to take care of sick sailors. As for the Consul General, Evgeny Kiselev, he kept sending me to support rallies where I would speak on behalf of the Soviet Union.

The FBI finally made an attempt to entrap me, probably as a matter of course. One day I had two American visitors, who claimed to be lawyers for the Development Corporation, speak to me enthusiastically about the great advantages of Socialism, offering their services to accelerate its coming to America.

"Why have you taken this decision?" I asked them very calmly, since I felt I had to be very alert.

"Well, it's the future of humanity! We don't want to miss the boat."

"Very well! I think it's best that you join the labor movement. You must have a union in your company?"

They probably didn't expect such an answer but that's how I let things stand.

To be sure we sent one of our American agents to this Development Corporation and instructed him to ask the same questions that had been put to me by my two visitors. Our agent quickly understood that the company did not handle that type of business. Therefore, it could only be one of two things: the company was either an FBI cover, or my two "lawyers" had picked that name at random, not expecting us to check it out.

Despite all our worries about the FBI, our work proceeded very efficiently for reasons that were unrelated to the fact that it took place in the United States, because the situation was similar for our services in other countries. I have already mentioned the purges at the end of the 1930s that had decimated Soviet foreign intelligence. Yet that period of the 1930s and 1940s was to be among the most productive of all. The INO and the GRU[22] were able to penetrate Europe, America, and Japan, creating a huge illegal network of over three hundred sources of information. During the war the "Red Orchestra," led by Leopold Trepper in Nazi Germany, was able to transmit to Moscow, under the very noses of the Gestapo, some of the most sensitive information on Wehrmacht plans and operations. Over eighty agents led by Harro Schulze-Boysen and Arvid Harnack put their lives on the line and many were to die after the network collapsed in 1942.

Alexandre Rado in Switzerland directed the illegal network "Rote Drei" ("the Three Reds"). This network had many sources inside the Third Reich and even some high-level Abwehr officers of German military espionage were its informants. It was in England that the best known network, the legendary "Cambridge Five," was created. Its members—Kim Philby, Donald Maclean, Guy Burgess, John Cairncross, and Anthony Blunt—held extremely sensitive positions, during and after the war, within British intelligence and the Foreign Office. During this crucial period of history most of the state secrets of the mighty British Empire landed on the desks of the Lubyanka and the Kremlin.

The technical and scientific intelligence gathered by the New York Rezidentura alone was no less impressive. I didn't know it at the time but my friend Yatskov and our boss Kvasnikov directed the most important network—actually the only network—dedicated to atomic espionage. It was thanks to Klaus Fuchs, Theodore Hall, the Cohens, and a few other agents who have not been identified to this day, that the USSR was able to create its own atomic bomb. Another network of prime importance specializing in radio electronics, aviation, and ordnance was the one headed by Julius Rosenberg. It so happens that from 1943 to 1945 I directed the secret Rosenberg network and that, from 1947 to 1949 in London, I became the case officer of Klaus Fuchs. I shall discuss these operations in detail later.

The secret services recruited their sources mostly among the support staff—secretaries, typists, translators, code clerks, couriers—by manipulating human and character problems. Some excellent informers agreed to work for foreign intelligence services because they felt frustrated in their ambitions, because their work was not appreciated, because they loved gambling, drinking, or women. Yet during the period I am writing about none of these archetypes applied to any of our recruits! Many times they were part of the best society, had easy lives, were often well educated, intelligent, talented, and had good, even brilliant, careers. Understanding what could prompt people as brilliant as Maclean or Fuchs to hand over their country's secrets to a foreign power deserves careful scrutiny.

First of all, in the 1930s and 40s, Marxist and Communist ideas had a powerful influence on many people. Many workers and intellectuals were looking with great hope toward the country that was attempting to build a society of equality and justice. The Soviet Union also attracted much sympathy because of the hostility surrounding it, that many people in the West disapproved of. Naturally this good will receded dramatically after the signing of the German-Soviet Non-Aggression Pact, which was seen as a betrayal of democratic ideals by the USSR. However, once Nazi aggression began in 1941, the feelings of sympathy toward my country resumed even stronger than before.

If so many foreigners decided to engage in the dangerous activity of espionage by giving us jealously guarded state secrets, it was because they were disgusted by the situation: they felt it unjust that the Soviet Union should fight the German war machine alone, while the Western leaders, despite their promises of opening a second front, allowed the Soviets to exhaust themselves in their superhuman effort. Everywhere in the world people became convinced that liberation would come from the east. So, to bring about victory over the common enemy faster, the West's intellectual and technical elite decided to make its contribution to the military effort of the USSR.

The popular view of the work of secret agents appears to be something necessary, but dirty and demeaning for both sides. This view casts the case officer in the role of a cynical Mephisto, preying on human frailties to feed upon one of the most shameful human vices, that of treason, while the source is portrayed as cowardly, greedy, lustful, an alcoholic or someone seeking revenge against his superiors.

When I started out in the shadow world this was not the case at all. Almost all of my informers were persons of high moral character who were extremely brave and acted according to their convictions, out of devotion to the Communist cause or simply because their understanding of the notions of good and evil went beyond everyday politics. The currency of our trade was not the dollar but human solidarity, helping others, anti-fascism, and rejection of the deals that each day would cost thousands of lives at the front, where the outcome of the war was being decided. I have no reason to find other motivations for my foreign agents who were putting their welfare, their freedom and even their lives at risk for their ideals. I can only feel admiration and gratitude toward them. These are the feelings that prompted me to write this book, certain parts of which have been published against the judgment—if not the actual prohibition—of those now responsible for the Foreign Intelligence Service of the Russian Federation, the SVR.[23]

Those men, my brothers in combat in the silent struggle where the front line was invisible, also faced the troubling question of treason. But I am quite sure of the answer they would have given to that question. To the best of them, the most disinterested, collaborating with a foreign intelligence service was not at all revealing of a personal vice or a short-term view, but rather more of a broader vision of things to come. Their homeland was not the United States or Great Britain, but the World itself and their compatriots were all the inhabitants of the earth. It is in the name of this community for the common good that they shared secrets with us that appeared too dangerous to be held by one side alone.

The best example of this type of thinking is the atomic bomb. Without the choice of people like Klaus Fuchs, Allan Nunn May, and other secret agents of Soviet intelligence whose identity has not yet been revealed; without the sense of danger that Niels Bohr or J. Robert Oppenheimer felt in having the atomic superweapon under one country's control that could easily shatter such a fragile peace, we would have had few chances of avoiding another world war. It is very significant that the three main secret Soviet intelligence networks that were operating before, during and immediately following the Second World War (the Cambridge Five, the Rosenberg Group and the Atomic network), did not survive the opening shots of the cold war. The most vital work had already been accomplished: Nazism was defeated and the atomic balance had been reestablished. Once global threats had been avoided, the time for national missions and civic loyalism had returned and the great idealistic spies finally disappeared from the scene: tragically like the Rosenbergs, dramatically like Fuchs or Sobell, bitterly like Maclean, Burgess and Philby, energetically like Barr or Sarant, or without fanfare like so many other unidentified agents. Their time had passed.

The next generation that would still include so many top people who sympathized with the USSR and believed in Communist ideology was to be very different. Payment became the rule and new techniques of agent handling—from blind treatment[24] to out and out blackmail—were now the norm. It is also for these reasons that, even though my activities during the 1960s and 70s were full of surprises and adventures, I shall not mention the agents I managed during that time. This book is not intended to be dedicated to them.

8

My entry into the world of intelligence was long and slow and I did not become truly operational until the summer of 1943. During my first New York posting I was, in technical terms, managing ten "human resources of valuable information" and three additional agents.

The story of the first agent I recruited was typical of the mindset of the times. It goes to show that to cooperate with Soviet intelligence in the midst of the war against Hitler was not at all debasing. A former tsarist colonel who lived by a high code of honor was my first guide. Like many White émigrés he came to see me at the Consulate. He was shaking indignantly because his son, as he told me, was serving in the OSS and had told him some fairly disgusting details. OSS officers had begun a massive debriefing of Russian and Ukrainian émigrés, seeking information about their relatives residing in the USSR and the Soviet ports in the Far East, the Far North and the Black Sea. Clearly the United States was preparing a scenario that included a landing in Russia. Officially, this plan was only to be activated in the event of the USSR's military defeat. However, it was not clear whether the purpose was to help the Red Army or to grab a piece of the pie were the Soviet Union to collapse. The colonel was more inclined toward the second possibility.

"I never would have expected such treachery on their part!" he said. "The Americans are getting ready to knife us in the back! Be careful!"

During the conversation I learned that his son, who had passed on the information to his father, was also indignant that America was letting the USSR fight alone against the common enemy. Since he lived in New York, I carefully suggested that perhaps I should meet him.

"Why don't you come to the house!" said the colonel. "My son will be delighted."

A week later, along with a political intelligence colleague, I went to see my new friends. Even though he was more American than Russian, the colonel's son agreed, without much hesitation, to hand over to us confidential information regarding the OSS and its activities.

That officer did not feel he was being disloyal in making this commitment. Prior to the war the United States had many intricate connections to various political, economic, financial, scientific and cultural organizations in Germany, Italy and many other countries in Europe. Furthermore there were millions of immigrants in America who had arrived from the very countries with whom she was now at war. These numerous sources allowed the OSS to gather valuable information on Axis plans, including those intended for the Eastern front. Alas, Washington had no intention of sharing them with the main target, i.e., the Red Army. We could only lay our hands on them via the underground.

At the end of 1942 Zarubin ordered me to establish contact with two American agents who were radio operators like me. The first, "Andrei," was of Polish origin; the second, "Koum," was a Serb. Like many other foreigners from Eastern Europe who had established themselves in the United States, they were enrolled in one of the many training centers in America and Canada set up by the Anglo-American special services. They would then be dropped back into their native countries by parachute to organize secret resistance groups and gather intelligence that would be transmitted back to London by radio.

Andrei had arrived in the U.S. with his parents at the age of seventeen in 1935. He was working in a radio repair shop in 1942 when he was drafted and sent to an OSS radio school. He learned how to use a transmitter, was trained in secret operations and in parachuting out of a plane, while the other part of the training was essentially political education.

The officers in charge of training explained that the Polish government in exile in London sought to recreate after the war, with the assistance of Britain and the United States, a greater Poland "from sea to sea." Andrei even gave me a map of this future state, which not only included regions that had become part of the Soviet Union in 1939—Byelorussia and the western Ukraine—but also a large portion of southern Ukraine, including the region of Odessa. The strangest part of the story was that Andrei, like most of his colleagues, was actually Byelorussian and for him the Poles were the oppressors. He and his friend were disgusted by these imperialist projects and even wanted to leave the school in protest, but we obviously convinced them not to.

Before he left we set up a calendar of radio dates between him and Moscow and gave him a permanent rendezvous point in Warsaw. Koum also received his calendar of radio meetings with Moscow, but he gave me an address in Yugoslavia where he could always be reached. I thought of them many times after they left but never found out whether they survived the chaos of the war.

During this first tour of duty in the United States, I personally recruited two agents. It may appear a simple matter of finding the right man, meeting him, becoming his friend and little by little drawing him into collaborating with you. For starters it's useless to recruit as many sources as possible. In reality, even though the officer in charge does most of the work, a recruitment implies a whole series of procedures undertaken by five or six other officers. This is what is called "studying the target." To get the green light for recruitment, the potential agent must fulfill at least four requirements.

The first question is whether the target really has access to confidential information. If the target is only to be used as a courier or liaison agent, then the first question is unnecessary and one can skip directly to the second: is the target a sensible person, serious, brave, capable of following all the rules of secret operations and not endanger, in a moment of panic, his own security and that of

69

his comrades? Intelligence work is not for eccentrics, for people who tend to overestimate their capabilities, or daredevils. The third rule is to discover what is called "the basis for recruitment." In the best case it will be devotion to a common cause or because of political or ideological beliefs. Greed or perpetual money problems, even though they do not foster friendly or deeper relationships, can be just as effective. Other reasons to betray (revenge, women, alcoholism, narcotics, or gambling) are not as good and clearly none of these character traits tends to add to the trustworthiness of the source.

Finally, it is important to be sure that the target is not a plant by the other side, a mole with a mission of infiltrating your network like the two "lawyers" of the Development Corporation the FBI had sent to sound me out.

Studying the target takes some time. The Rezident supervises the mission of the operational officer and assists him as needed, while three other persons at the Center (another operations officer, the section commander and his assistant) are also involved: their job is to do as much research on the target and his friends as possible within the imposing archives of the intelligence services. Since they are neither on the spot nor part of the action, they have the necessary detachment to follow the relationship with the target being studied and give their more or less unbiased opinion regarding his recruitment. If these five persons agree to "approach" the potential recruit, a request is submitted to the director of intelligence or his assistant, either of whom has the final say.

It would be too good to be true, naturally, if every recruitment were to succeed! It sometimes happens that those approached refuse to collaborate. Some politely refuse: "It's not for me, I have my family. I'm not in good health, I talk in my sleep," etc. Failure in such cases has few consequences, but if there is the risk that the person approached will inform his own country's authorities, it becomes necessary to change his mind by using arguments that are unfavorable to him. To avoid such a negative result, should the outcome of a recruitment attempt be in doubt, a special recruiter is generally brought in from overseas to handle the approach. In case of failure, he would be able to leave without compromising the

Rezidentura. Fortunately or unfortunately, life always unravels the most complicated theoretical constructs.

During my first tour in the United States, I was able to successfully complete all my recruitments. However, the reasons for my success were due less to my professional and psychological skills than to the high motivational level of my agents who were all devoted to the cause of fighting Nazism. This said, my very first experience, without being a real blunder, was a valuable lesson as far as I was concerned.

My target was a handsome well-built young man to whom I gave the code name "Zhemchug," or "Pearl" in Russian. He was a radio technician and lived in a worker's hostel. Originally from Galicia, he had arrived in the United States as a tourist in 1939 and, being Ukrainian, he did not want to return to his country, which was now under Polish control. Once most of Galicia became the western Ukraine and part of the USSR, owing to secret protocols of the German-Soviet Non-Aggression Pact, he requested Soviet citizenship. He came to the Consulate and spoke with me.

I met Zhemchug in the evenings and we spoke of many things but mostly about politics. These conversations convinced me that my friend was sincere, and I was able to complete a positive file on him while the investigations made by the Center also turned out favorably. Zarubin, the ace recruiter, favored a gradual type of recruitment and proposed the following plan of action.

I was to tell Zhemchug that the USSR needed specialists. Rather than going back to the Ukraine as a low-level technician, it was best for him to remain in the United States for a few years, go to school and get some work experience in an American factory, which would make him much more useful to his country. This suggestion was reinforced with the offer of a small "scholarship" to pay for his studies, while at the same time I was to begin training him in intelligence tradecraft by first asking him to write reports on articles taken from technical publications. Then I was to convince him to become an American citizen and get a job in a research lab.

Zhemchug accepted the idea of furthering his education in the United States with enthusiasm, but unfortunately for us he became too involved and too successful. At first everything went along fairly well: I would meet him in a cafeteria, he would bring me press articles on radio technology, and I'd hand him $25 every month. Then we encouraged him to go to Washington to take a one-year radio course, where there were American and Brazilian officers among his classmates. Not only was our man an excellent student, he also showed aptitude for business: for $50 a month he rented an apartment where he kept one room for himself and sublet the other two rooms for $40 a month. He also got a license as a radio repairman, and worked at repairing radios in his room from four in the afternoon to eight in the evening. His reputation grew and within one year his private repair shop was generating $200 to $300 a month. At the same time he continued to provide me with written reports and information he gathered from conversations with the other trainees. However, once his year of training was over, he was unable to get a job because he was not yet a naturalized citizen.

In 1943 I was to take over a very important secret group, the Rosenberg network. Since Zhemchug's production was by now insignificant, Kvasnikov no longer allowed me to go to Washington, to avoid arousing suspicion with the FBI. It just was not worth the risk and Zhemchug was left inactive. One year later I went to Washington on other business and was curious to find out what had become of him. If he now had a more interesting job, it would then be high time to reactivate him. I leafed apprehensively through the phone book, and found him listed, but at a different address. He was very pleased to hear from me and later, as we were having a beer, he proudly told me how his life had changed. In the middle of the war every family had a radio so that his new repair shop was constantly busy and couldn't handle all the work. He had hired another repairman, had bought a used car and a house with a mortgage he was paying off and, on top of all that, he had $2,000 in the bank.

He was a good fellow and I was happy for him, but the more he talked about his new life the less I had any reason to be satisfied. Zhemchug liked being his own boss in his own repair shop and he had no desire to become an employee once again, even with the best of companies. He was also making plans to get married and had no intention of leaving the United States. He assured me that he was deeply grateful, because it was thanks to my suggestions and the support he received at the beginning that he had been able to create such a good life for himself. In intelligence though, you rarely take someone completely off your lists. At the end of 1945 we urgently needed someone like Zhemchug, but unfortunately he was not in the new phone book and there was no answer at his old number. For ten long years the Washington Rezidentura tried to locate him but failed. He had probably been drafted and may have died during the war.

I had better luck with my other agents. My friend Yatskov passed me one of his sources, whose code name was "Dayvin." Anatoly had met him in October 1942. At that time, one of the hardest moments of the entire war, we would see between thirty and forty persons per day at the Consulate, where many came to express their support. Dayvin was of Ukrainian descent; his father had come to America in 1908 and remained a Russian patriot. At the very beginning of their relationship Dayvin told Yatskov:

"If I did Russia any harm and my father got wind of it he'd rip my head off!"

Dayvin was born in 1913. His mother was American and he spoke only English, which to us was very positive. Better still, he had never joined the Communist Party or any other left-wing organization, and his wife was also American, a practicing Catholic for whom Communism was the work of the devil. For us, it was ideal: on the one hand, Dayvin shared our beliefs, and on the other, no one could suspect that he'd collaborate with the Soviets. Obviously we strongly encouraged him to keep up appearances, and even though he was an atheist, Dayvin often went to church with his wife and had the reputation of being a hard-line conservative with his friends.

He was quite handsome and solidly built but was not drafted because of his poor eyesight. He worked as a foreman in a factory that made klystrons and magnetrons for radar systems. Manufacturing these empty tubes was top secret and riddled with so many technical problems with such huge wastage that the factory had to make fifty tubes before getting one that could function. Dayvin brought several of these tubes to Yatskov rather quickly as proof of his admiration for the heroic struggle of the Red Army. Since I was better trained than Anatoly in radio technology, Kvasnikov transferred the agent to me in October 1943.

As specialists we were able to go much further and I asked Dayvin to write very detailed reports on the way the assembly line was organized, the molding and oxidation of certain parts, the calculations used for soldering and other technical details. In addition to the tubes, he brought me miniature resistance elements, crystal processing units and other devices to produce electronic warfare material. At first Dayvin was not paid any money but since he only made about $50 per month, the couple's finances took a turn for the worse after the birth of his son. Our Rezidentura asked the Lubyanka for a monthly bonus of $50 but since the material he was passing on to us was so valuable the Center immediately authorized $75. Dayvin was pleased. On top of that I also gave him a yearly additional bonus of $550 to $600. He used the money to buy a second-hand car, which he drove expertly in making sure he was not being followed.

I liked managing Dayvin. He was a born agent: well disciplined, cautious, he was able to hide his feelings and remain all the while one of our most productive sources without ever causing any reason for suspicion either at home or on the job. He looked so straight laced that one day he came to a meeting wearing a new hat that made him look like a federal agent. This didn't help the kind of relationship we had: cops are singled out rather easily in a crowd and Dayvin ran the risk of being approached by one of them at a critical moment.

"You have to change that hat," I told him in no uncertain terms. "You look like a cop."

"Oh really? No problem."

Of all the agents I ever managed, Dayvin was the one who consistently gave me the feeling that our collaboration could go on indefinitely.

In November 1945 we learned to our great surprise that Elizabeth Bentley, one of our liaison agents, had long since been "turned" by the FBI. The "Red Spy Queen," as the papers called her, had exposed more than one hundred of our American sources. Faced with this media barrage, the Center ordered us to deactivate almost all our sources to avoid a complete collapse of the underground networks. Dayvin was one of the very rare exceptions. Nonetheless, out of caution, I set up a complicated security routine with him to cover our backs in all cases: before making contact we would cross paths in the street. If there was nothing suspicious, one turned left and the other right, and we would circle the block to cross paths once again in the street that was parallel to the first one. If after all this the coast looked clear we would meet and talk in a bar.

Dayvin listened to me carefully and smiled:

"Alexander, it's you Soviets the FBI is watching. There are too many of us Americans. If the Feds ever nab me it will be because of one of your mistakes."

Dayvin remained slippery until the end, and we had our final meeting in June 1946 when I temporarily deactivated him. One of my colleagues took over his management six months later. Our farewell meal was quite moving: we parted company like two soldiers who had gone into battle in the same platoon, and Dayvin dreamed of visiting Yatskov and myself one day in the Soviet Union. He was never to get his wish, for at age fifty it was discovered that he suffered from an incurable illness. Before he died he asked his case officer to take care of his children. He had been working for us for fifteen years by that time and he was right to appeal to those whom he considered to be his best friends. The KGB was able to assist his family without ever revealing the origin of the funds.

One of my very first agents was a great help to me in organizing my work. I'll call him "Setter." He was American-born, an enthusiastic ham radio operator, and an engineer at a large electronic equipment manufacturer, mostly radar and sonar for the U.S. Army. He was recruited because of his progressive ideas by one of our most trustworthy American agents during the summer of 1942. Another way of limiting the risk of exposure in recruitment is to have a local citizen make the approach because those kinds of agents who are really good at spotting talent do not necessarily have access to sensitive information and are less likely to be subjected to counterespionage surveillance.

I took charge of Setter in 1943. He was tall, over forty, with graying hair, and a distinctive face that made him stand out in a crowd. During our very first secret rendezvous, his angular features betrayed signs of great stress. I attributed this to the large number of documents he was carrying to his new case officer, in addition to not knowing how much he could trust me. When I finally asked why he was so jumpy, Setter felt relieved to open his heart to someone, since secret agents don't have that many confidants.

"I had another fight with my wife," he admitted. "You know how women are. Mine, in any case, is extremely jealous and, to top things off, she's pregnant. She made a scene as I was about to leave, accusing me of having a mistress. To be able to leave the house I actually had to push her away. And she's expecting a child! What a bastard I am!"

I smiled to comfort him since he appeared to need it badly.

"It would have probably been reassuring to her if I told her I was going to meet a Russian spy!"

Setter lived some 350 miles away from New York, and he had been cursing himself for the entire trip.

"You're wrong not to explain anything to your wife," I said. "Obviously you can't tell her what you're really doing, but you could say you're active in an anti-fascist organization. An American organization, obviously! But if word gets around it might affect your job. That way your wife will not tell anyone and will be reassured."

Setter felt better immediately.

"Yes, you're right. That's what I'll tell her, but I must say that my nerves are very raw. I can't sleep, and when I finally do sleep I have nightmares and wake up in a sweat."

I tried to reassure him and I concluded rather quickly that the main cause of his nervousness came from taking sensitive files out of his office, walking around with them all day and then having to put them back without alerting any of his colleagues. That was only one aspect of the problem because, as soon as Setter parted with those explosive papers for a few hours, it would be my turn to sweat! I ran a thousand times the risk of being stopped and arrested by the FBI when I returned to the Consulate to microfilm the documents. And then he naturally would be unable to bring the compromising material back to his office.

It was obvious that we had to organize ourselves differently. Instead of doubling the risks by having two meetings, one to receive the materials and the other to hand it back, the agent could photograph the documents himself and bring back the undeveloped film. Should there be any danger, all one had to do was open the roll of film exposing it to erase everything. I explained my idea to Setter, who was very satisfied since he knew photography quite well.

A few days later, during a brush pass, I handed him a Leica with the necessary accessories. That put an end to his worries and from that point on we met every thirty to forty days, preferably on a Sunday morning. I would leave the Consulate at six or six-thirty, when the streets were empty and discovering any type of tail was child's play. Following a security itinerary within Manhattan, I would take the bus to the small town where he lived or to another town halfway between New York and his home. I would take some precautions before actually reaching our meeting place, where Setter would pick me up in his old Ford. Together we would take another security itinerary before talking for a half hour in his car, in a drugstore, or a park. We rarely had any conversations that would allow us to get better acquainted, since he was always in a hurry to get back to his wife. He'd drive me back to the bus stop to New York and at the very last minute hand me the roll of film. As far as he was concerned the danger ended right then and there.

Between meetings Setter had time to take home two or three batches of documents from his office. He would take a short stroll after dinner with his baby boy, saying that the child needed fresh air, but really to make sure his house was not being watched. Then, about 9 p.m., he'd close the curtains but, as an added precaution, he made his microfilms in a large closet, which had been prepared expressly for that purpose. Once this system began functioning normally, Setter became a different man, a regular American, in control of his emotions and able to face any situation. He never missed a rendezvous. Each time he would bring seven or eight rolls, each with thirty-six exposures, rolled into one another along with blueprints and descriptions of the latest devices. The Center classified most of the documents he gave us as "valuable" and "very valuable." Setter was deactivated at the end of 1945, when I thanked him profusely and gave him money for his future expenses.

As soon as I understood the advantages of the system I had set up with Setter, I used it with all of my agents, and since all of them were technicians, they had no problems with photography, which was not always the case with a lot of our agents. Many case officers did not have it as easy as I did. Of course Klaus Fuchs, the famous physicist working at the Los Alamos research center in New Mexico, and who was under the tightest possible security, could only write his reports in longhand before handing them over to his case officer. Some agents communicated through "dead letter drops,"[25] but every other procedure required two meetings for each packet of documents.

Another event was to turn me into an expert photographer.

The Rezidentura and the Center were communicating through two separate channels, Western Union telegraph and my secret transmitter. The latter channel was used for urgent and very short messages, encrypting long correspondence, such as agent reports and blueprints would have required an army of code clerks. The documents were therefore photographed on microfilm by the operators or the agents themselves with the film being developed immediately to check each exposure. Should there be any bad exposures we had time to start over at once. I became so confident that after taking the pictures I would hand the documents back right away without even developing the film. All in all I thought it was better that way: each additional minute could be fatal to an agent who had given me the material and was expecting it back.

Our internal correspondence was an entirely different matter. Operational officer's reports, analyses, and general reports were much more sensitive documents. After all, should the FBI intercept microfilmed documents transmitted by our agents, it was not so easy to spot the actual source of the leak: many people had access to one confidential file or another and such an investigation—assuming it was successful—could take months or even years. Our reports to the Center, however, did mention the agent's code name, sometimes even the real name, address and other details that could lead to the agent's identification, the places of our meetings and the substance of our conversations. Therefore everything was typed, microfilmed and, as an added precaution, shipped to Moscow as undeveloped film.

All film, whether developed or not, went into the diplomatic pouch. It was shipped about once a month via couriers having diplomatic status, many of whom were former NKVD officers who for one reason or another were inadequate for operational work. The pouch took about three to four weeks to reach Moscow via Seattle and Vladivostok. At that time security procedures were extremely strict even though not all documents sent over were top secret, as the Americans like to say. Most of the time the material was actually very ordinary printed matter, such as American newspapers and magazines, press items, etc.

One day this ordinary pouch was made up of twenty-five large trunks! Two courier officers refused to be responsible for such a huge shipment: it was impossible for them to check on so much baggage when they also had several canvas bags that contained ultrasensitive material. As usual, Zarubin ordered me to accompany the "bags" to Chicago, where our couriers were to change trains on their way to Seattle. We loaded and unloaded our entire shipment under the disbelieving gaze of the FBI agents following us. At the station we formed a convoy of three carts stacked up high like skyscrapers. The red caps were out of breath just like us. When we finally reached the platform, the train had not yet pulled into the station. I smiled at one of the FBI agents, a big likable fellow, who was following us.

"What are you carrying that's so heavy? Is it lead?" he asked.

Whenever it's possible you must always tell the truth.

"Don't bet on it," I answered. "It's much heavier than lead! Here, why don't you pick it up!"

He took my word for it.

"So what is it?"

"One whole month of *The New York Times*, *Life* magazine, etc. It's the only way to ship the American press to Moscow."

"Thank you very much," he answered knowing he'd certainly be congratulated for having shed light on this intriguing mystery. "We can help you load it if you wish."

Obviously this only concerned unclassified documents. Secret materials on paper were shipped in double-lined, sealed canvas bags. Secret materials classified "D," which was the highest confidential code, were all placed in a small handbag with a very complicated opening mechanism that the courier was always supposed to carry by the handle. Better still, if there was any danger that the secret correspondence could be compromised, he was under orders to destroy all "D" documents by swallowing them. According to the rules, the total weight of the package that could be swallowed could not be more than two hundred grams. It is not difficult to imagine the expression of the courier who was handed a handbag with five or six pounds of film classified "D"! And that happened almost every month.

Fortunately for our diplomatic conveyors, a metal lining was quickly developed to transport the film, and it only took pressing a button in case of danger. Instead of stomach juices, an acid destroyed the films. The reason I know all these procedures is that, besides my work as an operations officer and radio operator at the Rezidentura, I was also in charge of the photo lab. The Consulate had an employee who handled false passports, false rubber stamps for visas, and did photographic work, but the man was not terribly efficient and after a serious instance of negligence that caused an important document to be damaged, Zarubin sent him home, to Moscow.

With my usual sense of detail I began by purchasing a few books on photography to guide me in my new job. I learned a thousand useful little tricks: that there was special film for microfilming documents or that it was best to use a brown rather than a black ribbon when typing documents to be microfilmed. From that time on I only worked with brown ribbons that I bought not just for my own use but also for my fellow officers, our agents, and our secretaries.

My biggest problem in New York, as far as photography was concerned, was the heat! My very unromantic room in the attic could be as hot as 35°C, while film must be developed and rinsed at no higher than 18°C, at higher temperatures the emulsion would melt. It was because of such a mishap that my predecessor had damaged the document, resulting in his being fired. I skirted the problem by adding ice cubes to the water and by keeping track of the temperature with a thermometer. I must say that I was right to make all the improvements I could in every detail of my intelligence activities because the volume of work I had to do was growing every month.

9

Most agents, just like Setter, are very much aware of that psychological barrier beyond which fear shows its relentless and often paralyzing face. They are like those soldiers who need to be shot at so they won't buckle each time a bullet whistles by. A good case officer must help the fearful informer cross the threshold so that when he faces a crisis he is able to keep cool, analyze the situation, and control his reflexes. I learned all this thanks to another agent I was managing early on in my career as a case officer.

Even though he was never identified, I can call him by the code name used in our encrypted reports and in his file at the Center. "Antelope" was French, and it was my idea to give him that name because timidity was his greatest character trait. He had completed his studies in electrical engineering in 1937, and in 1940 he came to New York after fleeing the occupation of his country by the Wehrmacht. He quickly found a job, married an American woman who worked in a bookstore, and had a daughter.

A friend introduced us around the end of 1942 at the opening of a Soviet film. After the show the friend invited us to dinner at a French restaurant, and as we parted company, Antelope and I exchanged business cards. Our relations quickly became very friendly. From time to time we would meet for dinner and since I was paying it was never a good restaurant. It was a time of austerity and Zarubin would not have paid for a gourmet dinner. In any case no one in my group gave it much thought since we were living through the most dramatic moments of the war. Two or three times Antelope invited me to attend receptions given by exiled French anti-fascists. He hated the Nazis and, naturally, we mostly discussed the fighting, but also French politics. The Allies had just landed in North Africa and Antelope, a passionate Gaullist, was openly indignant at the Anglo-American policy of giving their support initially to Admiral Darlan—whom he considered a "collaborator"—and then, following Darlan's assassination in December 1942, to General Giraud. Only de Gaulle, according to Antelope, had the stature to lead the liberation of his country. My French friend had Socialist ideas and sincerely sympathized with the struggle of the Soviet people.

I slowly found out that Antelope worked at a weapons plant where he had access to confidential documents. Since he was an excellent artist and designer he was often asked to draw technical specifications and would be allowed to consult blueprints and photographs of secret instructions for military equipment. The following summer I was told to recruit him. I had thoroughly prepared the groundwork and the Center's background checks didn't indicate anything worrisome. Six months is long enough to study a man's character so I was well aware of how much Antelope was fearful by nature. To avoid alarming him, I proceeded very slowly, giving him enough time to get used to each new stage in our collaboration; but then it was time to begin.

At the time Antelope had access to ultrasecret information on radar, which was of supreme importance to us, and during our conversation that day I was looking for a pretense to get it on the right track. My French friend admired the valor of Soviet soldiers, who had successfully reversed the tide of war after the victory at Stalingrad.

"You can help our Cossacks get all the way to Berlin!" I told him, alluding to the window of Old Russia on Fifth Avenue I had told him about. "And therefore shorten the time when General de Gaulle will enter Paris!"

Antelope understood and, in fact, had understood everything from the beginning.

"But what can I do?" he asked, hesitating nevertheless.

"What you can do? The instruction manual for radar would be very useful to all anti-fascists, not just the Americans."

Antelope lowered his head and then, gathering his courage, he looked up at me like someone who had made up his mind.

"I'll get it for you at our next meeting!"

One week later I saw him walk toward me on the sidewalk across a quiet street in Soho.* It was after office hours but the blacktop had softened because of the temperature and the many thousands of shoes still exuded heat mixed with that smell of ozone that is so unique. Following my recommendations, Antelope stopped in front of a storefront window to give me a chance to check that no other person behind him was slowing down. Since there was no one tailing him, I crossed the street and went right up to him. His handshake was flabby and his eyes avoided mine.

"I couldn't do it!" he said. "There was no time when I could."

I hid my disappointment and we set up another meeting eight days later. But, once again Antelope returned empty-handed. He was distraught and didn't try to explain it away.

"I can't control myself," he admitted as he stuttered nervously. "I was right there in front of my desk and I just couldn't bring myself to open the drawer, take the file and put it in my attaché case. No way, Alexander, no way! I'm just a good-for-nothing and I hate myself!"

I comforted him as best I could. Since he never took any vacation time, he must have been extremely tired and his nervous system was not responding well to stress. I took him to dinner and was careful to avoid talking about our secret activities at the table. Antelope was obviously expecting me to press him to deliver the documents at the next meeting, but I was careful not to make any demands.

---

* In the 1940s Soho was referred to as the "South Village," meaning the southern part of Greenwich Village.

"Suppose the four of us go to the country next Sunday?" I proposed as we shook hands. "To the lake, as usual?" Antelope happily accepted the suggestion.

That Sunday my wife and I left the house very early. Our private "guardian angel" (the old woman from across the street) must have been fast asleep. While constantly checking behind us, we bought newspapers and had breakfast in a coffee shop. Since the coast was clear, we went to the spot where Antelope and his wife were expecting us in their car; coincidentally we lived in the same neighborhood.

The lake was about forty miles from New York and the weather was magnificent. While our wives made small talk, Antelope and I read the papers and exchanged some comments from time to time. When it got too hot we would dash into the water to cool off, swimming out toward the middle of the lake. It was our third picnic there and every time I challenged Antelope to swim on to the other side of the lake but he would quickly turn back to the dock looking frightened. He did it again that Sunday.

For some unpremeditated reason, I suddenly swam ahead of him and blocked his path, saying:

"No! Today we're going to cross the lake together!"

To my amazement Antelope obeyed and fifteen minutes later we reached the opposite side. Without a word we started walking around the lakefront to reach our wives. Suddenly Antelope stopped:

"Alex, why don't we swim back across rather than do all this walking?"

I didn't quite expect him to say that and I thought for a moment before answering. I didn't want to risk having my friend freeze up with fear while he was in the middle of the lake, but I also didn't want to play down my decision; in some strange way that lake was to Antelope what the Rubicon had been for Caesar. I answered that I was tired and preferred walking back. Three days later Antelope delivered the radar instruction manual, followed by two years of continuously providing me with extremely valuable material. He was so committed that I often had to slow him down.

Toward the end of 1945 two events put an end to the golden age of Soviet espionage in the United States. In September, Igor Guzenko, a GRU code clerk at the Soviet embassy in Ottawa, defected, and in November Elizabeth Bentley, one of our liaison agents, was "turned" by the FBI and named about one hundred "Red spies." To limit the disaster, the Center gave an incredible and exceptional order to shut down all our sources. In effect, this meant stopping all intelligence activity in the United States. We had to dismantle with our own hands what had taken so long and so much patience to weave together in the face of so much danger. But an order is always an order. We obviously didn't just drop our agents suddenly or without explanations, and I made the rounds to see my comrades one by one, informing them of this decision. I told them they had nothing to fear personally since their actions were not being targeted. It simply meant that, faced with the renewed energy of American counterespionage, we had to avoid any possible failures.

To make sure none of the agents strayed away, we agreed to a fixed rendezvous with each one of them. All of them were to let six months go by and then, on a given day, for instance the last Monday of each month, they were to show up at a specific location. Since someone other than myself could reestablish contact, I also gave them special recognition signs. One would be reading *The New York Times* of the previous day while his contact would be wearing shoes with shoelaces of two different colors and bend over to tie them. The agent also had to memorize the recognition words he was to exchange with his new case officer. Some of them were relieved and even happy to get the news that their activity had been terminated. With the end of the war, the general attitude toward us was changing. Collaboration with the NKVD was no longer viewed as a contribution to the common victory over the Nazis and was causing a crisis of conscience for some people. Antelope was not beset by such scruples. He wanted to continue and was unhappy to stop working with me. We parted on excellent terms.

I didn't know at the time that Antelope would cause so many tense moments and make me feel, in turn, something of his own emotions of a few years before! Obviously my character and my childhood as a street fighter had prepared me to face fear much better than he did. I was not surprised to run into him in a convenience store in February 1946, since we lived in the same neighborhood. He told me his company was sending him to Europe for a few months and invited me to his home for dinner. Despite my orders I accepted the invitation, since I didn't want to hurt his feelings. That evening the conversation revolved around familiar topics among friends and we decided to have a game of chess before I left. Antelope's wife said she was tired and went to bed, leaving us alone. As if he had been waiting for that signal, my agent got up and handed me two thick bound files that were on top of his desk, without uttering a word. They were technical documents regarding aircraft carriers.

"You can hold on to them until tomorrow," he said calmly. "I'm due back at the office the day after tomorrow."

I leafed through the files and saw they were extremely interesting; then, still silent, I placed them back on top of the desk. We returned to our match: Antelope was pressing me on my left flank, and I was resisting him weakly.

What to do? The Center had expressly forbidden any contacts with our former agents without specific authorization. The very fact I was there was a serious breach of the rules. I only did it because Apresyan, the Rezident, had been recalled to Moscow and Yatskov, whom I could always speak to in confidence, was replacing him. If I took the material it would be microfilmed and sent to the Lubyanka, in which case I would have to explain why I had not followed orders. I was not quite sure that I could believe the old proverb "Winners are never questioned." And what if, God forbid, there were a hitch? What if I burned my agent and got caught myself? I, alone, would be held accountable. In those days you did not joke around with orders signed by Beria.[26]

I kept looking at the chessboard but all I could see was the face of my supreme leader as he was portrayed in all his official portraits, behind his pince-nez those hard eyes that made every country tremble. On the other hand, I had been managing Antelope for three years. I knew him by heart and couldn't imagine him being part of a double cross against me. I had helped him overcome his fear and couldn't appear to be lazy in his eyes. Finally, I was sure I had not been followed that day.

I also reasoned that rules and orders could not account for every circumstance. It was just like war. When you see the enemy you don't run to your commanding officer to ask if you can start shooting. In a regular situation, no. But in peacetime you would since it could be disastrous if your shots brought in reinforcements, causing unjustifiable losses in your own ranks. Each one must decide for himself in such cases. Even if I had the time to ask and secure the Center's approval, how could someone thousands of miles away be able to assess the situation better than I could?

At this point an event I still cannot explain took place, which I can only recount here just as it happened. Even though my eyes were riveted to the chessboard, the only thing I saw was the picture of Beria. Suddenly another image came into focus in my mind's eye and grew, quickly invading my mind completely to the point of sweeping away the terrifying face of my supreme leader. It was Lydia, my professor and companion during my training period at the NKVD school, the one who told me to think of her in difficult times. It appeared almost like a hallucination because at that time I had never seen a television screen, not to mention a computer screen. Lydia gave me her usual quiet, peaceful look and nodded in approval. I knew I could go ahead!

"I'd only be a weak and cowardly pencil pusher if I don't take these papers!" I said to myself energetically. Yet taking up my friend's generous offer didn't end any of the doubts and questions I had. I spent a sleepless night, one of the few of my entire life.

The following day, when I left my apartment with my wife, I was carrying both files in my bag. "What will I do if it turns out to be a trap after all?" I asked myself. I decided that if I saw the FBI following me, I would throw the bags under the continuous flow of cars on Broadway during rush hour. Zina got into the subway at Columbus Circle to go to Amtorg on Madison Avenue. I had to walk along Central Park before feeling secure with my load of dynamite. Yatskov, my new boss, had just returned from Moscow and had the smell of the Lubyanka clinging to him. He listened to my explanations as he leafed through the files, looking more and more somber as I spoke. He finally mumbled something and left the room; it was his turn to be on desk duty at the Consulate. His temporary job was off to a bad start.

I returned to my photo lab, a place where I could definitely be useful. Whatever happened to me I knew that the material I was microfilming would reach its destination and help my country. But that day I understood that I had just placed a tough choice before my best friend, since it was just as risky to hand the documents back as it had been to take them in the first place. At noon I walked past Anatoly, who pointed to the ceiling and said:

"After lunch!"

That was also a bad sign because most of the time we had lunch together, and if we were in a hurry we'd go to a coffee shop close by. On special occasions we walked all the way to Joe's on Second Avenue, a small family restaurant we discovered during the war. Joe supported the Red Army's struggle and had become a friend. He sometimes complained that he didn't see much of us but I must say that, with the small amount of money we had left over after all the deductions for the war effort, we simply couldn't eat at his place too often. To liven things up we'd say to him:

"We'll come every day when you complete the sign outside to read "Joe Stalin's Place!"

For most Americans, Stalin was "Uncle Joe." At other times Yatskov and I would have certainly gone to celebrate the previous evening's harvest at our friend's restaurant. And here I was, chewing on my hot dog all by myself, lost in my darkest thoughts.

A half-hour later, at the Rezidentura, I told Anatoly:

"Listen, you don't need to back me up! I'll handle this on my own and if there are consequences, I'll be the one to pay for them."

Yatskov thought a while, which was his way of handling situations. Once in action he was very quick but not before taking his time to make a decision.

"No," he said finally. "We'll go through the security routine in my car, one hour before your rendezvous. If there's nothing suspicious, I'll drop you off somewhere and you'll be on your own from there."

I can still remember that day as if it were yesterday. We had barely left the Consulate at around 6 p.m. when the weather changed. The sky darkened and the sun appearing between the clouds looked yellow and menacing as a sudden wind kicked bits of paper and cigarette butts into our faces. A newspaper tumbled across the street quickly folding and unfolding its pages. We just had enough time to jump into the staff car about fifty feet from the entrance of the Consulate; the first big drops of rain, as large as peas, were already beating down on the windshield and in a flash the storm was upon us. Amid all the thunder and lightning I understood the meaning of the expression "opening heaven's gates."

We couldn't see much beyond a few feet even with the windshield wipers, and cars were stopping at the curb because of poor visibility. But Yatskov drove on almost blindfolded while I tried to make sure that we were not being followed through the fogged rear view mirror. What I did manage to see was certainly no cause for alarm and the street looked completely empty. There was a subway station a few blocks from the Consulate.

"Let me get in there," I told Anatoly. "It's useless to keep on going."

In such circumstances we were synchronized like clockwork. In spite of the rain Yatskov let me out about fifty feet before the subway entrance. Before disappearing into the station I looked back; if Anatoly saw anything suspicious he'd blink his headlights for me. But he didn't. Two precautions were better than one and inside the subway I went through another complicated security itinerary, changing trains twice before reaching my destination. A half hour later, when I resurfaced, Antelope was waiting for me in his car as agreed and started the engine as soon as I got in. He was smiling broadly at me and for once my nervous friend looked much more relaxed than I was. We drove around for about a mile before I left my explosive package on the seat and got out of the car.

The rain stopped just as suddenly as it had started. I barely had time for a few steps before feeling strange and entered a coffee shop to sit down. I thought of myself as having nerves of steel but just then I felt completely drained. I was in a cold sweat, both from the rain and my state of mind. I slowly drank a glass of warm milk, followed by a cup of coffee as I read the paper. It took me a full half hour to feel good enough to go back home. I spent the next morning writing my report to the Center, and fortunately the files on aircraft carriers were considered so valuable that my stretching of the rules had no adverse consequences on the rest of my career.

10

"Rupert" was a real ghost.[27] Since July 1944, when I had been given this agent to manage; I regularly went to the entrance of the Astoria Theater on Broadway on the second Friday of each month at 8:45 p.m. The conditions of this permanent rendezvous were spelled out in a short letter from the diplomatic pouch. There was also a physical description of the man, a blurred photo that could have been of any nine out of ten men, and even some women, and naturally the Center's orders to establish contact with the agent. The seasons went by. It was good to be outside after a hot day indoors in the summer; but starting in November, more and more, I'd get out of the wind and rain and stand near the box office, while in the winter I changed from my raincoat to a heavy dark gray overcoat that my wife referred to as my "spycoat." But it was all to no avail, Rupert would not show up.

Contrary to popular belief, the first weapon of those on the other side is not an ordinary Walther PPK,[28] but lots of patience. In the world of espionage, long hours spent waiting can produce dazzling successes. Whenever I reported another missed rendezvous the Lubyanka would invariably answer to keep on going! I did, but as far as I was concerned I was becoming more and more skeptical. On the second Friday in February 1945 I took Zina to a different movie theater on Broadway. A movie house is the ideal place to find out if you have a tail. In this theater movies were being shown continuously and people would come and go at any time. In the middle of the film I got up and left my wife in her seat, but before going into the lobby I turned around to check that the other spectators were all sitting down, munching their popcorn and drinking Coke. Everything was in good order. As a precaution, however, I lingered in front of the movie poster for the following week's show and could see that the coast was clear. Out of habit I checked behind me by walking a few blocks to the location of the rendezvous. I really did not expect to actually meet the mysterious Rupert and I only went there because orders must be obeyed.

None of the people standing in front of the Astoria looked like the description of the agent. The one who came closest was a major who walked up and down in front of a billboard. He was the correct height, but he was thin while Rupert was supposed to be chubby, so I went through the motions anyhow and decided to make the approach with the prepared phrases:

"Excuse me, you're waiting for Helen, right?"

The major gave me a broad smile:

"You must be her cousin James?"

The probability that a complete stranger would be waiting for a "Helen" whose cousin's name was "James" was extremely remote. Yet I decided to go through a few more lines to be absolutely sure that I was finally meeting my Rupert. In a corner of the bar, while we had a beer, my contact explained the reason behind his long delay. Since he was fluent in several oriental languages, including Japanese, he had been transferred to the code-breaking unit of the U.S. Army Signal Intelligence Service known as SIS. [29] He had just spent the last few months in Hawaii and on other islands of the Pacific.

"I do have something important to tell you," he said. "We have broken the Japanese codes and we can now read their military and diplomatic correspondence. In particular we are reading all the correspondence between Moscow and Tokyo. We know that Molotov often meets with the Japanese ambassador, who is pressuring your foreign minister to sign a non-aggression pact. Since you Soviets are not hiding this from us, our leadership is aware that you're playing fair with America and that's very good!

"Beyond proof of Soviet loyalty the decoded messages also yielded extremely important information to the Americans. Washington knew of every movement of Japanese troops and, thanks to decoded documents, the U.S. Air Force was able to shoot down the supreme Japanese commander, Admiral Isokuru Yamamoto, in an air attack.

"Since the end of last year we're winning every battle in the Pacific. In part, because of the messages we can read, but also because of the quality of the radar and vision devices our Navy is equipped with as well as much more powerful cannon," he concluded.

His words confirmed what I already knew because of information I was getting from other sources. This kind of equipment was already being studied in the USSR. But what Rupert said next made me very anxious.

"You must also know that our code breakers are spending much time and effort trying to break your correspondence codes with Moscow. In 1942 our analysts were able to partially decode an Amtorg dispatch. They feel that from there they will be able to read all your messages."

My beer suddenly tasted bitter. I could instantly assess the enormity of the disaster that was looming over our heads.

"Do you know the date of that dispatch and its contents?"

If Rupert was an analyst and a linguist it was clearly because he possessed natural talent: he recited from memory the date and contents of the message. He also promised to find out more details and let me know during our next meeting. We scheduled a rendezvous exactly one month later at a different location. I asked Rupert to come in civilian clothes from now on. Zina was waiting for me at the entrance of the subway as agreed. She immediately knew that something was bothering me.

"Everything is fine!" I protested. "But let me review everything in my mind so I don't forget by tomorrow."

Obviously we took no notes of any kind. The next day at the Rezidentura, I wrote a rather thick report. The next "pouch" from the Center brought a list of questions for Rupert.

Our next meeting was also the last. Following the rules I first asked Rupert about his entourage to be sure that there was nothing alarming in his unit or at home. He then answered each question I had memorized, one by one. He also gave me some additional information regarding the Amtorg dispatch that had been about seventy percent decoded by the Americans. Finally, I told him his new case officer in Washington would be one of my colleagues, Tikhon, whom he knew quite well and who would appear five minutes after I left. I never saw Rupert again but the decoding operation of secret correspondence between Soviet stations in the United States and Moscow is still making waves to this day and is known as the "Venona files."

The decoding operation by the SIS of messages going from the Center to NKVD Rezidenturas in America began in February 1943. While the expression "intercepted message" is often repeated within the Venona documents, it is not what one might imagine. For the most part these were copies of Western Union cables, which, as I already mentioned, filled an entire warehouse. Only much later did the NSA place hundreds of stations around the world to intercept radio messages from the Soviets, the Germans, and the Japanese. As for the famous Amtorg dispatch, it gave rise to a myth and many misconceptions and speculation. Amtorg in fact could not have a code service because it also employed U.S. nationals. The Soviet employees of that company—the intelligence officers as well as the "clean" engineers—who needed to communicate secretly with Moscow used a special office located at the Consulate. Within the batch of coded cables from our services it was impossible to detect the origin of a particular message. My conclusion is that, before coming to the Consulate to encode his message, the Amtorg employee who had written the message had also prepared a draft that reached the FBI one way or another.

The codes used in our correspondence are normally unbreakable, even using very powerful computers that did not even exist at the time. The breaking of the code was made possible only because our Rezidentura violated the rules of secret communications. In the middle of the war when the diplomatic pouch functioned only intermittently, our code clerks had run out of one-time pads. Once the Lubyanka found out, it allowed them to break the first rule in such matters: a pad must only be used once. Each time it was used the number of possible comparisons increased exponentially, allowing the specialists on the other side to find a key, which is exactly what happened.

SIS ace Meredith Gardner was able to break the five main encoding systems used during the five previous years by NKVD Rezidenturas in America before 1946. This obviously took place by trial and error. After succeeding in reading a small part of the text, say 5%, SIS passed along the result to the OSS, military intelligence, the FBI, the State Department, and other organizations that might be interested in the message in question. The comments and suggestions which came back from these channels allowed more of the text to be read, up to, say, 10%. The new result was returned to the same offices and the entire cycle started all over again. This work was dramatically accelerated after the first Soviet atomic bomb was tested in 1949, which is the reason why most decoded messages concerned the Manhattan Project.

Between 1946 and 1952 the Gardner team decoded—partially or completely—about 2,200 secret messages that uncovered many operations and identified many Soviet intelligence officers and agents. At the expiration of the secret classification period, a first lot of forty-nine messages was made public by the NSA in July 1995. The bulk of the decoded messages filled six large volumes. I don't know how it was possible, starting from pseudonyms and code names in our correspondence, to really identify so many Soviet secret agents, projects and locations. It is possible that a few traitors or turncoats assisted the American special services. Soviet espionage did have a large number of moles inside the NSA. It was such a secret establishment that its acronym was jokingly said to stand for "No Such Agency."

For the most part, I must admit that, apart from a few errors, the decrypted messages are genuine. It also happened that the person signing the cable could make mistakes, as was the case of Kvasnikov. I will discuss a typical example of this in the chapter regarding Joel Barr and Alfred Sarant.[30]

At the time I handled Rupert I could scarcely imagine how much the Venona fallout would continue during my career. I also couldn't foresee how another one of my agents would be involved in atomic espionage. I shall refer to him as Monti. Just like many other sources in this book, he has never been identified nor even mentioned in the decrypted messages within the Venona files. His real code name is useless to researchers, whether they are historians or spy hunters.

I never actually handled Monti myself and never even saw him. I don't know whether he was short or tall, fat or thin, handsome or ugly. I managed him through a cut out,[31] who was also Russian and whose name I shall also keep secret, because it would be easy to identify Monti through this man since they met openly. I shall call him Pyotr Lastochkin.

Lastochkin came to see me at the Consulate during the summer of 1942. He had worked at Amtorg for ten months before the war, then in November 1940, when the United States put an end to trade relations he was sent back to the Soviet Union. He was returning to New York as a chemical engineer attached to the purchasing commission. We quickly discovered that we had something in common: his brother, who was fighting at the front, had been one of my classmates at the university. This coincidence, which is very important in the tightly knit world of a small foreign colony far from home, led us to become great friends. We loved to reminisce about Moscow, talk about the war and the ambiguous attitude displayed by our American allies. Sometimes on Sundays we went to the movies or spent two or three hours at the Manhattan Chess Club. Even though he was much older than I was, he became a closer friend than his brother had been.

At first I was careful not to let Pyotr know my real mission in New York. Once I got to know him better, I thought he could be part of my secret activities. He was very enthusiastic about his job; he spoke English very well and was constantly improving it; and much of his spare time was dedicated to reading specialized publications in libraries. He always attended lectures at universities or scientific societies and these activities greatly widened his already impressive circle of contacts among his American counterparts. One of them, named "Monti," stood out because of his interesting profile.

Pyotr had met him during his first tour in America. Monti was in charge of a team of engineers who were building chemical plants in the United States and overseas. He lived very well in a beautiful house in the Manhattan suburbs, which did not prevent him from being a sincere friend of the USSR. Monti became very worried when the Red Army was being defeated and he also felt terrible about the huge human losses affecting my country. He was openly critical of the Anglo-American attitude; he felt human solidarity to be more important than national interest.

The main interest our intelligence services had in Monti, had to do with his professional skills. At that time Kellex, the company he worked for, was completing the construction of a top secret pilot factory in Oak Ridge, Tennessee. The plant was supposed to process gas diffusion to produce the explosive that would revolutionize not only technology but also the future of humanity itself, uranium 235.

In those days my knowledge of atomic energy was extremely limited. Kvasnikov had explained to me what critical mass was and that was about as far as I got. The Manhattan Project to create the atomic bomb was the responsibility of my boss and of Yatskov, even though from time to time I would back up Anatoly at an important meeting. In August 1945, I covered his rear during a very important rendezvous—he used all sorts of additional precautions—with a mysterious woman. I found out many years later that this was Lona Cohen returning from Albuquerque with the crucial documents she had been given by one of our main agents at Los Alamos named Mlad.[32] I knew that project Enormoz—the code name the Lubyanka gave to the effort to create the American atomic weapon—was the top priority of Soviet intelligence.

I therefore had to recruit my good friend Pyotr. I told him about my being an NKVD officer and gave him the Center's orders to collect every possible piece of information regarding the development by the Americans of a new and very powerful weapon. I did not hide any of the dangers inherent to such collaboration. Because of his conversations with Monti, Pyotr knew even better than I that the future belonged to the atomic bomb. He had no qualms about it:

"I will do everything I can. Just like you, for me it's a duty. If I can help those fighting at the front, I'll run any risk."

I thanked him from the bottom of my heart, and then I explained my plan in detail. He was to proceed smoothly and tactfully with his American friend. I told him to ask a few questions without letting on that he was interested in the plant at Oak Ridge, such as the time frame of its being placed into service, the main operational blueprints and other details. Pyotr succeeded with my plan two weeks later: Monti talked a lot without holding anything back. He answered all the questions my "submarine" asked and pointed out that the U.S. government considered this construction site a top priority and was sparing no expense.

"Your scientists should get to work on producing uranium 235. It's the most promising element in existence today and not just for military purposes."

Pyotr seized the opportunity.

"Could you write me a little report on the subject?" he asked innocently. "I'll forward it to our Academy of Sciences, confidentially, of course."

Monti did not need to be prodded and at their next meeting he handed my friend Pyotr the technical blueprint of the plant at Oak Ridge. Kvasnikov grabbed the papers from my hands when I told him about my latest catch. As far as he was concerned, Monti had absolute priority. Even my most active network, the one headed by Julius Rosenberg, became secondary. The Center, which rarely extended any praise, transmitted its very high satisfaction for this document. Warmly thanked by the "Academy of Sciences," Monti agreed to answer other questions from Soviet scientists and our material reached research institutes and secret laboratories.

Even though I was not assigned to the atomic project at the time, the Rezidentura never withdrew Monti's handling from me, since the quality of human relationships often overshadows any other consideration and I was on the best of terms with Lastochkin. I had also demonstrated my skill as a case officer, so why change anything? Monti was a rich man who was so eager to help us that we never offered him any compensation. Pyotr even thought he would have given us money had we requested it. The meetings between Pyotr and Monti were irregular because the engineer traveled a lot to Brazil, Mexico, and Canada. However, every piece of information he passed on to us was priceless. Pyotr had to return to Moscow in the summer of 1945 while Monti was overseas, and wrote him a letter apologizing for leaving without saying good-bye, adding that the person carrying the letter was a very good friend who would also become his friend. Even though Monti had never been formally recruited, he certainly must not have been fooled by the kind of relationship he had with the friendly Russian. He agreed to meet with the new representative without reservation.

As I began the task of managing agents, I hardly realized that I was to control one of the best producing groups of agents in the history of Soviet technological espionage, the Rosenberg network. Few episodes in intelligence history remain so mysterious and have produced so much legend and conjecture. Since I am now the last of the Soviet participants in these tragic and distressing events, I feel it is my duty to tell the truth.

PART THREE

Fighting Comrade and Fellow Soldiers

11

I n the thousand-year history of the secret services, it is hard to find anything that comes close to stirring world public opinion more than the Rosenberg case. During the early 1950s tens of millions of people in every country around the world protested against the death sentence that American justice handed down to this couple accused of passing on the secrets of the atomic bomb to the Soviet Union. In spite of the fact that Julius and Ethel Rosenberg proclaimed their innocence, they were executed amid universal outcry on June 19, 1953. None of the many books written about this case has ever given the Soviet point of view,[33] the obvious reason being that not only the KGB but also the SVR (the current external intelligence service of democratic Russia) have both denied the existence of any connection between the couple and the Soviet Union.

Fate has decided that I should be the last witness to this handling of agents, which ended in a horrible tragedy. Three years ago, at the age of eighty-four, I decided to tell the truth about this unwritten chapter of recent history for a number of reasons. I must admit that to speak of these events created a crisis of conscience for me and I have had to wrestle between my memory and my duty. The Rosenberg case is seen in the West from a single, mostly specious, point of view. A small group, whose ranks are thinning ever since America rejected the cancer of McCarthyism, remains convinced that the Rosenbergs were despicable traitors who placed their Communist ideals ahead of the security and prosperity of their country. By handing over to the Russians the secrets of the atomic bomb, they had endangered the peace that exclusive American control could ensure for the world. The consequences were the Korean War, where tens of thousands of American soldiers died, and all the other conflicts of the postwar period that pitted the free world against the Socialist bloc. For others the Rosenbergs were innocent dupes who had been unjustly accused and convicted of espionage during the anti-Communist and anti-Soviet hysteria of the McCarthy period, and, despite the protests coming from all over the world, they were executed.

Neither of these two points of view is anywhere near the truth.

The decoded Venona files revealed the existence of the Rosenberg network to the West. Later I will describe in detail the disaster that ended with the shutting down of this secret group and the arrest and execution of Julius and Ethel. Dozens of books have been written about this subject in the U.S. and Europe, but none with a Soviet contribution, and even the most serious of these books cannot claim to tell the whole story. On the other hand, the rules of confidentiality that are the hallmark of secret operations compel me to remain silent, but there is much to be gained in hearing, as the saying goes, "what the other side has to say." What is false then becomes true, pure idealists suddenly appear as cowardly traitors, while despicable characters pass themselves off as heroes.

Whether one is a Communist or a bourgeois liberal, on one side or the other of the divide that until recently defined the world, there are such things as universal values meaningful to everyone. Obviously, not all my readers will share my admiration for Julius Rosenberg and his friends, nor will they accept my ideas, but I am the only one who can fill this vacuum and no one else. I do know that this vantage point will give a more objective picture of that group of exceptional agents, some of whom went undetected and still remain unknown to the public to this day.

The first draft of my reminiscences regarding my operations in the United States during World War II dates back to 1987-1988, written for the eyes of KGB personnel only. In 1990 I asked my Service for permission to publish a book on some operations of Soviet intelligence in Great Britain and the United States during the Cold War. Finally, I was allowed to add some chapters regarding my first tour of duty in the United States from, 1941 to 1946. That book was published in Moscow in 1994 under the title: *Beyond the Ocean and on an Island. Memoirs of an Intelligence Officer.*[34] The story of Julius Rosenberg, named "agent Stanley," and his network was portrayed in such a veiled form that it was barely recognizable.

As *glasnost* took hold, more and more voices within the KGB called for publication of material regarding the operations of our anti-fascist agents. Leonid Kvasnikov, Anatoly Yatskov, and I, insisted that we pay our respects to Julius Rosenberg and his friends who, in a disinterested way and placing their own lives in danger, had contributed so heavily to the Soviet war effort. The leadership of Soviet intelligence was against it. In 1991 and 1992, Kvasnikov and Yatskov, who knew the history of the Rosenberg network very well, decided to ignore the ban. During a few interviews given to foreign journalists they admitted that Julius had collaborated with the Soviet Union while pointing out that he had nothing to do with atomic intelligence and that Ethel Rosenberg was innocent. Since I was more disciplined than they were, I refused to discuss the matter despite many requests coming from various quarters.

My best friend, Anatoly Yatskov, found out at the beginning of 1993 he had cancer and that his days were numbered. Before leaving us he repeated to me several times:

"Sania,[35] it's my final wish. You must tell the truth about Julius. We can't keep silent about what he did for us during the war, or why he and Ethel died. They did not betray us, and we will betray them if we don't tell the whole story. My time is up but you must do it."

Yatskov had no trouble convincing me. I handled seventeen foreign agents during my career as an intelligence officer. With each one I was able to establish a relationship of sympathy and confidence, but Julius Rosenberg remains to this day the only one I truly considered as my friend. I still required the approval of my superiors and I began by writing a report to the SVR director. Evgeny Primakov, the future Prime minister, received me on January 27, 1994.

"I read your document," he said. "Despite your reasons, I think it would not be appropriate to admit that Julius Rosenberg was our agent, but if you wish to pursue the matter we'll examine your report at the next director's meeting."

I decided to go ahead, and one month later I was informed that my request had been rejected. I wrote a second report stating my case in much stronger terms. Another month went by and I had a meeting with Primakov's assistant: the leadership had not changed its mind. I requested a written answer that never came. Since time was marching on and nothing could change the SVR's mind, I decided to act on my own. In 1996 I accepted a proposal from American film producer and director Ed Wierzbowski to appear in a documentary about the Rosenberg case. I returned to New York in order to be filmed at the locations where Julius and I had met and recounted a few events that involved us both. And yet this experience was a disappointment for me because many important scenes were edited out and the main thrust of my message is nowhere to be found. I understood that the only way to tell the whole story was to write a book.

The SVR reacted strangely to the documentary. After all, I had broken the rule of silence but the film said so little about Rosenberg and his network. Nevertheless, my intention to tell the story in a book worried the Service and like any good officer, albeit retired, I had sent in my manuscript for approval. In December 1997 I had a final meeting with SVR representatives who tried to persuade me not to publish the history of the network. I stood my ground and, seeing my determination, they gave me a final reason:

"As an intelligence officer you have signed a pledge never to divulge the information you received while you were operational.

Do you understand that should you break the pledge there could be legal consequences?"

"I am eighty-three and a decorated Hero of the Russian Federation," I answered. "If you want to take me to court, go right ahead!"

We parted on these words and I never changed my mind on the subject.

I have been an intelligence officer all my life, in active service from 1939 to 1974, and as a contract officer from 1974 to 1986. I have been in retirement for over thirteen years but I have never stopped being an officer. As far as I am concerned, I am not guilty of insubordination in disobeying the orders of my Service. I am only doing my duty, and I hope that at the bottom of their hearts the heads of the SVR, who must follow rules and regulations, understand and approve of my motivations.

This is the untold story that I have attempted to reconstruct as truthfully and in as much detail as I could. My conscience has freed me from any oath, and I have no reason to embellish, alter, or omit anything, but one thought does sadden me. The pages that follow will distress those few persons still alive, the two Rosenberg sons and Morton Sobell, who have already been sufficiently traumatized by this event. However, I am convinced that to hear the truth is better than uncertainty and dark suspicion. In the case of the Rosenbergs and of Julius' friends, it will only do them honor.

I have already described the spectacular tightening of FBI surveillance after our victory at Stalingrad. Some of us were being followed so closely that we simply could not operate efficiently. That was what happened to Semyon Semyonov. During the summer of 1943, the Amtorg engineer—my master in agent handling, the man who handled agent Khvat—went to San Francisco. At the time his friend, Grigory Heifetz, the Soviet vice consul and INO Rezident on the west coast of the United States, was about to infiltrate the Los Alamos center where a brilliant team of world-renowned physicists was putting together the atomic bomb. Heifetz personally knew J. Robert Oppenheimer, who was the scientific director of the "Manhattan Project," the most secret undertaking our Anglo-American allies were working on. The FBI must have suspected that Heifetz was up to other activities besides his ordinary work as a vice consul or gathering donations for the Red Army fund. I still ask myself to this day why such a seasoned professional, who knew he was being watched so closely, took the risk of having dinner with Semyonov in a kosher restaurant in San Francisco rather than meet with him only within the confines of the Consulate. Unless an FBI agent decides to reveal this in his memoirs or some secret document is released for publication, no one will ever know the extent of the risk they took with that meal or, possibly, in other circumstances. In any case, U.S. counterespionage was convinced that Semyonov was working for the NKVD.

Perhaps for diplomatic reasons or because of the popularity of the USSR with American public opinion, or simply because they had no motive, the FBI did nothing to stop him. I think the first reason is the most plausible; as soon as he returned to New York, Semyonov was under tight and overt surveillance, indicating that J. Edgar Hoover's men wanted to discourage him from pursuing his activities. Day and night, teams of agents wouldn't let him out of their sight. From the moment he left his apartment or his office a mobile unit would follow him in full view. In any country and at any time this kind of action means, "We know who you are but we're being nice about it. So all that's left for you to do is to pack up and go home."

The consequences of such a message were easy to foresee, Semyonov was missing every rendezvous with his agents and was quickly becoming useless to the Rezidentura. The Center therefore decided to withdraw him from handling any agents, and some time later, since he had been living in America for five years, he was recalled. Semyonov didn't want to return to his homeland in the midst of a war and managed to remain in New York as long as possible. Using the excuse that his son needed an operation on his leg and other pretenses, he stayed on four more months and left early in 1944. At the time I was just beginning to manage agents. Zarubin, who never missed a detail, must have been suffi-

ciently satisfied with my work and since Kvasnikov, my immediate boss, was also giving me favorable marks, he decided to transfer to me one of Semyonov's best agents, Julius Rosenberg. It is
possible that Semyonov's recommendations also played a considerable part; since I began helping him he had the opportunity to
form an opinion about me. I knew that Julius existed without ever
having met him. At first, toward the end of 1942, he was only an
agent with no name and no face. I only took over the documents
Rosenberg gave Semyonov during brush pass encounters, which
occurred two or three minutes before I would appear. I would microfilm the documents before handing them back to Semyonov in
the same manner. Obviously, during such operations, the source is
never present.

Later, since many documents provided by Rosenberg concerned radio technology, Kvasnikov ordered me to study them
and draft reports for the Center. I worked with Semyonov, who
also handed me additional information on the agent's capabilities.
All things considered, I was clearly the best candidate to handle
him. Once the decision had been made, Zarubin allowed me access to the file on Julius that we kept at the Rezidentura. His code
name at that time was "Antenna," but this was something I didn't
know. In September 1944 that pseudonym was dropped and
changed to "Liberal." When I remember him, I think of the af-
fectionate nickname of "Libi"* that I gave him at the time. It is
amazing but the code name feels closer to me when it is written
rather than spoken because of the rules set by Kvasnikov that we
never speak our agents' names at any time, even inside the
Rezidentura.

The file included a clear photograph of Rosenberg. He was
about twenty-five, with regular features and a thin, carefully trimmed
mustache. Through his glasses his eyes appeared to belong to an
intelligent man, who was perhaps something of a dreamer. The
son of Russian-Jewish immigrants, he was born in 1918 and had
grown up on Manhattan's lower east side, the melting pot of immigrants from Eastern Europe at the turn of the century. He

---

* Pronounced LEE-bee [NDT].

went to Seward Park High School as well as a Jewish school, the Downtown Talmud Torah and Hebrew High School. In February 1939 he graduated as an electrical engineer from CCNY, the City College of New York, but did not find a permanent job right away. In 1940 he was finally hired by the Army Signal Corps at a salary of $2,000 a year. He was to hold that job until February 1945, when he took a better position with Emerson Radio, a company that manufactured radio electric devices for the army.[36]

Like many young men of his age and background, Libi was active in left-wing circles as a student. He would always be a militant labor organizer wherever he was hired thereafter. I was not concerned as to whether or not he was a member of the Communist Party of the United States. At that time to advertise one's membership in the Party entailed some risks and many Americans were using aliases when paying their party dues. In any case, the moment he began working with us we insisted that he avoid any Communist rallies or draw attention to himself under any circumstances. Yet, every week, Libi paid his Party dues through his friend Bernard Schuster.

Julius was married at twenty-three, a few months after graduating from CCNY, to Ethel Greenglass, who was three years his senior. At the time he was working for us the couple had a child, Michael. Beyond the file, my other source of information on Rosenberg was Semyonov. He gave me a somewhat idealized portrait of his agent: a man of left-wing ideas, pro-Soviet, completely dedicated to the fight against fascism, totally disinterested. "Julius never accepts any kind of compensation," said Semyonov. "He will no doubt be shocked if you take him to a fancy restaurant and order expensive wine. He feels we have no right to celebrate since our country is at war." Knowing Semyonov, I had no reason to doubt such a flattering portrait, since he was ordinarily quite cynical. After spending some time with Libi, I later understood how correct his initial assessment had been.

Rosenberg came to the attention of the Rezidentura in the spring of 1942 through his friend Bernard Schuster, who was active in Communist labor organizations using the alias "Chester" and working with Soviet intelligence under the code name "Ekho" (Echo).

His case officer, Konstantin Chugunov, was one of the best operational officers in political espionage. Rather short, with a ski jump nose and blue eyes, Konstantin was seriousness personified and spoke only to make reasonable and useful statements. The reports he submitted to the Center were so perfect that the Rezident signed them without making any corrections. When Zarubin found out that Rosenberg had access to scientific and technical secrets, he decided that Kvasnikov's team should be responsible for the actual recruitment. Kvasnikov then passed Julius on to Semyonov, one of his best case officers.

Julius was approached during a Labor Day rally on September 7, 1942. A podium was set up on a lawn in Central Park with a few rows of chairs for labor leaders, public figures, cultural personalities and Soviet representatives, surrounded by a dense crowd of up to 50,000 people at times. Schuster attended the rally with his friend Julius Rosenberg. His case officer, Chugunov, introduced them to Semyonov. Rosenberg was delighted; he had never met any Soviet nationals before, while wholeheartedly supporting their struggle against Nazism. He quickly found interests and other points in common with Semyonov and showed no disappointment when Schuster and Chugunov walked away, leaving him alone with "Henry"— Semyon's pseudonym for the occasion, since he was usually known as "Sam" by his American informers.

Julius invited his new Russian friend to have lunch at a restaurant and throughout the meal he fired away questions about life in the USSR, the attitude towards Jews, their extermination by the Nazis, and the harshness of the fighting on a front that was several thousand miles long. A spontaneous friendship, at least on one side, was born between the two men who decided to see each other again. As a seasoned recruiter, Semyonov didn't want to push things too far too quickly, but Julius' enthusiasm towards the Soviet Union was so friendly and sincere that he decided to make his pitch at the third meeting. Semyon said that America, in spite of its commitments, was hiding its latest technological innovations from its ally who needed them very badly. Rosenberg was quick to volunteer:

"I find it unfair that you should be fighting the common enemy alone. If I can do anything to help, you can count on me."

That was it. At their next meeting Julius brought his friend a first batch of confidential documents. I was quickly able to assess the content and the volume of the information—his usual delivery was between six hundred to one thousand pages long. Not satisfied with placing his own security at risk, Julius felt it was his duty to bring two of his friends into his activities. Since contacts among Americans were much less risky, he collected the information they produced and handed it to us for a few hours. Rosenberg was not just a very valuable source himself; he was also the linchpin of a network growing in importance from month to month.

I had to reestablish a contact that had been cut off for several months since the deactivation of Henry, alias Semyonov. The simple way would have been to phone Rosenberg at home, but this was unanimously rejected: since Julius had access to secret documents, his phone could be bugged. The best solution was to meet at his home. I began by exploring the location. The Rosenbergs lived in lower Manhattan, near the Brooklyn Bridge, at 10 Monroe Street, in a large low-rent project called Knickerbocker Village. They lived in a modest three-room apartment on the 8th floor of Building G, a dark brick ten-story tower. I found it easily enough. There was a sort of walkway held up by a metal structure connecting the sidewalk to the entrance. I also noticed that to open the front door one needed a code or had to use the intercom.

I set up a plan that Zarubin and Kvasnikov reviewed and completed. We decided that I'd go to see Rosenberg next Sunday afternoon at about 2 p.m., the most likely time I'd find him at home. As an introduction I would say that I came from Henry. I'm always nervous the day before an operation and went over the smallest details in my mind, trying to imagine every unforeseeable circumstance that could possibly occur, while on the day of the operation I am perfectly calm and collected. If ever I felt any emotions surfacing I would just say to myself that my two brothers were facing death every day on the battlefield. What was I doing that was so dangerous in the peaceful traffic of New York streets?

On that particular day I was in tiptop shape as I left my house an hour and a half ahead of schedule. I followed the itinerary my superiors had approved and walked along Central Park like someone who doesn't know how to kill time on his day off. Then I'd suddenly cross the street. It's my favorite move, you must look left and right and this allows you to see, without showing it, what the situation around you looks like. At Columbus Circle I took the subway down to Little Italy and I could not detect anything suspicious. I took the bus back uptown to Grand Central Terminal and had a hot dog in the midst of a busy crowd, where idle individuals stand out conspicuously. I had no further doubts: I could go! I took the bus downtown once again.

I was alone on the sidewalk when I pushed the intercom button to the Rosenberg apartment.

"Yes?" answered a man's voice.

"Hello, I'm looking for Julius Rosenberg," I said, trying to give my voice all the self-assurance I possibly could.

"That's me."

"I am a friend of Henry's," I introduced myself. "May I come up for a minute?"

"Okay, come in."

The electric lock buzzed and the door opened. I was in a clean, well-swept hallway in spite of the modest appearance of the building. On the eighth floor the man who met me in front of the elevator was Julius Rosenberg. He looked me over for a few seconds from behind his steel-framed glasses with those watchful eyes of his. Feeling a bit awkward I shook hands and he gave me a strong handshake in return. The initial contact was firm and open.

I explained quickly why Henry had dropped out of sight. "I'm the one who will come to see you from now on," I added.

"Excuse me but I can't let you come in. We're entertaining a couple of friends," said Julius apologetically.

"It's okay. I just wanted to set up an appointment."

"Very well. I'll come with you downstairs. Let's take the staircase."

As we descended the eight floors we were able to set up each detail. We were to meet next Tuesday at Childs, a cheap restaurant around 30th Street where he used to meet with Semyonov. I asked him not to bring anything so that we could talk quietly. As we parted on the ground floor I noticed that the tension I experienced at the beginning had now disappeared.

Secret meetings with our agents, as a rule, took place in the evenings because they all worked and were available only after office hours. On the day of our meeting, around 7:30 p.m., I stood on the sidewalk across the street from Childs and pretended to look at the window of a bookstore. Julius appeared on time. I watched him enter the restaurant and, after making sure no one was following him, I also pushed the lacquered wooden door. A little bell announced my arrival. Julius had had time to sit at a small table for two at the far end of the dining room. He motioned me with his hand and kept looking at me with his faint smile as I made my way toward him. We were now sitting facing each other. A waiter came with a notepad and I asked Julius to order. At the time I spoke English easily but, as my American teacher at the advanced class at Berlitz told me, "Your vocabulary is very extensive and your flow of speech is good, but your Slavic intonation betrays you." I was well aware that many waiters and bartenders were police or FBI informants and consequently I thought that two precautions were better than one.

But I took no precautions with Julius. I read somewhere that in order to establish a confidential relationship with someone you must begin by opening up your heart. I told him straight away that my name was Alexander and that I was Russian. I stopped to let the waiter pour the wine and once he had walked away, I proposed a toast to my dinner companion's health and the success of our future collaboration. As we had appetizers, I spoke of my childhood in Moscow, my family, my two brothers at the front, my two sisters who had the hardest time reaching Moscow after digging trenches near Bryansk, which was encircled by the German offensive. Julius listened to me with the greatest interest, showing that he was clearly amused, worried, relieved, and sympathetic as I spoke.

He then talked to me about his small family, and his wife Ethel, whom he obviously adored.

"So she's nice?" I asked to please him more than anything else.

He closed his eyes and blew a kiss into his hand. The fact is, I never did meet Ethel. I was only to learn much later some biographical details about this woman whom I could not identify too well behind all the tenderness and love her husband expressed for her. In many ways the couple's itinerary had been very similar. Just like Julius, Ethel came from the lower east side, the neighborhood of many Jewish immigrants from Eastern Europe. Like her husband she had attended a Jewish school and Seward Park High School. However, while Julius was interested in technology, Ethel's main interest was music. She played the piano, and sang for a year at Hugh Ross' Schola Cantorum. She was also interested in modern dance and did some amateur acting at Clark House and the Henry Street Settlement.

Ethel had taken secretarial classes to earn a living right out of school when she was 16. She became a militant union member on the job. After her marriage and the birth of Michael, she became a housewife. Yet, unlike many women who were even younger, Ethel had not faded into domesticity. She continued to improve her education, taking courses in psychology and music for children and educated Michael, and then Robert, who was born in 1948, after I left. A feeling of mutual confidence quickly marked the relationship between Julius and myself. The conversation turned to Henry, my predecessor. Semyonov was still in New York at the time, and was being harassed by the FBI. His father, living under German occupation in Odessa, had not been heard from. Julius, who knew the situation, asked if Henry had received any news. The answer was negative and a painful frown darkened his face.

"Why do the Germans hate the Jews?" he asked clenching his fist. "What harm did we do to them?"

I didn't know what to answer.

Naturally, I also had to prove to him that I really was a Soviet intelligence officer. I asked him questions to find out if there was anything amiss around him and his friends Joel Barr and William Perl, who were also working for us. I made sure I used their real names and showed that I knew many details about both of them.

"No, there is absolutely nothing suspicious!" Rosenberg answered. "My friends are in place. Since I had no further contact from Henry, I asked them to stop bringing me anything, but they're ready to start again."

I already knew the type of material the network had provided. The list of projects they were involved in was very exciting to me. The United States was spending fantastic amounts of money to produce even more advanced military equipment. Rosenberg and his friends were working on the production of new planes, artillery pieces, shells, radar, and electronic calculators. Julius was very dedicated. I still didn't know how involved he could become and how impatient he was to do more. He was the kind you have hold back all the time.

During those first meetings I didn't know the place that this agent, among so many others, was to have in my life.

12

I met Libi about fifty times altogether in Manhattan and some
times in Brooklyn or the Bronx. In the first few months, we
would meet once almost every week during the evening after he got
off his job. He was not just giving us priceless documents "borrowed" by his friends Perl and Barr, but also technical drawings,
technical manuals and other information on the devices produced
by his company. I ordinarily took delivery through a brush pass. We
crossed paths mostly in the darkness of a movie theater. Julius arrived first and sat in the next to last row, since young lovers usually
took up the last one. He would come in and I'd watch his back
before taking a seat myself. Since I would sit in the same row, he
would have to stand up when I went by his seat. As politeness requires, I would be standing face to face with him and he'd quickly
pass his documents on to me. At other times we took advantage of
overcrowded buses at rush hour or the crowd at a boxing bout on
Friday nights at Madison Square Garden. I then rushed back to the
Rezidentura to microfilm the information, which I would hand back
to Libi very early the next morning.

This system obviously doubled the risks, so I quickly got Julius
into photography by providing him with a very simple Leica with a
special lens the Center had sent me. The extractable lens could be
adjusted, allowing perfect microfilming of documents, even though

an amateur photographer could make mistakes in setting up the distance. The camera was placed on a tripod face down, 15-20 inches above a table that was under one or, even better, two side lamps. This was the way we went about microfilming our reports at the Rezidentura before shipping them out in the pouch. To avoid any suspicion I bought the film myself in entire loops of about 10 inches in diameter. Back at my lab I cut them into sections of 36 exposures and I even had a special wood plank to cut the curved end of the film. Julius quickly got accustomed to this system. Our brush pass contacts took place every six weeks. I'd hand him about twenty new rolls of film and he would give me the same number of exposed, but still undeveloped, rolls.

Rosenberg didn't like the long stretches between our meetings; he felt we weren't seeing each other often enough and had it been up to him he would have been bringing me documents every day.

"Listen Alexander," he would say. "Your country has achieved such great things and now everything is in ruins. You have to rebuild all that! I want to help you but you must help me help you!"

Julius always addressed me as Alexander, while all my other American agents called me Al. It was his way of showing respect even though we were on friendly terms. I tried to explain to him that his contribution under such conditions would soon come to an end: the FBI was not sitting on its hands. Julius shrugged his shoulders; deep down inside he was convinced he was doing nothing wrong! Most of the time he was very disciplined but sometimes he would be as carefree as a teenager. I can still remember him during our second or third meeting, crossing the street to meet me on the same sidewalk. He looked happy and was smoking an expensive cigar, something he couldn't ordinarily afford. When he saw me a few feet away he waved and said:

"Hello comrade!"

I was stunned. Hadn't Semyonov drilled him about the basics of covert activities? A few minutes later in a cafeteria, I explained to him, choosing my words carefully, to avoid hurting his feelings, how foolishly he had behaved. To make sure security regulations are followed is one of the essential tasks of any case officer. Naturally, it has to be done smoothly so as not to anger the source to the point that it could break off any contact. I slowly persuaded Julius to stop subscribing to left-wing magazines, not to attend Red Army support rallies, or to openly associate with his Communist friends. Those meetings where we had nothing compromising in our pockets, "instruction meetings" in bureaucratese, fell between our brush pass encounters, every six weeks. We would meet for a friendly dinner which allowed us to get to know each other and strengthen our friendship. Naturally, fifty years later I can't remember every one of our meetings. Yet, having had the privilege of knowing this exceptional man and being one of the last witnesses to his actions, I want to recall everything I can of our conversations.

We rarely went to real restaurants, even cheap ones because the Rezidentura was under orders to cut down on expenses. Pastelnyak would even go so far as to reimburse only half the bill, the part relating to the source. In any case police informers always infiltrated those types of establishments. The few times when we actually decided to have a real meal we always went to Eastern European restaurants: Romanian, Hungarian, or Austrian. Most of the time we met in cafeterias, self-service places, or bars that served snacks. In the noise of the crowd of ordinary New Yorkers we could speak without having to worry too much about our neighbors. Julius could spend hours this way.

"I know you may not be aware of it, but our meetings are among the happiest moments of my life," he'd say to me. "I have a wonderful wife and a son whom I adore. But you are the only person who knows all my secrets, and it's very important to be able to confide in someone."

I honestly had as much pleasure in our conversations but, contrary to Libi, I knew the implacable rules of "konspiratsya": the more time a case officer spends with his agent, the greater the likelihood of their running the risk of falling under the watchful eye of counterespionage. I was therefore pressed to keep our meetings to no more than ninety minutes. Many things strengthened our bond. The more we met the more we found we had things in common. I was five years older than Julius and had grown up in different social and economic circumstances but our lives seemed to echo one another. Both of us had started working while we were still kids because our fathers' salaries couldn't support their respective families; we shared the same passion for technology and were both radio engineers.

Julius liked to hear me talk about my home, where I'd sleep on the wood prepared for the winter, of my youth as a street fighter and theater-goer, of the locomotive depot where I'd experienced moments of happiness in front of a vise with a file in my hands, of running in my shorts in temperatures of minus 20°C, or about the poorly dressed and hungry student I had been for five years. Through my experience he tried to envision the life of so many simple people who were building a society that represented for him, just as it did for me, the future of humanity. Everything concerning the USSR was of interest to him: our day care centers and our schools, our clinics and our stores, sports, political, and labor activities. I described gigantic factories and electrical plants built in just a few years, collective farms, workers' universities and the Communist Youth. Julius was nearing thirty and the father of a child, but he lost nothing of the great adolescent enthusiasm where there were no such feelings as selfishness, self-interest and the excessive caution stemming from laziness rather than wisdom. His optimistic, energetic personality was marked by his attachment to Communist doctrine that had such a mesmerizing effect on people like him. His Socialist ideas were new, clear, and brilliant and, through my descriptions, they became tangible. I was also happy to speak about my country because it was a way of going back to Russia.

Libi had read the great classics of Socialism: Marx, Engels, Lenin, yet during our meetings his statements had a childish revolutionary naïveté, which was part of his personality. He abhorred wealth, among other things.

"I don't know if I'll live long enough to see gold-plated urinals," he would tell me. "Hey, Lenin wrote that we would have them some day, and I sincerely hope so!"

Another time he said:

"I don't understand the rich. Do you understand them? They have amassed so many riches. Why don't they want to give a bit to those who have nothing?"

I knew that Julius had been very much affected by the Great Depression. Many Americans were very fearful of another crash and the resulting unemployment, fearing it would all return once the war was over. It was one of the reasons that the land of Socialism, since it had done away with unemployment, was a beacon of hope. That was certainly the reason why Julius, even before meeting a Soviet citizen, attended rallies in support of the USSR, and was in fact still attending them. I remember him being impressed at one of these events by a speech by the Soviet writer Ilya Ehrenburg, who was demanding the opening of a second front in Europe as soon as possible.

"Don't you realize?" he would tell me full of excitement, "Ehrenburg ended his speech and everyone gave him a standing ovation! Can you imagine that, the applause of twenty thousand people?"

However, his enthusiasm didn't overshadow his common sense.

"Obviously," he said sarcastically, "his anti-fascist speech couldn't move the capitalist hearts. They have other things to do than go to a rally meant to shorten a war that brings them more cash every day."

I fully understand how our commitment to Communist values, hatred of the exploiters and sympathy for the oppressed, the sincere enthusiasm in working at the creation of an era of equality and social justice may appear ridiculous today. Nevertheless, like millions of men and women all over the world, we believed in those ideals from the depths of our soul and we were ready to sacrifice our lives for them. Was Julius in the dark about the purges, the political trials and the repression of the Stalin era? He never discussed the subject with me and appeared convinced that the revolution could not avoid violence. He had read a lot and spoke to me about Cromwell, the French Revolution and Robespierre, and was not at all surprised that the Reds and the Blues had tried so hard to kill each other. The class struggle couldn't fail to appear after the civil war. For him the bloody episodes in the building of Socialism didn't change the fact that the system was much more equitable than capitalism.

Our ideological agreements were also strengthened by the thought that the human race was fighting an enemy attempting to erase thousands of years of civilization in the name of a demented idea. The choice was a simple one: either Nazism or us. For all those with a clear view of this clash, the disputes and the games of influence in the Allied camp appeared as particularly harmful activities. Nothing, we thought, should distract the anti-fascist coalition from its main task of destroying Hitler at any price. I am not preaching propaganda and my only purpose is to explain the motivations of people such as Julius Rosenberg, John Cairncross, Donald Maclean, or Klaus Fuchs, who were considered traitors in their own countries but who, as far as I'm concerned, are real heroes. Their contribution to the war effort of the USSR certainly helped save hundreds of thousands, perhaps even millions, of the lives of my own countrymen, including perhaps my own brothers Boris and Gennadi.

Julius saw his collaboration with Soviet intelligence as a kind of religious calling, which was his way of fighting, indirectly, but no less effectively, his personal enemy: fascism. The issue that most troubled him was the extermination of the Jews. At almost every rendezvous he asked for news of Semyonov's father, who was thought to be caught inside occupied Odessa. One day, I finally reassured him that he had been evacuated to Barnaul in Siberia. Even though Julius Rosenberg was living in New York, his heart was beating in the eastern hemisphere. The war that was raging thousands of miles away from his home was his main preoccupation. When I first met him, the Red Army was already pushing the enemy toward the west, sweeping from one victory to the next. Most of our meetings would begin with a sentence such as:

"Did you see? Belgorod (or Kharkov or Kiev) has been liberated!"

To him the announcement of a victory was never simply a few lines in a newspaper. He imagined the thousands of soldiers who had given their lives for it, who lay dead on the battlefields or in the mass graves. He was always thinking there were so many because his country wasn't doing enough to help and he felt ashamed and remorseful because his own efforts couldn't repair this injustice. I tried as much as possible to prove to him that he was doing everything he could. He was full of admiration for the resistance fighters struggling behind enemy lines in Yugoslavia, France, Italy, Greece and the USSR most of all and sometimes he would ask me:

"Can you explain to me how in the dead of winter, when it's freezing and there's snow everywhere, the partisans manage to survive for months on end in the forests?"

I would answer that the soil doesn't freeze up completely and that they dug shelters where they slept covered by branches of fir trees.

"Okay, but what about... the women!"

"The women live just like the men."

"That's easy to say! No, to me it's inconceivable!"

One day Julius asked me something he probably had been thinking about for a long time:

"Tell me truthfully, Alexander. Do you think my friends and I are like partisans as well?"

"Yes of course!" I answered. "Obviously you stay in your offices while others are in the trenches or the forests but you take risks just like they do. It requires the same kind of courage and you help bring about our victory just as much as the partisans do."

Julius pursed his lips to avoid showing his happiness and nodded affirmatively. What I told him was true and Libi quickly became top priority in my operational work. He gave us immeasurably valuable technical documentation of the radio device that allowed anti-aircraft defenses to distinguish between friendly and unfriendly aircraft. The importance of his work was confirmed when, at the beginning of 1944, he gave us a number of blueprints and spare parts relating to the proximity fuse, a revolutionary device that was manufactured by Emerson Radio. Until then shells only exploded upon actual contact with a plane and if they didn't damage one of the plane's vital systems, the aircraft had a very good chance of being able to land or even return to home base. The proximity fuse had been designed to make the shell explode at a short distance from its target: the fragments were scattered in balls, and at least some were guaranteed to cause irreparable damage to the plane. The other advantage was that it automatically corrected the path of the explosive charges toward the location of the plane itself, making it a precursor of future missile homing devices.

Despite the little mishap I discussed previously, when Julius greeted me loudly in the street, he was very serious once engaged in covert action. I can't remember him ever missing a rendezvous or being late. He enjoyed excellent health, but suffered from hay fever at the beginning of every summer. His reddened eyes watered, he sneezed and never was without his handkerchief. When I saw him in that condition I would schedule our encounters even further apart. We were a real team: I was the confirmed professional but he knew his own country, his fellow citizens, their frame of mind and their reactions, and workplaces, far better than I did. Often in discussing the technical possibilities of obtaining this or that document, or the details of our next meeting, Libi would listen to me without interrupting before he would completely change my initial plan. I didn't need to ask for his advice, he always volunteered it himself.

Julius was completely indifferent toward material things. He dressed properly but without elegance. The only object of any value that he carried was his wedding ring. In restaurants he was always careful to order the least expensive dishes; a bottle of wine to celebrate something was a luxury for him. Semyonov had warned me that Rosenberg adamantly refused any compensation. However, from time to time, I found an excuse to offer him some money. Ethel wasn't working and clearly Julius' salary made it difficult for them to make ends meet. I was very tactful and courteous in trying to avoid offending him, but to no avail! All I could reimburse him for were his travel expenses and the restaurant bills he paid for his colleagues who, unwittingly, became our informers, so I was lucky to get him to take $25 per month, yet his contribution was such that even millions would not have compensated him for its true value.

13

Even in the middle of a war Christmas was a sacred holiday for all American families, though religious holidays were never observed in the USSR. A beautiful Christmas tree was set up in the middle of the skating rink in Rockefeller Center. On the main thoroughfares like Broadway and Fifth Avenue, storefront windows were decorated with tinsel, Christmas decorations, Santa Claus with bags full of presents, or even just a branch from a Christmas tree. People walked around with beautiful boxes tied with red, pink and green ribbons. I also wanted to give Julius and his family some presents. For over a year we had been through risks, disappointments and successes together. Julius had by now become more than just a source of information and he was more like an ideological companion, an army buddy.

I wanted to give him a wristwatch, to help him remember me long after we had parted. A plush animal would be fun for little Michael. As for Ethel, I had never met her and had no idea of her tastes, but I did know how much Julius loved her. I couldn't get just anything, so I looked for something that would please her. I thought about it for several days and finally I asked Julius.

"You know what she'd really like? She's been dreaming for some time about a new handbag, the one she has is old and out of fashion."

Since I'm not very clever at these things I asked my wife Zina, who knew Manhattan stores very well, to help me make a choice. I thought I was about to waste an entire morning in the pre-holiday rush, but to my amazement we found everything we wanted at Gimbel Brothers. In the toy department we settled on a beautiful teddy bear; then, remembering Libi's dislike of gold, we chose a handsome Omega stainless steel watch with a bracelet made of the same metal. My wife bought a large brown crocodile handbag she would have picked for herself. To make our presents look like family gifts, we placed the watch and the toy inside the handbag, which was then packed in a beautiful box with wrapping paper and lots of ribbons.

All this was far removed from konspiratsya, I must admit, but at times the quality of the relationship is more important than an excess of caution. I met with Julius on December 24, 1944 at 7:30 p.m. at the Horn & Hardart cafeteria on West 38th Street, right near Broadway, to give him the gifts. I had cased the location a long time before and it had two positive features for secret meetings. First, there were no waiters, only automatic distributors. You put in the amount of coins, made your selection, pressed a button and a small glass door opened, giving access to the chosen plate or drink. The other advantage was that it had two exits, one on 38th Street and the other on Broadway.

Following a rather long security itinerary, as usual, I reached the location about fifteen minutes early and stood on the opposite sidewalk. I used the extra time to look at some posters and buy a newspaper as I surveyed the surroundings. Then I saw Julius arrive with a brown carton in his hand; he walked into the cafeteria without noticing me. Through the window, as in a giant aquarium, I watched him set down his package on a low windowsill and place his hat and coat on a rack before getting a cup of coffee from the machine. He came back to the table and spread out a newspaper. Everything looked perfectly normal so I walked in and, just like my friend, placed my box on the windowsill next to his. As I took off my winter coat, I could see that Libi was surreptitiously watching me as well. To kill the taste of what Americans call coffee, I also bought a sandwich. Then I sat facing

Libi and began reading the paper. That was how we exchanged our greetings without looking at each other.

"Don't forget to take the box I brought you," I almost whispered to him. "Those are your Christmas presents." Julius smiled.

"Thanks. Your present is in the big carton. Careful, it's pretty heavy."

That was something I didn't expect, but Libi didn't give me any time to respond. He wished me a Merry Christmas and got up. Before putting on his coat, he placed his *New York Times* on the box meant for him, and a few seconds later he took it as naturally as could be. I finished my sandwich without hurrying, pretending to read my paper. No one seemed to have noticed our little exchange but before grabbing my gift I decided to wait for two women chatting near the window to leave. The carton was tied with a string and Julius was right, it must have weighed 14 or 15 pounds. I had planned to get back to the Consulate by subway but I was afraid the string would break from the weight. I walked for a block or so, to be farther away from the meeting point, before hailing a cab.

Once inside the Consulate I walked directly upstairs to the Rezidentura and opened my package. At that hour there was no one in the large communal office and the scene that followed had no witnesses. It's too bad because I must have had a totally flabbergasted expression on my face. What I was looking at was the famous proximity fuse! This was the short-range fuse, the one that exploded automatically when it got close to the plane, guaranteeing the plane's complete destruction; it was the very item the Center had designated as being a priority in intelligence gathering. What I had were not drawings or descriptions but the complete device, in working order, brand new, smelling of metal and oil, with an additional supply of miniaturized replacement metal tubes fastened to the top.

Christmas Day was not a holiday in the Soviet Union, the Orthodox Church celebrates it on January 7, so I spent the day working at routine chores, receiving the visit of a cargo captain and the second officer of a Soviet cargo ship that had arrived the day before. I had a long phone conversation with a journalist from CBS who was preparing a radio broadcast on *The Allies at War*, in which

I was to participate. The editor of a small Russian émigré newspaper brought me about one hundred dollars he had collected from his readers, but I couldn't stop thinking about my magnificent new present. Even as a child I had never felt such joy in thinking about my presents. That feeling lasted until lunch time when my boss, Kvasnikov, appeared. At first he displayed as much excitement as I did, turning the priceless little rocket around in his hands. But, konspiratsya! His mood quickly darkened.

"What's the problem?" I asked, suddenly feeling nervous myself. Kvasnikov narrowed his eyes.

"How could Libi walk out with such a large object? In his secret factory, the smallest part, even if defective, is under control. Can you give me an explanation?"

I didn't have one and, instead of congratulations, I was reprimanded for having loosened control over my agent. I was hurt but not worried because I trusted Julius. At our next meeting Libi told me the whole story. The idea of this Christmas present had come to him three months before when he had been able to take a proximity fuse that had been rejected and hide it in a corner of the workshop. Little by little he managed to replace the defective parts until the device was in perfect condition. Then he hid it behind a box on a shelf where spare parts were kept, so that now all he had to do was find a way to smuggle it out.

The opportunity came on the day before Christmas because the factory would discard defective parts accumulated for an entire year just before the holiday. Since these were secret devices, everything was shipped to a safe place to be destroyed under the watchful eye of the engineers. Julius was named to ride in the van that was transporting the parts and he decided to make an attempt. He wrapped the rocket in a carton that looked like all the others. On December 23 he helped the workers load the van he was to accompany and, before taking his seat next to the driver, he placed his treasure close by. The driver started the engine and drove to the exit. This was the critical moment of the operation because the guards were under orders to check the papers and the contents of the shipment in each vehicle. If any one of them had decided to be thorough that day and open the carton, it would have been the end.

The guard, a stocky fifty-year-old, with a red face, walked up to the van slowly and the driver handed him the paperwork.

"It's the last run to get rid of all the garbage," said Julius. "Now all we have to do is clean up the house for the holidays!"

The guard answered in kind:

"Then you can keep the van, if you have as much garbage as we've got here!"

The three men laughed, the guard folded the papers and handed them back to the driver.

"Merry Christmas, guys!"

"Merry Christmas!"

The electric gate moved slowly to one side and five seconds later Libi and my gift were outside. Julius had carefully planned the rest of his task so that when they passed by a store he asked the driver to stop in order to buy some groceries for the holiday. He bought food that was packed in a carton of the same size as the rocket and placed them next to each other in the van. All he had to do then was to convince the driver to make a small detour to his home.

"Can I help you take that upstairs?" asked the driver.

"No thanks, it's not that heavy," answered Julius.

He walked around to the back of the van, took both cartons and disappeared inside his building, returning five minutes later.

"Thanks, we can go now."

I was on the edge of my seat during the whole time.

"Julius, you shouldn't have gone into this crazy scheme," I said. "It could have gone very wrong. Next time you feel like jumping headfirst let me know in advance. We'll think about limiting the risks."

"It's not a crazy scheme at all!" replied Libi. "I planned my moves step by step and I brought them to fruition at the moment of least risk. The day before Christmas people are only thinking about the holidays. One week before or after and it would never have worked."

He smiled at me disarmingly.

"Honestly, I wanted to set up my own operation that would be, well, not so heroic, but at least daring! Millions of Russians are taking even bigger risks every day, and I don't want to live off their sacrifices."

I tried to convince him that his being cautious would be much more useful to our cause than his daring actions, but I wasn't so sure of that myself.

The consequences of this matter were far-reaching. The sample of the proximity fuse was carefully examined by Soviet specialists and, based on their conclusions, the Council of Ministers of the USSR created by emergency decree a special laboratory and factory to produce these devices. Modified by our engineers, the fuse was quickly put into production and thanks to it, the American U2 reconnaissance plane flown by Francis Gary Powers was shot down over Sverdlovsk on May 1, 1960. After that incident the Eisenhower administration dropped the idea of a law on freedom of the skies.[37]

Many years later, while I was working at the Center, I learned from the American media that of all the technical innovations that had been created during the Second World War, the proximity fuse came second after the atomic bomb. In order to enhance the device, the U.S. spent about one billion dollars. I think my 1944 Christmas present was the most expensive one individual ever received from another!

Alexander Feklisov, alias "Alexander Fomin" and code named "Kalistrat," was an NKVD officer in the Consulate General of the USSR in New York City working undercover as a low-level trainee in 1941. He was to handle the Rosenberg espionage network, among several others, in the United States.

Anatoly Yatskov, alias "Anatoly Yakovlev" and known to most of his agents as "John," was specifically focused on atomic bomb espionage. Yatskov also worked out of the New York Consulate and was Feklisov's life-long friend and colleague.

left

Leonid Kvasnikov, code named "Anton," was the overall supervisor of the atomic bomb espionage project, known as the "XY Line" in the New York Rezidentura of the NKVD. He spoke very little English and was rarely seen outside the building. After World War II Kvasnikov headed the KGB's technical espionage services in Moscow.

right

Semyon Semyonov, known to his agents as "Sam" and "Henry," was the NKVD officer who actually recruited Julius Rosenberg. Semyonov was pressured to leave New York in 1943 by intense FBI surveillance.

left

Gaik Ovakimian was the NKVD officer who recruited Harry Gold. He also headed the New York Rezidentura until his entrapment by the FBI in 1941. Because of the Nazi attack on the Soviet Union, Ovakimian was allowed to return home in July of that year.

left

Vyacheslav Molotov just before the Nazi attack in 1941, when he was Foreign Minister and Prime Minister of the USSR.

below

Lavrenti Beria, head of the NKVD since the demise of Yezhov in 1938, was also in overall charge of atomic bomb espionage known as Project "Enormoz."

Elizabeth Bentley was part of the espionage network run by Jacob Golos, which included Abraham Brothman and Harry Gold. Her defection to the FBI in 1945, as well as that of Soviet code clerk Igor Guzenko in Canada, was a major blow to Soviet espionage in North America.

above
Julius and Ethel Rosenberg at Coney Island in 1939.

below
Morton Sobell *(right)* was arrested in Mexico in August 1950.

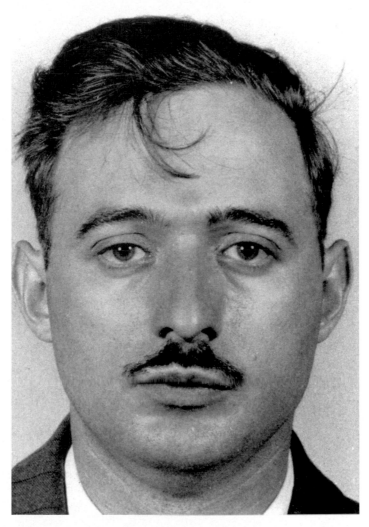

Julius Rosenberg on the day of his arrest by the FBI, July 17, 1950.

David Greenglass was identified by Harry Gold
and arrested on June 15, 1950.

Klaus Fuchs in Dresden, East Germany, in 1960 after being freed from the Wormwood Scrubs prison in England.

The Nags Head pub in London where, on September 27, 1947, Feklisov met with Klaus Fuchs for the first time and reactivated the scientist as a KGB agent. Fuchs passed secret data on the atomic and hydrogen bombs to Feklisov.

The Spotted Horse pub, another meeting place of Klaus Fuchs and Alexander Feklisov.

above
Klaus Fuchs married Greta Keilson, whom he called "Margot,"
27 years after they first met in Paris.

below
Morris and Lona Cohen fly back to the Soviet Union
in a spy exchange after spending time in a British prison for espionage.
Lona Cohen was the other courier at Los Alamos who passed on atomic bomb secrets
she received from Theodore Hall, code named "Mlad."

Feklisov *(middle)* was in charge of security for Nikita Khrushchev in September 1959 during his state visit to the United States. Nina Petrovna, Khrushchev's wife, is standing between them.

above

John Scali held secret meetings in Washington with KGB Rezident Feklisov as a back channel to the Kremlin during the October 1962 Cuban Missile Crisis.

right

Nikita S. Khrushchev in 1962.

John F. Kennedy listens to Nikita Khrushchev at the close of their
only face-to-face meeting in Vienna on June 4, 1961.

President Kennedy meets at Hyannis Port on November 25, 1961 with Nikita Khrushchev's son-in-law and chief editor of *Izvestia*, Alexei Adzhubei *(right)* and journalist Georgy Bolshakov *(second from right)* a KGB operative and back channel contact of Pierre Salinger. State Department interpreter Alex Akalovsky is holding his notepad.

14

Beyond his own activity Julius had built a whole network of friends and close relations who were ready to work with Soviet intelligence. With only one exception, they were all under thirty and had been classmates of Rosenberg's at CCNY. The exception was a man named Alfred Sarant, who was of Greek origin. When I was in charge of handling Julius, his network included only two other members and when it was deactivated, at the end of 1945, it had grown to two more sources and two liaison agents. I must say that, besides the proximity fuse, the production by Julius' friends was greater than his own.

Julius was a born recruiter who could communicate forcefully and passionately his boundless faith in Socialist ideals. His desire to help the USSR in its fight against Nazism often drove him to find the right words to overcome the hesitations of his recruits and the fact that he was a secret agent was not humiliating to this partisan fighter in the streets of Manhattan. You can only convince others by setting an example and Libi's was sure to catch on. Since he was American-born and above suspicion, it was much easier for him to meet his fellow citizens than for a foreigner with an FBI file. For this reason Julius held secret meetings with his sources and would collect documents himself. Once American counterintelligence began reorienting its efforts against Soviet intelligence after Stalingrad, this system vastly increased the risks for a go-between such as Libi because he was not only meeting with his friends but with his case officer as well. At the end of 1943, to ensure Rosenberg's security, the Center decided to transfer the agents he was handling to a Soviet case officer. That case officer was none other than this writer, Alexander Feklisov, alias Alexander Fomin, a trainee at the New York Consulate, who, in the worse case, would only risk being declared persona non grata. Around that time I had already exchanged my four-panel identity document for a real service passport, which still did not give me diplomatic status, but at least guaranteed immunity with U.S. authorities. That was how I became acquainted with most of the members of the underground network, one of the most effective in the history of Soviet technological espionage.

The first acquaintance of Julius' to participate in his covert activity was Joel Barr, whose father had fled Russia in 1905 and who also came from an impoverished Jewish family. Upon arriving in New York the Barrs were desperately trying to make ends meet. Once, when they were unable to pay the rent, the police threw them into the street. Barr and Julius went to the same school and the boys became friends. They both passed the tough entrance examination to CCNY where college tuition was free. Those four years drew them even closer together because they shared the same ideas, joined the Young Communist League, and later joined a Communist Party cell. For two years they worked at different labs for the Army Signal Corps at Fort Monmouth, New Jersey[38] and shared many interests; they had the same Communist ideals; they were part of a study group of Marxist literature and sympathized with the USSR. Half the students at CCNY were members of the Young Communist League. From the start of our relationship we asked them to hide their opinions and refrain from any activity that could draw attention to them.

Despite their ideological similarities, Julius and Joel were two very different personalities. Julius had the makings of a leader and was passionate about the smallest of his activities, talking about it eloquently. Joel was a much more reserved type, more inclined to observe than to speak out himself. He preferred isolation and acted only after having given something a lot of thought, which probably explained why he was still a bachelor. Those differences did not prevent the two friends from genuinely admiring and feeling close to one another. Rosenberg recruited Barr at the end of 1942 when the latter worked as an engineer at a Western Electric plant in New York, designing improvements on radar devices to be fitted on B-type bombers. Barr was much appreciated by his employers and had access to most of the secret documentation available in his field.

The procedure established by the Rezidentura to handle this very important agent, whose code name at the time was "Scout" (in December 1944 he became "Meter"), was not exactly a simple one. On the evening of a delivery (the dates were set several weeks in advance) Barr would lift a confidential file as he left his office and had to replace it the next morning. He handed it to Julius, who then rushed to meet Semyonov, who passed it to me, and I in turn would hurry to the Consulate to photograph the material. I handed the documents back to Semyonov, who passed them back to Julius, who returned them to Joel! When Semyonov left, the chain was greatly simplified by one link. Once Julius began microfilming the documents, security improved because he could now photograph the documents he had received at any time between our encounters. But since I was to handle Barr personally, I insisted that we cut the risks even further by having him microfilm his own documents.

As far as I was concerned things couldn't be better, since Barr lived alone in a rented two-room apartment at 65 Morton Street in Greenwich Village. Kvasnikov disagreed. He pointed out very shrewdly that the apartment was empty during the day and there was nothing to prevent the FBI from searching it surreptitiously. Joel and I then created two hiding places under the floorboards, one for the camera and the accessories, the other for the exposed or new film. On top of that he still had his own room in his parents' apartment where his younger brother and his sisters lived and where he kept his books, records, a record player, and could even hide microfilm. That's what we decided to do.

Barr was easy to recognize. Like the Soviet poet Boris Pasternak, he had a long equine face and a piercing look behind his glasses.[39]

Even though he was extremely perceptive and very cautious, he didn't have the makings of a good spy, lacking courage at critical moments and having trouble controlling himself. When he had to hand me the film, he would look around with an anguished expression on his face seeing an FBI agent in anyone walking by. At our instructional meetings he was less anxious, but he automatically became nervous every time a new customer entered the establishment where we were meeting. Since it was in his nature to be nervous I attempted to radiate calm self-assurance in his presence, even more than usual.

An anecdote will illustrate the difference between Barr and Rosenberg. One day I had scheduled a meeting with Julius in Brooklyn. As I got off the streetcar at a stop, I sensed a hostile presence in the area. Among the professionals, this business ends up refining one's senses and teaches you how to trust your intuition. The danger I felt was a couple getting off behind us.

"Julius," I mumbled, "I think we're being followed. Take the subway right away; I'll make them follow me."

Libi gave me a look that meant he'd gotten the message and would execute the plan, without hesitation. His eyes showed neither fear nor concern. We turned a corner and Julius ducked into the subway. I bought a paper and stood around, which is the best technique in such cases to check your back. The suspicious couple crossed the street, strolled into the crowd and disappeared. The next day we found out from the papers that the aircraft carrier *Roosevelt* had been launched at the shipyards of Bethlehem Steel. Eleanor Roosevelt, the First Lady, was the guest of honor at the ceremony and the entire neighborhood was swarming with policemen and plainclothes agents. My subconscious fear had not failed me. When I told Libi at our next meeting, he was happy to find out the key to the mystery. Barr, however, who had been told the story by Julius, didn't react the same way.

"It's not such a great idea to meet in cafeterias or in the street," he said at our next meeting. "We've got to do it in a taxi!"

I was about to reply but he insisted:

"Please let's take a taxi!"

I hailed a yellow cab.

"You tell the driver where we're going," I said before getting in with my agent, since I feared my accent would give me away.

Pleased at having obtained what he wanted, Barr gave the address to the driver with a self-assured voice and then fell silent. With a witness only three feet away, no confidential conversation is possible. He had to admit that totally secure solutions were not always practical. Cautious as he was, though, Joel Barr was no slouch and never missed a single one of our meetings.

Barr was a classical music buff. He could play the piano and the violin fairly well and often went to philharmonic concerts. Johann Sebastian Bach was his idol. More than once he tried to convert me into becoming an unconditional admirer of the German composer and only partially succeeded, since I was much too busy. However, this passion of his drew him closer to one of his friends, Alfred Sarant, an amateur guitar player. Sarant had an attractive professional profile; he was a talented engineering designer in charge of a study group and worked at Bell Research Laboratories developing radio electrical devices for military applications.

Joel and Alfred were good friends and spent a lot of time together. I must admit that Sarant had the makings of an undercover agent; he was a cautious young man, yet full of resolve, with progressive ideas. Before we recruited him though, he had to pass a test. Barr asked Sarant to borrow some secret documents to which he had access because he, Barr, needed them for his personal use. Alfred did not hesitate in helping his friend and in the meantime the Center approved a bona fide approach. This assignment was given to Barr, but he obviously didn't like the idea. He hesitated and procrastinated without giving a specific reason. He could have simply said that he feared outright rejection, which would have ended their friendship. Instead he kept on repeating to me: "It's not as easy as that!" I think Rosenberg had to step in to allay his fears.

We decided that the best way to convince Sarant was to use a simple idea, the Soviet people were giving their blood in the struggle against fascism for the common good of all humanity. The war effort prevented the release of necessary funds for research into new weapons that the USSR needed even more than its allies. Barr was to tell him that a Soviet friend had requested his help and that he'd agreed to give it a long time ago. Now it was his turn to make a decision. Actually these points were absolutely true. Much to Barr's relief his friend accepted immediately, and since he was of Greek ancestry we gave him the Anglo-Saxon-sounding code name of Hugh. Sarant's recruitment had a positive effect on Barr, who no longer felt alone and could sleep better. Sarant even moved to Greenwich Village to share his friend's apartment; they helped each other microfilm documents and avoid any possible tails.

Danger was never very far away, the two young bachelors received the visits of many pretty girls. Barr didn't hide any of this from me, and I found it all quite alarming, because since the dawn of history the pillow has always been the best way to break a secret. Because we had no way of opposing this behavior, Kvasnikov kept on repeating to me that we had to constantly reemphasize the risks they were taking.

At every meeting I would ask Joel to be cautious. Beyond that Barr was no problem for me. Like most of my agents, he would automatically refuse the money I attempted to offer him and his usual answer was: "You certainly need it more than I do!" Naturally, he was speaking of the Soviets at war. I insisted that collaborating with us meant expenses to "grease" some colleagues or take extra precautions, and he and Sarant had to dip into their personal accounts to be efficient. I thought it absolutely normal to reimburse them. At that point Barr would admit that there were some books or some records they hesitated to buy and he'd reluctantly accept my modest offer. One day he admitted to me that they didn't spend all that money but saved some for emergency expenses.

For security reasons at that time I never did meet Sarant. I only knew from his pictures that he was a handsome, dark-skinned Mediterranean young man with curly hair. But I was meeting with Barr every two weeks on average. Once a month, early in the morning, he would slip me a roll of about twenty films representing about 400-500 pages of documents. The instruction meetings always took place in the evenings. My two music-loving friends allowed us to keep abreast of the most recent studies at Bell Research Laboratories and Western Electric. Better still, Barr and Sarant allowed the

Rezidentura to carry out, by pure chance, an extraordinary feat of espionage that was to be long remembered.

During the war, the Center would give very general assignments, such as "gather information on the new radar, aiming and other electronic devices created by the Americans." Yet on one occasion the request was extremely precise: "Just outside London, an ultra-modern device, the SCR584, automatically determines the speed and path of German V2 rockets and sets the firing of anti-aircraft batteries. Take every step to obtain more information on this facility." The cable reached us the day before a brush pass meeting with Barr. The next morning at 7 a.m. we were crossing paths in a cafeteria and, before taking the rolls of film under a table, I slipped Joel a piece of paper describing in a few words what the Center had asked of us. He smiled at me and said:

"That's funny! We must have a crystal ball! Five days ago we read your minds and got the technical manual of this facility. We just finished photographing it last night at 2 a.m. There are 600 pages of text and drawings."

I thanked him very quickly because another customer was coming to sit at our table. As I was developing the film, I realized that we indeed had been handed exactly what the Center had requested and circumstances worked in our favor all the way through. The diplomatic pouch was leaving for Moscow two days later; the film was placed in the container with the walls full of acid and was taken by plane under the watchful eye of a courier. It crossed America, stopping along the way, to Alaska, and then over our immense country from one end to the other, finally landing on Pavel Fitin's desk in the Lubyanka. Just one week after he had signed the order, the head of Soviet intelligence was looking at the result of an operation that ordinarily would have taken months to achieve. For the first time since I had arrived in New York, the Rezident and I were congratulated for the speed with which we were able to accomplish such a vitally important mission. The same message ordered us to pay a special bonus of $1,000 to Barr and Sarant. It was a large amount of money that would have allowed them to buy an entire library of music recordings. And yet Barr refused the envelope; he didn't want it. As for Sarant, Barr told me he would bring back his answer at our next meeting. Just as I expected, Sarant also refused.

Many years later, when I became the head of the American section of the First Directorate of the KGB, I was able to consult the files of all my former agents. That was how I found out—when I was in action I didn't even think of such things—that between 1943 and 1945, Barr and Sarant gave us 9,165 pages of secret documents relating to more than one hundred programs in the planning stages. On several occasions I could verify that this material had been very highly thought of by one of the topmost authorities on the subject, the academician Axel Berg. The name made me smile because it was the same name used at the time by Joel Barr who, in the Soviet Union, had become Josef Veniaminovich Berg. But we shall discuss that later.

15

William Perl was another classmate of Julius Rosenberg's at CCNY. Perl majored in aeronautical engineering and the two students met regularly, especially to discuss the great classics of Marxist-Leninist literature, which they read diligently. Just like Rosenberg, William, known as Willy to his friends, felt that the values of social justice, equality, and brotherhood were paramount; he hated the independently wealthy who did no work and lived in the lap of luxury.

After graduating with honors, Perl was offered a job at NACA, the laboratory of the National Advisory Committee for Aeronautics, in Cleveland, Ohio, where he worked on the design of new fighter planes. Since it was a government contract, Perl had access to all secret documents sent in by other companies and government agencies. When Rosenberg told Semyonov and Zarubin of this friend of his who had such an interesting profile, they immediately contacted the Center. Fighter planes were a very exclusive area and the Lubyanka quickly gave its approval to proceed with Perl's recruitment under the code name "Gnom," later switched to "Yakov."

Perl traveled from Cleveland back to New York about once a month to spend Sunday with his parents and see his friends. Like many of Libi's contacts, this romantic twenty-three year old agreed to help the Red Army's struggle, and from December 1942 regularly brought back a large brown briefcase filled with confidential material. He arrived by the night train, and passed along his explosive lode to Julius Rosenberg in a location agreed upon in advance before visiting with his family. The briefcase was just beginning its journey. A half hour later it was in Semyonov's hands, then relayed by me to the Consulate. That same evening it would travel the relay in reverse until it reached the train about to return to Ohio.

During the summer of 1943 the network was interrupted because of the increased FBI surveillance of Semyonov. When I took over the Rosenberg network, Perl was reactivated and the chain resumed, but Julius would now pass the briefcase directly to me. The documents Gnom provided were so valuable to us that the Center decided to add a security liaison. Should Julius be burned, I had to be able to contact Perl directly. Our first meeting took place at the beginning of 1944 in Julius' presence.

When I met Perl I understood the irony of his code name, Gnom, which means "midget." In fact Perl was a well-built, handsome fellow, over six feet tall, and a smart dresser. We met in a cafeteria to talk and, as usual, I avoided places that were too small. The best locations were a bar or a drugstore large enough for thirty or forty people, providing lots of noise, with a free table surrounded by tables already taken to prevent anyone following us from sitting down.

"Delighted to meet a real friend," I told William. "We greatly appreciate your fraternal help, which is vital to us."

Perl, no doubt, found my words somewhat pompous.

"I'm only doing my duty as any normal person would," he answered simply.

These initial meetings, which appear to be an exchange of courtesies, are actually very important for "taking stock" of the other person. Perl appeared to be very trustworthy and I assume he came to the same conclusion about me. From that point on we would meet directly but this was far from solving all the problems we encountered.

The scrutiny we were subjected to became tighter every day. A whole army of detectives permanently surrounded the Consulate, day and night, including Sundays and holidays. The FBI surveillance center at the Pierre Hotel recorded every one of our comings and goings and no sooner had a Soviet citizen left the building than a whole team would follow him. From my office window I could always see two or three agents standing on the sidewalk, and sitting in the row of cars parked nearby. They became suspicious of weekend visitors when the Consulate was supposedly closed. I was living on West 89th Street with Zina and had no real reason to go to the office on holidays. Besides, it was impossible to go to the Consulate on a Sunday morning at 9 a.m. carrying a briefcase filled with documents and then leave two or three hours later. That would really attract a whole posse of agents. How we missed the peace and quiet of just a few months before!

Fortunately I could count on Anatoly Yatskov who, besides watching my back during my secret meetings, also helped microfilm the documents Perl delivered on Sundays. We did this at my home or at the home of a Soviet Amtorg engineer. Since I was also assigned to prevent any infiltration of that company by American secret services, I needed good informers who would not ask useless questions. Anatoly and I worked quickly, while one of us snapped the picture and loaded the next frame, the other placed the next page in front of the camera; but then we still had to return to the Consulate afterwards to be sure everything was safely stored. We had to find ways to avoid exposing ourselves to unnecessary risks.

The obvious solution was to set up a liaison agent in Cleveland. I spoke to Julius about this and he promised to look among his own acquaintances. Since that person had to be of unimpeachable loyalty, it took Julius three months to propose a candidate, or rather, candidates, since it was a husband and wife team. Rosenberg had known Michael Sidorovich since high school. The son of Russian-Jewish immigrants, Sidorovich was born in the United States and had already proved his courage and attachment to Communist ideals by volunteering for the international brigades in Spain. His wife Ann was also the daughter of Russian immigrants, but neither one spoke the language of their parents and they had no children. Michael was a locksmith in a factory, while Ann was a housewife who supplemented the family income by sewing dresses for her neighbors and relations. Still, the Sidoroviches had a hard time making ends meet.

Julius sounded them out very cleverly and assured me that they would be very proud to be asked to carry out a dangerous mission for the USSR, provided that the proposal come directly from a Soviet citizen. After the usual checks, Kvasnikov gave me the green light. I'll always remember my first meeting with Michael and Ann. One evening after work, Julius and I took a suburban train. It was already dark outside and when we reached their town, it took us quite a while to find the house. The weather was damp and cold and we were slipping and sliding on the rain-swept streets, but our troubles were not over even when we reached their home. We were wet but the Sidoroviches were drenched because they were repairing a water break in their small garden. Julius introduced me as his Soviet engineer friend. We rolled up our sleeves, quickly repaired the plumbing, and were finally able to dry up.

The living room furniture in the Sidorovich house was rickety and an old tattered lampshade let a bit of light seep through, but the hospitality offered was very warm. After changing clothes, Michael, whom I immediately renamed Mikhail, offered me a beer while his wife prepared some sandwiches. As usual in those days, the conversation turned to the war in Europe. I complained about our allies and their hypocrisy because of the delay in opening a second front and their refusal to supply the Soviet Union with offensive war materiel. Michael agreed:

"Yes, they're playing a double game. America doesn't want a strong Russia after the war."

We finally began speaking quite openly and at one point Julius said:

"We are here for a very sensitive reason."

Ann immediately got up:

"Then take care of your business and I'll go tend to mine."

She cleaned off the table and left us alone.

"We need someone we can trust to help the Soviet Union fight the imperialists," I said finally. "But it's dangerous and there must be absolute secrecy."

Michael was so moved I could see beads of perspiration cover his forehead.

"It will be an honor for me to fight against Russia's enemies. I'll do anything I can."

I explained to him that his job would be to receive confidential documents from an American friend, and once he had photographed them, hand them back along with the film. But to do this they would have to relocate to Cleveland.

"I'm ready to do what's necessary," answered Michael. "That's not a problem. But I'll have to tell Ann. Besides, I know nothing about photography."

I had no problem in his sharing his secrets with his wife, whom I felt was sympathetic enough, and our plan could not succeed without her participation. We therefore called her back in and explained our proposal. Ann must have been in the habit of relying completely on her husband, and since Mike had already said yes... I told them we would pay for their moving expenses, reimburse them for any losses they might incur in selling their house, and would also support them since it would take Michael some time to find another job. The following Sunday I promised to come and teach them about photography, and thus every obstacle was removed.

The Sidoroviches had never held a camera in their hands and I had to return there twice. I also took advantage of those two weekends to teach them the rudiments of clandestine work, how to spot a tail without letting the other side know, how to make brush pass contacts, how to hide the special lens and exposed film. They were eager to learn everything about operational work and neither one displayed any kind of fear or hesitation. By the second Sunday we had become fast friends.

"Practice without me," I said, getting back on the train. "I'll come back next Sunday to test you."

They passed with flying colors and after having imparted my final instructions about the move and the money they would need, I left them feeling secure. The Sidoroviches never suspected that this lesson in photography had inspired their code names: Michael became "Linza" (lens) a feminine word, and Ann, "Obyektiv" (objective), a masculine word. We purposely inverted the gender of their code names. Such little tricks may appear meaningless, but sometimes they can avert a disaster. Since initially the Center had only planned for Michael's recruitment, the couple would operate under the single code name of Linza. Two weeks later, our amateur photographers moved to Cleveland and found a good apartment convenient to their meetings with Perl. Michael had no trouble landing a job; there was plenty of work everywhere during the war. Once they were set up, Rosenberg went to Ohio to introduce Perl to our new agents.

Our plan was for William Perl and Michael Sidorovich to meet twice a month and for Perl to hand over between three and five hundred pages of documents. The couple photographed them at home and handed them back to the engineer the next day. Once a month Ann—or Anya as I called her, Russian style—took the exposed but undeveloped film to New York. Since her train arrived early in the morning I met her before going to work, but obviously I wouldn't be waiting on the platform carrying roses. All my meetings with agents who lived outside New York took place far from their normal itineraries. I waited for Ann on 9th Avenue where she'd change buses. I sat in the bus behind her, and in the commotion she would slip me a roll of film as big as a large apple wrapped in black paper.

Our first contact, following this scenario, took place on a Tuesday in January 1945 and went exactly as planned. I ran to the Consulate, leaving Ann to enjoy her brief stay in New York, see her parents and do some shopping. Her train to Cleveland left at 8 p.m. Naturally, I gave her a quiet briefing at 6 p.m. in a cafeteria near Washington Square. Even though she had already taken a security itinerary, I still checked to make sure she had not been followed before joining her at a table inside. As I always did with all my agents, I began asking her about their lives, attempting to detect any alarming sign that she and her husband might have missed.

"Oh, things are very quiet," answered Ann. "Mike is working, I'm in the house cooking and during the evenings we read. We listen to the radio and sometimes we go to the movies. On Sundays we take a walk in the park. All our neighbors can see that we lead the same kind of life they do, but that's only on the surface. Thanks to you our lives have meaning."

I knew Ann was sincere and the Sidoroviches now had trouble understanding how so many other people could be content with their routine lives when their own had become so exciting. To go through such a transformation one had to join a great cause, making one feel involved in the events that were changing the world. The couple was always ready to volunteer for any dangerous mission. Even though the system we had perfected functioned like clockwork, a case officer is always uneasy operating at a distance. In February 1945 I went to Cleveland to supervise what was happening on the spot. I was used to traveling from one rally to the next, and I had been all over the northeastern United States. Yet this time I wanted to keep my trip a secret, so before boarding the night train I took a long security itinerary throughout Manhattan. When I reached the entrance of the station Yatskov's car was there, passing me by without flashing its headlights. The coast was clear!

Compared to New York's demented swirl of activity, Cleveland appeared like a little Garden of Eden. In the streets where the few pedestrians walked slowly, it was almost impossible not to notice if there someone was following you. I had breakfast and savored the rare pleasure of not feeling the huge eye of the Octopus, as we referred to the FBI in our correspondence with the Center, upon me. At noon, after a walk on the banks of Lake Erie, I rang the Sidorovich's doorbell. Anya and Michael were expecting me for lunch. There was a bottle of wine and an excellent meal on the table, and the couple tried to make me feel as comfortable as possible. It was just like a vacation, but I was there to work. Michael took me to the bathroom, which in a few minutes became a photo lab. He hid the Leica and the film in his bedroom, beneath a loose floorboard, under his bedside table. As a precautionary measure I took him back to the bathroom where I used the noise of the running faucet to cover our voices.

"Cleveland really is a quiet town but that must not deaden your sense of vigilance," I told him as I sat on the edge of the tub.

"Don't ever forget to check your back when you meet with Willy or when Ann goes to New York. If you suspect anything unusual, cancel the meetings without hesitation."

"Okay," answered Michael.

"You must also put a dead bolt on the front door, a good one. The bolt must be at least half an inch long. That way, if the cops are trying to break the door down, you'll have enough time to destroy or expose all the film."

"I had already thought of it," he answered. "I'll do it first thing tomorrow."

Everything I had seen at the Sidorovich house was very reassuring. I gave them some money to encourage them and cover their expenses. I also had to meet with Perl.

It was already nighttime when his dark Oldsmobile stopped in front of me along a quiet street. I got in and we went to the lakeside. Cars were parked there randomly, at some distance from one another to give the passengers privacy, making it the ideal place, and not just for lovers. I wanted to be sure that Perl's attitude at work didn't make him stand out among the other engineers.

"Aren't you taking out more confidential documents to study than the other engineers? Or more often than they do?" I asked him.

He gave me a broad American smile.

"No way! Don't worry about me. I'm above suspicion."

I still insisted on him being more vigilant, and told him to reduce the volume of information he was providing down to about four hundred pages per month. Since taking material out was risky, it was best to eliminate the least important documents straight away.

"I'm very happy about our friend Mike," said Perl. "The new system is great I realize now how many neurons I was losing every time I traveled to New York."

"The system will only work well as long as you switch the techniques of your meetings often enough," I answered cautiously. "You're creative; think of how to diversify them without letting it become something permanent. Every new arrangement must offer as many guarantees for security as the one before."

We also discussed the world situation. The Western Allies were already thinking about reducing their military assistance to the USSR while the war in the east was far from over and William was indignant about that.

"You're right, but keep your reactions to yourself. Whatever may happen, be sure not to show your real feelings to your colleagues."

It was cold inside the car; the fogged windows blurred the streetlight nearby. Willy started the engine and wiped the windshield with a cloth. We could once again see the parked cars with the lovers and I began thinking of something completely different.

"Are you thinking of getting married, Willy?"

"No," he answered. "I have two girlfriends but I wouldn't marry either one. I like my life as a bachelor too much."

Like a good scientist, he began explaining his theory. The ideal woman, able to capture his heart, had to fill a whole list of requirements: beauty, intelligence, sensitivity, and the potential of becoming a good housewife. In addition to all this there had to be psychological compatibility. I was hearing this term for the first time and he had to explain it to me. His conclusion was as unusual as he was: for a responsible person, marriage was only a theoretical concept. Yet coming from him this didn't sound macho or conceited to me, being the good husband I was. These mental constructs were just fun ideas to Perl.

He was unquestionably an elegant man who knew how to charm women and men, and above all he appeared trustworthy. He drove me back to town, dropping me off in front of the railroad station. In the bathroom I met Michael Sidorovich, who passed me the roll of exposed film because it would not have been safe for me to take it that morning and carry it all afternoon.

Once in a while it's good to put yourself in the place of those you manage, and that was one of those times when I got my fill! Once inside the compartment, I took the top berth and carefully buttoned up the curtains separating me from the other travelers so that I'd have a better chance of waking up should anyone try to frisk me while I slept. Yet to hide the film under my pillow seemed imprudent, as it would be too easy to just grab it from under me.

So I wrapped the film in a towel and put it under my pajama top. Despite all these precautions I was barely able to close my eyes and I'd wake up suddenly to be sure my film was still there. I wondered whether Ann also went through such a terrible time during her monthly night trip.

The network began functioning smoothly very quickly. Perl was passing us material on aircraft projects and the first missiles, and in the process he provided Soviet intelligence with the complete blueprint of the first American jet fighter, the Lockheed P-80 Shooting Star. Another time Ann told me as she passed the documents during a meeting, "Willy asked me to tell you that there are two odd documents in there."

At the Rezidentura, once I developed the film, I discovered two ultrasecret reports written in Russian and full of incomprehensible formulas, regarding rockets. As soon as they reached Moscow, the Center asked us to find out through which channel these documents had landed in the offices of NACA. Perl was unable to provide an explanation to this mystery but those reports had clearly been obtained in the USSR by British or American intelligence.

It was a real pleasure for Kvasnikov and me to handle the Perl-Sidorovich group and I was quite surprised when my boss, after a few months' activity, let me read, without offering any commentary whatsoever, the following dispatch:

> Because of his hasty and unconscionable acts to have Linza [Michael Sidorovich] move, to organize a "cache" at his home, and give him $500 for moving expenses without checking for the agreement of Artemis [the INO], Anton [Kvasnikov] is hereby reprimanded. Should any similar occurrences repeat themselves, the resulting expenses will be deducted from his personal salary.

This warning greatly agitated Kvasnikov. While the FBI was widening its activity and each weekly delay had potentially disastrous consequences, our decision was necessary to guarantee the security of a valuable source. And that was the way we were rewarded!

Kvasnikov was not the type of person to allow himself to get depressed. As convinced as I was that our decisions were timely and absolutely correct, he wrote a long letter to the heads of the Service, justifying his decision in detail and requesting that the undeserved reprimand be lifted. Contrary to normal procedure, that letter was left unanswered. What could we possibly do under those circumstances? Should we simply execute orders from the Center without thinking? Avoid any kind of action without its authorization? Kvasnikov and I agreed to behave as if we had never received the coded reprimand, which turned out to be the right move because one year later we received another cable:

> By creating a "cache," our section [the New York Rezidentura] performed very useful work that benefited the management of Yakov [Perl]. He has provided us with a lot of very valuable material that will greatly help our industry. The usefulness of the work consists not only in increasing the volume and quality of the documents received, but also because the "cache" has increased the security of the management of the agent in question.

The Center later told us that, in just one year, Perl had provided 98 complete studies of secret material, totaling about five thousand pages. Of these documents, 50% had been classified as "very valuable," 40% "valuable" and 10% "of informational interest." Unfortunately, the letter coming from the INO made no mention of the previous letter of reprimand received at the beginning of this successful operation.

16

The Rosenberg network included another agent, who is still alive as I write these pages. His name is Morton Sobell. I used to call him Morty, but his code name at the Center was "Senya." Kvasnikov and I gave him another nickname that we thought appropriate because it really described him best: Coy. There was no pejorative connotation intended; Sobell was neither two-faced nor a hypocrite nor even secretive, and his modest and withdrawn attitude actually concealed a great deal of activity. That's why it makes me feel somewhat uneasy to describe him.

Morton Sobell was born in New York City in 1918. He went to Stuyvesant High School and then to CCNY from 1934 to 1938, where he became a left-wing militant and a friend of Julius Rosenberg. He graduated as an electrical engineer, was hired by the Navy Bureau of Ordnance and moved to Washington, D.C. Sobell received a master's degree from the University of Michigan in 1941 and, in spite of the general draft following the Japanese attack on Pearl Harbor, he was deferred from active military service because he was a top specialist in his field. He moved to Schenectady, New York, after being hired by General Electric, and this allowed him to travel often back to his hometown to visit family and friends, including Julius Rosenberg.

Libi, in his new job as a recruiter, was fully aware of how important his friend was to the cause. Sobell was involved in radar engineering and had access to other confidential documents inside GE. Rosenberg recruited him during the summer of 1944 and handled the first two deliveries of documents. Then, very quickly, as with all the other members of the secret network, I stepped in to deal with Sobell. The young man I met was of medium height, with dark hair, regular features and expressive eyes. As soon as he spoke, I understood that he was a modest and good person. His simple way of dressing confirmed my impression. When I asked him if he could microfilm his own documents, he replied it was not a problem since he knew photography quite well. At our next meeting I brought him a camera with the necessary accessories and a small stock of film.

Every thirty to forty days, during a brush pass, Morty would hand me a roll of exposed film. When I returned to Moscow I saw from his file that his production totals were also very impressive. Our agent Senya gave us forty complete research documentations representing thousands of pages of text and drawings. In 1945 alone there were two thousand pages but quantity was not the only criterion; most of Sobell's production, and especially the documents on sonar, the use of infrared rays, and the aiming devices for artillery pieces, was rated "very valuable." Morty told me that some prototypes had reached such precision at aiming at a target, that American engineers called them "the third world war sights." He provided us with the first information about missile guidance systems, which would be used for the atomic bomb.

Agent Senya also gave us secret reports on the meetings of the Coordinating Committee for Radio Technology, which were priceless documents allowing our specialists to follow all the studies undertaken in the United States in that area, revealing the direction research would be taking in the years to come. Sobell was so valuable to his employers that he was not affected by the wave of layoffs that followed America's victory, and continued his research on military systems with German scientists who were the prize catch of America's war effort. Just like the entire Rosenberg network, Morton Sobell was collaborating with us out of ideological conviction. The Center asked me repeatedly to hand him a modest sum of money to cover his expenses, but I only succeeded once or twice.

The nickname "Coy" was well deserved because I only found out bits and pieces of his private life. It's true that we would see each other on average only once every two months for dinner in a cafeteria, and those meetings never lasted more than an hour. All I knew was that Morty was very much in love with Helen, a physics teacher he married in 1945, who had progressive ideas and even knew about her husband's secret activities; this was an additional risk, but there was nothing I could do because Sobell adored her.

Shy as he was, Morty never expressed his feelings and I was to find out indirectly what he really thought of me. Less than one year after we started working together, I was ordered to transfer him to one of my colleagues from military intelligence because I was handling too many agents, in addition to working full time at the Consulate. My replacement was Alexander Rogov, codenamed "Svet," an Amtorg engineer specializing in the same areas as Sobell. A few weeks went by; then one day Kvasnikov called me into his office. True to konspiratsya, without saying anything he handed me an envelope with the words "To Whom It May Concern" written on it in English. It meant that he wanted me to translate it, since my boss spoke no foreign languages and I helped him with that sort of thing. I read the letter and something made me wince.

"Who wrote this?" I asked him.

Following his own rules inside the Rezidentura, he took a pencil and wrote *Coy* on a piece of paper.

"And how did this reach you?"

Through Rogov, was the written answer.

"So, what's the problem?" he asked me, speaking at last.

I pointed at the two names on the piece of paper going from Coy to Rogov and said:

"Basically this one here doesn't want to work with that one."

Kvasnikov chuckled sadly. Sobell had passed along this message at his third meeting with his new case officer.

"In that case," he told me, "why don't you take him back! If you don't mind?"

That's what I did, but I'm not proud of this incident. It only went to confirm my basic rules concerning the importance of the confidential relationship that must exist between a case officer and his agent. To deserve that confidence one must be candid, talk about oneself and one's own life, and never lie.

I must say a few words about someone close to Sobell who was to play a key part in the dramatic changes that would upset my life some four years later. Max Elitcher was Sobell's longtime friend, going back to their days as classmates at Stuyvesant High School and CCNY, and worked in the same section of the Navy Bureau of Ordnance. They had even shared an apartment in Washington. In September 1941, when Sobell left to get his degree at the University of Michigan, Elitcher remained in Washington and they continued to meet off and on for a few years.

In June 1944, Elitcher got a phone call from Julius Rosenberg. They were both CCNY alumni but barely knew each other. In any case Max agreed to meet with Julius and invited him to come to his apartment. During the meeting at one point, Libi asked Elitcher's wife to let them talk alone. Julius said that many people, Morton Sobell among them, were helping Soviet Russia by passing on secret information on war materials. He asked Max to join him, but Elitcher did not respond one way or the other.

Nevertheless, Max made a good impression on Julius and I trusted my friend's conclusions since he was in a much better position to judge when Elitcher would be ready to be formally recruited. He tried again in September 1945 but once again Max was noncommittal. After that meeting, Libi told me with a sad smile:

"Elitcher has changed."

I knew him well enough to understand what this statement meant. I discussed the matter with Kvasnikov and during our next meeting told Julius:

"Forget about Elitcher. It's not that important."

Still attempting to do better, Rosenberg and Sobell tried recruiting Max again after I had left the United States. They were far from anticipating how their insistence would be detrimental to their own future...

I must now introduce the final character in the tragedy, which was about to unfold. In September 1944, during one of our working dinners, Julius talked to me for the first time about David Greenglass. Julius' wife, Ethel, had three brothers. David, the youngest, was barely twenty-one years old at the time and already married. He had just been drafted and transferred to a military installation in the desert of New Mexico as a machinist. His wife Ruth had been down there visiting him and that was where the story became interesting: David was stationed at an ultrasecret base where a very powerful weapon was being developed.

None of us at the time knew what this was all about but we clearly understood that it was a highly sensitive project. David fit the profile of the typical NKVD agent; he had progressive ideas, was anti-fascist and pro-Soviet. The only thing against Greenglass was his youth, but Julius was intent on having him join our cause and I immediately approved, since all of Libi's recruits were of the highest quality. I asked him to write a report of his conversations with Greenglass, so I could include it in my cable to the Center. He was to ask his brother-in-law many questions regarding the base, details about his work, and the weapon that was being prepared; but first and foremost Greenglass had to be vetted politically because no one could be allowed to work at such a top-secret facility without having been subjected to a thorough security check.

Compartmentalization is a basic rule of all clandestine work. Each member of the network must only know the very minimum required for him to carry out his mission. In cases of betrayal or leaks the damage will be limited. However, through bits and pieces of information, I was aware that my colleagues Yatskov and Kvasnikov were looking for information on a "super bomb" that top Western scientists were working on somewhere in the American southwest. I was therefore not surprised by Kvasnikov's reaction when I told him of my latest conversation with Rosenberg.

Despite his natural reserve, my boss was unable to hide his excitement. He jumped to his feet and began walking around the room as he interrogated me in great detail. He immediately understood that David Greenglass was working at Los Alamos on the "Manhattan Project." Perhaps he was in daily contact with Oppenheimer, Fermi, and the other originators of the "baby" about to be born, which would alter the course of the war and perhaps even the evolution of humanity itself! He asked me a million questions about the smallest details of my conversation with Libi and ordered me at once to write a report, which gave rise to many other questions. Kvasnikov then had a long discussion with Yatskov. Events would confirm the paramount importance this matter would take.

Three days later, after an exchange of cables with the Center, Kvasnikov asked me to begin planning, with Rosenberg, for the recruitment of David Greenglass. Julius was to assess whether his brother-in-law did indeed possess the skills required of a secret operative. I broached the subject during my next meeting with Julius and told him that at twenty-one years of age one doesn't yet have very strong convictions. At that age one is a revolutionary, but a few years later the same person can become a staunch conservative, very much at home in the society he once passionately desired to reform. Furthermore, would David have the courage and toughness to face the many challenges a secret agent must respond to?

As usual, Julius listened to me patiently without interrupting until it was his turn to answer. His voice was very steady. His brother-in-law, he said, was part of his own family, of the same blood as his wife Ethel, devoted to our cause and one hundred percent reliable. After a pause, Libi summed up how he felt with a sentence that would resonate painfully in my mind a few years later:

"I'll give my right hand to be chopped off if he lets us down!"

He was very convincing!

In November 1944, Ruth Greenglass, David's young wife, went to spend two weeks at Albuquerque to visit her husband and celebrate their first wedding anniversary. Julius, who trusted Ruth as much as he did his brother-in-law, asked her to ask David if he would agree to help their Soviet friends by supplying information on what was taking place at Los Alamos. Ruth had no problem in undertaking that mission.

I met with Julius again on December 5. Ruth Greenglass had just returned from Albuquerque and David had agreed to help us. Since Libi knew nothing about nuclear physics, he suggested that one of our specialists meet with David upon his return to New York on leave, in January 1945. Our memorable exchange of Christmas gifts, on December 24, 1944, had been too short for either of us to discuss the topic, and David Greenglass was still in the New Mexican desert. Yet by our next meeting, on January 3, 1945, David had already spent a few happy days with his family. Julius had asked him questions about his work at Los Alamos and, at his request, David had even made a drawing of one of the lens molds he was working on with a few written explanations. We could not go any further than that because I was just as ignorant as Julius was on the subject.

"It's very important that David be able to talk to one of your specialists. Is that possible?" asked Julius.

Excellent idea! I proposed a meeting on Wednesday, January 10, between David and the expert who was none other than Anatoly Yatskov, alias Yakovlev, in his official capacity, "Aleksei" in the coded messages with the Lubyanka, and "John" to his American agents. After making the introductions, I immediately left them alone; for me the entire matter ended there.

Because of the sacred "need to know" rule, I was not to find out what happened that day until after I left the United States in September 1946. I never discussed the matter with either Kvasnikov or Yatskov. I was to discover the sequence of events only many years later, and to maintain the chronological progression of this story, I would rather discuss it later on.

17

Since I had been handling all of Rosenberg's agents, our meetings had become less frequent because of the need for tighter security. Julius was unhappy about this change and, during one of our instructional meetings in the spring of 1945, he had a heart-to-heart talk with me.

"Alexander, I understand why you removed all my comrades from my supervision and I accept that. I don't see them that often and I even avoid calling them up. I don't even see you that much anymore. I understand everything but it makes me sad. I'm bored... I was used to being involved, seeing people, convincing them, making plans. That was my life! And now...."

We were sitting across from one another. His gray-blue eyes, usually so happy and sweet-looking, were clouded with melancholy. I attempted to cheer him up as best I could. The war was almost over and the U.S. government was looking at the USSR more and more as a rival in the future reshaping of the world. The FBI was tightening its surveillance of Soviet citizens posted in the United States and of Americans with left-leaning ideas. They could unravel our secret activities through Julius as much as through me. I told him to make the most of it and use his free time to take Ethel out on the town or to the country with little Michael. Seeing that he was still looking very sad, I added:

"You can also take advantage of the time to meet new people who could be useful to us in the future."

But I knew my words didn't sound convincing because the situation had worsened considerably for us. After the defection of Elizabeth Bentley and Igor Guzenko, in December 1945, Julius Rosenberg was kept inactive for six months, just like every other agent. At that time I knew I was getting close to leaving New York, but my replacement had not yet arrived. My departure was decided only in August 1946 and I couldn't leave my friend without saying goodbye. I found a good enough reason: more than six months had gone by and it was time to renew contact with Libi again. Once an agent is left hanging, he may panic or decide to break with us. I knew there was no such risk with Julius, but it was a very powerful argument for the Center. After Kvasnikov returned to Moscow, Yatskov had officially become my immediate boss and he accepted my proposal without a fuss. I was authorized to meet with this important agent for our reactivation rendezvous.

For our farewell dinner I wanted a place that would be an improvement on our usual cafeterias and self-service restaurants, where we could be comfortable and take our time. I decided on *The Golden Fiddle*, a good Hungarian restaurant on the West Side. We ordered the specialty of the house, a kind of sautéed veal with spicy sauce, and a bottle of Portuguese red wine. We hadn't seen each other in eight months so there was a lot of catching up to do about our families and common acquaintances, as well as world affairs. The restaurant featured a violin player who walked from table to table with a small orchestra playing Hungarian gypsy music. The band was excellent and created a happy atmosphere for Julius, who was very pleased to see an old friend who knew everything about him and with whom he could open up completely, knowing he'd find security and understanding. For me the entire meeting was already full of nostalgia. I had a difficult time telling Libi that I was about to leave, since he looked so happy, and yet I had to do it, there was no other way.

The waiter had just finished filling up our glasses and taking away the empty plates when I leaned in toward my friend.

"Listen Julius, I have to give you some news. I'm about to leave New York in a very short time. I'm going back home."

Julius stopped, looking at me wide-eyed. A few long seconds went by.

"What do you mean?" he asked. "You're leaving me? Why?"

"You know the normal stay abroad is three to four years. I have been here for five and a half years."

"So?"

"So if I stay too much longer *you-know-who* might start getting suspicious. Even for your sake it will be best to lay low for a while. In about six months one of my colleagues will contact you in the manner we have set up together."

"You're sure you can't stay longer?"

"No, Julius. It's not my call."

The orchestra began a new song and we fell silent. The bald violinist, with his chiseled features and long tapered fingers that ran up and down the strings of his instrument, approached our table, his eyes half closed as he played. As each melancholy note sounded, we both kept silent, lost deep within our thoughts. Once the orchestra stopped playing, Rosenberg got up, took something from his jacket pocket, went up to the violinist at the back of the room, spoke to him, and gave him some money.

"You know what that song was?" he asked as he sat down. "A Hungarian song called *The Storks Fly Away*."

We exchanged a knowing glance that expressed more than words, just like the tune we had just heard. Our meetings, so full of danger and warmth, were about to end. We reminisced about the best moments of our work together: the proximity fuse, the recruitment of Sarant and Sobell, our visit to the Sidoroviches. Julius was dreaming about a trip to the Soviet Union someday to see for himself the society he thought represented the future of humanity. We were about to have coffee and I had already paid the bill. Julius turned around and nodded at the violinist, who closed his eyes and nodded back. He stopped in the middle of his tune, throwing his fellow musicians into a panic. Then he played the slow song about the storks flying away and I felt quite moved. The musician came up to our table and slowly walked all around it, looking at us briefly each time, somehow understanding this was a farewell dinner and playing to our nostalgic thoughts.

It was already dark outside when we left the restaurant but we didn't want to say good-bye just yet. We slowly walked along Riverside Drive, then we sat on a bench to admire the ocean liners, with their fully lit portholes, on the Hudson River. I had Julius repeat the date and location of the reactivation rendezvous as well as the passwords he was to use with his next contact. Then, following instructions from the Center, I gave him one thousand dollars for any unforeseen emergencies.

It was time for us to part. I wished Julius every success, happiness and prosperity for himself and his family. He wished me a good trip back home and we gave each other a fraternal hug as a ship let out a long whistle. The next whistle I would hear deep inside me would be on the plank of a ship sailing for Leningrad.

PART FOUR

A New War

18

I n those days intercontinental travel by ship was a real vacation and a time to sum things up.

Zina and I were entranced at the prospect of going back home and so was our daughter Natasha, who was only six months old and yet seemed to sense something happy was about to take place. Naturally, just one year after the end of the war living conditions in the Soviet Union were extremely harsh but it didn't matter, we'd be back home! Besides pieces of cloth to make dresses, we brought back shoes, canned food, butter, sugar, and flour.

The Soviet government, to save on foreign currency, would not allow its citizens to make transatlantic crossings on anything other than Soviet cargoes. I had the pleasant surprise of meeting my good friend Ivan Afanasyev, the captain of the *Stary Bolshevik*, who told me the epic story of his previous trip while the war was still raging.[40] When I told him we were going back to the USSR, he offered us a cabin. His ship was to be the first to sail back into Leningrad after the mines had been removed from the Gulf of Finland. Just like last time the ship was packed to the gills, but now it was carrying enormous tubes for the construction of the great Soviet gas pipeline between Saratov and Moscow. They filled the hold and formed giant pyramids on deck, leaving only narrow passages to walk through.

I had prepared a debriefing for my chiefs at the Lubyanka. Even though I did not know all the numbers at that time I was aware that from 1943 to 1946 I had handled one of the most productive networks for scientific and technical intelligence. The five top agents who made up the network—Julius Rosenberg, Joel Barr, Alfred Sarant, William Perl, and Morton Sobell—held very sensitive positions within the laboratories and planning departments of the American defense industry. They had given me over 20,000 pages of technical documents plus another 12,000 pages of the complete design manual for the first U.S. jet fighter, the P-80 Shooting Star. Yet statistics are not enough to gauge the production of secret information. A few sentences scrawled on the back of an envelope can be much more valuable than hundreds of volumes. One day, as a joke, while we were preparing the diplomatic pouch to be sent to Moscow, we weighed the documents on a scale, comparing the results of the political section to ours. They were both the same weight. Such a method is just as rough as counting the number of pages to evaluate the quality of the information gathered.

In a somewhat indirect way I had also participated in the top priority target of scientific information gathering of that period: the "Manhattan Project," the program to create the atomic bomb. My part, however, had been very small and I only transmitted documents already received. I was far from imagining what the future would bring.

The crossing lasted 19 days. After the first week the trip was almost interrupted by a violent storm. For one whole night our ship felt like a ping pong ball bobbing on the waves. The next morning a waitress told us at breakfast:

"When you're seasick, there are only two things you can do: eat and lie down."

Our tiny Natasha was the only one who could follow this advice: she had not even woken up during the entire night. After the storm died down, the tablecloths in the dining room were kept wet so that the plates wouldn't slide off, and soup was served in aluminum bowls. The crew was indifferent to all this, as though it were a normal occurrence, but I felt something was wrong.

"So what's going on?" I asked the captain in the hallway. Ivan Ivanovich couldn't hide the truth:

"We avoided disaster by the seat of our pants. The steel cables that hold the tubes together on deck were close to snapping. Everything would have been swept away, including the deck. We've been very lucky!" And the captain made the gesture of spitting over his left shoulder as if to ward off evil spirits. It would have been very ironic for his defenseless ship to sink in an ordinary storm after having already survived an entire armada!

Floating mines all over the North Sea made it necessary for us to hug the Irish coast and cross the English Channel. At the entrance to the Kiel Canal, I was very surprised to see two rather aging German pilots come on board. I couldn't believe my own eyes! I was still thinking of the citizens of that nation, including these happy-looking fellows with graying hair and round red faces, as Nazis, krauts, our worst enemies. As if it were the most normal thing to do, the pilots gave the second in command a military salute and went up to the bridge.

As we crossed the canal we gazed intently at the landscape of what for years we had considered the Belly of the Beast. Seeing the Soviet flag, some German youths ran alongside to insult and threaten us with clenched fists and one of the pilots tried to calm them down from the bridge. Once we got through the canal the captain invited the two men to eat with us in the officer's mess, offering them wine and a carton of American cigarettes each. The war was definitely over!

When we reached Leningrad at the beginning of October, a freezing wind swept over the sea. Zina and I, holding tightly to the railing, looked at the land we had been away from for so long. The longshoremen, who were carrying the pulleys and installing the gangplank, were wearing patched-up and shapeless clothing, boots and shapkas. Their faces were emaciated and unhappy. For 900 days they had defended the besieged city, four long years they had fought for my homeland, my freedom and my dignity. I felt strange in my unlimited gratitude toward these unwelcoming people and of the joy of being able to return to my homeland. I felt guilty for not having faced enemy bullets alongside them. Of course I had done my duty in a different way and had hoped just as strongly as they did for the moment of our victory, but this guilt feeling was to haunt me for many years.

The train reached Moscow at 10 a.m. and all our families were on the platform: my mother, my brother Boris, my two sisters, Tasya and Anya, as well as Zina's mother and brother, whom I was meeting for the first time. They all looked as bad as the long-shoremen at the Leningrad piers, with their sunken cheeks and bags under their eyes. Threadbare clothing hung over their bodies as if they were coat hangers. After many hugs we piled our belongings aboard an NKVD truck and drove off to the Lubyanka. The fact was that we had no place to stay in our own city. My entire family, two brothers and their families, my sisters, my mother and grandmother, were all living in a small three-room apartment. Zina's parents were in the same situation. So we spent the whole day in the truck while my colleagues attempted to find us a hotel room, which turned out to be impossible! Only at 8 p.m. was I handed the key to the room belonging to an NKVD officer and his family who were traveling on a mission overseas. Two other families were sharing the communal apartment and they gave us a reasonably warm welcome.

We spent the next few days recounting the war years. My family had been hit very hard: both my father and grandfather had died; my brother Gennadi had been wounded during the fighting; my two sisters had dug trenches near Bryansk and had worked, along with my mother, on a collective farm in the Urals where they had been evacuated. When they returned to Moscow in April 1943, they were drafted to work in a factory. Anya, who was only 17 when the war began, came down with tuberculosis. I felt worse and my heart sank as I listened to the hardships my family had endured. I did my best to help them with the food, clothing, and money I had brought back, but I always felt privileged and that a terrible injustice had been done to them.

One week after my return I was given a new identity card of the MGB, [41] the new name of the state security services, and went to the Lubyanka where I met Lev Vassilevsky, who headed the brand new department of technical and scientific intelligence. His staff included Andrei Rayna and my old boss, Leonid Kvasnikov, who had returned to Moscow in December 1945, after our agents were deactivated. The next day I met with Pavel Fitin, head of the First Directorate, the PGU, the new name of the INO. It was mostly a formal meeting and the general appeared to know about my activity through my reports and my personnel file. He thanked me for my work and asked if I had any problems. I handed him a written request for an apartment, which he immediately approved and signed. Despite this, we were only able to get one room in a communal apartment a few years later. Finally, before leaving on vacation, I wrote a long report that answered the innumerable questions the specialists in my department had asked me. I also took the opportunity to volunteer my personal opinion on how to reactivate some of the agents I had previously deactivated. My New York work was rewarded with the Honorable Insignia, a prestigious decoration rarely given to intelligence officers, compared to combat troops. I must reiterate that, for anyone not on the inside, I was only an employee of the consular service and even kept my alias, Fomin. It may seem strange but the "konspiratsya" was just as important inside my homeland as it was outside.

After one month's vacation, I returned to my cover job at the Foreign Ministry. My "official" boss at the personnel office, Mikhail Alexandrovich Silin, future ambassador to Czechoslovakia, ran me through a kind of interrogation. Many officers were being demobilized, every vacancy was accounted for and Silin was trying to be a good manager, making sure an employee of special services would not be depriving a good veteran of a job.

"Are you certain that you are not part of another organization?"

Following the orders of my real chiefs I did the best I could. It was easy to deny my belonging to the Big House, because in New York, only two "clean" staff members knew my true identity: the consul, Evgeny Kiselev, who was on excellent terms with Zarubin, but in any case would never have spoken to anyone about it and who was still back in the United States, and the Consulate's accountant, a curious and solid kind of man, and it was not in his interest to say anything.

"But you never did any training with us!"

"I never had the time. The Japanese offered to give us a few transit visas and everything had to be decided very quickly."

I imagined myself shifted back to the building on the opposite side of the square and in that case, goodbye konspiratsya! But Silin found nothing more to say.

I was given the rank of third secretary and placed in the newly created United Nations section headed by an old-time Soviet diplomat, Sergei Vinogradov, who had just returned from the sensitive position as ambassador to Turkey. I shared an office with three younger diplomats, one of whom, strangely, had the same last name I was using, Fomin. To this day I wonder whether it was real, or invented like my own. Another colleague of mine, Oleg Troyanovsky, was to become a well-known diplomat and historian. They all had taken courses under the auspices of the Foreign Ministry and each one, to earn some extra money, was writing articles on world events, but with my real job I had no time for such things and stood out a bit.

My days would begin wearing a diplomat's hat. Foreign affairs personnel, the MID as it was known, would leave the building at 6 p.m. However, I couldn't leave the office so early: the MGB would stop for a break between 5 p.m. and 8 p.m. Using the excuse of additional work, I would linger on beyond regular hours and built a reputation as a hard-working functionary. I would leave around 7:30 p.m. and, since the Lubyanka was on the opposite side of the square, all I had to do was walk across. I continued to follow the same security procedures as in New York and I walked around a bit, stopped for tea and a few sandwiches, entering the MGB building only when I was absolutely certain no MID personnel could see me.

The staff of the First Directorate was still very small right after the war. I estimated the entire personnel to be no more than 600 people if I remember correctly the general meetings we held. The scientific and technical intelligence department included about thirty officers to handle all the industrialized countries. Half of them were covering the American and British "lines" as they were called. I was placed in the American section that occupied one single office, yet I was assigned no specific task and just did whatever was handed to me. For example, I gave three lectures on my New York experiences. My colleagues were extremely interested in my observations at the first two and the things I had found out and asked me many questions, but for the third one I was clearly lacking in the theory and techniques of intelligence gathering.

In May 1947 I was shifted to the British section. I knew nothing about the United Kingdom and began reading everything I could find about its history, political system and parties and, naturally, its scientific and technical organizations. I could also consult the reports from the London Rezidentura and our agents' files. Once again I was not given a definite area to concentrate on and I asked no questions, but it took me some time to understand why. It was not in my character to try and figure out such administrative quirks. Life in a country devastated by war was very hard. During the spring of 1947, most Muscovites were given a few parcels of land, some five hundred square feet each to plant potatoes, and on Sundays we would water our crops and tear out the weeds. I was hoping to spend two or three years in Moscow before being sent abroad once again. I had to help my family, for whom I was the main breadwinner. Zina and I were dreaming of an end to the nomadic life we had been living, to finally have our own room and be able to buy furniture and take care of our little Natasha, but those were to remain impossible dreams.

I was in my office at MID one day in the middle of May when I received a phone call asking me to come to the personnel department. When I entered, Georgy Zarubin, the Soviet ambassador to London, was expecting me.[42] He was a tall, imposing man, with ruddy and handsome good looks framed by bushy eyebrows, wearing a perfectly tailored suit with a dark, elegant tie. Zarubin asked me about my work, my family, and my stay in New York. Another colleague from the British section, whom I did not know, was also present at the meeting and asked me a question in English and I answered him in the same language. In five minutes he was able to tell the ambassador that I spoke fluent English and had a very good vocabulary. Zarubin, who had been leafing through my file, finally closed it and said:

"I actually wanted to offer you the job of Second Secretary, which is going to be vacant in London. What do you think?"

I didn't expect such a proposal.

"It's an important decision, and I would like to be able to discuss it with my wife," I answered, to give myself some extra time.

Once the ambassador found out that Zina was a professional translator, that she had taken a course at Columbia University, and had worked as secretary to the President of Amtorg, he assured me that she would certainly find similar employment in London, but he understood my request for some time to think it over. In truth, when I asked for time I was not really thinking of my wife but more about my superiors in the building across the square.

Vassilevsky's reaction came as a surprise to me:

"Say yes! There's nothing to think about! We've been looking for an excuse to send you to England anyway."

That was the reason why, since my return from the United States, I had not been given a specific job. My bosses just wanted me to rest a bit before putting me in the front lines once again. The next day at MID I accepted the offer. My new boss would again be a Zarubin but a different one and the ambassador was very pleased.

"You won't regret this! You'll gather some real diplomatic experience in this job. I will give instructions to expedite the red tape very quickly. Take a vacation. You won't have any more time once you reach London."

Even though he did not know everything about me he wasn't too far from the truth! Zarubin addressed me in the familiar form, which led me to believe that I was already part of his team.

My job in London, among other things, would be to represent VOKS, the All Soviet Association for Cultural Relations,[43] which was a very important propaganda and foreign policy tool geared to the masses, leaving official relations to the embassies. The interaction of the Soviet Communist Party with its foreign counterparts was quite limited in scope. Contacts with the outside world, of such prime importance during the Cold War, were maintained through friendship organizations, artist tours, film festivals, art exhibits or literary meetings. Since these events were not openly ideological, the most well-known personalities had no trouble participating in them or even in joining their steering committees. How bad could it be to celebrate with some Soviet veterans the victory over the Nazis or inaugurate the new tour of the Bolshoi?

My U.S. experience of support committee rallies and radio speeches made me take all this in stride, but to get back in the swing of things and establish the right contacts in Moscow, I spent some time at the offices of VOKS. The second in command at that institution—which was used by many intelligence officers as a cover—was an MGB man making the key introductions even though, as far as everyone else was concerned, I was only an MID functionary.

Some of the other preparations were of a different nature. My assignment was to handle an agent whose identity I still didn't know but who was passing us information on nuclear physics. I had to acquire some knowledge of the subject, enough to be effective as the intermediary between the agent and the Soviet team of physicists, who, following the Americans, were about to complete our atomic bomb. I was able to accomplish this after several meetings with a young and talented scientist, Yakov Terletsky, a tall, frail-looking man who, as soon as he began speaking, made you immediately forget everything else. He was extremely intelligent and the assurance in his voice made a rock-solid impression. He explained the entire concept of the bomb and the terminology being used both in the Soviet Union and Great Britain. His English was very good and, point-by-point, we examined the ten questions I was to ask during the first meeting with our informant.

In mid-July, Zina and I took Ambassador Zarubin's advice and went to a spa in Batumi, on the Black Sea. From the outside everything looked idyllic, a beautiful beach with white sand, palm trees, lots of sunshine all day, but at night the couples were separated. I went back to the men's dormitory where we slept six to a broken bed while Zina did the same in the women's section. It was my second vacation in Georgia and, oddly enough, history was to repeat itself: less than two weeks after we arrived, I was called to the local MGB office to find a cable summoning me back to Moscow at once. This time the cloistered lifestyle of our resort and its food did not encourage me to delay, and Zina was also happy to leave.

On August 3, 1947 I knocked on the door of my supervisor's office at the Lubyanka. Vassilevsky told me I was going to London on August 30 on the ship *Beloostrov*. My mission was to handle the very important job of assistant Rezident for technological intelligence. Furthermore, I was to manage our main source of secrets on the atomic bomb, a weapon only the Americans possessed and their main trump card in restructuring the postwar world. I would meet our agent twelve days after arriving in England, and I only had three weeks to prepare.

At the Lubyanka, I studied all British MI5 counterespionage techniques and how to organize our secret meetings with the head of the British section. I read everything available on this man whose security would be my responsibility from now on, and he was quite young, just like Terletsky, tall and thin with the wide forehead of the intellectual, quiet and intelligent eyes behind his round glasses. His name was Klaus Fuchs and his code name was "Charles."

At the end of August, during a rainy autumn night, Zina and I boarded the train for Leningrad. Two days later, less than one year after we had arrived in that same harbor, we watched the pier and its cranes, its shabby warehouses, and the gray shadows hurrying back and forth among the metal noises from the deck of the *Beloostrov*. We were sailing off once again.

19

The *Beloostrov*, together with another Soviet cargo ship, waited for the high tide to enter the Thames. We stood on the deck looking at the banks of the river but England refused to lift the veil to those looking at it for the first time. Through the thick fog we could sometimes make out a small cottage with a brick chimney or the crest of a tree, then the North Sea waters rose and washed into the mouth of the river, driving back the tired flow of the Thames. A tugboat drew our ship into the sifter of one of the locks and a heavy metal door closed behind us like a fortress. This was a country that made you feel twice a prisoner, because it was an island and because it walled itself in.

The capital also made us feel unwelcome. The consular employee who helped us from the pier took us to a shabby old hotel that had been hit by German bombs. The room looked dreary with strips of wallpaper peeling off here and there. The curtains had not been washed since the reign of His Majesty King George V. Our guide explained that the bombing had devastated London and there were no hotels with vacancies. It had taken him one whole week to find that room, and we had to accept our fate. The next day I brought up the problem with the ambassador and Georgy Zarubin confirmed the extreme dearth of housing space but promised to help find a solution. Eight days later we moved into a large two-floor wooden house that had been damaged in the bombing and purchased for a very low price six months before by our commercial section. Following some very minimal repairs, the building had become a temporary residence for Soviet missions visiting London. However, we were unable to live there for more than two months because the fireplaces were the only way to heat the place. The air was rank and dusty, and every morning we woke up with violent headaches.

Zina and I decided to look on our own through the classified ads, and finally found two furnished rooms rented by an elderly couple who lived in a third room. The rent was high, £33 out of my salary of £90. But the brick building was in good condition and the rooms were so inviting that we agreed on the spot. We were able to accept the high rent for about six months before taking over, at a fixed rate of £10, a municipal apartment being vacated by a Soviet diplomat who also sold us his furniture for a reasonable price. The two-story building was old and not very comfortable, and the water heater above the tub was coin-operated, so to take a shower shillings had to be inserted one by one. However, the low rent made it very attractive and we lived there until the end of our tour.

Once Zina found a part-time job with the Soviet film distribution company, our financial situation improved. The head of Sovexportfilm spoke no English whatsoever so Zina, as translator, receptionist and even accountant, was the inevitable go-between with the outside world. She was very happy to contribute to the family budget and improve her English while being free all afternoon to do family chores. Our daughter Natasha was two and went to a private day care center where she began babbling in English. On weekends she played alone or with a little English playmate at the entrance of our building while we watched over her from the window.

The difference with America, which had experienced war only at a distance, was palpable. The British lived modestly; you could see it by the way they dressed. Most foodstuffs were rationed, but it didn't create long lines as in Moscow. Monarchy or not, everyone was subjected to the same treatment whether they were British or foreigners, and we also received monthly ration coupons. Meat was imported from Argentina in refrigerated ships and once it thawed it turned a very unappetizing gray-blue color. British meat was red just like before the war, but it cost four times as much. Even those regular English staples of tea and sugar were rationed, but as far as we were concerned, since we did not have five o'clock tea, the ration was sufficient; but sugar was not, so we would ordinarily barter with the neighbors.

While our daily relations with British people were pleasant and friendly, it was the exact opposite with government officials. Two years after winning the war, it was a far cry from the enthusiasm of the early days. After crushing Nazism, the West was turning on its old enemy, Communism, which, although victorious, was barely left standing after four bloody years of war. Great Britain had naturally remained the ally of the United States, only the war had reversed their roles and the United Kingdom was now very much weakened while America had created the strongest economy in the world. The older cousin had become dependent on the younger one and was feeling sick about it, so that British officials were just as suspicious and aggressive toward the Soviet Union as they were about their American allies. Churchill himself would be the one to embark upon a crusade against Communism with his March 5, 1946 speech at Fulton, Missouri.[44] The truce was indeed short-lived and, having spent the entire Second World War in New York, I was now in London in the midst of the Cold War just two years later.

I was to experience this vividly a few weeks after I arrived. From November 25 to December 15, 1947, London was the venue for the fifth session of the Council of Foreign Ministers, of the four powers: the USSR, the United States, the United Kingdom, and France. Vyacheslav Molotov led the Soviet delegation with the assistance of Andrei Vyshinsky.[45] The United States was represented by Secretary of State George Marshall, the architect of the famous plan to help Europe; Great Britain by Ernest Bevin, well known for his pro-American positions, while Georges Bidault, his French counterpart, was more in favor of a European union. The meeting was to draft a peace treaty with Germany. Molotov wanted a democratic government for the entire country and demanded that Germany quickly pay to the Soviet Union the reparations that had been decided upon at the Yalta and Potsdam conferences. The West feared that Germany would trade the swastika for the hammer and sickle and stated that before it paid any reparations, the Germans had to rebuild their economy and pay back their loans to the capitalist countries. The meetings took place in an acrimonious atmosphere of mutual accusations and Molotov would often light a cigarette while he silently listened to the various speakers, which, to those who knew him well, was a sure sign of frayed nerves.

I remember a poisoned arrow aimed at Molotov coming from Ernest Bevin, who was proud of his own "proletarian" origins:

"You have no right to speak in the name of Soviet workers; you are a Menshevik from a bourgeois background."

And Molotov firing back:

"You're correct, Mr. Bevin, we are both traitors. I have betrayed the bourgeoisie to defend the workers' cause, and you have betrayed the working class to defend the bourgeoisie."

During the conference I saw Molotov twice, since my job was to make sure there was a permanent, 24-hour connection between our embassy and Moscow. On the first day of the conference I obtained a line through Paris to West Berlin. The local telephone operator easily put me through to East Berlin, but at that point a Russian military operator refused to give me a line to Moscow without his captain's approval. The officer told me that the decision was too important for him to take without orders from his superiors and at 4 p.m., when Molotov had to speak with Moscow, the line was still not operational. Zarubin asked me to explain why. I found the ambassador sitting next to Molotov on a sofa. After listening to my explanations, the minister displayed no anger.

"Just tell the officer in Berlin that Molotov must speak with the Kremlin," he said simply.

That was like an "open sesame": in two minutes I had the line, and during the next few days contact was made in a matter of seconds. And no wonder, because the voice at the other end had that Georgian accent every Soviet citizen easily recognized. It was possibly to rehabilitate me in Molotov's eyes that Zarubin, who, as promised, had helped me considerably when I first started, asked me to write a report on the British Pilgrim Association, which had requested the foreign ministers of the four countries to speak at an official meeting. My report was due by 11 a.m. the next day but, having just arrived, I didn't know how to go about such things. Fortunately, among my London contacts was a British journalist who agreed to help me. He was very obliging and simply went to the head office of this organization, and by 9 p.m. delivered a stack of documents describing it in detail. I was then able to draft a brief note where I explained that rich pro-American conservatives who were hostile to the USSR controlled the Pilgrim Association. I delivered my report on time to the ambassador's assistant, who immediately took it in. Zarubin asked me to wait for fifteen minutes, then called me into his office and I saw Molotov reading my report.

"This is good work," said the minister, "but what's missing is your recommendation. Should I attend or not?"

I didn't expect the question because I couldn't imagine myself giving any advice to such a powerful man. With all the courage I could muster I answered calmly:

"In my opinion, agreeing to go wouldn't be such a good idea, comrade Molotov. The environment would prove completely hostile to you."

Molotov looked at Zarubin.

"Well, Georgy Nikolayevich, shall we take this young man's advice?"

Zarubin only smiled.

"I agree," said Molotov. "This Pilgrim Association is not for us. But next time be sure to always make recommendations in your reports."

I doubt the minister was trying to impart a lesson to a lowly diplomat who had already made a mistake. The criticism was obviously aimed at Zarubin for not having briefed a staff member thoroughly enough.

I have always been lucky with people named Zarubin. Vasily Mikhailovich taught me a lot of things about intelligence work back in New York and his namesake, Georgy Nikolayevich, became my mentor in London. I have already mentioned that, in those days, intelligence officers took at least as many precautions in guarding their true identity from their "clean" Soviet colleagues as they did towards the "natives." This was to change shortly after my arrival. In March 1947, the two intelligence services—the MGB and the military GRU—were merged into a new organization, the Committee of Information. The CI was officially under the Council of Ministers and directed by Molotov, who was both Deputy Prime Minister and head of the diplomatic service. From then on our services were working for the Foreign Ministry and, consequently, the ambassadors had to help the Rezidents. That was how Zarubin found out I belonged to the Big House.

Zarubin, for no apparent reason, had been very friendly toward me during our initial meeting in Moscow and the news came as a jolt. He took it somewhat emotionally since he'd already had a problem with the secret services when he was our ambassador to Canada in 1945 and Igor Guzenko defected. Zarubin walked over to me in the embassy courtyard at Kensington Palace Gardens, on land belonging to the royal family and where we even had a tennis court. In foreign countries the fear of being recorded by counterespionage quickly became second nature. Inside the embassy, we would whisper to discuss delicate matters in the center of one of the three large rooms, as far away from the walls as possible because they could hide "bugs."[46] It was much less risky out in the open. The setting was perfect for Zarubin. When he saw that I was out playing tennis, he entered the courtyard. He didn't have to wait long because I'm a terrible tennis player and I lost very quickly. As I was returning to the embassy to take a shower and change my clothes, Zarubin took me by the arm and, while attempting to joke about it, actually began reprimanding me:

"You're a real bastard! You misled me! You pretended to be someone else and, fool that I am, I believed you!"

He quickly understood that I could certainly have behaved differently and that his accusations were all to my credit but his anger abated quickly because he was the main beneficiary of the close collaboration with the Rezidentura. Due to our excellent rapport, he got many clues directly from me and did not have to wait for them to pass through the various MGB, MID, and Kremlin filters. Because of us, Zarubin always appeared as well informed as the minister every time Molotov came to London. When the four foreign ministers met again in Paris, Molotov asked Nikolai Rodin, the Rezident in London, to accompany him because two of our priceless sources, Donald Maclean and Guy Burgess, were part of the British delegation and would immediately inform our Rezident as to the intentions of their chiefs. I had nothing officially to do with politics, technology, and even less with intelligence work. My line was cultural relations and, just as in New York, I was careful to work hard at my cover job.

20

I have always been fortunate throughout my career and my luck held up here as well. I mentioned previously that, due to the growing State bureaucracy, secret intelligence officers often follow each other using the same cover jobs in every country in the world. As soon as an intelligence officer's identity has been penetrated, his replacement will be under increased surveillance even though it may not always be easy to detect. In New York I had replaced a staff member who had no connection to the Big House and had therefore already deflected any suspicion by local counterespionage. These favorable circumstances were to repeat themselves in London.

My official boss, first secretary of the embassy Boris Ivanovich Karavayev, a "clean" diplomat, had been in London for four years and headed all non-political relations with trade unions, cultural organizations and others. Since his tour was coming to an end, I was promoted as his second in command to familiarize myself with his activity and take over effectively once he left. As far as MI5 was concerned, there was no visible sign linking me to an affiliation with the MGB, which was also the case for my other embassy colleagues. Karavayev, as much as his chiefs in Moscow, had no clue as to my real job and, as far as he was concerned, I was a former MID official on the United Nations desk who had been trained at the VOKS offices.

Karavayev was a rather dour person as his position warranted, and when he smiled it looked more like a smirk. However, I was able to establish good relations with him until he left nine months later. After my experience with support organizations and press contacts in America, I had no trouble organizing my work in Great Britain. The great solidarity of the war years was now a thing of the past. On November 7, 1947, the anniversary of the October Revolution, I went to a rally that had been organized for the British with Georgy Zarubin. It was a small, shabby meeting room with a capacity of 900 people at the most, including Communists, trade unionists, members of friendship associations, and workers. I remarked to our ambassador how shameful it was that so few of our former allies had come to celebrate the national holiday of a country that had given so much for the common victory.

"Are you some kind of idealist?" answered Zarubin. "Where have you been? The war is over and Stalingrad is ancient history by now."

I disagreed with him.

"I don't think so. Let me organize the event next year and you'll see for yourself!"

"Go right ahead! It's part of your job anyway."

I could not change my mind once the challenge had been accepted and I had to make it work. London's largest hall for such events at the time was Earl's Court, which accommodated 10,000 people and was used mostly for boxing bouts. I went there some months ahead of time during the summer of 1948, but the director was very skeptical: only a heavyweight boxing championship would fill the hall!

"Okay," I replied. "Since you don't want to share in the ticket sales with us, I shall rent the entire hall myself."

It was a risky gamble and obviously VOKS had its own budget separate from the embassy. I went as far as I could and paid the director an advance, so that on November 7 Earl's Court would be mine. Now my job was to get the crowds to show up. I contacted Harry Pollitt, the General Secretary of the Communist Party of Great Britain, who showed little enthusiasm for my project. He had enough worries and didn't want to get involved in something that could make him and his comrades look ridiculous in the newspapers.

"With a party such as yours it must be child's play to mobilize 10,000 people!"

"You're not fully aware of the situation," answered Pollitt.

Those who were supposedly our natural partners were not very helpful, yet thanks to the Party's smallest cells and to the trade unions, the activists of the friendship organizations and the many sympathizers, the last ticket was sold a few weeks before the event. The 10,000 spectators were not disappointed. Zarubin sent Molotov a cable at my request and we brought in the best of Soviet intelligentsia of that time: composer Dimitri Kabalevsky, the poets Alexander Surkov and Pavlo Tichyna, historian Vyacheslav Volgin. It was a memorable evening. The huge hall was filled to capacity, the participants were ecstatic and the entire operation ended up with a profit of some £800. My Communist Party partners then demanded half the amount for their newspaper, *The Daily Worker*, and newsman Bill Wainwright, who also happened to be President of the England-USSR Association, pursued me relentlessly. I was adamant, since I hate people who only want to share in success and are unwilling to take risks. Knowing that insubordination was a major sin in our type of system, Harry Pollitt complained to the ambassador but Zarubin was well informed of my problems and decided not to use his authority against me. Like the good diplomat he was, he wrote to Moscow and obtained a contribution for the Communist newspaper, allowing me to have the final word in the whole matter.

My counterparts in the associations were much easier to deal with. Even though the Nazis had not invaded them, the British had experienced the horrors of war and, unlike the Americans, they were well aware of the dangers they would have faced had Hitler defeated the Russians. Our victories in the East were also their victories and therefore, despite the "Iron Curtain" and the Cold War, England had three independent friendship associations: England-USSR, Scotland-USSR, and the Association for Cultural Relations with the USSR, whose president from 1933 to 1969 had been the well-known attorney Dennis Pritt, and included the world-renowned physicist, John Bernal, on its board. Faced with the hostile policies of the Attlee government, which had forbidden any Labor Party members from joining the associations, our friends were able to set up scientific, art, and even "sister cities" exchanges: London and Moscow, Manchester and Leningrad, Coventry and Stalingrad, among others.

In the course of these activities I was to meet twice with George Bernard Shaw. The first time was the screening of a new Soviet film at the embassy. Like most local celebrities, G. B. Shaw was invited to all our important events and receptions but he never appeared. To everyone's surprise, at the end of 1948, he did come, accompanied by his secretary. He was immediately surrounded by his fellow citizens like a star and at one point Mary Pritt, wife of Dennis Pritt, who was just as much of a militant activist as her husband, waved over and introduced me to Shaw as the cultural affairs director at the embassy.

"You happen to be the person I'm looking for," said the writer as we shook hands.

I answered that I was there to help and gave him a very earnest speech on the honor and pleasure it was to speak with such a well-known writer, whose books were being constantly reprinted in my country and whose plays were part of the repertoire of our theater companies. An unsmiling Shaw listened to me in silence.

"That's all fine and good," he said. "Then why is it the Soviet Union has not paid me any royalties?"

His question silenced me while people around us began to laugh. Leaning on his cane, Shaw glared at me until I felt embarrassed. It took me some time to detect the twinkle in his eyes and I told him that the USSR had not joined the Bern Convention, meaning that Soviet authors also received no royalties when their works were published overseas.

"That's true," said an Englishman. "If our radio stations and orchestras had to pay even just for the works of Prokofiev, Shostakovich, and Khachaturian, it would mean tens of thousands of pounds every year."

Shaw nodded and the conversation shifted to something else.

"Actually, I'm here because of another issue. My publisher is preparing an edition of my complete works. Each volume will be illustrated with a picture of me, but I don't much like what our painters have done. One painting I do like is by Pikov. Do you know him?"

Mikhail Pikov was an excellent book illustrator; his engravings for Dante's *Divine Comedy* were considered the best of their kind.

"I've written to him two weeks ago to ask for a woodcut engraving that we could use here to make a print," continued Shaw. "Could you sort of speed things up a bit?"

I promised him that I would and walked him back to his car. The following day Zarubin signed off on the report I had prepared on this conversation and Moscow's answer arrived very quickly, stating that, as an exception, Bernard Shaw would be paid his royalties. As for the engraving, it would be in the next diplomatic pouch. I called the writer once the pouch was on my desk and he invited me to his house at Ayot Saint Lawrence, near Hartford, some 50 miles north of London. I drove and had drawn the directions on a map spread out over the passenger's seat. It took me a good half hour to leave the industrial suburbs behind in my little Vauxhall, but after that the trip was a real pleasure: a beautiful sunny day in the country, cows and sheep in the green meadows, neat little farmhouses and manors surrounded by their landscaped parks. I must admit, however, that I felt quite tense. I was ready for the meeting and had read everything I could find on the Nobel Prize-winning author, but he was one of the more paradoxical minds of our time. What sort of joke would he dream up to make fun of me?

The roads got narrower and the potholes multiplied. Finally, I turned onto a dirt road and came to a house surrounded by a tall green fence at the end of the village on a hill. A woman in her late forties came to the door with a white kerchief over her reddish hair, like a peasant. While I was explaining the reason for my visit, the master of the lodge appeared on the threshold. Seeing my Vauxhall, he said, "Park the car inside the courtyard!" as he walked to the gates, obviously ready to open them. I knew that Shaw was 91 years of age and answered:

"Don't worry. My car can stay outside."

The writer glared at me:

"Do as I say!"

I dared not disobey him. The gate was shut just as in Russian villages, with a long wooden bar locked into the two panels by metal fasteners.

"Let me help you," I said, trying to unlock the doors before he did, which made him very angry.

"Go away!" he yelled. "I'm strong enough to do it myself!"

I stood aside and looked on fearfully while Shaw unfastened the bolts one after the other, and then, like a staggering weightlifter, took the bar and settled it far from the passageway.

"Go ahead, get your heap inside!" he ordered.

I drove in and the writer pointed to the precise spot where the car should be parked.

"Stop here! Cut the engine and pull the hand break!"

I followed all his orders and looked at him silently—the red-haired nurse stood next to him without uttering a word—while he repeated in reverse order all the operations to place the wooden bar back in position on the doors. Once that was done, he trotted back towards me in his elderly man's shuffle, took off his straw hat and wiped his face and neck with his handkerchief. He was out of breath, his hands were shaking and he was obviously barely able to stand up, but his light gray eyes were full of pride and made me feel ashamed of being young and energetic. Levin, his secretary, appeared and Shaw, still out of breath, ushered us back inside. We sat down in the large room on the ground floor where every wall was covered by shelf after shelf of books. I recognized *Quiet Flows the Don* by Sholokhov, *Days and Nights* by Konstantin Simonov, the works of Ilya Ehrenburg. On the left side I could see only books by George Bernard Shaw published in every language imaginable.

After the housekeeper served us tea and biscuits, I handed over the original engraving by Pikov. Shaw looked at it closely and appeared satisfied, then he set it aside, promising to give it back to me once the print was made. We talked about his library and his theater. I observed him as he spoke; he was wearing linen pants and a Tolstoy-style shirt of the same material, with a braided rope for a belt that had a little tassel at each end. His body looked faded and discolored and his hair, beard, eyebrows, and eyelashes were all immaculately white. His hands were full of large, protruding veins, and covered with parchment-looking skin, and yet his face was clear, without any old age spots, and his mind, to which he owed his success, was intact and functioning.

To each one of my compliments he'd come up with an answer intended to contradict the high opinions his contemporaries had of him. He felt he had done nothing terribly good in a long time; he didn't write any more, but scribbled all day as he argued with his entourage and his publishers as well as some Labor Party leaders. I spoke about the royalty issue and told him that my government intended to pay a first installment of £20,000. Shaw had been listening to me with his eyes half closed and then he suddenly perked up; there was an ironic smile on his face. Levin gave me a card with his bank information.

"You can wire the money to this account."

I had barely put the card away when Shaw said in a rough voice:

"In that case most of that money will wind up in the hands of my enemies."

I was puzzled.

"I'm talking about Stafford Cripps, the Chancellor of the Exchequer, and Ernest Bevin, the head of the Foreign Office. I don't want that!"

He fell silent, looking at his hands, and Levin explained:

"This year Mr. Shaw received many royalties from various countries around the world. Your royalties would only contribute to paying income taxes. Could you pay us the same amount in stock certificates?"

I explained that in the Soviet Union, where every enterprise belongs to the State, stocks did not exist.

"Perhaps they could be paid in precious stones then," said the secretary.

I had to answer that such a question could only be decided in Moscow. Shaw, who appeared to be lost in his private thoughts, opened his eyes.

"Oh no, not jewelry! That's illegal. Cripps and Bevin would be only too happy to throw me in jail as the biggest English Bolshevik, because that's how they refer to me, you see! No, I don't wish to die on the straw in a prison cell. After all is said, I don't even want these royalties. We are all indebted to the Soviets if we can live at peace today. Your country needs that money more than I do. Keep it!"

Shaw fell silent once again and buried his head in his hands, closed his eyes, and seemed to be asleep. I told him that the embassy would be ready to help him and then Levin and I tiptoed out the room. The secretary had already opened the gate when the writer appeared on the threshold. He smiled at me and waved good-bye. George Bernard Shaw died in that house three years later, but I was not to see him again.

21

The very first postwar years were to prove how the patchwork of the anti-Fascist alliance had been unnatural in many ways. The state of war that had begun in 1939 had never really ended. No sooner had the Allies defeated the common enemy than they found themselves facing each other with their arsenals of weapons and their fighting instincts. Following a brief interval after the German surrender, hostilities resumed and the fact that they were cold rather than hot didn't make them any less real. When I arrived in England two years after the end of the war, the Anglo-Americans had identified the USSR as their main enemy. All Soviet citizens were suspected of engaging in espionage and were being treated as spies by MI5, which was deploying its vast apparatus to watch over us.

First of all, our "guardian angels" wanted to control all our movements. There was a permanent observation post in a building in front of the embassy, so that the teams assigned to tail us would know in advance which employee was going out and to photograph anyone who entered. MI5 was probably renting an entire floor, if not more. The people entering that building certainly didn't look like tenants. There were no children, no old people, very few women, and many working-age men who did not appear to be homosexuals. This observation post was always quite amusing to us. The best windows were partially blocked by an elm tree growing on the side-walk. What could have been an advantage soon became an obstacle as new leaves and branches were getting in the way of a clear view. In the spring and summer when we arrived at the embassy we could see that during the night one branch here and there had been sawed off. It was a strong tree and the patience of the MI5 agents had eventually run its course; one morning we found that it had been chopped down with only a stump remaining.

It's very important for an intelligence officer to get his "guardian angels" used to his comings and goings. I always made sure I had something to do in town every day, to go to a meeting, have lunch with some official, a press conference, a show, or an exhibit. These outings helped me get familiar with London and spot those locations where it was easiest to elude any surveillance if necessary. I was experienced enough at detecting anyone tailing me without making them suspicious. Most of my visits were completely innocent and I knew that sooner or later counterespionage would decide that it was wasting its time on me and would only watch me occasionally. I can still remember one of those tails. I made it a habit, a few days after receiving my paycheck, to go and purchase a good book for my collection. I would leave at about 4 p.m. It was foggy that day and no matter how much clothing you wore the dampness chilled you to the bone. I walked from the embassy directly to the closest underground station at Notting Hill Gate. On the platform I immediately spotted two men, one about fifty and the other possibly thirty-five. They glanced at me from time to time and they had too many idle gestures. "So there you are!" I said to myself.

I slowly browsed through the bookstores and the used book dealers, always checking for one or the other of my two fellows. Since I had found nothing of interest, I took a bus to a larger used book dealer farther away from the center. The older of the two agents jumped into the bus as it was leaving. Suddenly that dense fog the British call "pea soup" descended over London. You could not see five feet in any direction but Londoners are ready for such moments, and the driver lit a large lamp and handed it to the conductor, who walked out in front of the bus, lighting up the path. Since the bus was going very slowly and the door was open, I slipped off and disappeared into the fog. I went into the first pub I could find around the corner and ordered a beer. It was child's play and I had done it only because this time I was as clean as a whistle. Had I been meeting an agent I would have quite simply canceled the rendezvous. Sitting in front of my pint with a thick head of white froth, I was happy to be in this little bar where no one could possibly find me. Right then, out of the fog, a face appeared at the windowpane like a ghost: it was the younger of the two men who had been following me. Once he spotted me inside he disappeared again and the entire incident convinced me that we were facing a well-informed and very professional opponent.

The traditions and mentality of the people in each country force us to make adjustments in the way we work. Consider the typical case of my Rezidentura colleague, Yuri Modin, who was handling the liaison with three agents of the network that was to become famous in history as the Cambridge Five. He was in the habit of having breakfast at the same time every day in the same little café. Those who were following him found it more pleasant to get out of the rain and the cold and have a cup of tea inside as well. Modin would walk in, say hello to his "guardian angels," who often tipped their hats at him, and read the paper while he had breakfast. Then he would get up and wave at his followers, as if to say: "Well, gentle men, shall we begin our day?" On days when he'd have to meet secretly with an agent, Modin would make a simple change to his routine: he would leave one hour earlier after having breakfast at home. The next day the agents would be waiting across the street, not acknowledging his hello. Sometimes they would remain unfriendly for weeks before they would forgive his breaking their gentlemen's agreement and resume their usual meetings at the café down the street. Until next time!

MI5 held a big advantage because it could count on the complete cooperation of the London police. The Bobbies knew all the license plates of the Soviet mission's cars and could identify our people on sight. If they spotted a Soviet citizen, especially in a distant neighborhood, far off from central London, they would immediately inform counterespionage by phone or walkie-talkie. We also knew that our British neighbors, the greengrocer next door, for example, could be reporting in. And phone conversations were bugged both at home and at the embassy where His Majesty's Service delivered the mail to us.

This was both exaggerated and insufficient.

Exaggerated because a Soviet Union devastated by war had immense difficulties in recruiting qualified personnel for its intelligence services. Despite the "iron curtain," the opening to the outside world was very broad and each Rezidentura required high-level professionals and, furthermore, their chiefs at the Center needed to be better informed, more experienced and of an even higher caliber. There were only two officers in London at that time with any prior experience in Western countries.

Insufficient because our informers kept us abreast of the daily operations organized against the Soviets in London and our services had no major reverses for many years thanks to this information, while ordinary Britons for the most part maintained a favorable attitude toward us.

The war was still very much present in everyday life, both in the rubble of destroyed buildings as well as in the people's minds. The British had not forgotten the immense contribution made by the Russians, whom many considered their saviors. On the other hand, many Britons were unhappy to witness the reversal of roles with their American cousins.

One day, as I was boarding the plane to Glasgow, an elegant elderly lady, seeing an empty seat, asked the man next to it if she could sit there.

"Excuse me, sir. Is this seat vacant?"

"Sure!" he answered, with a strong American accent.

The lady gave him a dirty look and sat next to me, a few seats away. We exchanged a few words during the flight and at one point I asked her why she had not taken the seat next to the American.

"I don't like those people, and I'm not the only one in this country," she answered with some acrimony. "They're uncouth and common and behave as if they were in a conquered land. They're always building air bases and want to drag us into a war with Russia!"

Such attitudes were quite common with the older generation and among some youths, who were our best candidates for recruitment. They generally had no access to confidential information, but they did show much potential. Often the most talented would have very rapid careers, reaching the top leadership of some extremely sensitive organizations. When I arrived in London, temporary Rezident Mikhail Shishkin was replaced in November 1947 by Nikolai Borisovich Korovin, whose real name was Boris Nikolayevich Rodin. I had met him in New York where he had worked for the GRU from 1939 to 1944, and since both services had merged he was now my supervisor. Rodin was in his forties, had a military demeanor, and the direct and often vulgar language of the barracks. On the other hand he spoke excellent English and loved field work. He personally handled some of our most important agents, and there were many of them in London. During the postwar years the United Kingdom was the most productive country for the Soviet intelligence services. The Rezidentura had two key missions: to secure the most secret Anglo-American plans for a war against the Soviet Union and to track the development and improvement of atomic weapons.

I can immediately state that I played no part in the saga of the Cambridge Five or any other major sources handled by my colleagues of the political section. Only rarely did I help Yuri Modin, who shared my office, in translating the documents provided by his informants. I obviously did not know their identity and only found out about Philby, Maclean, Burgess, Cairncross, and Blunt many years later once I became head of the British section at the Lubyanka.

My purpose in this book is not to blame or justify the actions of the various participants during those crazy postwar years where, because of the nuclear monopoly of the United States, the entire planet was on the brink of a new world war. I can guarantee that anyone would have taken a position had they seen the kind of documents that crossed my desk. Most people found out decades later, once the archives were made public, that the world had been living under the threat of an American atomic attack against the USSR since 1945. One day I had to translate a very confidential report by a team of British and American military experts who were supposed to evaluate the most favorable moment to begin hostilities against the USSR. One chapter analyzed year by year the projections for demobilization of personnel from the various branches of the services and the drafting of young recruits. Another section in the report projected military production and evaluated planes, submarines, tanks, and artillery to be manufactured. A third chapter described the morale and physical condition of the Soviet population following the war and the postwar situation with the spread of tuberculosis, cancer, heart disease, intestinal disorders and mental illness... I can remember very clearly the conclusion as if it were yesterday:

"The most favorable period to go to war with the USSR is in 1952-1953."

Other documents were even more explicit. After the "Totality" plan, another scenario sent to President Truman in December 1947, called "Charioteer," set the start of the Third World War as April 1, 1949. The plan called for 133 atomic explosions on 70 Soviet cities over thirty days; 8 over Moscow and 7 over Leningrad. During the next two years, 200 more A-bombs as well as 250,000 tons of conventional explosives were to be hurled at the USSR. Then there was the "Fleetwood" followed by the best known of all these scenarios, the "Dropshot" plan, which was to become effective on January 1, 1950. The United States was seriously thinking of attacking the USSR from its bases in Great Britain.[47]

I was therefore convinced that my mission in London was to make sure none of these plans was ever enacted. As second Rezident for technological intelligence, my efforts were meant to break the American monopoly in atomic weapons. Some time after I arrived in London, I was able to recruit a promising source with access to sensitive information in this area. I also inherited from another officer a liaison agent to a very important source. Their names have never been revealed and I shall not be the one to do so.

On the other hand, I have no reason to hide anything concerning the man who was the real reason for my being posted in London in the first place. Without Klaus Fuchs the USSR would never have been able to create its atomic bomb in such a short time. Would the United States have decided to implement one of its sinister plans in the meantime? If so, then we owe it to this modest and quiet man that we were able to stay alive.

PART FIVE

The Puritan as Spy

22

K laus Fuchs was such an unusual personality as to be an exception in the shadowy world of espionage and requires a more detailed portrait than an ordinary spy. The man who became my agent was born in Germany from a family that treasured moral correctness, a sense of duty and sacrifice to a cause, all qualities that were passed from one generation to the next. Both his grandfather and father were highly regarded and respected leaders in the Protestant Church. His father Emil Fuchs was born in 1874 and died at the age of 97. He lived a long, eventful life, with strong beliefs in a Christian type of Socialism and in pacifism. As a leader of the Quakers, he spent his life preaching equality and social justice. He was firmly convinced that one should only follow one's conscience and ideals whatever the consequences may be. When he was very young, Emil Fuchs spent two years in Manchester among very poor working-class German immigrants who were deprived of any rights and were enslaved by British capitalism. He joined the SPD, the German Social Democratic Party, in 1921, thus becoming the first German Socialist Protestant Minister. In 1906 Emil Fuchs married Else Wagner and they had four children, two boys and two girls. Klaus was the third child, born on December 29, 1911. Ever since his earliest years he displayed an excellent aptitude for math and science and in 1928 he was awarded first prize as the best student in the high schools in Eisenach, where his family was living at the time.

Once he completed his secondary education, Klaus went to the University of Leipzig, but political militancy proved more attractive than his studies. In 1929, during the depression, he discovered the writings of Karl Marx, Friedrich Engels, and Lenin and just as his father, his brother Gerhard, and his sister Elizabeth before him, Klaus joined the SPD. He was frail and nearsighted, unable to see without his glasses, yet he still joined a youth paramilitary organization, the Reichsbanner, which engaged the Nazis in street fighting. The family moved to Kiel in 1931 where Emil Fuchs had been named to the chair of theology at the Educational Academy. His three older children had become disenchanted with the SPD, which they found too conciliatory and so, along with Klaus, they joined the KPD, the German Communist Party. Their house was open to all like-minded comrades and the Fuchs were nicknamed "the red foxes."[48]

A terrible tragedy was to leave its mark on this happy and very close family. One October day in 1931, as he returned home for lunch, Emil Fuchs found his wife in agony with horrible pains. This sweet and quiet woman, who was deeply loved by her family, had just swallowed some acid, seeking a horrible death. Her last words were "Mother, I'm coming!" Emil Fuchs would later find out that his mother-in-law had also committed suicide. This unexpected event was a terrible shock and became a taboo subject within the family. Klaus would never once speak about his mother to his closest friends nor to his wife to be. Despite their identical political ideas, Klaus was very different from his father, a charming and cordial man. His sister Kristel said that he resembled his mother more than his father because of his silent, introverted personality. Some people thought of him as being haughty, but this was not the case. He had a delicate and sensitive nature that sought to protect itself.

On January 30, 1933 Hitler was named Chancellor of Germany. On February 27, using the Reichstag fire as an excuse, the Nazis declared a state of emergency and blanketed the country with a wave of terror that was a foretaste of the horrors to come. Half of the 300,000 members of the KPD were either murdered, placed under arrest, or forced to leave the country. Klaus himself was barely able to avoid arrest. Very early in the morning, the day after the fire, he took a train to attend a conference of Communist students in Berlin. As he read the account of the fire in the newspaper, he removed the hammer-and-sickle badge from his lapel. In effect this amounted to a symbolic gesture: Klaus was going underground from that moment on.

The Nazi students at the University of Kiel had condemned him to death and the Gestapo came to his father's house to arrest Klaus a few days later. But he did not return home and in July the party decided to send him abroad, because the new Communist Germany would need all its scientists after its coming victory over the Nazis. The best minds had to continue their academic studies and Klaus first went to Paris and, a few weeks later with the help of the Quakers, he reached England as an anti-Fascist refugee. On September 25, 1933, he was in Bristol. He had no money and his only possessions were a small suitcase, a duffel bag ,and a letter of recommendation his father had given to him. He was lucky enough to meet Neville Mott, the future Nobel Prize winner for physics who was only 28 years old at the time and a professor at the University of Bristol. Mott hired the young German to work with two of his assistants who were also refugees and would, at various times, be Klaus Fuchs' supervisors: Hans Bethe was to become head of the department of theoretical physics at Los Alamos and Herbert Skinner would be Fuchs' friend and supervisor at Harwell laboratory.

Mott made an important observation confirming the strong Communist ideals Klaus Fuchs believed in. The professor and his assistant would go to the local section of the Association for Cultural Relations with the USSR, that very same association I was to be responsible for in London in 1947. They would organize reenactments of the great purge trials taking place in Russia at the time. Fuchs always wanted to play the role of Andrei Vyshinsky, the chief prosecutor, and as Mott remembered, "He played the role of the prosecutor accusing the suspects in such a cold, poisonous way that I never would have suspected in such a quiet and calm young man."

At 25 Fuchs successfully defended his doctoral dissertation and moved to Edinburgh in February 1937, where he was given a university position. He was fortunate to have Max Born as his department head, one of the creators of the most advanced school of physics, which was then undergoing a complete renewal. Born's previous students would all be part of the group that would revolutionize scientific thought in physics: Edward Teller, Rudolf Peierls, Otto Frisch, Hans Bethe, Leo Szilard. Later on Fuchs would have all of them as his colleagues and Max Born mentions him in his memoirs as a brilliant young man, shy, agreeable and well-mannered, with sad eyes, who had certainly suffered more than most others at the hand of the Nazis and who was passionately pro-Soviet. Fuchs worshipped his boss, and would write many years later: "He was and will always remain a beacon for me. I owe my place in science, whatever it may be, to Max Born."

Fuchs faced countless problems: his passport had expired and the German Consulate refused to extend it, demanding that he return to Germany. He requested British citizenship and the acknowledgment that his request had been received arrived in the mail on August 31, 1939. War broke out in Europe the next day and from one moment to the next the anti-Fascist refugee became an enemy alien. Fuchs was interned on the Isle of Man, then at Sherbrooke in Quebec. He had avoided the Nazi camps, only to be held behind barbed wire in a friendly country. Newspapers were forbidden in the camp and the treatment was a bit rough. Klaus didn't complain and even organized a popular university for young scientists, some of whom were to become famous later on. In December 1940 he was allowed to return to Great Britain, thanks to the efforts of Max Born.

Many things had changed and after the fall of the Netherlands, Belgium, and France, the United Kingdom faced the Nazis and their Axis partners alone. The Battle of Britain was raging and Churchill had replaced Chamberlain as Prime Minister, understanding full well that yesterday's suspects could become excellent fighters against the Nazi regime and that, in the case of Klaus Fuchs and other scientists, their contribution could have great potential. In March 1940, two émigré German scientists in England, Rudolf Peierls and Otto Frisch, estimated the critical mass for the fission of uranium-235 and sent a memorandum to the British government for the "creation of a superbomb based on the nuclear chain reaction of uranium." This document was the basis for the creation of an ultrasecret committee called the "Maud," to study the technical possibilities of the project. By the end of the year Britain had decided to build a factory to manufacture uranium-235 and authorized funds for studies to begin production of the atomic bomb. The work was to be parceled out to four university laboratories, including the one directed by Peierls at the University of Birmingham.

Money was obviously not enough. The right men were also required to undertake such a colossal task and the name of Klaus Fuchs came up very early on. Peierls had read and found his articles excellent, and the recommendations from Born and Mott were of the highest order. He knew that the young scientist had left-leaning ideas and Peierls was sympathetic to the USSR himself, having traveled to Russia twice and having even married a Soviet physicist, Evgeniya Kanegisser, whom he had met at a conference in Odessa. At the beginning of 1941, Peierls asked Fuchs to come and work with him, and he was to be more than a supervisor to the young man. Rudolf and Evgeniya Peierls had sent their children to the United States and felt very lonely in their big house. They invited Fuchs to come and live with them and for almost two years he became part of the family, handing his ration coupons to Mrs. Peierls and letting her purchase his clothes.

To gain access to confidential information, Fuchs had to be vetted. He was subjected to very close scrutiny and there were two problematic documents in his MI5 file: a letter from the German consul in Bristol in August 1934 identifying Fuchs as a Communist, and a recent report from an informer among German émigrés confirming that accusation. But British counterespionage felt that the contribution of the "most valuable scientist" at the Birmingham laboratory, in Peierls' own words, was more important than his

Communist antecedents. In June 1941 Fuchs signed the Official Secrets Act, the commitment to not divulge information, making him a full-fledged member of the British atomic program. Germany attacked the Soviet Union on June 22 of that same year. In a short time the Wehrmacht occupied a huge slice of territory and reached the outskirts of Moscow. At this critical juncture, Fuchs decided to help the cradle of Socialism and the Russians, whom he had learned to appreciate thanks to Evgeniya Peierls. As he would write in his confession:

> At this time I had complete confidence in Russian policy and I believed that the Western Allies deliberately allowed Russia and Germany to fight each other to the death. I had, therefore, no hesitation in giving all the information I had, even though occasionally I tried to concentrate mainly on giving information about the results of my own work.[49]

Theoretically, Klaus Fuchs was innocent of any crime. Hadn't Churchill even offered the Soviet Union "every technical and economic assistance that we could possibly give and that could be useful [to the USSR]"? In May 1942 this was to be confirmed by the British-Soviet mutual assistance agreement that was to last twenty years and entailed the exchange of "all information, including specifications, plans, etc., concerning weapons, blueprints or procedures in existence or being planned for the pursuit of the war against the common enemy." Obviously, England had no intention of sharing its plans for the superbomb with Moscow. The physicist therefore took it upon himself to correct this sleight of hand.

Klaus Fuchs contacted Jürgen Kuczynski in London to make the connection to the Soviets.[50] Kuczynski was not a formal Soviet agent, but he helped Soviet military intelligence, the GRU, for many years and even had a code name, "Caro." He introduced Fuchs to "Alexander," who was really Semyon Davidovich Kremer, a GRU officer operating since 1937 undercover as secretary to the Soviet military attaché. However, Fuchs was very quickly handed over to "Sonya," who was really Jürgen's sister, Ursula.[51] In 1942 and 1943 Fuchs and Sonya met six times, every three to four months in the vicinity of Banbury. They would reach their meeting place by bicycle halfway from each other's homes.

On June 18, 1942, Klaus became a British subject, backed by the strong recommendations of his fellow scientists because the restrictions placed upon him were detrimental to his work. He was now allowed unlimited access to secret files. He was also asked to evaluate the progress of atomic research in Germany based on information obtained by MI6. These missions reinforced the confidence MI5 placed in Fuchs, not suspecting that the scientist was passing everything on to Sonya and the Lubyanka. The scientific information given by Fuchs, under his code name "Rest," with a few exceptions, was not of primary importance. Soviet scientists were working at the theoretical level in the USSR in the same direction and were very close behind their British counterparts. Two items Klaus was able to provide turned out to be very important: that the Germans were going down the wrong path and the Anglo-Americans had begun manufacturing components for atomic bomb production. This information added credence to the recommendations of our scientists who were pressing the Soviet government to urgently initiate a similar program.

Great Britain, while in no hurry to share any atomic secrets with the USSR, began doing so with the United States by the end of 1940. At first Washington didn't consider London an equal partner, until the August 19, 1943 agreement at the Quebec conference signed by Roosevelt and Churchill, combining British and American joint efforts to create the superbomb. It proclaimed three basic principles: both countries would never use the weapon against each other, they could only use it with each other's consent and they would not share the information with any third country. Despite the clauses of the British-Soviet treaty of 1942, there was no intention to share A-bomb secrets with the USSR.

It was reasonable from every point of view to build nuclear reactors and other industrial facilities in the United States, as far away as possible from potential bombing and destruction. From the point of view of infrastructure, the Americans were way ahead of the British. Since the summer of 1942, the project was under the command of General Leslie Groves, who had no knowledge of physics but was a formidable organizer. The secrecy surrounding the Manhattan Project was absolutely total. Even the Vice President of the United States, Harry Truman, would learn of its existence only upon becoming President once Roosevelt died on April 12, 1945. British scientists who were at the same level as their American counterparts would also benefit from improved working conditions and tightened security in the United States. In the autumn of 1943, J. Robert Oppenheimer, the scientific director of the American program, asked the best British scientists to join his large team. Klaus Fuchs, Rudolf Peierls, Otto Frisch, and others did not hesitate. Fuchs told Sonya at his next meeting that he was leaving for the United States. Since Ursula Kuczynsky operated the radio link to Moscow herself, she brought Fuchs his instructions at their next meeting. Fuchs' contact would be a man named "Raymond," whom he would meet in early February in New York.

23

It feels strange for me to describe the risky saga of Klaus Fuchs in the United States. I was close to those events even though I knew nothing about this agent at the time, including the simple fact that he even existed. Klaus was staying in New York hotels that I would walk past every day and he could have been in the same streets I was in. I also knew some of the protagonists of this extraordinary story, like my friend Yatskov or my boss Kvasnikov. But professional requirements are such that I knew absolutely nothing until I became directly involved in handling our agent. I actually found out the essential facts of this whole affair decades later, while going through the files in the silence of my office when I was head of the British section at the Lubyanka or asking Yatskov directly about one episode or another.

When he arrived in the United States, Klaus Fuchs was among the top world specialists in the separation of gaseous isotopes from uranium. This technology had to be perfected to separate uranium 235—the atomic explosive—from uranium 238, which doesn't activate chain reactions. This was the main reason Oppenheimer asked Fuchs to join the Manhattan Project. Fuchs arrived at Norfolk, Virginia, on December 3, 1943 after an Atlantic crossing. The British scientific mission was located in New York and the physicists had accommodations at the Taft Hotel, near Times Square. Later they moved to the luxurious Barbizon Hotel with its magnificent view of Central Park. Fuchs took advantage of this peaceful life without air raids or ration coupons or any of the restrictions of a country at war. In order to save money he found a furnished apartment at 128 West 77th Street. We were practically neighbors without even knowing it, since Zina and I were living on West 89th Street, only a fifteen-minute walk away.

Fuchs spent the holiday season at his sister Kristel's house, in Cambridge, Massachusetts. They hadn't seen each other in seven years, since the family had been scattered by the maelstrom of war. The Gestapo had arrested their older brother Gerhard and his wife Karin in 1934. After two years in prison they managed to emigrate to Prague. Gerhard had contracted tuberculosis and went to Switzerland for treatment just before Czechoslovakia was annexed by Germany, leaving his wife and child behind in Bohemia, not knowing what had become of them. After the war, he found out that they had vanished inside a Nazi concentration camp. Fuchs' other sister, Elizabeth, was even worse off because her husband, Klaus Kittowski, had been arrested in 1936. She swam across the Elbe River to help him escape from the camp and they also moved to Prague. But the family curse was to strike once again: Elizabeth threw herself under a train in 1939 and Klaus Kittowsky ended up in a concentration camp. A Nazi court condemned the father, Emil Fuchs, in 1935 to 10 months in prison for "anti-government agitation." The Quakers protested vigorously and he was freed one month later. Emil was living in Germany with his grandson Klaus, Elizabeth's child.

Kristel had better luck. She had emigrated to Switzerland and then to the United States in 1936. With the help of the Quakers, she had been able to finish her studies and marry a German-American, Robert Heineman. Despite three children, including a newborn, a baby girl named Kristel, after her mother, it was not a happy marriage and the young woman wanted to separate from her husband. Klaus felt very close to his sister, his niece and nephews, and wanted them to live with him in New York. Naturally, he did not mention his work to Kristel. The isotope separation from uranium took place in a gas plant in a location that remained secret, even to Klaus himself. In fact, it was run by the Kellex Corporation at Oak Ridge, Tennessee, where my generous agent Monti was employed.[52] The theoretical work and blueprints for the project were being prepared at Columbia University, in a laboratory financed by the same Kellex Corporation.

The planned meeting with Raymond almost didn't take place, because by February 1944 most of the British physicists had already returned home, except for Rudolf Peierls, Tony Skyrme, and Klaus Fuchs, the three most important research scientists from the Birmingham labs who were to remain in the United States.

On Saturday, February 4, 1944, as planned, Klaus Fuchs was standing on the sidewalk in front of the Henry Street Settlement on the Lower East Side in Manhattan. He was holding a tennis ball in his hand, which seemed odd for such a cold winter day, but after all, this rather slight young man could also be attempting to exercise the muscles in his forearms. Soon a rather short, stocky little man with a sad-looking face and a slight double chin, walked up to Klaus from the crowded street corner. He was holding a pair of gloves in one hand and a green book in the other. After an exchange of conventional passwords, Fuchs was sure that this was indeed Raymond.

Raymond's real name was Harry Gold, but his code name between the Rezidentura and the Center was "Guss."[53] The son of a Russian-Jewish émigré, Efim Golodnitsky, Harry was born in Switzerland on December 12, 1910. The family moved to America in 1914 and Harry studied chemistry while he worked as a laboratory assistant at the Pennsylvania Sugar Company in Philadelphia. When he left the company in 1946, he became an engineer. Without being a Communist or even a progressive, Gold was very fond of his parents' homeland and Gaik Ovakimyan recruited him in 1935. Harry started out by passing confidential information to Amtorg on certain chemical manufacturing formulas his company was developing. In addition, he was a liaison agent while studying at Xavier University in Cincinnati from 1938 to 1940 and reactivated once he returned to Philadelphia. Gold's new case officer, Jacob Golos, was also a Russian Jew, employed by the Association for Technical Aide to Soviet Russia, who had become an American citizen and a Communist Party member. From 1934 until his death in 1943, Golos was in charge of a small secret network, which included his secretary, Elizabeth Bentley, and Harry Gold. The fact that Gold had been associated with the "Red Spy Queen" would later become important, even though this connection had lasted only a very short time. By the end of 1940 Gold was transferred to Sam, alias Semyon Semyonov, the recruiter of Gold's friend, Abraham Brothman, whom we shall discuss later on.

By that time Gold's industrial information had become virtually worthless and he was being used less and less. But right after Germany invaded the USSR he was reactivated as a courier. Early in 1944 Sam ordered Gold to drop all his connections to Soviet agents and told him he was being given an extremely sensitive task. Gold became part of the atomic espionage network. However, as I explained earlier, a short time later all of Semyonov's agents were reassigned to those officers of the Rezidentura who were under the least suspicion. I took over the Rosenberg network while "Guss" was assigned to "John," alias Anatoly Yakovlev, who was my friend Yatskov.

Between February and July 1944, Guss met with "Rest"—Klaus Fuchs—five times.[54] The scientist passed on all the information he had regarding the Oak Ridge processing plant as well as all the reports written by the British scientific mission. Then Klaus Fuchs disappeared. He failed to show up at a rendezvous at the Bell Theater in Brooklyn and at a back-up meeting in Central Park. By the end of August, Yatskov, who was handling Gold, was considering every possibility. Since the information coming from Fuchs was so valuable Yatskov, with the approval of Kvasnikov and of the Center, decided to take some risks. He asked Gold to go to the physicist's apartment ostensibly to return a book he had borrowed. The superintendent and an elderly neighbor said that Fuchs had gone away "on a boat."

At the end of September Gold traveled to Cambridge to meet with Fuch's sister. A lady, probably the building manager, told him that Kristel and her family were still away on vacation. Gold returned one month later on a weekday to be sure the husband wouldn't be around. On that occasion a maid opened the door and showed him in. Kristel met with Gold and told him that Fuchs was somewhere in the southwest but that he was coming back to spend Christmas with the family in Cambridge. Gold had introduced himself as a friend from New York who was in Boston on business and left a sealed envelope for Fuchs. There was a phone number typed on a page with instructions for Fuchs to call at a specific time, any day of the week, and say: "I'm in Cambridge for so many days."

Actually, Fuchs had not left on a ship at all and was in the southwestern United States. In January 1944 he had been authorized to visit the atomic experimental centers, specifically Location Y or Camp 2, depending upon the classification used, which was the newly built Los Alamos laboratory in the desert of New Mexico under the supervision of J. Robert Oppenheimer. On August 14, 1944, Fuchs and Rudolf Peierls joined the T-1 team of the theoretical division headed by Hans Bethe. Taking advantage of so many eminent scientists who had fled Nazi Germany and Fascist Italy, as well as the goodwill of most of the civilized world in facing the Axis powers, the United States was able to assemble the very best of the world's scientific minds to participate in the atomic project. In this melting pot full of secrets, where races and nations were mixed, leaks were inevitable and Fuchs was providing them by the armful.

The United States would later accuse the USSR of having stolen their atomic secrets. This is true. I was in a position to know that Soviet nuclear weapons were very closely based on American prototypes. In my country we have asserted that only the first bomb built by Kurchatov was a replica of the one made by Oppenheimer. This is not altogether the case; the second and the third bombs were also replicas. The Soviet hydrogen bomb generally attributed to Andrei Sakharov was, just like Teller's H-bomb, as big as a hotel room. The fact is that, because of the information provided by Klaus Fuchs, we were able to reduce its size and easily deliver it to the target. Can the first atomic bomb created at Los Alamos be thought of as an American bomb? It was certainly financed by the United States but intellectually it was the result of an international effort. Americans, like Robert Oppenheimer and Harold Urey, were being seconded by Germans, like Rudolf Peierls, Otto Frisch, Hans Bethe; British scientists, such as James Chadwick and John Cockcroft; Italians, like Enrico Fermi and Bruno Pontecorvo; Hungarians like Edward Teller and Leo Szilard; Russians like George Kistiakowski and Georgy Gamow, to name just a few. The Americans paid for their services in cash, while the collaboration of Soviet intelligence with its agents was based upon ideological values. To me, this was the only difference.

I feel that atomic weapons were created by all of humanity facing the threat Nazism represented to the civilized world. This same humanity, through a group of nuclear physicists, decided to redistribute these weapons between the two rival blocs to guarantee its own survival. With the benefit of hindsight, we may judge the protagonists of this story, both scientists and spies together, according to the results. We must avoid any ideological disputes and examine the facts objectively because there can be no "ifs" in history. There is no doubt that without the discovery of nuclear weapons and both blocs not having them in equal measure, it would have been impossible to avoid a new world war. But this is an aside.

Many years later, in East Germany, Klaus Fuchs reminisced about his two years at Los Alamos:

> I had the good fortune of working with the best scientists of this century, whose names have practically become legend: Niels Bohr, Enrico Fermi, Hans Bethe, Richard Feynman, Emilio Segré, James Chadwick, Rudolf Peierls, Otto Frisch, and many others. On the scientific as well as the human level, it was to be, without a doubt, the high point of my life, and also of the lives of many other researchers who were to be awarded the Nobel Prize and would begin new scientific schools. Los Alamos was to be for me both a human and academic school that could not be duplicated.

The average age within this community was twenty-five and there was potential for every kind of behavior. For security reasons General Groves wanted the information to be isolated and separated among the researchers, but Oppenheimer was against it: only the free flow of ideas would allow him to give birth to the A-bomb in the shortest possible time frame. Fuchs could therefore get a general idea of what was going on in other laboratories. He was even in contact with Edward Teller, who had preceded Peierls as head of T-1 and who was concentrating his efforts only on building the super thermonuclear bomb, of which the A-bomb was to be the "matchstick."

The very existence of the Los Alamos research center was one of the best-kept secrets. The area was surrounded with barbed wire, every entrance and exit was closely checked and, inside the compound, a second barrier protected the laboratories themselves. To leave Los Alamos—the closest town was Santa Fe, about thirty miles away—the scientists and their families needed a special pass that was issued by counterespionage. All incoming mail at the U.S. Army Corps of Engineers, Post Office Box 1663, Santa Fe, New Mexico, addressed to personnel on the facility, was opened and subject to military censorship. However, the letter sent to Mrs. Robert Heineman in Cambridge, Massachusetts, didn't appear suspicious. Dr. Fuchs was informing his sister that it would not be possible for him to spend Christmas with her and her family.

Klaus was unable to leave Los Alamos before February 1945. As soon as he reached Cambridge, Kristel gave him the envelope left by Harry Gold. Klaus called the number and three days later our agent arrived at their home. Fuchs spoke briefly about the Los Alamos laboratories and two days later, in Boston, he gave Gold a large envelope containing a detailed report summing up everything he knew about the creation of the atomic bomb. A special section of that report discussed the problems relating to a plutonium bomb, including calculations of the value of the critical mass of the metal. Its final design was being held up by the choice of the shape of the powerful explosive that would start the chain reaction, whether it would be a sphere or a system of special "lenses." I mention these theoretical points here because these lenses were to play a dramatic role later on.

Since work on the A-bomb was entering its critical phase, Klaus was well aware that he would have to stay in New Mexico for at least another year. He therefore suggested that Gold come and visit him there. Gold agreed because he was scheduled to take a vacation in June anyway. Fuchs had thought out every detail and gave his courier a map of Santa Fe where he had marked the location of their rendezvous and even the bus schedule. Harry Gold gave Fuchs a wallet as a Christmas present, which had obviously been purchased by Yatskov. He also had an envelope in his pocket containing fifteen hundred dollars and attempted to discuss financial needs; however, Fuchs answered in such a harsh and uncompromising manner that Gold dropped the subject and returned the envelope to Yatskov.

The physicist, who had discovered ways of calculating the power of the bomb, took part in an expanded meeting of the coordination council of Los Alamos, chaired by Robert Oppenheimer, on June 4, 1945 to discuss Trinity, the first test of the plutonium bomb. A few hours later, Klaus drove his dilapidated blue Buick to the Castillo Street Bridge in Santa Fe. He handed Gold a complete description, both physical and mathematical, of the plutonium bomb. He also informed his Russian friends that the United States was intent upon using the two types of bombs, uranium and plutonium, against Japan. The next meeting was set for September 19, near a church in the Santa Fe suburbs.

The whole world had changed between those two meetings. Gold was struck by the worried look on Fuchs' face when he met with him again. Klaus had witnessed the first atomic explosion at Alamogordo on July 16. The monstrous destructive violence unleashed by the new weapon had been an enormous shock to him. Three weeks later the atomic bombing of Hiroshima and Nagasaki on August 6 and 9, 1945 created tremendous anxiety and alarm among the scientists at Los Alamos. Furthermore, Japan's capitulation and the end of the Second World War notwithstanding, the United States was continuously reinforcing its atomic arsenal. American reactors were still producing one hundred kilos of uranium 235 and twenty kilos of plutonium per month. The idea that the bomb could be used against the Soviet Union was being discussed.[55]

Fuchs thought he would leave the United States in October or November and Gold gave him instructions to reestablish contact in London. Actually Fuchs was to remain in the U.S. for one more year. After Oppenheimer left in October, the new head of Camp Y, Norris Bradbury, asked him to take part in writing the final report, which was called the "Los Alamos Encyclopedia." Fuchs was also to analyze the results of the bombing of Hiroshima and Nagasaki and take part in many meetings concerning the development of the H-bomb. He went to Montreal on vacation on November 20 where John Cockcroft, the general scientific councilor of the British government, made him an offer to become head of the theoretical department at a nuclear research center under construction in England. The U.S. Navy asked Fuchs to remain until the end of the nuclear tests then being conducted on the Bikini Islands. He would leave Los Alamos permanently on June 14 and reach London at the beginning of July 1946.

24

D espite their involvement in the Manhattan Project, the British were far from certain that their good relations with the United States would remain that way forever. They quickly found out that their cousins were accommodating only when they wanted something. As soon as the British made a request the attitude would change. The Soviets were not the only ones seeking secret information about the atomic bomb. London asked William Stephenson, its security coordinator in the United States, to also try to obtain information. Every British participant in the Manhattan Project was to report secretly on his activity as well as on the work done by others in America. All these reports went to Hampshire House in New York where Stephenson had his headquarters.

These precautions were quickly justified because Washington made it clear that it wished to keep the invention to itself once the atomic bomb became operational. On August 1, 1946, the same day Klaus Fuchs began working at Harwell, the British center for nuclear weapons research in Berkshire, Congress passed the McMahon Act, which prevented the U.S. government from sharing any information on nuclear secrets with any other country. The United States pressured Great Britain to stop its own atomic weapons research, refusing at first to even transmit the results of the work of Britain's own scientists at Los Alamos. The U.S. also wanted to revise the terms of the Quebec agreements of 1943, because the British right to veto the launching of an atomic bomb on Moscow, for example, was upsetting to some senators. Fuchs knew of these negotiations and was well aware of all the disagreements.

The British were so fearful of being completely dependent upon the Americans for atomic weapons that in the summer of 1945 Prime Minister Clement Attlee created a secret committee to build atomic weapons production facilities. The government released £100 million for the project without even informing Parliament. The program was under the supervision of the Ministry of Supplies and included the construction of nuclear reactors and a plant to produce plutonium at Windscale, in western Scotland, another for uranium 235 production at Capehurst, Cheshire, and a research facility at Aldermaston. The scientific and administrative center of the program, headed by John Cockcroft, was created at Harwell, near Oxford. The exceptional talent of Klaus Fuchs had been much appreciated at Los Alamos. Once the Manhattan Project was completed, Robert Oppenheimer asked him to work at Princeton University. But Fuchs wanted to return to Europe and accepted the position of head of theoretical research at Harwell, the third most important post in the British program after those of director and deputy director.

As soon as he was back in England, Fuchs tried to contact his family. He missed his father very much, and remained attached to him all his life, making every effort to have him come to Great Britain. It was to take almost one year before Emil Fuchs finally arrived in the fall of 1947. Klaus had been able to visit him three times in Germany. Since Fuchs was considered extremely reliable because of his security clearance, he had been deeply involved in the analysis of the secret reports from MI6 concerning atomic research done by the Third Reich and had participated in the debriefing of Otto Hahn, a captured German physicist.

Klaus Fuchs had had no contact with Soviet intelligence since his return to England in July 1946. Fifteen months is a long time and he was anxious to pass along the information he had gathered and that he knew was of enormous importance, especially when world peace was endangered because the USSR did not possess nuclear weapons. Despite the fact that he was a very disciplined agent, Fuchs decided to contact the Soviets on his own and against the strictest orders of the Center. He once again went to the local German Communist Party underground. However, Jürgen Kuczynsky[56] had returned to Germany and no one knew what had happened to Sonya.[57] Fuchs had a friend in London, Johanna Klopstech, alias Martha, who was a member of the Freier Deutscher Kulturbund, a German émigré cultural association founded by Kuczynsky in 1938.[58] She was a prewar contact of Fuchs' when he had been active in the association. When he saw Martha in London he asked her to contact his Soviet comrades. He had gone to the right person, even though Johanna Klopstech was not a secret agent. Instead, she was what is known as a "reliable person" within Soviet intelligence. The first meeting between Fuchs and his new case officer was scheduled for Saturday, September 27, 1947, at 8 p.m., in a remote part of London. Visual contact would take place at the Nags Head, a pub near the Green Wood underground station.

Before leaving for England, I met with the head of intelligence at the time, Lieutenant-General Sergei Romanovich Savchenko, who was later to become Minister of the Interior. Leonid Kvasnikov was also present at that meeting, which covered the following points: at that time the entire country was completely engaged in the construction of the Soviet A-bomb and Klaus Fuchs was one of the key elements in this effort; my mission was to organize the handling of this agent and satisfy all his requests, but also be completely responsible for his security; I was to make contact with him in person only if I was absolutely certain that neither of us was being watched or followed. The West was now paranoid about spies everywhere and, beyond the fact that an arrest would be in and of itself a serious setback, any kind of problem could be potentially disastrous for Soviet scientific research.

Only two people at the London Rezidentura, the Rezident and myself, knew of the existence of agent "Charles." I always preferred to act alone. If one man goes to a secret rendezvous there is a risk, but if two of them go the amount of risk doubles, especially if the field agent is inexperienced, which was the case of most of the London operatives. Yet, for this first meeting with Fuchs, I went with one of my colleagues. We took the security path to the far-thest side of London with respect to our meeting place, then doubled back by underground and by bus. I had been to the location a few days before to get to know the place and yet I arrived there fifteen minutes early. It was a foggy evening when I emerged from the Green Wood underground station. The Nags Head was across the street and I opened a newspaper, pretending to be waiting for a bus. Everything appeared quiet and clear. At ten minutes to eight a man came around the corner and went into the pub. He was tall and thin and held his head high as he walked. He had a pleasant face, wore glasses and looked like an intellectual. I knew it was Fuchs even before he entered the Nags Head. I waited a few minutes to make sure no one was following him and then walked up to the pub myself. A little bell chimed every time someone opened the door. I went in.

Inside, the warm pub smelled heavily of beer and tobacco. The better British pubs generally have four different areas: the saloon, where you can also order sandwiches, the bar for regular patrons, the larger pub area for transient guests, and the sales office for take-out beer orders. The saloon area was the best one from every point of view, and following this first try I continued to use pubs for all my secret meetings. The man I had seen enter was sitting on a high stool at the counter nursing a beer. He was reading the *Tribune* as we had agreed, which was actually not such a good idea because it was too left-wing for scientists who had been given the highest security clearance. He had blond hair and a high, receding hairline. There could be no doubt this was our agent "Charles." We exchanged a brief glance and he had certainly spotted me as well, since I was holding a red book as my sign of recognition. I sat a bit farther away at the bar and ordered a draft beer. This was the criti-cal moment, for if there was someone tailing either one of us, the persons following would enter now.

The door suddenly chimed and two red-faced retirees, over-dressed for the season, walked in, speaking in loud, boisterous voices. From the way they greeted the bartender it was obvious they were regular patrons. They ordered a pint of Guinness and went into the lounge. Since I only knew Fuchs from a single photograph and he knew nothing about the way I looked, some passwords had to be exchanged besides the signs we used. I was to say:

"The stout is not as it should be. I prefer lager."

Fuchs was to answer:

"Nothing can compare to Guinness."

I had memorized these sentences before leaving Moscow, but neither Fuchs nor Johanna Klopstech, being seasoned professionals, liked them very much. It was too common, too simple and any pub patron could say something like that to our agent and listen politely to his answer. Klaus and his friend had thought up a different password. Mikhail Shishkin, who was still the Rezident when I arrived in London, showed it to me on paper but dared not say it aloud for fear of anyone eavesdropping. Klaus had obviously noticed my book because he got off his stool and walked over to a corner where there were some photos of British boxers. A few patrons were standing around arguing about their favorite prize-fighters. I slowly wandered there myself. Despite my accent I was fluent enough in English and since foreigners were not out of place in London, I had no fear of drawing undue attention to myself. Without looking at me, Fuchs said the conventional phrase:

"I think the best British heavyweight of all time is Bruce Woodcock."

I immediately answered:

"Oh no, Tommy Farr is certainly the best!"

The argument heated up once again but without us. Fuchs finished his beer, said goodbye to the bartender and left. I watched him from the window to check which way he was walking. No one was following him. For added security I waited one more minute before leaving the pub. Fuchs was walking slowly and I had no trouble catching up.

"Klaus? Hello! My name is Eugene, I'm happy to see you."

"Hello, Eugene! I'm happy as well. I thought you had forgotten me."

We shook hands as we kept on walking. Contact had been made. One of the first tasks of a case officer is to get to know the kind of environment his agent is living in. Sources often fail to react to small details, which can set off all kinds of bells for anyone knowledgeable about counterespionage techniques. I started by asking Fuchs about his life at Harwell. The ultrasecret research center was just as unattractive as Los Alamos: barbed wire fences, checkpoints, faceless buildings perpetually under construction, horrible "Rezidential areas," each one furnished in the same standard way, mountains of red tape, and endless security requirements—in short a closed world that would have been unbearable had there not been the work at hand. Soon after his arrival, Fuchs had left this scientific ghetto and moved to a boarding house in Abingdon, a luxury he could afford because he had a car that also came in handy for his secret meetings.

Fuchs had been warmly welcomed. Fourteen years after his arrival in Great Britain as a brilliant university student and following his experience at Los Alamos, he was no longer considered a foreigner. Henry Arnold, the head of security, liked him and they were friendly even outside the compound. Klaus was also friends with Herbert Skinner, a fellow student at the University of Bristol who had become deputy director at Harwell. Even though they were at odds politically, Skinner being rather conservative, they nevertheless spent a lot of time together. Because of his position and his personal prestige, Klaus was well informed of every aspect of the atom bomb project. On his own initiative during our first meeting, Fuchs handed me some very important documents he had been unable to obtain in the United States on plutonium production techniques. I also had a list of technical questions I had memorized and that he answered straight away. I gave him some cigarette paper, which could easily be swallowed, with a list of information we were interested in for our next meeting. Klaus read it carefully and handed it back to me:

"No problem. You'll get all this next time."

I would have preferred to see him take some notes in code in his daily reminder, just to make sure he wouldn't forget anything, but if he trusted his memory that was all right too. His Lubyanka file had stressed his phenomenal memory.

We made plans for our next rendezvous and a backup meeting should problems arise. It was a lot of detailed information and as a precaution I asked him to make some coded notes. Klaus smiled.

"Don't worry, I remember everything."

"But you don't know the layout of the location!"

"I'll go there right away to make sure."

I became insistent:

"It's not that I don't trust you, but it is quite important."

"All right," he smiled, and then proceeded to repeat, point by point, every detail of our coming meetings.

The security arrangements for our meetings were my responsibility and I would have to answer for them personally. I made it very clear that he was never to come to a meeting if he had the slightest suspicion of being followed. I also gave him a security itinerary that would allow both of us to check each other's back, and we agreed to always hold our meetings in pubs. However, once we left the pub, rather than meeting right away, each one would walk around the block in a different direction. Once our paths crossed on the parallel street we'd be able to spot any tails and would only make contact if the coast was clear. Intelligent and experienced as he was, Fuchs understood everything immediately. Now it was time to split up because there were too many risks if we kept on chatting away.

"I'm very happy to be with you again," said Klaus looking at me straight in the eyes. After a moment he added, "I hope your baby is born soon!"

I didn't understand.

"Which baby?"

"Your bomb. From the questions you're asking me I estimate it will take you one to two years. The Americans and our own research scientists think it'll take you seven or eight years. They're very wrong and I'm delighted.

Before parting he gave me a notebook with about forty-odd pages covered in tiny but legible handwriting. Fuchs had wanted to give it to me at the beginning of our meeting but I took the documents at the very last moment. Should our meeting have been broken up by counterespionage, the source would have a better chance of explaining things than if the documents were in the pockets of a foreigner.

"Thank you!" I said simply as I was about to leave.

"My pleasure," answered Fuchs. "I shall always be indebted to you."

He was obviously alluding to our victory over the Nazis.

The notebook contained information on the Windscale plutonium plant. I microfilmed everything at the Rezidentura and shipped the undeveloped film to the Center. I only sent the originals in the diplomatic pouch after receipt of the film was confirmed. Later I always proceeded in this manner. It would have been impossible for me to copy or type the material passed on by Fuchs: sometimes it was a scratch pad full of formulas, graphs and sketches that were totally incomprehensible.

The documents followed a chain of transmission; at the Center they reached the 10th Department——Technical and Scientific Intelligence——of the PGU.[59] Information concerning the atomic project was placed in the ultrasecret Enormoz file—a word taken from the English "enormous." Then a special department, called Department S, and supervised by General Pavel Sudoplatov, was to depersonalize the production so that it would be impossible to trace it to its source. The information would reach the group of Soviet physicists under Igor Kurchatov of the famous "Labo number 2" only after these procedures.

The evaluation of the first batch of Fuchs' documents reached us six weeks after its transmission. The message was longer than usual and the material was classified as "extremely valuable" and went on to say that it would allow us to save 200 to 250 million rubles and reduce the timing of the problem's solution. Much to my surprise, Georgy Zarubin knew about our success. He called me into his office and, after having congratulated me, said:

"Let me know if you need anything."

I thanked him, but obviously I preferred to solve my own problems within the "family."

25

I had six covert meetings with Klaus Fuchs from September 1947 to April 1949, one every three to four months. I had located other good meeting places in various London neighborhoods and we rotated from one to the other. I would tell him the location of our next meeting at the end of each rendezvous. He didn't require too many explanations since he was *the* perfect agent. When I'd ask him how he would reach London and what precautions he would take, Fuchs would give me one of his shy smiles, like a child who answers his parents to say how good he's been. Despite his experience of covert operations, he never refused to offer a complete explanation to my cautionary questions.

Fuchs would drive from Harwell, which was some 50 miles outside London, in his sports car. On roads with little traffic, it was easy for him to detect whether or not he was being followed. Nevertheless at midpoint he would park his car at a railroad station and board the London train at the last minute. I also insisted that he use a security itinerary in town. He could enter a building with two separate exits, go though a courtyard or into a continuous movie theater just before our meeting was scheduled. That was my favorite place; you could enter at any time in the middle of a show, sit in the last row to watch everyone coming in and, after a while, go back out through another entrance.

I would also organize myself accordingly. I always liked to drive, but I could use the embassy chauffeur as well. Volodya Kudryavtsev was a tall and resourceful young man I had nicknamed Tyorkin.[60] Because of his personality he was the ideal assistant, and I asked the Center for permission to use him in my secret activities. Without suspecting anything and while he was still in London, Tyorkin was thoroughly investigated in Moscow. I was finally given the green light and told him that I was an intelligence officer. Tyorkin immediately agreed to help me; it amused and excited him very much. No one, except Rezident Rodin, knew anything about our collaboration. We would carefully study the itinerary in advance on the day of a secret meeting and Tyorkin would very quickly identify several locations that suited our complicated maneuverings. At a certain point he would drive faster as though we were late: anyone following us would be required to do the same and give themselves away in a few seconds. If we were assured that our back was safe, Tyorkin would slow down once again to better fade into the flow of traffic. We avoided intersections where policemen, who could quickly report our car's diplomatic license plates to MI5, were directing traffic.

After driving around for about a half hour, Tyorkin would pull into a side street and suddenly stop. I would quickly get out and go into a shop or a pub. The car would take off once again with my hat resting on the back window as if I were still sitting inside. Since we would go through this routine in a neighborhood that was far removed from the meeting place, it would then take me one to one and a half hours to get across town by bus, underground and another bus. At the meeting place I was quite certain that I hadn't been being tailed and my only worry was to make sure Klaus was safe.

Even though it's much more secure to have a confidential conversation outdoors, in a deserted street or in a park, bars are the best place to make "visual contact," as we say in spy jargon. That's where you can wait for someone without attracting attention and check that no one has been followed as they come in. I would only enter the pub once Klaus was safely inside and I was sure there was no one behind him. Once I went through the door it would be his turn to check and make sure there was nothing out of the ordinary. This entire checking exercise just took the time of downing a beer. I didn't like lager that much, but a London pub is not the kind of place where one orders whipped cream. The more I met my agents in beer halls the more I got used to drinking beer and having tried many different brands, my favorites remain light draft beers.

Our second meeting was in a London suburb at Golden Green. It was easy to find the place: there was a huge tree close to the pub. But when I returned to London in 1993, for a documentary entitled "Red Bomb," the tree was no longer there, just the stump.

The circumstances of another one of our meetings were quite different. In downtown London some parts of the street were paved in wood and would become very slippery when it rained. One evening early in 1948, I lost control of the embassy's black Vauxhall; that veered sharply to the right and hit an oncoming car. Although I had not lost consciousness, my right leg was broken and I was unable to get out of the car. I asked a passerby to call the embassy and a few minutes later my faithful Tyorkin lifted me on his back like a sack of potatoes and carried me over to his car. Fifteen minutes later I was in the emergency room of the nearest hospital.

The look on the faces of the doctors around me clearly meant that my fracture was not an easy one. This was bad news, as I was supposed to meet with Fuchs five weeks later. I asked, as delicately as I possibly could, whether the surgeons could handle the case or whether I should go elsewhere. Clearly my question was not at all appreciated. "To the operating room!" ordered a stern woman in a white smock. I still remember the name of my surgeon, Leslie Turner. Despite all his efforts, when I had to meet Fuchs the cast was off but I needed a crutch to walk around. Tyorkin found all this very funny.

"You don't need a security itinerary!" he said "You're in such bad shape that no one will suspect you."

The meeting was to take place in the Odeon cinema on Haymarket Street. When I limped in, Fuchs was already at a table. He winced when he saw me but immediately controlled himself.

"Are you using this disguise on purpose?" he asked with a twinkle in his eyes once I sat down next to him.

"I broke my leg a short time ago."

"Then why did you come? I would have understood that you were sick."

I hadn't even considered the possibility.

"To delay once again? Apart from all the other complications we have? No."

That time we didn't linger. As we parted company, instead of describing our next meeting place, I told Klaus:

"We'll meet at Nags Head."

He nodded:

"Okay, just like the first time."

All our meetings were necessarily very short. The Cold War was escalating and every Soviet citizen was thought to be a spy. The holder of the greatest state secrets was already at high risk traveling to London to see me and every extra minute increased the possibility of running into counterespionage with one of Fuchs' relations or one of my own official contacts. I'd be lying if didn't say I knew the physicist well under such circumstances. We were like two members of the same fighting unit facing the same danger and trusting one another, yet without having shared the same information. Even though he was reserved, Klaus was a most engaging fellow and I regret not having known him as well as Julius Rosenberg.

Beyond any human considerations, it's essential from the professional point of view to get to know your agent as thoroughly as possible. The sequence of events proved this in the Fuchs case: it is probably because of a lack of contact with someone who knew his secrets that a crack appeared in his own defense mechanisms. I was always trying to slip in an instructional meeting. The Center would often tell me: "Next time, no document exchange. Go and have some small talk, communicate, get to know him better." But then, at the last minute, I would receive yet another list of precise questions relating to problems encountered by Kurchatov's team. Even at such a distance, Klaus Fuchs was a full-fledged member of that team. How can you have dinner quietly with an agent when you know that the papers he's carrying aren't just dynamite but plutonium! The Soviet Union was locked in a deadly race and it was lagging behind its opponent; this fact overshadowed everything else.

It has been said that at every meeting I would ask Fuchs ten questions. That's simply not true. I would not have been capable of such a feat. Like all my colleagues, I trained my memory to the degree that I could remember the license plates of at least nine cars one after the other, but how could I remember words written in a different alphabet such as Greek or Hebrew? That was the impression I gathered in dealing with the bomb, whose underlying principles I understood only in theory. When the question was, for example, to know why the implosion method was better than the detonation method and the effect of the acceleration of the particles in the case of symmetrical pressure, no one could clear up that complicated story for me. Since Fuchs didn't want to take any piece of paper from anyone outside his lab, the risk of asking such questions in writing was unacceptably high. The only way was to memorize everything like a parrot, going in and coming out of the meeting. I had to limit the number of questions to no more than five, since I couldn't promise to remember more.

Klaus listened to me attentively without interrupting. Then he'd answer slowly, in a calm voice, gauging my reactions. As soon as he saw I no longer followed him, he would start over again using different terminology. Because of his nature or his upbringing, or perhaps both, he never lost his patience but remained very calm and collected. He was truly a man of quality and class. He was so knowledgeable that, no matter what question I asked, he'd always answer straightaway. Not once did he ever request time to think it over, find out or check a number, and this despite the fact that Kurchatov would run into a wide spectrum of problems. Klaus was also very much aware of my own problems. He would try to formulate his answers by using the same language of the question. I would file everything in different drawers within my memory and then rush back to the Rezidentura. Once I was back in my office, I'd empty each drawer one by one, and put on paper what had been said in that language I didn't understand.

Fortunately, Soviet physicists were beyond the purely theoretical stage and my experience as a steelworker and radio technician came in handy. When dealing with air or water-cooling systems, or the configuration of graphite rods for the circuit, I was able to ask for additional explanations. Once, it must have been in November 1948, I felt very much at ease in asking Klaus some questions regarding the aluminum shield around the uranium rods: what should the thickness of the shield actually be? And the height of the cooling flanges?

"Well, well! Your physicists are now very close to success," he commented.

I displayed my complete ignorance on the subject.

"I can see it from the questions you're asking me," he said. "Your baby will be born very soon and he'll start screaming!"

Besides his verbal answers to my questions, Fuchs would come with written answers to the questions Kurchatov had asked and to which he'd add, on his own initiative, other documents or calculations on the plutonium and hydrogen bombs. From September 1947 to May 1949, Fuchs handed me ninety extremely sensitive documents as important as the diagram of the principle behind the hydrogen bomb and the theoretical underpinnings for its design as planned by British and American scientists. These outlined the calculation of the power of the explosions at Hiroshima and Nagasaki; the formula to calculate radiation intensity according to distance; the plans for the construction of an isotope separation plant; detailed blueprints on nuclear reactors and the plutonium facility at Windscale; the comparative analysis of batteries cooled by air or water; the results of American tests on the uranium and plutonium bombs; reports on U.S.-British cooperation in nuclear weapons production; and many other issues.

These documents were highly rated by my superiors in Moscow, and I never failed to inform my agent how valuable they were. One day as he thanked me for those encouraging words, Klaus replied:

"I'm sure that my Soviet comrades are capable of producing the atomic bomb on their own, but time is getting short and I want to be sure they don't waste it chasing after the wrong problems."

It's always better to be extra cautious and documents were always exchanged just before we parted, by brush pass, in some out of the way place or in a deserted alley. I would then take the bus or the underground back to the embassy. Officially I took no risks and used my diplomatic passport and the foreign Rezident card issued to me by the Foreign Office. But protocol would not have mattered in a case as vitally important as atomic intelligence. If MI5 thought I was carrying confidential documents they would find an excuse to stop and search me thoroughly.

Obviously these risks were rather small compared to those taken by Fuchs. One day, at the beginning of our relationship, I asked him how he took out his written material, calculations, graphs, and sketches. What if someone found out while checking his ID card just as he was leaving Harwell?

Rather than playing the role of the brave but low-key hero, which was not his style, Klaus gave me his usual ironic smile.

"Simple. I'll tell them: 'But no one ever said I have no right to take my own notes with me. I work nonstop for twenty-four hours and an idea can come to me at home just as easily as in the lab!'"

I still asked him to be very cautious. The press had whipped up the spy hysteria into a frenzy and it was about to engulf the peaceful community at Harwell. Klaus told me that three young researchers had been dismissed because they were Communist sympathizers and that his colleagues now avoided saying anything positive about the USSR. I sensed that he was now much more at risk, yet every time he would wave all my objections aside: he was already as cautious as possible and it would be paranoid to do any more than that.

As I found out with Klaus this type of assurance is useless when one is confronted with the unforeseen. The day of the meeting I was waiting in front of a pub as usual. He'd always arrive some ten minutes early and when my watch struck the meeting time of 8 p.m., I began having a first anguished thought. At 8:10 p.m. he was still not there. I had been on the sidewalk for over thirty minutes, pretending to wait for a bus, and felt that by now I had become very conspicuous. I entered the pub and ordered a lager.

All those who have been stood up know the kinds of thoughts that were running through my mind. Had Fuchs really understood where the meeting place was? We had already met there before, so the answer was yes. Had he misunderstood the date or the time? It was the usual time, eight o'clock in the evening, and this was the second Saturday of the month. And what if he had missed his train? Impossible, he would have taken his car into town. And what if the bus had been late? That would be unlikely because if he were running a little late, he would just shorten his security itinerary, which ordinarily took about an hour. So what could it be?

I ordered another beer and wiped the perspiration from my forehead. I was sweating profusely and a wave of high anxiety overtook me. There were times in New York where an agent had failed to appear, but I was never in this condition. It wasn't because the Soviets and the Americans were allies at the time, while now we saw each other as enemies. Why was this happening to me, then? Was it because I knew how high the stakes had become? Or was it simply because I was older? I tried to calm my nerves by reasoning that Klaus was just sick or had some work-related change at the last minute, a meeting he could not avoid. He could have also decided to avoid any risks after spotting something alarming. What if he had seen that someone was following him? Deep down I refused to think about the possibility, but supposing he had been arrested? The back-up meeting was set at the same location, same time and day one month hence. I had to wait a whole month. Suppose he didn't show up a second time? That would be a horror story.

Fate took pity on me. After a few days of terrible uncertainty, I was called into Rodin's office to read a decrypted message that had just arrived. The Center, which carefully monitored every major newspaper in the world, informed us that an American daily announced the visit of a group of British scientists, including Klaus Fuchs, to the U.S. The Lubyanka could now explain why agent Charles had stood me up and wished to reassure us all. Klaus did appear at the back-up meeting. He was sitting at the counter and smiled when he saw me walk in right after him. That night the lager tasted very good indeed and I could have posed for a painting entitled "The Beer Lover." Six months later Klaus stood me up again. He had to attend an important meeting at Harwell because, besides his usual job, he was also on several committees and responsible for many activities, from anti-nuclear defense to the recruitment of young research scientists. That time I worried for one entire month and yet it was nothing compared to what was about to happen.

The danger became apparent during the summer of 1948. We received a long message from the Center informing us that Fuchs could be placed under surveillance by MI5 at any moment. This memo was written in the somewhat alarmist terms that were atypical of the Center. I was ordered not to contact the scientist if there were any unusual signs. Most of the time in such circumstances the agent at risk was usually placed in "hibernation." But Fuchs was giving us immensely valuable information and every month counted.

We decided to try another procedure that has the advantage of avoiding all contact with the source: the dead letter box, or DLB. We had a secure agent in London, an Englishman by birth, who was handling another informer. He lived in a cottage on a deserted suburban street. A fence made of large square poles, which were set about ten inches from each another with a thick, shoulder-high and well-trimmed hedge behind them, hid the lawn. It would be easy to slip one's hand through the poles of the fence to throw a small package, an envelope, or a box behind the hedge. The object would remain invisible from the sidewalk but the owner of the cottage could see it very clearly.

I asked Fuchs to test this out before one of our meetings. He walked along the fence and once he was sure the street was empty, he tossed a copy of *Men Only* magazine through the hedge. The owner of the cottage brought the magazine to his handler the next day. However, we rejected this method for a simple reason: never mix two separate networks. The informant already using this dead drop was equally important and should Fuchs have come under surveillance, his bizarre comings and goings would have looked suspicious, multiplying the dangers for himself and the other network as well. Despite the considerable risks of covert meetings, I was ordered to continue handling Fuchs, but, as in any human enterprise, the security effort was not always perfectly efficient, as one specific incident would show.

The Soviet colony in London was rocked by a defection at the time I was Fuchs' case officer. A polyethylene specialist, who had a British mistress, requested political asylum. The Rezidentura was asked to investigate what had happened to him and what his plans were. I had an excellent contact in the Association for Cultural Exchange with the USSR, where there was a scientific section, one of whose members we suspected of being an MI5 agent. Rodin asked me to pump him for information. I refused because the man in question could think that I worked for Soviet intelligence.

"Be clever about it," said Rodin, "just hint at your question."

I was not afraid of my cover being blown, but I also believed that every risk required some justification.

"Clever or otherwise I won't do it, Nikolai Borisovich. I just can't endanger the security of agent Charles for a little two-bit defector."

I had managed to avoid conflicts with Rodin, who was my boss, but this time he saw red.

"I don't give a shit what you think!" he screamed at me. "This is an order!"

"Very well, in that case I'd like to have it in writing."

"I'm the one who decides what gets written and what doesn't."

"No, Nikolai Borisovich. I will do nothing until I get a written order approved by the Center."

"So you want to get the Center involved? Very well!"

I knew I was right but still it was not such a smart move on my part, since the Rezident was the captain of the ship. A few days later I was ordered to report to the Lubyanka immediately. Rodin was beaming, positive that I would not return from that business trip. In Moscow I had to justify my conduct not only in front of General Savchenko, who was the real head of intelligence, but also to Valerian Zorin, the official director. They were both in a delicate situation: if they backed Rodin, I would have to remain in Moscow; if they sided with me, Rodin would be censored. Diplomacy won after all and Savchenko ordered me back to London and even requested that Ambassador Zarubin continue to extend his full assistance to me. Strangely, Rodin did not bear any grudges. Once the conflict had been resolved, our relations remained good, in London as in Moscow later on.

I still remember vividly one meeting with Fuchs in February 1949. We needed to have a quiet conversation without exchanging any documents. I used the procedure that Semyonov had taught me back in New York. When we left the pub—it was called The Spotted Horse—I took the notes Fuchs gave me and we immediately walked away from each other. A block away near an underground station, where a crowd was hurrying to get downstairs, I passed the packet on to one of my people who took it back to the embassy. I turned back and met Fuchs in the Putney Bridge Park near the pub. It was late on a Saturday morning with typical London weather, cool and cloudy. I sat on a bench next to Klaus. Some kids played nearby while their parents read the papers or were deep in conversation, as they kept an eye on their children.

It was the rare occasion when we had some time to talk, without too much risk. But it was all business once again. I wanted Klaus to describe Harwell in detail, its atmosphere, his relations with his colleagues, his supervisors and the security people. Had he seen anything out of the ordinary? Did he still have complete access to all documents? Was he sure that his apartment had not been discreetly searched in his absence? Klaus would answer me in his usual low and quiet voice: no, he hadn't noticed anything suspicious. Oppenheimer had come to Harwell and had once again offered Fuchs a job working with him at Princeton. Klaus had refused. Peierls and Cockcroft had proposed his name for membership in the Royal Society. There seemed to be no reason for Fuchs to worry.

A woman sitting near us got up to place a woolen cap on her daughter's head. The child was losing her patience and the mother held her still by the scruff of her overcoat. We both watched that simple and charming little scene.

"Why don't you get married?" I asked Klaus. "Aren't you tired of being a bachelor?"

He shrugged his shoulders.

"I think about it from time to time. But you know I'm walking through a minefield. One false move and it will all blow up. I can accept the worse case scenario but I can't involve a wife and children."

Even before he answered, I was about to say that a family would have been very useful to us, making him appear more trustworthy. He would be invited with his wife to social occasions and would have more opportunities to meet important people and further his career. Now I felt slightly ashamed of using those arguments.

"Furthermore," said Klaus, "to have a family in England is not part of my plans for the future."

"What are your plans?"

He sounded very assured, as if he'd made a decision after giving it much thought.

"I'd like to help the Soviet Union until it is able to test its atomic bomb. Then I want to go home to East Germany where I have friends. There I can get married and work in peace and quiet. That's my dream," he said with a smile.

"I hope your dream comes true. Do you have any news from your family?"

Klaus was happy to talk about his loved ones. He had seen his father for three days in Abingdon some time before. Emil Fuchs was about to leave for a one-year stay in the United States. He was to preach at Quaker communities and lecture on Nazi persecution and the future of Christian churches in the new Germany. In October he had spent some time with Kristel and his grandchildren in Cambridge, Massachusetts. Klaus' older brother, Gerhard, was still in Davos, recovering from tuberculosis. They had not seen each other since Christmas 1946 when Fuchs had gone to Switzerland to spend the holiday with the Peierls. Gerhard had become hopelessly obese from his illness and his constant coughing painfully shook his massive body. He had retained his Communist ideals and desperately wished to return to East Germany to build the workers' and peasants' state. His illness would not allow him to leave Switzerland, where Klaus sent him funds for his expensive treatment.

I quickly jumped in when he said this. The Center had been asking me for some time to pay Fuchs a formal subsidy while being very discreet about it. I didn't know he had rejected out of hand the previous offer made by Harry Gold in Massachusetts. I took the envelope I brought to each one of our meetings but never found the right opportunity to give it to him.

"Klaus, I know you're not working for the money and want none for yourself. But we do wish to help you with your daily financial problems. I hope you will not feel offended if I offer this small token of our gratitude."

Fuchs hesitated for a moment and understood that this was a friendly gesture. He took the envelope and put it in his pocket.

"Thank you. I don't need money, but I do appreciate your offer. I'll send a money order to my brother right away."

We parted company at the entrance of the park. Our next meeting on April 1, 1949 was to be the final one.[61]

26

T he defection of Igor Guzenko, the GRU cipher clerk at the Soviet embassy in Ottawa, in September 1945, allowed American
counterespionage to begin hunting down the "Moscow spies." Investigators were questioning a mathematics professor, Israel
Halperin. Klaus and his sister Kristel were both in the professor's
phone diary. Kristel Heinemann had been under FBI surveillance
since 1946. Investigators quickly established that in 1945 an unknown American had come twice looking for her. The first time,
while she was away on vacation with her family and he had asked
the building superintendent for information, and the second time,
the Heineman housemaid had actually seen the man. It was Harry
Gold, alias "Raymond," alias "Guss." But the FBI didn't know this
and the description of a complete stranger was useless, akin to looking for a needle in a haystack.

It was because of Elizabeth Bentley's betrayal that Gold came
to the FBI's attention. Bentley had been Jacob Golos' secretary,
and an INO courier. She was a widow and the FBI had suspected
her for some time while one of its agents was keeping her company. The man turned out to be very clever and managed to pry the
information out of her. Caught in a vise, Bentley went from being
an obscure bookstore employee to the role of "spy queen" who
was to testify at innumerable trials in the years to come. Bentley

named Gold and Abraham Brothman as "Moscow's spies." The two men were placed under surveillance. By mid-June 1947 they began testifying in front of a grand jury in New York. The hearing lasted almost one year without ever going to trial because of insufficient evidence. Gold was still under suspicion; however, there was nothing to link him to the stranger who had been seeking out Klaus Fuchs.[62]

On August 29, 1949 the Soviet Union secretly tested its first plutonium atomic bomb. A WB-29 spy plane gathered radioactive particles in the atmosphere east of the Kamchatka Peninsula, confirming what America had suspected for some time. The impact was enormous. The Truman administration and the Attlee government each held a secret meeting and came to an identical conclusion: the Russians could never have reached such a result so quickly without stealing the secrets of the bomb from the Western countries. In both countries, counterespionage went into high gear and anyone who had worked at Los Alamos would be very carefully scrutinized.

At about the same time a strange document was linked to the names of Klaus and Kristel Fuchs in Halperin's diary. Gestapo archives retrieved by the Americans and the British after V-E day indicated that Klaus Fuchs was listed as number 210 among those persons who were to be sent to Germany immediately if they were captured by SS units in occupied Soviet territory. This was the equivalent of a search and seizure warrant for a Communist Party member, and would not have surprised the British, who were aware of Fuch's past and had taken the risk of giving him a security clearance in the middle of the war. But to the Americans, in the throes of an anti-Communist campaign, it looked very much like a red flag.

On September 22, the day before President Truman officially announced to the world that the USSR now had the A-bomb, the FBI opened a criminal file on Klaus Fuchs under the code name "Foocase." They would do the same in October for the Heinemans, placing a tap on their phone and reading their mail. At the beginning of September 1949, FBI agent Robert Lamphere, who handled the Soviet section, informed his colleagues at MI5 that there was a leak of confidential information relating to the Manhattan Project from the British delegation and that leak probably originated with Klaus Fuchs. These very serious allegations were tantamount to an accusation.

One can imagine that the British were not thrilled at the thought that the greatest thief of military secrets of the time was a subject of His Gracious Majesty. Prime Minister Clement Attlee ordered an in-depth investigation of the physicist. He was immediately placed under surveillance; all his movements were carefully monitored, his phones tapped, his mail opened. However, this naturalized German refugee had been under observation ever since he arrived at Harwell.

The initial investigation had taken place in the summer of 1946 at the request of Henry Arnold, Harwell's chief of security. It lasted five months. At the time Fuchs had just returned from the United States and was not in contact with Soviet intelligence. In November 1947, Arnold made another inquiry because he felt that Fuchs' behavior was too good to be true. Arnold was about fifty years old; he wore glasses, a mustache, and looked like a university professor but was, in fact, a first-class policeman. He was also intelligent, ambitious, and capable of improvising. Counterespionage officers, just like their intelligence counterparts, also use psychological methods besides technical information gathering. I can't say for sure whether Arnold deliberately decided to befriend the suspected mole and it's possible that he felt some genuine sympathy towards the young scientist. His special relationship with Fuchs allowed him to gauge his mindset, check his mistakes, ferret out moments of weakness and influence his decisions.

Arnold's mission became much easier because in August 1949, a few weeks before the FBI's warning signal, Fuchs had left his boarding house in Abingdon to go and live at Harwell. He had been offered a nice apartment in a brand new building and Arnold was his neighbor on the same floor. The head of security would invite Fuchs to dinner from time to time and regularly visited his apartment for a cup of tea or some small talk. Arnold performed his mission flawlessly. Considerate and tactful, he never elicited any confidential information. Fuchs later explained that Arnold was the only person he trusted completely.

Suddenly, on October 15, 1949, Klaus received a letter from his father. Emil Fuchs wrote to his son that he had been offered a chair in theology at the University of Leipzig and that he was going to establish himself in the German Democratic Republic. The GDR had just been founded on October 7, 1949. The news came as no surprise for Klaus. The summer before, as he returned from his long trip to the United States, his father had spent a month with him and they had had many long talks. The theologian felt that democracy had failed in the West and that true freedom was to be found in the east.

This decision was bound to have an impact on Klaus. Just like any employee with high security clearance, Fuchs had to discuss the matter with his security chief. It was obvious that if the Communists could have some leverage on the father of a physicist engaged in extremely sensitive research, there was a very good chance that they would try to do so. Arnold, being an excellent psychologist, immediately discussed the problem on a purely sentimental level. The management of the institute would ultimately decide but he would do all he could to help his friend.

Arnold couldn't know that I was the only person in London who knew the truth. He was convinced that Fuchs would be very unhappy to lose his job at Harwell where he did interesting work, enjoyed high status and a comfortable salary. Actually, what would have been thought to be an unpleasant incident in the career of a respectable and well-regarded physicist fit rather well with the plans of the Soviet agent who hoped to fulfill his dream of moving to East Germany once his mission was accomplished.

Arnold's advantage over me was that I couldn't see my agent for more than a half hour every four months and, because of his natural shyness, I was far from detecting that he was undergoing a psychological crisis, which more than anything else played an essential part in the events that followed.

William James Skardon handled the investigation that Attlee had ordered MI5 to undertake when the FBI file was delivered to the British in September 1949. A good psychologist, Skardon also specialized in the USSR and had studied Fuchs' background. He understood that threats or blackmail wouldn't work with an anti-fascist militant the Nazis had condemned to death. Yet since Fuchs himself had brought up the issue of his father choosing to live in the GDR, MI5 had a reason to begin a series of conversations with him that would quickly become police interrogations.

It was like a play in four acts. Act one: rather than having Fuchs come to London, Skardon went to Harwell on December 21, 1949. The conversation took place in the scientists' office. The investigator asked Fuchs questions about his family and himself. When Fuchs talked about his work in New York, Skardon asked him point-blank:

"During your stay over there were you ever in contact with a Russian to whom you gave information about your work?"

The question took Fuchs by surprise and he indignantly denied any such thing, before adding:

"I don't understand. I never did any such thing!"

Skardon became even more aggressive after lunch, repeating several times that Fuchs had passed along secrets to the Soviets. Even though Fuchs denied everything, Skardon returned to London convinced that the physicist was guilty. He also realized that Fuchs was undergoing a deep psychological crisis and opted to let things take a natural course.

Act two: at Harwell Fuchs' position had become more and more strained. On December 29 he celebrated his thirty-eighth birthday as one of the main research scientists at the laboratory. The next day he was a suspect once again, under hostile interrogation in his own office. The officer was clever enough to say that the matter was not as serious as it may have appeared. If Fuchs admitted his espionage activity, he would simply be fired for security reasons. Fuchs continued to deny everything.

Act three: the tone changed and the climax was at hand, while all action was suspended before the final explosion. John Cockcroft, the director of Harwell, was finally informed of the investigation's progress and deeply shocked. On January 10, 1950 he explained to his friend Fuchs, whom he had known for many years, that it would be best if he resigned. He even promised to keep him on as a consultant. By now everyone at Harwell knew that Fuchs was a suspect and many of his colleagues averted their eyes when they encountered him in the facility. Klaus said later that he was moving as if in a kind of soft emptiness, among shadows he couldn't touch. Henry Arnold was among those who had not turned on him, but he was really playing the role of midwife.

Act four took place on January 13 in Arnold's office at Harwell. He fell into Skardon's helping hands, ripe for the taking. Fuchs was at the end of his tether, psychologically spent; he admitted that since 1942 he had been giving the USSR information regarding atomic research.

The rest of the story is just a long epilogue. As strange as it may seem Skardon did nothing. MI5 officers were not allowed to make arrests. He returned to London and made no moves. Long endless hours ticked by and still nothing happened. After ten days the prey could no longer endure the pressure and requested that Skardon return. On January 24, Fuchs told Skardon the whole story of his eight years of collaboration with Soviet intelligence. But he said that he did not know the identity of the agents he worked with. Surprisingly—and against any kind of logic—the island mentality of the British makes them truly different in such things from the rest of the Continent: the spy was still not taken into custody. He was even allowed to remain free after the next interrogation, on January 26. On the 27th he went to London on his own and Skardon was waiting for him on the platform at Paddington Station. They walked to the War Ministry where Fuchs signed his confession. In a strange twist Fuchs refused to reveal details of the information he passed along to the Soviets, saying that Skardon didn't have a high enough security clearance! He then quietly returned home to Harwell.

Three days later, on January 30, he went to Shell-Mex House in London to meet Michael Perrin, the inspector for the State Commission for Atomic Energy, whom he had known since 1942. Perrin was quite knowledgeable and Fuchs related to him the amount and nature of the information he gave the Russians. He then returned to Harwell alone, once again. On February 2 he was asked back to Perrin's office to "clear up some details." This time he returned to London to be arrested, at last, some three weeks after having been charged with espionage.

A trapped fox will bite off his own foot to break free, but Fuchs, the "red fox from Kiel," didn't live up to his nickname. The question as to why secret agent Charles, knowing his cover was blown, failed to attempt to make a run for it is very complicated. The answer can only be found by examining each angle of this case.

In a business as risky as intelligence one must plan at the beginning of any agent handling for its ultimate conclusion. The possibility of failure requires preparation for what we refer to as "evacuation procedures." The agent must evade those watching him and seek refuge in a safe house where he can be rescued by his handlers and smuggled to safety out of the country. Later on this procedure was built into the handling of every important agent, but at the time of the Fuchs case it was not yet the rule. This was what happened during my London tour; we never planned to take Fuchs out of England. Later on when I returned to Moscow I learned that the exfiltration of Klaus Fuchs had in fact been planned.

On March 23, 1948, an alarming article by Chapman Pincher, a journalist who specialized in intelligence matters, appeared in *The Sunday Times*. He wrote that, according to reliable sources within the counterespionage community, three foreign scientists at Harwell had been found by MI5 to have concealed the fact that they belonged to "international Communism." Pincher stated that the files of these disloyal research scientists were already on the desk of the Minister of Supplies, who was to decide their fate. The Center became alarmed and set up an evacuation procedure for Fuchs, seeking a job for him in our nuclear research program in a note to the Soviet government. Molotov annotated the document, writing "We will be delighted." But this turned out to be a false alarm and the procedures to be used were never transmitted to the London Rezidentura.

On the other hand, Fuchs was a very experienced agent. He had almost certainly understood that he was being watched. Because of the importance of the case, two surveillance teams, meaning two cars and about ten agents, had to be following him closely. At Harwell security had almost certainly been reinforced, placing Klaus in such a vise that he could not reasonably think of breaking loose.

Another key point: MI5 conducted the investigation with great skill. Another more "direct" agency would have immediately arrested the suspect, attempting to pressure him into making a complete confession to save his life and so on. The British acted differently. Until that fateful day of February 2 when Fuchs was placed under arrest, counterespionage treated him civilly, allowing him freedom of movement, confident that he would behave like a gentleman. After all, Fuchs was a world-renowned research scientist, who had been privy to the most sensitive state secrets, including those of MI6, and he had always displayed exemplary conduct in that area. Until the day he was imprisoned in Brixton, when he understood he was going to be charged with espionage, MI5 had led him to believe that he would not have too much to worry about: at the most he'd be stripped of his security clearance and lose his job at Harwell.

Actually, I am convinced that solution would have fulfilled one of Klaus' wishes. He had even told me that once the Soviet Union had its own A-bomb, and his mission would be accomplished, he could at last retire after 16 years of covert action, first as an anti-Nazi militant, and after 1942, as a Soviet agent. He also dreamed of going back home to his own country, that part of Germany that was building Socialism and a better future. He would resume a normal life, marry, have a family, and work in a civilian laboratory.

Since I never saw him again, I can't vouch for it with any certainty but one may assume that, following the successful Soviet atomic test on August 29, 1949, Fuchs felt he had completed his mission and was grateful for his father's letter providing him with an excuse to resign from Harwell. I even think—but this is only conjecture—that Emil Fuchs knew about his son's secret activities and how he planned to end them. Once the preacher found out that the Soviet A-bomb had become a reality, he decided to take the job offer at an East German university, an offer he had probably requested, to give Klaus an excuse to break away from it all.

Fuchs played the role of the absentminded scientist who had committed serious but understandable mistakes and was not worried in the least of being followed because he had no intention of making a run for it, having decided to trust the wisdom and leniency of the authorities in his new homeland. However, the psychological crisis Fuchs underwent was the source of his problems, and he probably would have been able to withstand the pressure of interrogation by British counterespionage otherwise. He had dropped his defenses at a critical moment of his life, just as his mother and sister Elizabeth had done much more tragically before him. These memories had troubled his mind and paralyzed his willpower. That was the key to his breakdown because what he was being accused of could be corroborated only by his own admission.

27

Why did Fuchs confess? The question remains unanswered in the greatest atomic spy case.

There are two first-hand sources dealing with this very difficult moment in his life. The document of his confession to MI5 is the first one. To my knowledge the original text of this signed confession remains classified in the United Kingdom, though it is assumed that the text MI5 sent to the FBI is complete and identical. I do have one reason to doubt this and shall explain why later on. It seems to me that this version, which was made public in the United States in 1980 following the Freedom of Information Act, indeed contains the most important parts of the Fuchs confession. The authenticity of that document and the sincerity of the accused have never been challenged. My view is somewhat more specific: I find that much of the description Fuchs gives of his state of mind is true. When he was in prison and indicted for espionage, Klaus was convinced that he would be executed. He saw his confession as belonging to history and eternity, but there are two points preventing me from taking his confession as the whole truth.

First, there are several omissions and pieces of information withheld that can easily be explained. The confession, after all, had been written while he awaited the judgment of the court, and even though he feared the death sentence he could still hope that his life would be spared. Rather than admitting to more than was necessary, it was to Fuchs' advantage to provide a moral and psychological justification for his behavior. It seems to me that he could not have invented that subtle analysis of his own psychological state only in anticipation of the trial.

Furthermore, the confession had been written by an agent who was spying for ideological reasons and who had never gone back on his faith. Since I know this story from the inside, I can clearly see that many important aspects of his activity were not even mentioned. Contrary to many convicts facing the gallows who would gladly sell their mothers to save their own skins, the preacher's son does his duty, come what may. Far from accusing anyone else, he admits his guilt.

A second source reveals Klaus Fuchs' frame of mind at that critical time in his life and helps set some things straight. Long after getting out of prison and returning to the GDR, Fuchs told his story as a secret agent in a 1983 interview filmed by the Stasi at the request of Marcus Wolf, the head of East German foreign intelligence. Part of this interview remains classified but other parts have been published in specialized magazines and books. I think this version of the facts is closer to the truth than the much-publicized confession made to British justice. Fuchs, at the time, was free and among friends, in a country that considered him a hero. Some people may say that on the human level he would have tended to embellish his actions in Great Britain and cover up what could appear negative. This is possible, but Fuchs never tried to pose as a hero. Furthermore, as any good scientist, he calmly analyzed that period and admitted to the many mistakes he'd made, more so, in fact, than any outside observer could have discovered. Any sensible person would give greater credence to the second version than to the first one because of the circumstances in which they took place. What could then be said about me since I had access to information never before published?

My only regret is that, despite my rank within the KGB, I was never able to hear any of this from Klaus himself and I shall explain why later on.

The reason for this long digression is to introduce new information, never before published for the most part, that has never been divulged in Western books about Fuchs. But let's return to the main question: why did Fuchs confess to his espionage activities?

The answer may appear obvious to anyone who read his confession: Fuchs had lost his faith in what had originally prompted him to work for Soviet intelligence.

True, he was tied to the Soviets by strong ideological convictions that were thicker than blood relations. He thought that the American or Western monopoly of atomic weapons created greater risks of a new world war. This sophisticated intellectual, with his profound scientific knowledge and intuition, was also convinced that in passing nuclear secrets to the USSR he was helping build a more secure world for the entire planet. However, despite his Communist faith, Fuchs no longer was the young man in Bristol who attacked Stalin's enemies with the cold poison of a Vyshinsky. Having reached maturity, he could no longer accept the changes he saw taking place in the Socialist bloc. The new regimes being set up had all the characteristics of the Stalinist system: ideological intolerance, bloody repression of the opposition, personality cult. A wave of political trials swept Eastern Europe in 1949, affecting the veterans of the Spanish Civil War, the Communists who had escaped from the Nazis to the West rather than to Moscow, progressives who had fought the Third Reich on the side of the Anglo-Americans. Because he had worked at the development of the American atomic bomb, and had served as an expert for the British intelligence at MI6, Fuchs might think that, upon his return to the Soviet bloc, he would be suspected of being the perfect imperialist spy himself.

The crushing presence of the State in the intellectual life of Eastern bloc countries must not have appeared very attractive to the physicist. Following the "anti-cosmopolitan" campaign in the USSR that was heavily anti-Semitic, the Communist Party attacked entire scientific groups that were declared bourgeois, decadent, and false. After cybernetics and genetics, quantum mechanics was running the risk of disappearing "into history's trash can." Fuchs was

to remember much later how shocked he had been by the willingness of ideologues and scientists to attack a science to which he
had dedicated much of his own life. It was only because of
Kurchatov's explanation to Beria, the all-powerful head of the Russian atomic program, that all the physical processes of nuclear reactions were subjected to the rules of quantum mechanics that Soviet
physicists were spared. But Fuchs didn't know any of this.

There was another problem. Fuchs was not well informed ideo-
logically and he was only hearing one side of what was going on in
the Socialist camp. Throughout the eight years he worked with Soviet intelligence, he carefully hid his Communist ideas and his sympathy for the USSR. Following the rules of konspiratsya, he stopped
reading progressive publications after 1942 and obviously did not
communicate with like-minded comrades. Thus, from that point
on, that side of his mind remained deprived, losing its vital energy.
Two other elements did, however, influence his thinking: powerful
anti-Soviet propaganda and the liberal political views of the intellectual milieu in which he lived and worked. All infiltration agents,
be it in intelligence or narcotics, know the long-term involuntary
effects of being exposed to the values of an environment. I think it
was no surprise that Fuchs had ideological hesitations when he realized the shortcomings of totalitarianism. In doing so he followed
the path of many Western Communists. The Soviets were not too
far behind when they attacked Stalinist deviation at the XXth Congress of the Soviet Communist Party in 1956.

The ideological problem was also complicated by ethical considerations. Fuchs was a man of very high moral standards, and he
suffered from having to live a double life. As he stated, "there are
moral rules one has within oneself and cannot ignore." At the beginning of his work with Soviet intelligence he had only wished to
transmit his own research. It was only gradually and, due to circumstances, that he crossed that threshold. He was living in the
midst of scientists, many of whom were his personal friends and
who thought of him as their friend. He felt closer to these real
people who were intelligent, warm, and nice to him. By comparison, the Moscow scientists, whom he'd never met, became more
and more unreal, as if they were part of a virtual world. In order to

serve his ideological homeland, the cradle of Socialism, he had been forced to betray the country that had given him shelter, his co-workers and, in the end, himself on a daily basis. Faced with doubts, isolation and exhaustion, the secret agent disappeared, to be replaced by the preacher's son. His puritanical nature in perfect harmony with what he was doing during the war, now had trouble accepting the new situation where the enemies of the USSR were no longer the Nazis, who were hated just as strongly by the people he knew and liked so much in England and America.

Fuchs would describe his inner conflict in his 1950 statement:

> In the course of this work I began naturally to form bonds of personal friendship and I had, concerning them, my inner thoughts. I used my Marxist philosophy to establish in my mind two separate compartments. One compartment in which I allowed myself to make friendships, to have personal relations, to help people and to be in all personal ways the kind of man I wanted to be and the kind of man which, in personal ways, I had been before with my friends in or near the Communist Party. I could be free and easy and happy with other people without fear of disclosing myself because I knew that the other compartment would step in if I approached the danger point. I could forget the other compartment and still rely on it. It appeared to me at the time that I had become a "free man" because I had succeeded in the other compartment to establish myself completely independent of the surrounding forces of society. Looking back now, the best way of expressing it seems to be to call it a "controlled schizophrenia."*

I have no documents to back up the following, which is based upon the personal conviction of a man who knew Klaus Fuchs and has had access to many Soviet intelligence classified documents as well as inside experience of the workings of the intelligence services. I also had many conversations with Anatoly Yatskov, and

---

* From the original in R.C. Williams, op. cit. p. 184. See note 60. [N.D.T.]

after reading several books on the subject, I feel I can understand the nature and motivations of the other important player in this case, namely Harry Gold. Obviously one is not obliged to believe what I am stating, but those who disagree must seriously consider this as a possible explanation. In fact, I am convinced that Harry Gold had betrayed Klaus Fuchs long before the FBI decided to launch their media circus around him in May 1950. Fuchs, in turn, admitted his guilt, not just because of his inner conflict but because of the undeniable proof Gold had provided, which the FBI passed on to MI5 in the fall of 1949.

I will explain my reasons in greater detail further ahead. At this point I shall only provide a few elements which can be confirmed by publication of the relevant documents of the FBI and MI5. I am convinced that when the Americans warned MI5, the British demanded the FBI deliver proof that there had been a leak from the British scientific mission between 1944 and 1946. I am convinced that the famous map of Santa Fe that Fuchs had given to Harry Gold in February 1945 had not been found during the search of Gold's home on May 22, 1950, but had been actually handed by Gold to the FBI some time before, probably during the summer of 1949. In that case, the FBI had most certainly checked that map for fingerprints. Even four years later Fuchs' fingerprints could still be found on that piece of evidence. I am therefore convinced that it was because of the documents MI5 obtained from its American colleagues—the map of Santa Fe, with or without fingerprints and the photographs of Harry Gold—that Skardon was able to get Fuchs to confess on December 29.

The account given by the scientist himself partly confirms this possibility. Once in the GDR, Klaus admitted that from the moment MI5 began asking him questions he made mistakes in his behavior. His failure had a mesmerizing effect on his mind. The words "depression" or "stress" are not strong enough to describe the way he felt. During the long interview filmed by the Stasi, Fuchs recounted an episode that he felt was fatal to him:

> One day, Skinner, the deputy director who was my close friend, told me: "Klaus, accusations are being leveled against

you. If you give us assurances that this is not the case, we shall all be on your side. And we shall fight for you." This caught me by surprise. As a secret agent I should have been happy about it, but as a human being… I suddenly had to face the human relations problem, I had friends who were ready to trust me completely. It was at that moment that I betrayed myself.

But it was mostly during his long "chats" with Skardon that Fuchs understood Gold had betrayed him. The inspector from MI5 was able to discuss certain details known only to the two agents. Even the pictures of Gold they showed Fuchs led him to this sad conclusion: in some photos Gold was tense, anxious, his eyebrows curled towards his nose, like someone thinking very intensely; on others his face was relaxed, peaceful, and relieved. Fuchs thought that the first group of pictures had been taken before his betrayal and the others after. Faced with undeniable proof, Fuchs, by now psychologically spent, did not have the strength to withstand the attacks of his interrogators.

During these dramatic events I was without any news from my top agent. Our last meeting had taken place on April 1 or 2, 1949. Fuchs did not show up at our next scheduled meeting in July. I shall never forget the name of the pub where I waited for him: The Spotted Horse, near the Kew Gardens underground station where we had met once before. The other two times he had stood me up were for legitimate reasons. I was therefore not excessively worried. Yet when Klaus also failed to appear at the backup meeting, in August, I couldn't help but be alarmed. One day in the shower I was so absorbed in my thoughts that I was short a one-shilling coin to keep the water warm. Zina heard my screams under the freezing water and searched for a coin in her purse. I could remain hopeful as long as the truth was not forthcoming that Klaus could have gone off on a mission abroad or be in a hospital somewhere.

September 1949 was very warm. I returned to The Spotted Horse. My first beer quenched the thirst I had built up after a treacherous security itinerary. I quickly ordered one more, just for the pleasure. Deep down I knew something had happened to Klaus Fuchs, but by waiting there I hoped a miracle might happen: in one minute the door would open and a very cool Klaus, just another respectable gentleman, would be smiling at me. Actually, in the months following the Soviet A-bomb test, it was impossible to have regular meetings with him.[63] The press was crazy, seeing spies everywhere, and the British services were on edge. Along with the Center and Rodin, my boss, we thought Fuchs was under surveillance and would be at risk by meeting with his case officer. Yet every month I continued going to The Spotted Horse. The trees were now losing their leaves, and there were overcoats instead of raincoats on the racks in the saloon, and the pub's windows were the only protection offered to the usual customers against the low-hanging clouds.

28

S cotland Yard Inspector Leonard J. Burt arrested Klaus Fuchs on February 2, 1950. The following day at the Bow Street court, public prosecutor Humphreys read the charges to a very small audience. The charges against Fuchs were few and, despite the spy craze that was rocking the country, the wording was very objective, stating that at least four times, between 1943 and 1947, Fuchs had passed to persons unknown information on atomic studies that could benefit the enemy.

This confirms my earlier statement that Klaus had only admitted to the very minimum and was far from volunteering to confess everything to British authorities. If the authorities were rather unhappy with the result, British courts were satisfied for the most part because they wished to limit the damage done to the country's image. Fuchs' reputation was not distorted in the process and the prosecution introduced him as one of the most brilliant specialists in theoretical physics of his time. His supervisors had been very much impressed by his scrupulous adherence to security rules and had given him the highest security clearance. But deep down Fuchs was a dedicated Communist who served his cause out of idealism and not for personal gain; money was not a motivation for this act of premeditated treason. The judge decided that the case would be tried in criminal court.

The Fuchs case was akin to a bomb in the Western press. Less than four months after President Truman had announced the end of the American monopoly of atomic weapons, espionage returned spectacularly to the forefront. Tabloid headlines screamed that Fuchs was the most dangerous spy of the century. America demanded his extradition because he'd also spied on United States territory. Had London agreed to extradite Fuchs, he would almost certainly have been sentenced to the electric chair. Once again the British courts displayed their sense of fair play by rejecting the extradition request on the grounds that a British subject had to be tried according to the laws of his own country. FBI director J. Edgar Hoover offered assistance to his British counterpart, Percy Sillitoe, for the trial. An American counterespionage officer would help in the search for the truth, but once again the British rejected the offer. FBI agent Lish Whitson sat through the trial as an official observer of the State Department and nothing more. British authorities were intent on retaining control of the case to settle it quickly without publishing too many details.

They succeeded on every count. Fuchs was tried on March 1, 1950 at the Old Bailey courthouse in London less than one month after his arrest. Since the accused was pleading guilty the whole matter took less than an hour and a half, without a jury or any kind of cross-examination. There was a single government witness, William Skardon, and three short pleadings by the public prosecutor, the defense attorney and the accused. It was, however, a major news story and the trial proceedings were attended by hundreds of newsmen, including a reporter from TASS news agency. The public prosecutor, Hartley Shawcross, who had been one of the prosecutors at the Nuremberg trials, read the indictment. Fuchs had transmitted information about atomic plans and studies to unknown persons acting on behalf of a foreign power: the first time in Birmingham (rather than Banbury to suit the indictment) in 1943; in New York between December 31, 1943 and August 1, 1944; in Boston in February 1945; and finally in Great Britain in Berkshire in 1947. The defendant admitted that he had passed on information to the Soviet Union when it was an ally and later when it became an adversary of the United Kingdom. As the newsmen noted at the trial, the indictment was more eloquent for what it omitted than for what it stated.

Fuchs' defense attorney, Derek Curtis Bennett, said that his client had fought Nazism and that the United Kingdom had greatly benefited from his talent. The judge ruled that it was unnecessary to ask the accused any questions and simply read some excerpts from his written confession. Fuchs did say briefly that this had been a fair trial and he hoped that his admission of guilt would help lessen the harm he had done. Dressed in the traditional crimson robe laced with ermine, presiding Judge Goddard declared that the accused had done irreparable damage to Great Britain and the United States and that his crime was almost equivalent to high treason.

The fact that the British courts were so anxious to close the case, which in the U.S. would have become the "trial of the century," was proof enough that it was felt to be an embarrassment. The fear of having more leaks of nuclear secrets was not what worried the judges and magistrates the most. In my opinion, the British were much more concerned that they were losing points in the friendly but nevertheless tense competition between Washington and themselves. British authorities had failed to react in 1941 to the fact that Fuchs was a member of the KPD when they agreed to make him a member of the most secret team of atomic physicists. The Americans could now claim that the British didn't know how to keep secrets, a good excuse to keep them as far removed as possible from the U.S. nuclear program. Let us also not forget that British public didn't know that its government was going ahead with its own A-bomb project and, therefore, its research at Harwell could become public knowledge. From every point of view, London could only wish for a speedy end to the Fuchs case.

Years later in the GDR, Fuchs said that all he could remember of the proceedings at the Old Bailey were the steps leading up to the defendant's cage surrounded by a railing:

> Once I could no longer see anything around me, I sat there and my lawyer asked me,—Are you aware of what the maxi-

mum penalty could be?—Yes,—I answered, "death."—"No,"—he replied,—"at the most fourteen years in prison." Strangely enough, at that instant I felt nothing. I was convinced I would get capital punishment and was ready for it. That was my mistake: a real secret agent must fight for his life until the end. Then I felt what someone who is on death row must feel when he's told, "You will not be executed; you're going to live."

Fuchs had never considered the risks he was taking while he was working as an agent. Once he decided to work for the Soviets, he was ready to pay the highest price. The lawyer was right: British law distinguishes between high treason and violation of the Official Secrets Act. High treason is strictly a capital offense and would have applied had Fuchs been spying for a foreign power, such as Nazi Germany, and only in wartime. But during the war the USSR was an ally of Great Britain, becoming an enemy only when both countries were at peace. Fuchs received the maximum penalty for violation of the Official Secrets Act: 14 years in prison.

The trial of Klaus Fuchs caused a great deal of anxiety within the scientific community. Many of the "fathers" of the atomic bomb favored openness and even the exchange of nuclear secrets with the USSR once victory over the Nazis had been achieved. Niels Bohr had unsuccessfully attempted, as early as 1944, to convince President Roosevelt and Churchill to share at least general information regarding the Manhattan Project with Stalin. Albert Einstein, Bertrand Russell, Leo Szilard, and Joseph Rotblat all made public statements against American monopoly and against the use of these monstrous weapons in general. As one anonymous scientist was to say when questioned by the FBI at Los Alamos, Fuchs "was perhaps the only one of the group there who actually acted on a theory accepted by almost all of them."[64]

The USSR could not remain completely passive while a world-renowned scientist was being tried and condemned for having spied on its behalf. One week after the trial TASS issued a statement which, I was subsequently to find out, had been written by Foreign Minister Vyshinsky himself:

Reuters has published news of the trial of British atomic physicist Fuchs that took place in London this week. Fuchs was sentenced to fourteen years in prison for having violated State Secrets. The public prosecutor of Great Britain, Shawcross, who prosecuted the case, stated that Fuchs had transmitted atomic secrets to "agents of the Soviet government." The TASS agency is authorized to say that this declaration is a gross fabrication since Fuchs is unknown to the Soviet government and no "agent" of the Soviet government has had any contact with him.

This was an understandable, and I should say, normal reaction. The damage had been done and the USSR could do nothing more to help its agent. If we had admitted that Fuchs had passed atomic secrets to us, it would have only meant a further deterioration of international relations. What is more difficult to understand is the attitude the Soviet government was to have toward Fuchs, as we shall see later on.

It is no consolation but, whatever regrets I may have, I don't think I can blame myself for anything in this entire story. Had this failure been due to a mistake on my part I would always blame myself, but nothing I did could have harmed Fuchs once he had been arrested. At that time, when a secret agent was identified, his case officer had to return home immediately. The Center ordered me to do so, but Rodin, who in spite of his quirks was a good operations officer, had a different opinion. There was no question that MI5 had greatly increased its surveillance of Soviet operatives. Rodin wrote back to Moscow that if I were to leave in haste, however, as soon as the arrest of Fuchs was announced, MI5 would immediately understand who was running him. Once I had been identified, British counterespionage could arrest me as I was leaving, or find out about other meetings and increase the number of charges against my agent. The Center agreed with this position and decided to keep me in London until further notice. So, even though I could no longer undertake my main mission or even handle my two other agents, nothing was to change in my schedule.

In the final analysis what risks could I possibly be taking? Could I get beaten up in a police station while I waited for the Soviet consul to retrieve me? How much weight did that really carry compared with the deadly threat hanging over Klaus? Or to the hardships my family had endured during the war that still made me feel guilty? The former street fighter of Worker's Alley that I was didn't fear the blows, and the British would think twice before going too far. If they broke an arm or a rib while they beat me, a British officer would be expelled from Moscow wearing a cast. The law of retribution has always been followed by intelligence services. I was covered by diplomatic immunity for everything else; the British could only declare me persona non grata and expel me from the country.

Fuchs was to be as faithful to me as I was to him, which convinces me even more that he only gave the British a minimum of information. Obviously he didn't know my real name and at our first meeting I introduced myself as "Eugene." I don't know whether Klaus referred to me by that name; he knew it was a pseudonym and our meetings were very short. We spoke impersonally saying "you" to each other. He must have used some kind of name when he would think of me, but given his extraordinary memory I'm sure he remembered the name I used the first time. However, there is no "Eugene" in his confession and therefore Fuchs feared that from there MI5 could have traced its steps all the way to me. Either because of caution or lack of time, Fuchs never asked me any personal questions. He didn't even know whether I really was Russian. Skardon had nevertheless tried hard to get him to speak of his liaison agent in London, but Fuchs only gave a very sketchy portrait.

"How old is he?" asked Skardon.

"He's neither young nor old. Let's say thirty, thirty-five."

"Is he tall?"

"Well, yes, rather tall."

"How well does he speak English?"

"Very well. He's very fluent and has an excellent vocabulary."

"But does he have an accent?"

"Oh yes! He does have an accent."

"A Russian accent? Or Slavic?"

"I wouldn't know. Possibly Slavic."

We had enough sources within British intelligence at the time to find out all these details later on. Since Fuchs had been given a local liaison agent in Harry Gold in the United States, MI5 reached the conclusion that in London his case officer was also a covert agent—an "illegal" in Russian terminology—perhaps a Czech or a Pole who had been living in London for a long time and was probably a naturalized citizen.

Only amateurs would be satisfied with such evasive answers and I wouldn't dare insult British counterespionage that way at all. MI5 had the photos of all the employees of the Soviet offices in London. In the one I had furnished for my file I was wearing diplomatic-style clothes with a tie. Naturally I always wore business suits in town, but Klaus and I had met six times, and it would have been impossible for him not to recognize me! Yet he said nothing.

I stayed on in London for two more months following the trial, remaining a very well-behaved second secretary at the embassy. My activity as an intelligence officer couldn't even harm Fuchs anymore. British jurisprudence doesn't allow trying someone twice for the same crime. Even if they had been able to do so, the British wouldn't have reopened this explosive case once it disappeared from the front pages of the newspapers after three or four weeks. No doubt MI5 had come to the conclusion that Fuchs' case officer was an illegal rather than an intelligence operative under diplomatic cover. Nevertheless, I could no longer stay in London as though nothing had happened; there was the risk of being found out and I had become too useless to collect confidential information. I was recalled to Moscow in April 1950, enough time had passed for my departure not to appear precipitated.

The Fuchs case was actually only one of many episodes in an avalanche of trials concerning atomic espionage. U.S. justice, having been kept out of the legal proceedings against the main Soviet agent, would have its day of vengeance in a logical, legitimate but monstrously unpredictable way. The sentence that was handed down in the quiet halls of the Old Bailey would be followed by an incredible campaign of spy fever and anti-Communist hysteria in America that was to spread its cancer all the way into the sacred halls of American justice and the Supreme Court.

The FBI's interest in Klaus Fuchs after he was arrested was quite understandable. John A. Cimperman, the Bureau's representative in London, was pretending to be the U.S. embassy's legal officer. To avoid any problems during the arraignment and trial of Klaus Fuchs, he kept out of the news, operating through third parties. On February 12, 1950 he cabled back to FBI headquarters that the British scientist had not named any of his accomplices. Hoover was convinced that the British were inept at interrogation and demanded that Fuchs be questioned by one of his men. It was an unprecedented demand: British justice had never allowed foreign policemen to operate on its own turf. Yet, an exception was made given the seriousness of the matter and the fact that a good part of the crimes had been committed in the United States. After the legal deadline of forty days for an appeal had passed, the FBI was allowed to interrogate Fuchs with his consent. The physicist agreed on condition that William Skardon be present at the interrogation, but despite this friendly arrangement the matter was still viewed as humiliating by many newspapers.

What follows is the official version. I remain convinced that Fuchs, having understood that Gold had betrayed him, had identified his American liaison agent long before his own trial. Unless that part of his confession had never been given to the FBI or that the Americans wanted to corroborate this face to face.

On May 20, 1950, two FBI agents, Robert Lamphere and Hugh Clegg, spoke with Fuchs for one hour at the prison of Wormwood Scrubs. They reported that the scientist was cooperating. On May 22, Fuchs, in Skardon's presence, described his meetings with his American courier in New York and Santa Fe. Yet, according to this version, he persisted in denying that he had ever known the man's name or his identity. On the same day in the United States, during an interrogation by the FBI, Gold signed a long confession where he described in great detail his covert meetings with Dr. Fuchs.[65] Excerpts of this confession were immediately cabled to London where another interview with Fuchs was scheduled for the following day. Unable to deny the evidence, the prisoner identified Harry Gold. That day, May 23, Gold was indicted for espionage in Federal Court in Philadelphia. Bail was set at $100,000 and he remained in prison.

Lamphere and Clegg had two more meetings with Fuchs on May 23 and 26, dealing specifically with the kind of information he had given to Harry Gold. On June 2, 1950, when the two FBI agents returned to the United States, newspaper headlines were screaming that Fuchs had "named over one hundred red spies." The most important problem for any intelligence service, namely how to hide its true sources of information, had been solved. From now on any refusal by the FBI to comment on a new arrest would be interpreted as significant. For the press and the public, the original source that brought about the dismantling of Communist spy rings in the United States was Klaus Fuchs when, in truth, the scientist was only the first on the long list of those betrayed by Harry Gold.

29

T he Fuchs case continued to make many waves, and one major consequence was the deterioration of U.S.-British relations. The Americans resented being excluded from the questioning and trial of Fuchs by the British. The U.S. Congressional Committee for Atomic Energy demanded a report on all information that had been accessed by the Soviet agent. They were genuinely worried about the hydrogen, or thermonuclear, bomb, which was many times more powerful than the A-bomb. The report prepared by the Los Alamos research center and the FBI, after careful analysis, was devastating for the United States. Lewis Strauss, the Committee's President, admitted that in 1947 Fuchs had "transmitted information on the hydrogen bomb to the Russians." Not only had the Soviets been able to break the American A-bomb monopoly, they now stood the chance of creating their own H-bomb ahead of the United States!

On March 9, 1950, a special subcommittee of the National Security Council recommended President Truman speed up development of the H-bomb. The White House made it a national priority the next day. American analysts were right: since the first Russian A-bomb had been tested four years after the American bomb, the Soviet H-bomb was to follow the U.S. test by only one year, and *The New York Times* estimated that Fuchs had shortened research time by three to ten years.

Even though the accuracy of such calculations is only a guess, it was abundantly clear that the U.S. had many good reasons to be angry at their British allies, who were responsible for such frightening leaks. U.S. efforts to eliminate Great Britain from nuclear research were justified. London tried to patch things up and on March 6, 1950, a few days after the Fuchs trial, Prime Minister Attlee made the following statement in the House of Commons: "It was only in the fall of 1949 that Great Britain learned from the Americans that secret material had been transmitted during the war. MI5 quickly established that Fuchs was responsible for this leak. The security service acted quickly and efficiently and placed him under arrest."

The FBI disagreed with this assessment. How could British counterespionage have allowed a refugee with Communist associations to become involved in the atomic project? How could a Russian spy have operated for so long under the very nose of such efficient security? Why hadn't MI5 caught Fuchs in the act while he was passing classified documents over to his Soviet case officer? There were even rumors spread by the newspapers to the effect that Fuchs could never have succeeded without the protection of Soviet moles within the upper echelons of British counterespionage. Roger Hollis, the head of the Soviet desk at MI5, became a suspect. The Fuchs case had reopened the giant hunt for moles at the top of the organization, which continued unsuccessfully for decades. Following the icy relations between the British and the Americans in matters of scientific research, the intelligence services of the two countries were also at odds.

Some journalists, seeking revenge and encouraged by the intelligence services, were trying hard to use Klaus Fuchs to undermine Moscow as well. I was tracking the fallout from the Fuchs case very closely in the British and American press at the time. I remember an article stating that perhaps Soviet espionage had purposely sacrificed its agent, once he had passed on all he knew, to create friction between the United States and Great Britain and thus weaken their military and economic pressure on the USSR. Other journalists highlighted the ideological switch by the Communist scientist and his critical attitude towards Soviet policy. Others still talked about sensational information he had revealed and repeated the story about the "hundreds of red agents" he was said to have given away. The authors of the last two versions of these stories felt that Moscow now considered Fuchs, its most important former agent for the nuclear program, to be a turncoat and a traitor!

It doesn't appear that these problems affected Klaus that much at the time. His first years in prison were particularly harsh. Both the prison administration and the common criminal inmates looked upon him as a traitor to his country. There were times when Fuchs was even in fear for his life. He had very few visitors; security chief Henry Arnold was the first to speak with him. Arnold had managed the unusual feat of putting a man in prison while remaining on good terms with him and actually keeping his trust. His former boss Rudolf Peierls also came to see him. Otherwise Fuchs passed his time making canvas bags and in the evenings he would read. Gradually he managed to get the other inmates to trust him. They appreciated his intelligence and kindness and some even asked him for advice. Just as he did in 1940 in the internment camp in Canada, Fuchs was able to organize a sort of night school with the permission of the warden of Wormwood Scrubs. It made no difference that his students were now illiterate criminals instead of young researchers, that was not a problem for Fuchs; instead of physics he taught them a little of everything. His courses were good for the mental outlook of the inmates and kept things peaceful inside the prison. The warden and the prison administration now looked favorably upon Fuchs and he had every chance of being released before the end of his sentence for good conduct.

Emil Fuchs, who was then 83, came to London during the winter of 1957-1958 and talked with his son several times to arrange his eventual return to East Germany. There were many people with an interest in that trip. The preacher was not aware of the many KGB friends he had among the local Communists. One or two Stasi agents were also handling the file. Jürgen Kuczynski, Fuchs' first liaison agent, had become an important official in the GDR. As an economist and statistician, he held the chair of political economy at Berlin University before becoming director of the Institute of Economics at the Academy of Sciences. Since 1935

Kuczynsky had been the personal emissary of Walter Ulbricht, now the First Secretary of the SED—the Unified Socialist Party of Germany[66]—who also took a personal interest in the matter.

Klaus Kittowski, Fuchs' nephew, also paid a visit to his uncle with a private message: Margot was still alive and hoped to see him again soon. Fuchs had met Greta Keilson during a brief trip to Paris in 1933. She was active in the anti-Fascist committee headed by Henri Barbusse. At that time Greta, or Margot as Klaus called her, using her French name, was married and from time to time she would invite the young refugee, who was in Paris alone, to dinner with her and her husband. From London Fuchs had written her some funny letters. Greta left to work at Comintern headquarters in Moscow and they lost touch. But the memory of the skinny young man remained with her. Greta tried to get some news through the Party but she was told he had emigrated to another country. Since she was aware of covert action, she stopped her search. Only much later would she discover the truth, once the Fuchs case was in the news and her only thought was how she could help him.

In the spring of 1959, news of Fuchs' release before the end of his sentence was reported in the newspapers. The British government even considered offering him a teaching position in Great Britain or in Canada, unless he wished to live in the German Federal Republic. Kristel Heinemann had become a U.S. citizen in 1956 and offered to have her brother come to Boston. However, the McCarran National Security Act would not allow the former Soviet spy back into the United States, nor did he wish to live there. Klaus Fuchs got out of prison on June 24, 1959, having served 9 years of his 14-year sentence. He saw the London streets flash by in the car taking him to Heathrow airport. Everything had changed: the cars, the advertising billboards, the way people dressed and Klaus felt alien in that new London. He was only 48 and had a whole new life ahead of him.

He traveled under documents made out in the name of a Herr Strauss. Despite his much-trumpeted ideological metamorphosis, he boarded a Polish plane that took him to East Berlin's Schönefeld airport. Greta Keilson was there among the officials welcoming Fuchs with a bouquet of red carnations. As he descended the steps

Fuchs displayed some annoyance with Western newsmen who had badgered him with questions throughout the trip, but once he saw Greta he immediately called her Margot and reestablished the friendship they had back in Paris. He laughed because the other inmates had said before he left his cell that morning that a woman would be waiting for him in Berlin with a bouquet of red roses. To avoid photographers, Klaus threw the bouquet on the back seat of the car then jumped in over it. The driver took him to a house used by the East German security services. When he got out of the car he noticed that he had been sitting on top of the flowers and laughed:

"No problem. At least they weren't roses."

Greta Keilson was in charge of international relations at the Central Committee of the SED and was responsible for getting Fuchs settled into the GDR. Since the instructions came directly from Walter Ulbricht, every detail was instantly solved. Fuchs, the fugitive scientist and secret agent, had no problem fitting into the society of his homeland. On June 26, two days after his return, Fuchs was given East German citizenship and reunited with his 85-year-old father at his country house in Wandlitz where they talked for three full days. Emil Fuchs passed away twelve years later in 1971, at the age of 97.

The General Secretary of the SED wanted to meet the scientist, and Fuchs was enthusiastic following his interview with Walter Ulbricht. On August 31, he was named assistant director of the Institute of Nuclear Physics at Rossendorf. Ten days later, he married Margot, 27 years after they had met for the first time. He was 48 and she was 54. Greta Keilson had given her entire life to the Party. She went to see her supervisor at the Central Committee and said "I have had my Party card for 33 years and I know my duty as a Party member. Now my duty as a Party member is to help my husband. I must give him those things he has been denied all these years: a home and a family." Many Soviet comrades were also in touch. I found out Fuchs' reaction through my own professional activities. The KGB had made Fuchs an offer, through Walter Ulbricht, to come and work in the USSR. He turned it down, saying he wanted to live in Germany. Fuchs was also approached unofficially by one of our "confidential operatives" in the GDR. The

KGB wanted to know what it could do for their former agent. Fuchs thanked them but said he had no requests.

That was where things stood. The man who had allowed the USSR to reestablish strategic balance at a critical time in history and had put his own life on the line for the cause in which he believed, spending almost ten years of his life in prison in the service of the Soviet Union, was never to be rewarded for his efforts.

It is necessary to examine this rather strange situation. The KGB never had the reputation of being ungrateful nor indifferent to the life and security of its agents. In 1950 an American couple, Morris and Leontine Cohen, the key operatives within an atomic espionage network in New York, which handled another Los Alamos physicist code-named "Mlad," were spirited to the USSR through Mexico. One year later it was to be the turn of Donald Maclean and Guy Burgess, two of the famous Cambridge Five, to get away. In 1963 Kim Philby, the third man of the secret British network, also defected to the USSR. In 1966, following a hair-raising break out from Wormwood Scrubs prison outside London, where Klaus Fuchs had done time, George Blake was warmly welcomed in Moscow. And the list continues. The KGB never failed to use every possible device to get its agents out and made sure they lived well in their Soviet exile. Many were honored with prestigious decorations and the Cohens, the only ones on that list to have participated in atomic espionage, became Heroes of the Soviet Union after their deaths, just like Kvasnikov, Yatskov, and myself. But why not Fuchs? It almost appeared as if some leaders at the Lubyanka and the Kremlin considered Fuchs to be a "traitor."

That was a key word in Stalinist ideology. Soldiers who became prisoners during the war were considered to be traitors, whether they were captured in desperate circumstances, wounded, or unconscious, none of it mattered! Those who had fought like heroes and returned from Nazi concentration camps as martyrs were put on trial, sentenced, and marched off to the Gulag. Intelligence was a weapon to fight the enemy from behind the lines. Anyone falling into the hands of enemy counterespionage that admitted, even under torture, to being Soviet intelligence operatives were considered to be traitors with all the consequences this entailed. The name of

Richard Sorge was not even mentioned for many long years, only because he had failed to conceal that he was a Soviet intelligence officer when interrogated by the Japanese. As for Klaus Fuchs, the evidence he gave was to resurface at the trials of Harry Gold, David Greenglass, and the Rosenbergs. Everyone in Moscow was relieved that Fuchs opted to live in the GDR because it was no longer necessary to establish whether he had been a hero or a traitor.

The physicist had returned to science. Fuchs created an independent theoretical school at the Institute of Nuclear Physics, where he worked until 1974; he accepted a chair at the Technische Hochschule; and was elected to the GDR's Academy of Sciences in 1972. He actively championed the cause of peace and the end of nuclear testing through the Pugwash movement of international scientists, who favored disarmament. His many professional and social activities often led him to travel to the USSR, something I did not know at the time. His contacts in Moscow were limited to the Soviet Institute of Nuclear Physics, already named after Kurchatov, and with other scientific institutions. No Soviet leader ever met with Fuchs, the man who did so much for the USSR and, as far as I know, he had only a single meeting with KGB representatives in 1968. The final odd detail in this strange chain of events was that, as his former case officer, I was not asked to meet with him at all.

I was working in political intelligence in Moscow at the time. Yatskov, who had ended his career as director of the "T" (for Technology) section, was involved in another area of intelligence. Leonid Kvasnikov, who was director of scientific and technical intelligence, was designated to meet with Fuchs. My former New York boss was not gifted at creating a congenial atmosphere for the persons he dealt with and didn't even believe it was necessary. Furthermore, since he spoke no foreign languages, he had to communicate with Fuchs through an interpreter. The entire meeting was summarized in two pages that read like the account of a trade meeting of a plumbers union! Yatskov let me read them some time later as a friendly gesture and nothing in that summary shed any new light on the more obscure points of the Fuchs case. What had really happened? What was it that really gave our agent away? What had he revealed during the criminal investigation? I am certain that Fuchs would have told me everything and not held anything back, but I didn't even know he had come to Moscow.

Why all this? Beyond the very special links between the case officer and his agent, operational interest was at stake. How could we decide not to investigate and analyze one of the most painful fiascos in the history of Soviet espionage? Under normal circumstances I should have immediately been dispatched to the GDR as soon as Fuchs had been set free. Since I had been shifted to political espionage, I assumed someone else had been sent in my place. In this line of work no one asks useless questions. From every angle it still remains a big question mark to this day. It was possible, of course, that Kvasnikov wanted to be certain that I had made no mistake that could have drawn attention to Fuchs. Klaus would certainly not have told me directly but he could have spoken to one of my supervisors, because that was how Kvasnikov introduced himself.

I found out about that interview many years later, after Fuchs had died. Kvasnikov, Yatskov and myself were all retired and from time to time we would get together for dinner with our wives. The women would all go into another room after the meal to let us discuss more sensitive matters. Naturally I became very angry:

"Damn it! Why didn't you let me meet with Klaus? I'd have found out ten times more than you did!"

Silence.

"You could have at least told me you had invited him to come on vacation the following summer!"

The KGB had its own vacation spas and summer resorts in the most beautiful locations, at the beach, in the mountains, in the forest. Kvasnikov had invited Fuchs to come over with Greta, but that year he had no more vacation time left. Kvasnikov then invited him for the following year.

"Well, did you?" I asked.

Silence.

"I never would have forgotten to do so."

It was true. Not because I think of myself as being better than any of my colleagues but because Klaus was my agent. Little by little I found out more details. Kvasnikov did admit one grievance against Fuchs:

"Why did he tell MI5 the location of your meetings?"

Kvasnikov did not get that piece of information, which was news to me, from Klaus, and he never would tell me where it came from.[67] He felt Fuchs had no right to reveal such important information. I can attempt the following explanation: Skardon could have told Fuchs that he had been followed in London and the prisoner then revealed what he assumed the investigators already knew.

To best explain the silence surrounding Fuchs in the Soviet Union it should be remembered that at the time and until the 1970s, any mention of the KGB and intelligence was absolutely taboo. The very name "Committee for State Security" was only mentioned when its directors were named. Newsmen would use euphemisms such as "the competent organs," while the man in the street would continue to say "organs of repression," just as they did in Stalin's time. In any case these rare allusions only concerned counterespionage, whose job it was to break up the intrigues of imperialist agents and stop all spies and saboteurs. Foreign intelligence gathering did not exist officially, and the only window, barely opened on the secret world, hardly mentioned the successes of Soviet officers working against Nazi Germany. Even TASS press releases that referred to Western publications were considered "strictly confidential" when they touched upon espionage. It was only after the nomination of Yuri Andropov as head of the KGB in 1967, that the "organs" began, very slightly, to lift their veil of secrecy.

Since there was no such thing as "Intelligence," officially the credit for the creation of the Soviet A-bomb was attributed exclusively to Soviet physicists. Following the first successful A-bomb test in August 1949, the list of those who had taken part in its development was given to Stalin. Beria had established that list a long time before to be used for multiple purposes. In case the program failed, those on the list would be "held responsible for their actions to the fullest extent of rules applied in wartime." If they succeeded they would be rewarded accordingly. The fathers of the bomb: Vannikov, Kurchatov, Khariton, Zavenyagin, Zeldovich,

Shchelkin, Flyorov and Dukhov, were made Heroes of Socialist Labor, received monetary rewards, free cars, the right for their children to be admitted without entrance examinations to any higher education institution in the USSR, and the right for them and their families to travel free of charge throughout the entire country. In that first list there were only scientists and high-level civil servants.

A few days later, the Vice President of the Council of Ministers of the USSR in charge of the atomic program, Avrahami Zavenyagin, had a meeting in his Kremlin office with Igor Kurchatov and Leonid Kvasnikov. Kurchatov did not want to take all the credit.

"Surely, Avrahami Pavlovich," he said to the minister, "we owe a lot to Intelligence, I would guess about 60% of the credit."

"No, no Igor Vassilievich, you are too conservative, let's say 50-50."

"Okay, as long as our Intelligence colleagues don't hold it against us. Do you have plans to give them decorations as well?"

Zavenyagin handed him a second list that was to be submitted to Stalin. Kurchatov saw only five names he didn't know: Semyon Semyonov, Anatoly Gorski (NKVD Rezident in London and Washington during the war), Vladimir Barkovsky, who had been in charge of atomic espionage in London from 1941 to 1945, Anatoly Yatskov, and Alexander Feklisov. They were all to be decorated with the Order of the Red Banner for Labor. Kvasnikov was not on the list. Kurchatov insisted that he be added and Leonid Romanovich was awarded the Order of Lenin. No one thought of a decoration for the main purveyors of secrets, Klaus Fuchs being the first among them. In 1964 I submitted to PGU head, Alexander Sakharovsky, a proposal for a major decoration for Klaus Fuchs or to recommend his candidacy as member *honoris causa* of the Academy of Sciences of the USSR. The reaction of Academy President, Mstislav Keldysh was:

"This is not advisable; it would lower the image of our own scientists in the creation of the atomic weapon."

We had to wait for perestroika for the Soviet people to find out the truth about that unwritten page of their history. Central Television mentioned Klaus Fuchs' name openly for the first time in July 1988 in the course of the documentary "Risk 2." On that occasion, once again, Soviet scientists were far from unanimous. Some, like academician Yuli Khariton, took the opportunity to state their gratitude. It was the first time one of the fathers of the A-bomb publicly acknowledged that the Soviet bomb had been a replica of the American one, reproduced thanks to the British scientist. He said: "The entire Soviet people should be grateful to Klaus Fuchs for giving Soviet physicists a large mass of information." Others, such as the President of the Academy of Sciences of the USSR, Anatoly Alexandrov, were loath to share the credit with a foreigner: "There was something," he stated reluctantly. "But it did not play a significant role."

There were many reasons for this refusal to admit Klaus Fuchs' decisive contribution: the feeling that he had been broken during his interrogation; the ingratitude of Soviet authorities; the jealousy of his Russian colleagues; the need for secrecy; the lack of consideration on the part of the intelligence services. However, I still do not understand how all these issues clouded his heroic contribution—one should not shrink from using big words when they are appropriate. Klaus Fuchs died of lung cancer on January 28, 1988, without having been duly recognized. There wasn't a single Russian at his funeral, nor was there any Soviet decoration on the black cushion next to the Order of Karl Marx that his country had awarded him.

"I thought you had forgotten me," was what Fuchs had told me at our first meeting. He didn't know how right he was.

I never saw him again. In July 1989, 18 months after his passing and a few months before the Berlin Wall was torn down, I was invited to visit the GDR. Film director Joachim Helwig was making a documentary on the scientist's life and he wanted to interview those persons who had known him well. Once I reached Berlin I went to the cemetery where he was buried, placing some flowers on his grave and bowing three times. One of the persons accompanying me asked me why.

"The first time was for me," I answered, "because I had the good fortune of having met the man. The second time was for all my Russian fellow citizens, because Klaus helped us in one of the toughest challenges of our history. And the third time was to honor him in the name of all the people of the planet earth. He wished we could live in a safer world and we probably owe him our lives."

The next day I went to Dresden where Fuchs' widow, Greta Keilson-Fuchs (Margot) lived.[68] She received me at their home, a rather modest apartment with a view of the Altmarkt. After they were married the couple had been assigned a house with a garden, but Klaus had very little free time and couldn't do any gardening. He was also opposed to hiring anyone to do the work and the couple then gave up the house and went to live in Dresden. When she found out that I had known Klaus in England in 1947 and 1949, Margot immediately understood who I was.

"But why have you come so late?" she asked me immediately.

Then, understanding that it was not my decision to make, she added warmly:

"Klaus waited to see you for some thirty years. Lately he was saying that no Soviet comrade who had known him was probably still alive."

What could I possibly answer? I stuttered a few words about bureaucracy during the years of stagnation and how perestroika had just begun. I was not too convinced of it myself.

Margot told me that Klaus had no regrets about the course his life had taken. Had he not decided to help Soviet intelligence he probably would have a brilliant academic career. So many of his colleagues saw in him a future Nobel-Prize winner! That was not to be but Klaus harbored no bitterness toward the USSR, as the many friendly contacts he had with Soviet physicists and the shelves full of "matrioshkas"* and many Russian souvenirs attested. He suffered nonetheless from attacks by journalists and writers who called him a spy and a traitor. He had hoped that the USSR would recognize his work and protect him from those attacks.

"I'm heartbroken, knowing that he died with such bitterness in his heart," said Margot.

Perhaps this was not the case. During his filmed interview for the Stasi, Fuchs said, shortly before his death:

---

* "Matrioshkas" are traditional Russian dolls.

There have been things in my life that I must admit I would do differently. Looking back at those 72 years I have lived, I can see all the mistakes I made and those I could have avoided. But I am deeply convinced that, in spite of all their mistakes and their negligent behavior, if the line of your life still took you toward the goal you had set once and for all; if you were able to reach that goal, or at least get closer to it; if going in that direction you did not lose yourself, nor squander your strength, committed anything contemptible, humiliated yourself climbed over dead bodies, nor harmed others to get there; if you were able to maintain the moral course within your soul which in every language is called conscience, you can consider that your life is a success...

These words and the entire life of the scientist who was a spy can be summed up in the words of Rabelais: "Science without conscience is only ruin for the soul." Whether they were in conflict or in harmony, Klaus Fuchs possessed both science and conscience.

PART SIX

The Wrecking of a Network

30

A t the beginning of April 1950, after two years and nine unin-
terrupted months in England, I was on my way back to Moscow, alone. Zina and little Natasha stayed behind in London so that
I could find us a place to live back home. Five years after the end of
the war the situation had improved. At first I stayed at the Armenia
Hotel in Neglinnaya Street. Soon enough I was assigned a room in
a communal apartment that we shared with only one other family.
The six-story white brick building in Pestschanaya Street was brand
new and had been built by German POWs.

When my wife and daughter arrived one month later we were
overjoyed to gather all our belongings long scattered with various
relatives. The happy moment was very short lived for me because I
was overloaded with work.

I had mentioned earlier the merging in 1947 of the intelligence
services, PGU and GRU, into the Committee for Information, the
CI. The overall head was Vyacheslav Molotov, First Vice President
of the Council of Ministers and Foreign Minister, as well as the
second man within the Kremlin hierarchy.

With his political clout, Molotov had no problem in securing
the necessary space for the new structure. The old PGU moved

from a single floor in the old Lubyanka to vast new offices. The central offices went into the northern suburbs of Moscow, into a building belonging earlier to the Comintern, dissolved in 1943. We also had use of several smaller townhouse buildings in downtown Moscow. Directorate S, covert agents, was in Lopukhin Alley near Kropotkin Street and the office of personnel was near Gogol Boulevard.

The offices soon seemed to get even bigger as if by a miracle because the men of the GRU returned to their former headquarters. The marshals of the USSR had protested in unison, saying that the high command couldn't function without its own intelligence service. This change took place in February 1949, altering the status of the CI, which was shifted to the Foreign Ministry rather than reporting to the Council of Ministers. Our head from now on would be diplomat Valerian Zorin, who was mostly an administrator. Intelligence was under the leadership of Lieutenant-General Sergei Savchenko.

There were advantages to this new reporting line: the diplomats no longer considered us as intruders and we would get proper cover and diplomatic passports much more easily. Assignments to missions abroad took place faster, but many problems remained. As long as intelligence gathering (the Intelligence Service, IS) and counterespionage (the CE) were under the same roof within the MGB, there was between them a constant flow of agents, officers and occasional agents, despite the unavoidable rivalries. If the representative of a foreign company in Moscow had been recruited by the CE, the actual handling would be transferred to the IS as soon as he left the USSR. The best spy hunters were attracted to the IS, which held more prestige and the possibility of traveling abroad. On the other hand the CE was often a dumping ground for intelligence, rotating those officers whose cover had been blown, had drinking problems or problems with women. A Soviet intelligence operative abroad who helped the IS without actually belonging to it, like my chauffeur Tyorkin, was recommended to the CE once he returned to the USSR, for example to become a chauffeur for a Western embassy. It would be only at the beginning of 1952 that the leadership concluded that the merging of the IS and the CE was much more important than with the diplomatic corps. The CI was then dissolved and the SR returned to the MGB under its old name, the PGU.

In 1950 I did not have to take a cover job at the Foreign Ministry, I just went straight to the British section of the PGU. That service only handled political intelligence. Science and technology were part of the 10th Department. There were only 12 officers in our department at that time and the top position was vacant. One of the two deputy directors was Mikhail Shishkin, the Rezident who had trained me when I first reached London. I was to supervise the new Rezidenturas that had been created in Australia, New Zealand, and South Africa. It was my turn to be the "Center," but I first had to learn before I could lead. I had to acquire a useful knowledge of those countries in a very short time, select personnel for the Rezidenturas, and work at the recruitment or transfer of the first agents. By the summer of 1950 I was promoted to deputy head of the department.

My old friend Yatskov was also in Moscow. We had last seen each other in mid-September 1946 when my family and I boarded the *Stary Bolshevik* in New York harbor. The Yatskovs, including their little Victoria, who had won the bet her father had made against the Nazis, had also left shortly after us. By December 1946 they were stationed in Paris. When they finally returned to Moscow in 1948 I was in London, so I hadn't seen my friend in three and a half years. Yatskov was still part of the 10th Department. I expected to be extensively debriefed on the Fuchs case, which was still bothering me. For my colleagues in the scientific and technical department it was a well-known and humiliating fiasco. I had nothing to blame myself for and was ready to answer the most delicate questions. To my astonishment no one asked me anything. The only action the department took was to give Fuchs moral support. A few people would write to him and visit him in prison from time to time.

The three persons directing the 10th Department, Andrei Ivanovich Rayna, a heavyset balding man, with a round face and short nose, Leonid Kvasnikov, his deputy and my former boss in New York, and Yatskov, now head of the American section, all behaved as though everything was perfectly clear to them. They only asked superficial questions and I was the one soliciting them. Obviously they had other problems to handle. They answered very briefly and looked away and I was to discover just one month later the reason for their nervousness. Upset as I was by Fuchs' arrest, I was far from suspecting that worse problems were yet to come. A mole was digging underground tunnels and another building was threatening to crumble.

31

S hortly after Victory Day, on May 10, 1950, I peeked into the office of my friend Yatskov.

"How are you?" I asked.

Anatoly sighed, he looked drawn and his eyes were lifeless.

"Do you have a minute?"

Yatskov closed the door behind me.

"There's a traitor in our American networks," he said. "It's Gold, that strange bird!"

He had made a play on words: in Russian the word "guss" (the goose) was Gold's pseudonym. It was the first time I heard that fateful name. Both Kvasnikov and Yatskov had talked about Guss in my presence but I did not know the real identity of the agent or the fact that he had been used as a courier between Anatoly and Fuchs. Because I had been part of atomic espionage since 1947 he could discuss it with me. He filled me in on the highlights of Harry Gold's career and his work for our service.

Clearly Gold's usefulness as an intelligence provider was very limited, but as a courier he was extremely valuable. First of all, contrary to most of our American couriers, he was not a member of any progressive organization nor did he attend rallies or demonstrations of any kind; he was completely non-political and there was no reason for counterespionage to suspect Gold in any way.

He was also a paid agent,[69] meaning that we knew what we could expect of him. Guss lived alone, had no family ties and could adapt his schedule to suit his case officer's needs. Finally, he was flexible, very helpful and obedient; he loved to obey and carry out what others told him to do. This also seemed to be to our advantage since he was under our control, and no one thought that with his submissive temperament the opposition could turn him.

Even Yatskov had failed to consider that side of the equation. Yet Yatskov, the excellent observer, couldn't help but notice details in his agent's behavior, in words, actions and mannerisms, proving his lack of sincerity. Twice he had caught Gold lying, once when he said that he had not left Philadelphia, when Anatoly had seen him having a grand time with a girl in Manhattan. Gold was an adult and Yatskov wasn't playing the role of his father and, besides, there was nothing to say so why these little lies?

Yatskov, who was a real tough go-getter, despised the weakness of character of his courier.

"This guy is a weakling," he told me. "With a minimum of pressure he just rolls over on his back."

Anatoly was by nature a quiet and withdrawn person who kept his opinions to himself the entire time he handled Guss in New York. He preferred to judge his agent by what he produced. In 1946 Gold had not yet dented Yatskov's trust in him and was still under control. I also found out why, once his New York assignment was over, my friend Anatoly had been sent to Paris rather than back to the Soviet Union. His mission was to take over the handling of Fuchs in Europe.

Yatskov was clearly the best qualified officer for that assignment. Even though he had never actually met Fuchs, he knew enough about him and the kind of milieu he worked in. The Center decided that their meetings would take place in Paris rather than London. The situation in France was much more favorable, as there were Communists within the French government and the attitude towards the USSR was very positive. And, on top of that, in France, Fuchs would not stand out as the key part of an ultrasecret project, or run the risk of being followed—he would just be another tourist and MI5 would have found it difficult to organize surveillance in a foreign country without alerting French espionage! Furthermore, Yatskov spoke French. That was why Anatoly moved to Paris, where he first set up a "safe house" for his covert meetings with Fuchs. Harry Gold would also have to take a short trip to France to establish contact with the scientist.

Yatskov left New York in haste on December 27, 1946. He had a final meeting with Gold the day before. Anatoly told him to get ready to travel to France but then the two men got into a heated argument. Gold, who had temporarily lost his job, was hired by our former agent Abraham Brothman. Any American who read the papers knew that Elizabeth Bentley had exposed Brothman; the story was in the news on July 6, 1946. Gold was absolutely forbidden to meet with Brothman.

Yatskov lost his temper:

"Are you some kind of jerk? You're destroying ten years of hard work!"

He threw the money at the bartender to pay for the drinks and stormed out without even looking at Gold. But then again the simple fact that Anatoly had displayed his anger to his agent was proof that he still felt he could trust him. However, Yatskov was never to see Gold again. The original plan on how to handle Fuchs was quickly modified and the Center decided to manage the scientist in Great Britain after all.[70] I was to be the one to go to London while Yatskov would stay in Paris to handle other agents, but he was not to leave France voluntarily.

I have mentioned earlier the threats looming on the horizon during the summer of 1948 and the alarmist message sent by the Center to the London Rezidentura at the time.[71] Now I understood why and the alarm came from a very credible source. The French DST—Direction de la Surveillance du Territoire, France's counter-espionage—had received a communication from MI5 stating that Anatoly Yakovlev, officially on the staff of the Soviet embassy in Paris, was in fact a Soviet intelligence officer. The French services were invited to keep him under very close surveillance. It was therefore because of security matters that Yatskov-Yakovlev was urgently recalled to Moscow.

Having reached this point in his story, Yatskov removed a large file from the safe in his office and handed me a typed page.

"Look at that!"

It was the intelligence report containing the MI5 warning to the French, revealing the true identity of Yakovlev-Yatskov.

"As you know, I have never set foot in England and don't know a single Englishman."

He took a sheet of paper and drew a triangle as he talked.

"Look here. On the left is America, and here France. But the information," he drew two other lines completing the triangle, "comes from London. What can link me to that country? Fuchs! It is the only source I handled in the United States who went to live in England. But Fuchs doesn't know me and had no knowledge of my identity. Only one person knew both of us, and that's Gold. So, he's the one who betrayed both Fuchs and me!"

The Western press at the time was saying the exact opposite, namely that Fuchs was the one who betrayed Gold. I think we can now clear this matter up. I have shown how Fuchs had taken full responsibility while questioned by MI5. How was it possible that a man who hadn't betrayed me, who as a Soviet diplomat only risked being declared persona non grata, would turn around and denounce a U.S. citizen who risked the electric chair under American law? We also learned that under MI5 interrogation Fuchs was careful to change the description of his American contact. He described him between forty and forty-five and about 5 ft. 11 in. Actually Gold was between 33 and 34 years old when they met and not over 5 ft. 7 in. Such a description couldn't tie him to the chemist from Philadelphia.

Yet the notion that Fuchs was the one who revealed the secrets remains alive to this day. In their recent book *Bombshell*,[72] a serious and well-researched work, Joseph Albright and Marcia Kunstel write: "New York headlines said Fuchs had fingered scores of agents. As it turns out, he only helped identify only one person, his courier Harry Gold, but Gold would prove to be a critical link to others."

I thought the issue had been laid to rest at Harry Gold's trial on December 7, 1950 in Philadelphia.[73] Judge James McGranery ques-

left
President John F. Kennedy and
Attorney General Robert F. Kennedy
during the Cuban Missile Crisis.

below
Secretary of State Dean Rusk and
Foreign Minister Andrei Gromyko.

Ambassador Anatoly Dobrynin *(second from left)* and Andrei Gromyko *(middle)* both denied any presence of missiles in Cuba when they met with President John F. Kennedy.

MRBM FIELD LAUNCH SITE
SAN CRISTOBAL NO 1
14 OCTOBER 1962

ERECTOR/LAUNCHER EQUIPMENT

TENT AREAS

EQUIPMENT

ERECTOR/LAUNCHER EQUIPMENT   8 MISSILE TRAILERS

CONSTRUCTION

above
Soviet missile launch sites photographed by U.S. Navy
reconaissance flights over Cuba in October 1962.

below
Map of Soviet missile and military deployment
in Cuba in October 1962.

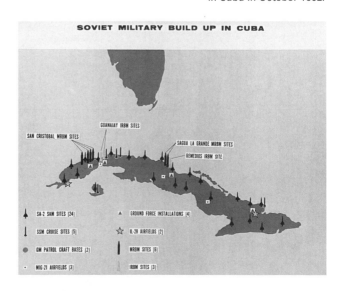

SOVIET MILITARY BUILD UP IN CUBA

GUANAJAY IRBM SITES

SAN CRISTOBAL MRBM SITES

SAGUA LA GRANDE MRBM SITES

REMEDIOS IRBM SITE

SA-2 SAM SITES (24)   GROUND FORCE INSTALLATIONS (4)

SSM CRUISE SITES (5)   IL-28 AIRFIELDS (2)

GM PATROL CRAFT BASES (2)   MRBM SITES (6)

MIG-21 AIRFIELDS (3)   IRBM SITES (3)

KASIMOV WITH IL-28 FUSELAGE CRATES ENROUTE TO CUBA
28 SEPTEMBER 1962

Soviet cargo ship *Kasimov* carrying crated warplanes to be assembled in Cuba.
September 28, 1962.

Khrushchev and Gromyko *(third from left)*, meet with Fidel Castro and the Cuban delegation at the Kremlin on April 29, 1963, six months after the Cuban Missile Crisis.

Feklisov *(far right)* officiates at meetings among other KGB veterans. Next to Feklisov is Vassily Zarubin, his boss as Rezident in New York in the 1940s.

From left to right: Anatoly Yatskov, Leonid Kvasnikov, Vladimir Barkovsky and Alexander Feklisov at the exhibit in the intelligence museum of the SVR, which is closed to the public. Their main decoration as Heroes of the Russian Federation was issued only in 1996.

Evgenyi Primakov *(right)* was head of the SVR, the Russian foreign espionage agency, before becoming Prime Minister under Boris Yeltsin. Vladimir Putin *(left),* was head of the FSB, the new initials of the former KGB, before being elected President of Russia.

Ruth Greenglass at the Rosenberg trial in 1951.

Harry Gold, a major Soviet courier, code named "Guss" and, later, "Arno," and identified as "Raymond" by Klaus Fuchs, at the time of his arrest, May 23, 1950.

left

Abraham Brothman *(left)* went on trial before the Rosenbergs in 1950.

below

Joel Barr disappeared from Paris when the Rosenberg case broke and escaped to Prague. Alfred Sarant would follow him through Mexico later on.

left

Alexander Feklisov and his wife Zina lived in this brownstone at 64 West 89th Street on Manhattan's upper west side during the period 1942-1946.

below

The Horn and Hardart Automat where Feklisov met Julius Rosenberg on December 24, 1944, for the famous exchange of Christmas gifts was located at Broadway and 38th Street. This sign is all that remains in 2001.

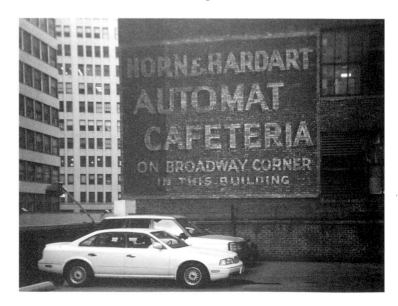

above
The Rosenberg network used apartment 6l located at
65 Morton Street in Greenwich Village to photograph documents.
Barr and Sarant shared the apartment for a time.

left
Knickerbocker Village is a
huge apartment complex in
lower Manhattan near the
Brooklyn Bridge. The Rosenbergs
lived at 10 Monroe Street.
Picture taken in 2001.

above

Feklisov was awarded the Order of the Red Star, a decoration given only to soldiers in the battlefield, by Kliment Voroshilov, President of the Presidium of the Supreme Soviet, after his first successful tour of duty in the United States in 1946.

right

Anatoly Yatskov in 1990 as he was dying of cancer. He wanted his friend Feklisov to tell the true story of the Rosenbergs.

Feklisov visited Pine Lawn cemetery on Long Island in 1996 and paid his respects to Julius and Ethel Rosenberg. According to Russian tradition he scattered some earth from his garden in Russia.

above
Klaus Fuchs at Los Alamos in 1944.

right
FBI counterespionage agents
Robert Lamphere *(right)* and Hugh Clegg
ready to depart from London in May 1950,
after Klaus Fuchs positively identified
Harry Gold as "Raymond."

tioned FBI agent T. Scott Miller, Jr., who had handled the Gold file from beginning to end:

> McGranery: I think it is very important for me to say, there has been some view that has gone abroad that this case probably was first exposed by Fuchs. That is not true. The Federal Bureau uncovered this matter, and Fuchs, as a matter of fact, as I understand it, had never cooperated in any way, shape or form until after the arrest of Harry Gold. Am I correct in that?
>
> Miller: I think the statement is, your Honor, that the identification of Harry Gold's picture was not made until after Gold signed a confession.
>
> McGranery: The point that I make is that Fuchs had never cooperated with the Federal Bureau. I am told that, by both the Attorney General and Mr. Hoover.
>
> Miller: That is correct, sir.

There should therefore be no doubt as to Fuchs' refusal to co-operate with the FBI: for a federal agent to commit perjury in court is not just a crime but also a serious violation of his professional code. It must be noted, however, that Miller's answer is both precise and evasive at the same time: "I think it has been established, Your Honor, that the identification of Gold's photograph took place after Gold had signed his statement." It is precise because—and this just goes to confirm what I have said—an officer of the law would never lie in court. It is also evasive in that it only refers to a single fact without getting into detail. Agent Miller actually solved a difficult problem: he was telling the truth—Gold had betrayed Fuchs and not the opposite—but also failed to mention another important point: Gold's admission of guilt could have been used to trap Fuchs long before Gold's own arrest.

After leaving New York, Yatskov never saw Gold again, but Gold did not disappear from the sights of Soviet intelligence.[74] At the end of December 1946, Gold was placed under the control of Ivan Kamenev, an intelligence officer who had been in New York since 1944. I remember him well: a bit older than myself, rather short, with thinning blond hair. Ivan was laid back, with a hooded, dreamy look and a slippery way of walking, which created an impression of someone who was unsure of himself. Since Gold was in contact with Brothman once again, to keep on handling him was tantamount to being criminally negligent. Agent "Arno," Gold's new code name since May 1944, was therefore put on ice. It turned out to be the right decision. Those tough orders issued by the Center and Yatskov were correct. Following Elizabeth Bentley's statements, Abraham Brothman and Harry Gold, under suspicion of espionage, appeared before a grand jury during the summer of 1947. Our service was naturally careful not to interfere in any way.

Brothman and Gold remained free since there was no evidence against them, and my meetings with Fuchs in London continued regularly. Everything led us to believe that our agent held up pretty well when questioned. By the end of 1948, once the interest in Gold had abated, the Center asked the New York Rezidentura to reestablish contact with the agent. The objective was not to reactivate Gold, who remained the weakest link of the whole network, but to convince him to leave the United States. Ivan Kamenev was still operating in New York and was ordered to reestablish contact. The meeting took place on April 10, 1949. Gold gave assurances to his case officer that he hadn't told the FBI anything, but he hid the fact that counterespionage had searched his apartment twice in 1947 and 1948. Kamenev told Gold that the FBI was not about to let up its surveillance. It would be in his own interest to leave the United States for some time. Gold's answer was noncommittal but he clearly didn't want to leave. His biggest problem was securing a good job. Kamenev gave him some money and, in parting, the case officer clearly told his agent not to contact Brothman again. The whole purpose of the meeting was to get Gold to leave the country, and that had failed.

By the following meeting on September 29, 1949, the first Soviet nuclear test had taken place and America was up in arms. Gold naïvely told Kamenev that the FBI was occasionally following him and that he knew this from Brothman. The tail came as no surprise, but the agent had failed for a second time to follow orders and stop contacting Brothman. Kamenev once again told Harry Gold that he must leave the country, but again he was turned down by the agent who said, contrary to any logic, that he hadn't noticed being followed. The final meeting took place one month later, on October 24, when the craze about atomic spies had reached its apex and Kamenev hoped that Gold, fearing arrest more than anything, would be only too happy to get out, but much to Kamenev's surprise this was not the case. Gold was very calm and in excellent spirits, offering even to resume delivering confidential information. He claimed that he had found a good job in a laboratory in Philadelphia that was engaged in secret studies on radioactive isotopes. Furthermore, he said, his brother Joe was working in an important facility of the U.S. Navy. But Gold had told Yatskov some years before that Joe had been killed in New Guinea during the war.

It had already been decided to send a more forceful officer to replace Kamenev, but following that meeting the plan was dropped. The only possible conclusion was that the FBI had succeeded in turning Gold! It became obvious that his new mission was to be used as bait. Had the Rezidentura taken that bait, Gold would have brought us some secret information concocted by U.S. counterespionage on atomic weapons to a subsequent meeting. When the exchange of documents was to take place, they would have sprung a trap on the Soviet intelligence officer and the FBI would have had irrefutable proof of atomic espionage by the USSR. To avoid such an unsophisticated trap, Kamenev skipped the next meeting scheduled for November. Two of his colleagues went to observe the meeting place, confirming that Gold was there on time, but the FBI plot fell through.

Therefore we have reason to believe that, despite Western statements to the contrary, Gold had started talking as early as 1948. The FBI, following the revelations made by Elizabeth Bentley, questioned him repeatedly. FBI agent Robert Lamphere, the U.S. specialist on Soviet intelligence, later admitted that those conducting the interrogation used special techniques; this could mean a polygraph test, hypnosis, or even drugs to make a person talk. Methods that would have broken some real tough agents worked very effectively on a weakling like Harry Gold. I feel he may have told everything he knew as early as the beginning of 1949. Now all the FBI had to do was use this unexpected manna from heaven, but the problem for the Americans was that most Soviet agents were still on ice.

There is one more reason to believe this possible explanation, because of the fact that Gold's apartment had been searched in 1947 and 1948. It's impossible to conclude that the FBI hadn't discovered in the basement the proof of espionage activity that it was to find "officially" in that very same place two years later. That's why I am convinced that the famous map of Santa Fe, which was supposedly "discovered" on May 22, 1950, had been used during the preceding winter to confuse Fuchs and lead him to admit his cooperation with the INO.

There is one more fact that proves a setup by U.S. counterespionage. Among the genuine documents the FBI provided MI5 in the fall of 1949 there was a forgery: a cable sent by the Soviet Consulate General in New York to the Center that Meredith Gardner's team was said to have decrypted. According to that cable, Fuchs and Gold held a secret meeting in January 1945 at Kristel's house. This forgery was planted for one purpose only: to protect the source, even from the British, so that it could be possible to say that the information didn't come from Gold but from a decrypted message.

If one accepts the fact that Harry Gold "gave away the store" during the first half of 1948, why hadn't the FBI immediately announced the capture of a red spy? Why wait for two years? To these questions there are two possible answers, which are not mutually exclusive. J. Edgar Hoover had obviously drawn his own conclusions from the fiasco of the grand jury espionage indictments following Elizabeth Bentley's testimony. The FBI was not well prepared for those hearings and did not produce evidence strong enough to secure the indictment of suspects such as Brothman and Gold. After that experience, counterespionage specialists decided to become very patient, keeping Gold out of jail in the hope that the Russians would attempt to reactivate him. Then they could track the agent for some time as he was being handled by his case officer, adding enough evidence at each meeting to end up arresting the agent and his officer in the act of exchanging secret documents. Nothing could be better for the FBI to come out looking like heroes after a sensational espionage trial! But our intelligence service made sure that plan did not succeed.

The other explanation is that during the grand jury hearings the FBI actually did have enough evidence to charge Gold but preferred to use him as bait, keeping him free until it could grab all his secret contacts and bring them to trial. Robert Lamphere was to confirm this indirectly when he wrote, "Gold was the biggest catch of all for the FBI. He informed on every one of the agents and Soviet officers he knew. The second half of 1948 was a great moment for the FBI when many important investigations were initiated." However, Gold had no incentive to tell all right away. He was after all playing poker with his own life and once he talked, the FBI would no longer have any use for him, and even though he had made a deal with them, he'd still be brought to trial. The best he could do was to extend this moment of limited freedom by doling out information piecemeal, hoping that the Russians would take the bait and making him irreplaceable for some time in the FBI's disinformation operation. For just a little bit longer, because sooner or later, his new masters were bound to use the fruits of his betrayal.

But in 1950 what could those fruits be, since Klaus Fuchs was already behind the gloomy walls of Wormwood Scrubs? The news Yatskov shared with me on that beautiful day in May, while I could hear the birds chirping from his open office window, came as a complete shock: Harry Gold had also been the courier for David Greenglass and from there the path went straight to the man who was as much my friend as he was my agent: Julius Rosenberg.

32

As far as I am concerned, both Harry Gold and David Greenglass have something in common: I have never met either of them face to face. In 1945 I barely missed an encounter with Ethel Rosenberg's younger brother. He was already at Los Alamos at the time.[75] Greenglass came to New York on leave on January 1, 1945 and gave Julius a few drawings of explosive lenses, which were used in the A-bomb, with explanatory notes. However, only a specialist could effectively debrief him. That was why, when I went to the meeting with Libi on the evening of Wednesday, January 10, I brought Anatoly Yatskov, alias "John," with me. Once I made the introductions I left John and Julius alone to talk. The two men walked around the block and got into a car where David Greenglass was waiting for them in the driver's seat.

David was an energetic young man, full of good will, with a ready open smile. Yatskov remembered him as someone who smiled a lot. It was quickly established that Greenglass actually did work at Los Alamos in the machine shop, but Anatoly's initial excitement was somewhat premature. True, our new agent did in fact work inside the most well protected research facility in the United States, but his theoretical and technical knowledge wasn't deep enough to allow him to comprehend the objectives of the research that was underway in New Mexico. David had a good enough visual memory to be able to reproduce the lenses he worked on every day, but he couldn't explain how they were being used. Furthermore, he didn't even know the other activities assigned to his unit. While the top scientists at Los Alamos were not cut off from each other, low-level personnel, such as David, had access only to what they needed to complete their assignments. Despite this shortcoming, the simple fact of having an additional source of information at Los Alamos was beneficial to us. No one could predict the future potential of David Greenglass. They shook hands, confident in a promising future. After Greenglass left, Yatskov and Rosenberg remained together a few minutes to set up the communication method with the new recruit at Los Alamos. Actually, Anatoly explained to Julius the procedures the Center had decided upon based on the reports the New York Rezidentura had transmitted. They went into a cafeteria and took a table in the back.

"Many soldiers' wives stationed at Los Alamos live in Albuquerque," said Yatskov. "It would be best if Ruth could move there as well. That way we could contact David every weekend."

Julius nodded since it was his own idea.

"Will Ruth agree?"

"I think so. I'll talk to her."

This way David Greenglass could leave the top-secret facility at Los Alamos to visit a city under intense scrutiny but still open to any U.S. citizen who didn't look suspicious. The information then had to be conveyed from Albuquerque to New York. This would be the job of my dear and brave Ann Sidorovich, code named "Obyektiv," who was William Perl's liaison agent. The Greenglasses met Ann at the Rosenbergs' a few days later. Since there could conceivably be yet another courier, Julius cut a Jello box into two pieces, giving one half to Ruth. The courier, whether it was Ann or someone else, would take the other half to Albuquerque.

Ruth moved to New Mexico in early March 1945. Since the secret meetings with Klaus Fuchs took place in Santa Fe, the Center felt that the courier used with Fuchs could also contact the new recruit inside the Manhattan Project. Harry Gold was scheduled to go to New Mexico that coming June. After he met with Fuchs he would visit the Greenglasses and pick up the information David had assembled. Gold was therefore handed the second half of the

Jello box. For added security, agent Guss was to use the recognition password: "I come from Julius." This seemingly logical and convenient arrangement had two monstrous and fatal errors built into it.

First of all, a basic rule was being broken, one that had been confirmed by innumerable bad experiences, namely, that two secret networks must remain compartmentalized, without communicating between one another. The person having access to both networks becomes a weak link: if that person should stumble both parts will fall together. Gold could already cause the discovery of Fuchs, and now he could also undermine the Rosenberg network, which was temporarily dormant but extremely effective. On top of this, Fuchs and Rosenberg, two extraordinary agents, were being exposed only because of a very young manual laborer who was providing low-grade information and had not been tested as a secret operative.

The second mistake was even more glaring and was, in fact, a made-to-measure piece of evidence against Rosenberg: the password itself. Since it was an entirely conventional phrase, they could have used something like: "I come from Chiang Kai-shek." But no, Gold was instructed to use Rosenberg's real first name, which was quite uncommon: Julius!

The liaison agent went to the Greenglass house at 209 North High Street in Albuquerque on June 1, 1945. The couple was finishing breakfast. Guss said the password, "I come from Julius." Both sides of the Jello box fit perfectly. That afternoon David handed the courier an envelope containing other lens drawings and explanatory notes, as well as a list of potential recruits for Soviet intelligence. Greenglass received an envelope with $500 that he left with Ruth. In September 1945, David returned to New York on leave. He gave Julius a sketch of the implosion bomb and about twelve pages of descriptive material and two lists: one was a list of the scientists working at Los Alamos and the other of those persons who could eventually be recruited. Rosenberg congratulated him and gave him $200. That was the extent of David Greenglass' collaboration with Soviet espionage. Compared to the crucial information passed on by eminent scientists such as Fuchs, his contribution as an agent was minimal. But the consequences were to be disastrous.

33

The Rosenberg case remains one of the most tragic in the history of the postwar years. The dramatic events of the case obscured the question of whether a real spy network even existed. The FBI supported its evidence by attempting to show that there had been a conspiracy, but mistakes made by the investigators produced vast inconsistencies and an absence of logic in the charges to such an extent that world opinion scarcely believed the government's case and considered the entire matter to be a setup by U.S. counterespionage and the judicial system.

To this day as well, Russian authorities, the SVR in particular, persist in not recognizing the very existence of the Rosenberg network. The principle that is being applied, to neither confirm nor deny, is a good one because it allows the private lives of former agents to be kept secret. But it also prevents any discussion about the destruction of the Rosenberg network, one of Soviet espionage's greatest failures.

The human tragedy I was involved in had its heroes, its innocent victims, and its villains, all of whom were to be crushed by the mill of history. When dominoes are lined up, the first one to fall draws all the others with it. That is exactly what happened: the disintegration of this secret network was the result of many betrayals, large and small. The path from Igor Guzenko and Elizabeth

Bentley led to Harry Gold. Among those he accused was a weak link, the Greenglass couple. The cowardly behavior of these despicable individuals was enough to destroy two wonderful persons and cause so much harm and anguish to their companions.

At the time the case began to unravel I was working on political intelligence within the British section and was not authorized to take part in the Center's attempts to save the Rosenberg network. Furthermore, because of the "need to know" rules, I had no access to information that didn't concern me directly. Following my long conversation with Yatskov, who obviously needed to unburden himself that day in May, the only thing I could do was to try and pluck some tidbits while we had lunch in the dining room. Only many years later would I be allowed to work in the classified archives, to question Anatoly and Kvasnikov quietly, while we were having a drink, read official publications and books that gave the true facts. This is why I can now reconstruct the chain of events leading to this tragedy.

Less than two weeks following Yatskov's unsolicited confession, the bad premonition of the 10th department—which I shared by now—became reality. On May 23, 1950 the FBI arrested Harry Gold. Disaster was now at hand. All those involved at the Center agreed that we should take strong measures to save our agents. But what could be done? And how much of a chance did they have while a wave of anti-Communist espionage hysteria engulfed the United States? If our plans failed it could make our friends' already complicated situation even worse. The adage "success breeds success and failure, failure" was particularly appropriate. Uncertainty and anxiety had a paralyzing effect. In America the arrests were following each other at dizzying speed. According to the newspapers all those indicted were immediately being labeled "red spies" and "members of the atomic spy ring," without even the semblance of the presumption of innocence.

The second person to be caught was Alfred Dean Slack, arrested in Syracuse, New York, on June 15. He was a foreman in a paint factory and accused of passing secret information on explosives manufacturing to Harry Gold in 1943-1944. His case had nothing to do with atomic espionage or the Rosenberg case. I personally had never heard of that agent and, in spite of his cooperation with the FBI, Slack was sentenced to fifteen years on September 22, 1950.

The next arrest came on June 16, 1950 and produced the chain reaction. The young man was David Greenglass, who was only 28 at the time, and didn't appear to realize the seriousness of the case that was destroying one of the best Soviet intelligence networks. It's difficult to say at what point he was fingered by Gold. It was obvious, though, that the FBI had kept Greenglass under surveillance for weeks before arresting him. The information gathered by bugging his phone and listening in on conversations among his friends quickly convinced Federal agents that Greenglass was in a state of panic. Two agents paid Greenglass a visit in January or February 1950. We may conclude that Gold had given his name at the end of 1949.

The Center had planned to get Greenglass out of the country at the beginning of 1950, long before Gold was arrested. However, that operation became impossible because, just like Gold, Greenglass didn't want to leave the United States. In February 1950, right after the arrest of Klaus Fuchs, Julius Rosenberg told his brother-in-law that Harry Gold, the man who had come to see him in Albuquerque, could also be arrested and that David should agree to go overseas. Greenglass would later claim he couldn't remember the conversation very well, and that it had not made an impression on him. Yet that same month, the FBI would question him for the first time. Once Gold was officially arrested on May 23, 1950, the New York Rezidentura was ordered to evacuate the weak link in the chain and Julius Rosenberg was given that task.

I had put Julius on ice just before leaving New York in September 1946. He was reactivated during the second half of 1948. His new case officer, Gavriil Panchenko, gave him the necessary funds and instructions to help David Greenglass escape. Greenglass was to get a tourist pass for Mexico. That document, which was not a passport, would allow him to cross the U.S. border into Mexico legally but would not allow traveling to another country. The issuance of a real passport took time and a man under suspicion of espionage would never have been able to get one.

Mexico was no guarantee of safety. The local police cooperated very closely with the FBI, which had broad freedom of action inside that country. That was why, once in Mexico, Greenglass was to write a neutral letter to the embassy of the USSR; for instance, praising the Soviet attitude at the United Nations. The signature "I. Jackson" would be the signal that he was inside Mexico. The meeting would then take place three days after the date of the letter, in front of the statue of Columbus. David was to admire the statue, with his middle finger slipped into the pages of a guidebook. A man would approach him, to whom he would say: "What a beautiful statue! I'm from Oklahoma and I've never seen such a beautiful statue before." The man would hand him a passport that would allow David to go to Switzerland. The next stop would be Prague, where Greenglass was to write to the embassy of the USSR announcing his arrival. Rosenberg gave him $1,000 and later another $4,000. But apparently his brother-in-law couldn't leave, or possibly didn't want to.

David Greenglass appeared unconcerned on the day of his arrest, June 16, 1950 and some newsmen noticed him even joking with the FBI agents. Turning to the reporters, he said with some arrogance, "I thought the United States was being very negligent in not giving Russia the information on the atomic bomb. They were our allies, after all." Bravado? Or was this part of an FBI scenario for him to send a message from the start? Something like: "It was atomic espionage after all, guys!" Had he, like Gold, already admitted to everything before his official arrest? Or did he break down shortly after? All we could do was pray that David Greenglass wouldn't betray his brother-in-law Julius Rosenberg. After all, he could also say he was being handled directly by a Soviet citizen, someone like "John" or "Sam." But that was like grabbing at straws.

All those belonging to the Rosenberg network knew that their days of freedom were numbered, but they didn't all react in the same manner. Some panicked, while others remained strong and kept their wits, but unfortunately, none of these reactions was enough to save them. The first one to crack under tension and try to make a run for it was Morton Sobell. He took off for Mexico on June 21, 1950 with his wife, without warning Rosenberg or the Rezidentura. Unfortunately, once he got there he was unable to get Soviet intelligence to effectively help him. In Mexico he could have contacted the Czech, Bulgarian, or Polish embassies, which were not subject to the same stringent surveillance of the Soviet embassy, but Morty did the one thing he should have avoided and contacted the embassy of the USSR. Since he hadn't informed anyone at the New York Rezidentura, the Mexico City Rezidentura didn't know anything about him. They needed time to check out his story at the Center. The Soviet embassy was under surveillance both by the Mexican police and the FBI. Sobell was followed as soon as he left the embassy and then arrested in Mexico on August 18, extradited to the United States and arraigned on the 23rd.

William Perl was still living in Cleveland where he had been kept dormant. Amid the hysteria of the times it was inconceivable to send a Soviet citizen to Cleveland to help him leave the country. Who, then, could possibly fulfill the mission? The underground network was disintegrating and every new contact could trigger new arrests. Yet time was of the essence and the PGU had to take some risks. Even though he had been hibernating for four years, Perl had been a very important agent and it was a moral duty to save him. My colleagues thought of using Vivian Glassman, a friend of Joel Barr. Perl had met her some time before in New York, when Barr, Perl, Sarant and the Rosenbergs would often see each other. Vivian was married. Even though she made no secret of her progressive views she was not at all connected to our Service. Perhaps she was even in the dark concerning her former lover Joel Barr and his activities. On July 21, 1950 one of our agents paid her a visit and asked her to undertake an important mission: go to Cleveland, contact Perl and warn him that he could be arrested, hand him $2,000 and detailed instructions to arrange his escape to Mexico.

Glassman had no prior record, had never been watched or questioned by the FBI, and therefore was not exposed to too many risks. But in the midst of a witch hunt you had to be very tough to accept such an assignment. Even though Perl's home may have been watched, our agent went there and fulfilled her mission apparently without a hitch. Yet the plan to evacuate Perl turned out to be a failure. The U.S. Communist Party was, at the time, completely infiltrated by the FBI. It was established later that, in some cells, one of every two or three members was an informer. Even the Child brothers, members of the Political Committee, were working for the FBI. Under those conditions no one trusted anyone else. William Perl had noticed that he was being watched for some time, and mistook the messenger for a provocation. He not only kicked her out but also promised to inform the FBI, and did so after consulting his lawyer.

On July 27, Vivian Glassman related her failure to another one of our operations officers and returned the money. To try to warn Perl again was meaningless. That brave woman was fortunate enough to avoid any further problems and was not even cited as a witness. Perl's arrest took place in March 1951, during the Rosenberg-Sobell trial. The FBI was unable to prove any espionage activity, and indicted him for perjury, he denied ever having met Julius Rosenberg, Morton Sobell, Helen Elitcher, and the Sidoroviches. During his trial on May 18, 1953, it was proved that he had known his classmates at CCNY but not Helen Elitcher or the Sidoroviches; he was sentenced to five years in prison. The Sidoroviches were picked up by the FBI as soon as Julius Rosenberg was arrested. In front of a grand jury Ann denied having seen David Greenglass in January 1945 or having ever met him; she only admitted having seen Ruth Greenglass very quickly. Without evidence, the couple was not prosecuted but would remain under surveillance for many years.

The main task from the Center's point of view was to get the key members of the network out, namely Julius Rosenberg and his family. To my knowledge ad hoc instructions reached the Rezidentura, but somewhat late. All necessary documents were ready. Gavriil Panchenko, Julius' case officer, had an urgent meeting with him, telling him to leave the United States as soon as possible. Rosenberg refused; he felt he couldn't leave his sister-in-law, Ruth Greenglass, by herself. She had been hospitalized because of burns to her body and was pregnant. We shall see later how Ruth was to repay that kind of thoughtfulness. Julius was arrested on July 17,

1950. His apartment was carefully searched but no one showed Ethel a search warrant. Federal agents even leafed, one page at a time, through three issues of *Parents* magazine. On July 29 it would be Harry Gold's former employer Abraham Brothman's turn, along with Miriam Moskowitz, his associate and mistress, to go behind bars. Neither one had anything to do with atomic espionage nor even with the Rosenberg network. Brothman, code named "Konstruktor" and subsequently "Expert," had worked with the INO but had only provided the results of his own research, which had no military value. His escape had not even been contemplated. As for Miriam Moskowitz, while she knew of her lover's secret activities, she had taken no part in them.

On August 11, less than one month after her husband's arrest, Ethel Rosenberg was arrested as she was leaving a grand jury hearing. She was not even allowed to return home to take care of her two young children and find them a place to stay. On the 17th she was accused of conspiracy to secure information relating to national defense for the USSR. On the same day the same charges were issued against former vice-consul of the USSR Anatoly Yakovlev, in absentia. The next day the FBI announced the arrest of Morton Sobell in Mexico.

The PGU was only able to secure the escape of two members of the Rosenberg network: Joel Barr and Alfred Sarant, my two Bach music lovers. Barr had actually been out of danger for some time. Since he was afraid of becoming unemployed, I advised him toward the end of the war not to wait to be fired but to resign and finish his studies at Columbia University. It would be much better for his resume. Soviet intelligence would pay for his tuition and give him a small monthly allowance of $50 to $70, which he accepted. He got his doctorate in September 1946 and found a job at Sperry Gyroscope, a company under contract with the Pentagon to make intercontinental missiles and atomic explosives. Barr needed security clearance. Despite his reputation as a brilliant scientist, his request was rejected because of his progressive positions in the past.

Barr was out of work by October 1947. He was 32 years old and his chances of securing a job commensurate with his qualifications after such a rejection were basically nil. His love of music took over and since at his age he couldn't hope to become a pianist, he wanted to be a composer. Joel told his new Soviet case officer—who was actually only a contact, since he no longer produced any information—that he wanted to go to Europe. Even for Soviet intelligence the change in its agent's life was not very attractive, the rule was to help all important sources in their enterprises and to thank them for what they had done in the past. Furthermore, Barr could also become an excellent illegal in the future. His case officer approved his plan. Out of caution, Joel first went to Belgium, but his destination was Paris. He began by learning to play the piano very well, but he didn't want to go to the Conservatoire because he had his own theory and system. In six months he learned the piano without doing scales, which he hated. He became a pupil of Olivier Messiaen, the famous composer and teacher. The very talented Barr quickly made many friends within international artistic circles. The PGU paid for his studies in Paris just as it had done at Columbia University, in New York.

Naturally, Barr was in contact with an officer at the Paris Rezidentura. After the arrest of Gold and David Greenglass, it became clear that he was running the risk of being arrested as well.[76] An escape route was set up. Czechoslovakia was at that time a hub between Western and Eastern Europe. Easily accessible to Westerners, the country was firmly part of the Socialist bloc. His case officer advised him not to request a visa in France since it was a NATO member and an ally of the United States. Barr went to Switzerland, obtained a visa, and on June 22 arrived by train in Prague. He was now safe.

At the end of the war his friend Alfred Sarant didn't need to finish his studies. After V-J Day he worked in the physics lab in a school and in 1946 he married Louise Ross. They quickly had two children. At the end of the year they became friends with another young couple, Weldon Bruce Dayton, a physicist specializing in cosmic rays, and his wife Dorothy Carol. The Daytons also had two children who were about the same age as the Sarants'.

During the spring of 1947 Dayton bought some land in Ithaca, New York, to build a house. The Sarants liked the place and also bought a small lot nearby. The Daytons finished the construction first and invited their friends to stay with them while they waited for the other house to be completed. This communal life lasted for one year and didn't dampen the friendship between the two families. Despite having been laid off at the end of the war Sarant, tinkered here and there and made enough money. He worked mostly as a house painter. His marriage however, was not a happy one. In search of affection, Alfred had an affair with Dayton's wife. Since she had two first names, Dorothy and Carol, each of the two men called her by a different name: for the husband she was Dorothy, and for the lover, Carol. Dayton knew his wife was cheating on him but didn't react. He was working on his doctorate and longed for peace and quiet.

This outwardly correct but strangely racy lifestyle was to be shattered on July 18, 1950. The FBI visited Sarant the day after the arrest of Julius Rosenberg. He was questioned for hours during the following days about his membership in the Communist Party and his friends Barr and Rosenberg. The FBI wanted him to admit to his collaboration with the Soviets and the fact that the apartment he'd rented at 65 Morton Street in Greenwich Village was being used for espionage purposes. Sarant denied everything. He felt the FBI didn't have a strong case against him, but the FBI was hoping to wear him down. Alfred was under stress and unable to sleep, exhausted by a long week of questioning and searches.

The Rezidentura had a hard time contacting Sarant at Ithaca to plan his escape. Furthermore, most of the officers were no longer go-getters like Yatskov or myself, and were thinking more of their own status than about their responsibilities. Those who had graduated from the prestigious Moscow Institute of International Relations were following two career paths: one within the MGB and the other in the MID. They hesitated in taking too many risks. If they were arrested and declared persona non grata they could forget about a career in diplomacy or intelligence. Therefore, our agent had to fend for himself. His arrest could come at any time and if he wished to avoid it he had to escape.

Late in the evening on July 25, after having put their children to bed, both the Daytons and the Sarants went out for a walk. Out in the open counterespionage agents wouldn't be able to eavesdrop on their conversation. Sarant explained his plan to his friends. Even though he'd been told to remain in Ithaca, he'd been given permission to spend a week in New York to visit his sister who was ill. He would have to check in with the local FBI office. Once he had done that, he would take advantage of the "leave" he'd been given to drive to Mexico. The Daytons approved the project. Weldon pointed out that to reach the Mexican border, some 2,000 miles away, Alfred would need to sleep several times. That was dangerous and he ran the risk of being arrested. Someone would have to alternate the driving with him. Weldon had to complete his dissertation and Louise didn't know how to drive. That left Dorothy Carol. The two lovers looked at each other incredulously. Weldon was giving them the opportunity to be together, even though he clearly told his wife not to accompany Alfred beyond the Mexican border.

Dorothy told the neighbors she was driving to Boston to visit a friend for a few days. The next day Alfred drove to New York City in his Dodge and on the following day, after making sure he had not been followed, he met with his mistress in a safe place before they both began the drive south. Dorothy had relatives in Tucson, Arizona. If the police stopped them they could always claim they were attempting to get away from a jealous husband. They drove day and night, in relays at the wheel. They were lucky and crossed the border into Mexico without a hitch.

I always thought Sarant was one of the more intelligent members of the Rosenberg network. Once he reached Mexico and knowing that the FBI was looking for him, he made no attempt to contact the Soviet embassy. He and Dorothy went to the Polish embassy and were lucky enough to meet an intelligence officer who, beyond helping them solve their problems, also told them not to come back there but gave them an appointment on a bench in a small park. The couple would have to be there at 3 p.m., five days hence. A Polish diplomat would contact them. If he didn't show up, the two fugitives were to return to that same bench at the same time every day without attempting to set foot in the embassy again.

Alfred told me later that when he shook hands with the Polish officer he felt he could rely on him.

That was exactly what happened. The same day the diplomat sent a cable to Warsaw. His superiors relayed the information to Moscow, where Yatskov and Kvasnikov were happy to learn that one of our men had succeeded in escaping the FBI dragnet. But Sarant was still far from being safe. The PGU asked the Poles to help convey the fugitives to the USSR. On the given day they waited at the bench but no one came. The next day they had a hard time waiting patiently for 3 p.m. to go back to the little park. They waited for over an hour pretending to enjoy the sunshine but no one approached them. Dorothy was becoming nervous. Perhaps they should try something else? But Alfred knew that losing one's nerve could lead to disaster. One week after their visit to the Polish embassy they were still on their bench, eating an ice cream and trying to make small talk. Finally a man approached the bench. He had blond hair and wore a suit but no tie.

"You can bet it's not for us," said Dorothy, to ward off bad luck.

"Obviously not," said Alfred who was playing the same game.

Yet, even before the man sat down on the bench, Alfred felt that their troubles were over. He sat a few feet from Sarant, opened a newspaper and began reading. The two lovers looked at each other in desperation. Then suddenly the man said:

"Are you Alfred Sarant?"

"Yes."

"I'm Winter. I work at the Polish embassy."

Alfred and Dorothy had to hide in Mexico for six long months. The couple had entered the country with a tourist pass that wouldn't allow them to travel to another country. They needed real passports, which took time, and they had to allow things to quiet down. The atomic spy case was all over the press, not just in the United States but also in Latin America. Borders were being closely watched and the local police were helping the FBI. The identities of passengers on all ocean liners were being carefully scrutinized. Sarant and his girlfriend modified their appearance as much as possible: a beard, a change in hair color, a different hairdo. Once they were completely unrecognizable they were given the passports of another country. One night they secretly crossed the border into Guatemala. From Central America they took a ship to Morocco and from there to Spain. They would feel secure only once they reached Warsaw. In the Soviet Union the couple was sent on vacation for six weeks. The most important thing was to allow them to relax and recover from the ordeal they had been through. There would always be time enough to think about the future.

We shall see later how useful the rescue of Barr and Sarant was to be for the USSR. Both men were to have long and productive lives ahead of them, but for their friends back in the United States the ordeal was just beginning.

34

T he trial of "the United States vs. Rosenberg et al." opened in New York Federal Court on March 6, 1951. The "et al." in the case were Morton Sobell and Alexander Yakovlev, who were being tried in absentia. The only useful function of the trial was to confirm a verdict that had been decided well in advance. Two key elements must be considered to understand the reasons that led the jury to swallow such a potpourri of lies.

The first was the Korean War, which began on June 24, 1950, allowing President Truman to whip up a new wave of patriotic feeling. After its tough fight against the deadly Nazi menace, America was forced to defend itself against the second sworn enemy of Western democracy: Communism. The Communist system had successfully broken the American nuclear monopoly, accelerated the disintegration of the colonial system and seized power in the most populous country in the world, China. The defeats of the first few months of fighting in Korea exacerbated the feeling that the poisonous inroads of Marxist-Leninist ideology must be eradicated everywhere, including in the United States, if the country was to avoid losing another battle.

The second element within this context appeared in February 1950. An obscure senator from Wisconsin named Joseph R. McCarthy stirred up anti-Communist hatred like a virus reaching epidemic proportions. For many years that citadel of pragmatic thinking and lucidity that was America became a country in the grip of uncontrollable hysteria. The mere fact of being, or having been, a Communist, was a crime, not to mention engaging in any activities favorable to the Soviet Union. Right-wing Hearst newspaper columnist Westbrook Pegler even wrote:

> The only sensible and courageous way to deal with Communists in our midst is to make membership in Communist organizations or covert subsidies a capital offense and shoot or otherwise put to death all persons convicted of such.*

Long before the trial began, American society in general, and the jury most notably, was convinced that the Rosenbergs were guilty of "the most heinous crime in the history of this country." The accumulation of evidence forged by the FBI, which would have been rejected a thousand times by an objective and detached jury, appeared rock solid to a country in the grip of such fever.

For the second time in one year some of my agents were being put on trial. I followed the proceedings of the Rosenberg and Sobell case from Moscow with a deep sense of dread. It was very clear that the verdict would not be as moderate as the one handed down to Klaus Fuchs at the Old Bailey. Furthermore, among the accused at risk of being sentenced to the electric chair was someone I considered a dear friend, Julius Rosenberg, and an innocent woman, his wife Ethel. In the morning on my way to the office, I would read the account of the previous day's hearings that the TASS news agency prepared for the Soviet press. Then I'd go to see Yatskov. Anatoly was just as affected as I was and he showed me confidential documents he had access to. Then we would exchange some ideas on the latest developments. Yatskov couldn't give me too much of his time. An internal investigation had begun within the PGU following Gold's arrest, to identify those responsible for the collapse of our American networks. The investigation was still in

---

* Schneir, op.cit. p.78 [NDT]

progress. On top of their daily duties, Yatskov and Kvasnikov were constantly writing up reports and making depositions to shed light on one detail or another. They would leave the office after midnight, just in time for the last subway train.

In New York the much-heralded "triumph of justice" was now becoming a tragic farce. Instead of the hundreds of witnesses who had been promised (including top-level people such as J. Robert Oppenheimer, George Kistiakowski, or Harold Urey) and hundreds of pieces of evidence that had been announced by prosecutor Irving Saypol, all the prosecution could produce one week before the trial was a handful of incriminating witnesses, all of them broken by the FBI or testifying with the promise of immunity, who were really nothing but hostages.

Saypol began by promising to prove that the Rosenbergs had set up, with the help of Soviet intelligence officers, a covert spy network which, thanks to David Greenglass, had allowed the secrets of the atomic bomb, a weapon vital to the survival of the United States and the free world, to be stolen.

The prosecution then attempted to prove that Morton Sobell was part of the conspiracy. The only witness was Max Elitcher, the former classmate of Morton Sobell and Julius Rosenberg, whom they had failed to enlist to work for the INO.[77] Even though we had decided to drop any attempt at recruiting him, Elitcher knew enough about his friends' activities, and besides, he happened to be a weak person. According to FBI agent Robert Lamphere, simple pressure had broken him. He was open to being charged with perjury when he denied his past Communist associations in 1946. Later on it was established that Elitcher's lawyer, O. John Rogge, had struck a deal with the prosecution. Saypol would drop perjury charges in exchange for Elitcher's testimony against Sobell and Julius Rosenberg. Elitcher told the court that Sobell, who was his only friend, had tried to get him involved in espionage activity and that he'd seen him going to a meeting with Rosenberg to hand him a spool of 35 millimeter film in 1948. Sobell had pled not guilty and denied these accusations, so that it was Elitcher's word against his.

Rogge, who was also defending David Greenglass, was clearly not only "negotiating" with the prosecution, which is common practice in the United States, but was also handling the accused for the FBI. Rogge was a well-known lawyer with an international reputation as a leftist, who often took civil liberties cases. He was active in the World Peace Council.[78] One day at the beginning of 1950 I met Ilya Ehrenburg who, like Rogge, was also on the Council's committee, at the Moscow apartment of the poet Alexei Surkov whom I knew since the rally at Earl's Court in London. The Soviet delegate was very much concerned by the attitude of the American delegate who was constantly obstructing every decision made by the movement. I am convinced that Rogge was a CIA penetration agent in the special section for international organizations under Tom Braden.

Rogge was probably working with the FBI in the United States, as is customary for agents of influence. Trial transcripts show on more than one occasion, the kind of secret activities Rogge was engaged in. For example, a few hours after his arrest, at 2 a.m., David Greenglass was allowed to call Louis Abel, the brother of his wife Ruth, to ask him to find a lawyer. But not just any lawyer! It had to be O. John Rogge. One might wonder how a simple mechanic such as Greenglass would even know the name. What could possibly lead him to think that such a well-known lawyer and a former deputy district attorney of the United States would defend an obscure individual accused of espionage for the USSR? Clearly, the answer appears to be that the FBI had suggested Rogge's name to Greenglass. When Louis Abel went to Rogge's office the next morning, the attorney sent one of his assistants to meet with David Greenglass. Personally, I have no doubt that there was collusion between Rogge and the FBI.

During the nine months preceding the trial, Rogge and a second lawyer, Herbert Fabricant, persuaded Elitcher and the Greenglasses to plead guilty and testify that the Rosenbergs were looking for people just like them, who were unstable enough to fall into their web. Actually it was to be these witnesses' defense that played a key role at the trial. Rogge, the man who brokered the deal between Elitcher and the Greenglasses and prompted his clients to lie, may be considered as one of the main movers in that deadly farce. The testimony of Ruth and David Greenglass was intended to demonstrate that Julius and Ethel Rosenberg had surreptitiously manipulated them into spying for the USSR. In previous chapters I have shown how Ruth, just like David, had freely agreed to help the Russians. Other documents, such as this excerpt of a cable decrypted by the Venona operation, whose authenticity has never been in question, will also confirm what I am stating:

> During his trip to Santa Fe, Kalibr [David Greenglass] told Ossa [Ruth Greenglass] that he agreed to provide information on Enormoz [the Manhattan Project]. He said he'd already been thinking about it. He said that security at Camp [Los Alamos] was taking every possible step to prevent information from reaching the Soviets and that the progressive thinking workers were upset about it. [...] Kalibr says that Oppenheimer and Kistiakowski are working at Camp right now. The latter is studying the thermodynamic process. *Document n. 37 of December 16, 1944. Anton [Kvasnikov] to Viktor [Fitin]*

David played innocent during the trial, testifying that he only found out about the atomic bomb being built at Los Alamos in November 1944 when Ruth went to see him at Albuquerque. He also described Julius as an expert in nuclear matters and the head of Soviet atomic espionage in the United States.

I, Alexander Feklisov, the case officer for Julius Rosenberg, have accurately described in this book the true role played by this extremely valuable agent and his precise contribution—which was very minor—in the Enormoz case. I have done so against the opinion of my superiors and even in defiance of the SVR's position. Thus, I have no reason whatsoever to distort the case at all. I can say that during my entire tour in the United States I had nothing to do with the gathering of information on the A-bomb and, consequently, I never spoke to Julius Rosenberg concerning the need to recruit agents for that specific purpose before September 1944 when his sister-in-law Ruth told him that her husband David was working at Los Alamos. Furthermore, Julius knew nothing about nuclear physics as the same Document n. 37 also indicates:

> Liberal [Rosenberg] recommends that an intelligence officer meet with Kalibr [David Greenglass] to ask him questions personally since he knows nothing about the problem. Let's ask for suggestions. Otherwise a questionnaire must be prepared for Liberal.

Clearly, Rosenberg was neither a specialist nor the head of an atomic network. As for the information provided by Greenglass, besides his notes and the list of his colleagues at Los Alamos, it was limited to three of the famous drawings of the explosive lenses, which Klaus Fuchs had also described to us around that same period. The Greenglass drawings were certainly not technical blueprints giving the size and dimensions or even just the proportions of the objects—but rather only childish sketches. One of them was attached to his first report which Julius gave me during our meeting in January 1945 and that I was able to look at before handing it over to Kvasnikov. It was a very rough drawing in a single dimension and without any specific proportion. Nevertheless, two prosecution experts, Walter Koski and John Derry (both former colleagues of Greenglass), manipulated by the prosecutor's questions, were able to agree that the three drawings—reproduced by the accused from memory for the trial—did allow experts to understand the working principle of the bomb.

As for the specialized witnesses who had been announced, physicists such as Robert Oppenheimer who had worked on the Manhattan Project, no one asked them to make an appearance, the prosecution having finally concluded that their testimony would probably be counterproductive and create even more doubts. Furthermore, when later on some important physicists examined the Greenglass drawings, they were to deny having any value. Philip Morrison said, "they were a rough caricature of the atomic bomb mechanism, full of mistakes without the necessary details to understand and reproduce it." Victor Weisskopf would speak of a "childish scribble without any value."

What was most impressive in the Greenglasses was that that infernal couple, following the guidelines set by the prosecution, was sending not just enemies or even strangers to the electric chair by their testimony, but their own closest relatives. At first David tried not to testify directly against his older sister, but once caught in the vise, he would accuse her without hesitation. His motivation was clear: between himself and his wife on one side and his brother-in-law and sister on the other, he had chosen what he cared for the most. Emanuel Bloch, counsel for the Rosenbergs, told the jury the witness was "repulsive, he can't stop chuckling and smiling":

"I wonder whether you have ever come across a man who comes round to bury his sister and smiles."

As I reread that sentence for the umpteenth time in the stenographic record of the trial, I remembered what Julius told me with such enthusiasm about his brother-in-law:

"I'd cut off my right hand if he lets us down!"

Libi was forever the idealist.

Two things didn't work in the deal struck between Rogge, the attorney for the Greenglasses, and the prosecution. The first problem was Ruth. She actually fit the profile of a suspect perfectly well: she had recruited her husband to work for the INO; she had agreed to be the contact with the courier who was to come to Albuquerque; she had brought the "password" and had taken the money Gold had given her. These facts alone were enough for her to be indicted as an accomplice. Yet the deal with the prosecution wasn't even for a lighter sentence because Ruth would obtain complete immunity for committing perjury.

The second problem was Ethel. She obviously shared Julius' ideals and was certainly aware of the fact that he worked for Soviet intelligence. However, she had never participated in his covert activities. The best proof is that she was never given a code name in secret cables with the Center (even Ruth Greenglass, despite her rather small contribution, had a code name: Ossa, the "Wasp"). The Venona files confirm this:

> Liberal [Julius Rosenberg] recommended the wife of his own wife's brother, Ruth Greenglass. *Document n. 25, September 21, 1944.*

Had Ethel been an agent she would have had her own pseudonym and it wouldn't have been necessary to use such a long sentence to identify her. *Dispatch n. 1657 [33]* of November 27, 1944 is even clearer:

Liberal has been married for the past five years to Ethel, twenty-five, a high school graduate, CP member since 1938, politically mature, she is aware of her husband's work and of the part played by Metr [Joel Barr] and Nil [unidentified in Venona] but she doesn't work herself due to poor health. A devoted person.

Since Julius Rosenberg was accused of having headed an atomic espionage network, his wife must have been involved—as far as the prosecution was concerned.[79] And so it was that someone as guilty as Ruth Greenglass would be set free while someone completely innocent, like Ethel Rosenberg, was convicted.

Ruth testified "like a gramophone record," as Rosenberg defense attorney Emanuel Bloch said. She had obviously memorized her testimony, which would replace any evidence against Ethel, for the simple reason that such evidence did not exist! According to Ruth, it was Ethel who had turned Julius into a spy and typed his espionage reports.

Other inventions caught the jury's imagination, such as the console equipped with an electric bulb built into a special drawer to microfilm documents when the lights were out in the room. His Soviet case officer was said to have provided Julius with the device to facilitate his work. Actually, I never would have thought of giving such a bulky and suspicious looking gift to any of my agents! Libi would photograph his material on a simple table with two lateral lamps by bolting his Leica camera to an enlargement tripod. Later on a receipt was produced, indicating that Julius had purchased the console at Macy's.

Besides the Greenglasses, the prosecution had another submissive collaborator in Harry Gold. His trial had already taken place on December 7, 1950 and he had been sentenced to thirty years in prison. Gold had not filed an appeal and was about to spend the rest of his life in jail. He was the key witness. All the Greenglasses could bring to the case, and they certainly didn't look like any great spies, was their meeting with Gold on June 3, 1945 in Albuquerque. Gold looked like an intelligence professional, which was why he was questioned for four consecutive days during the proceedings.

The problem was that he could only discuss the same incident. To get around this problem, the prosecution questioned him in great detail about his meetings with Klaus Fuchs and Anatoly Yakovlev (Yatskov). This additional information made the Rosenbergs appear to be at the center of a vast Communist conspiracy, and the theft of atomic secrets seemed plausible since, until then, it had only been tied to three childish drawings.

American historians Walter and Miriam Schneir were able to prove that Gold had been manipulated during the trial. The Schneirs consulted the stenographic record of Gold's confession to the FBI before his indictment and during the preparation of his own trial, as well as his meetings with his lawyer, John Hamilton. During his pretrial hearing Gold described his meeting with Yakovlev in New York in November 1945. Once the chemist reminded his case officer that Greenglass was due to arrive shortly on leave, Yakovlev's answer was unexpected: "Let's forget about him!" Gold concluded that the information provided by Greenglass was worthless and there was no need to risk another meeting with him. At the trial Gold would state that Yakovlev called the Greenglass production "excellent and very valuable." Walter and Miriam Schneir conclude that Gold had been carefully rehearsed for the trial and the FBI and prosecution had told him what to say.

Many newsmen covering the trial noticed that, strangely enough, no FBI agent was called to testify. Actually this was not an odd occurrence. The lawyers could have asked questions and the answers could have been unfavorable to the prosecution. For instance, what was the evidence of espionage activity against Ethel Rosenberg? Just one question of this kind could make the entire structure disintegrate. In another strange twist, Judge Kaufman and prosecutor Saypol insisted on questioning the Rosenbergs about their attitude toward Communism, their membership in the party and the fact that they read Communist newspapers such as *The Daily Worker*. That was the true purpose of this travesty of justice: to prove that Communist ideals were tantamount to treason toward one's country!

35

After hearing the witnesses, the court adjourned for a few days. Then, one by one, the accused were called in to testify. An America in the grip of McCarthyism was out for blood. The only way for the Rosenbergs and Sobell to save their lives was to go along with the situation and confess their collaboration with the USSR (which, at the time the facts in the case had taken place, was an ally of the United States), while rejecting at the same time the false accusations of atomic espionage. They refused to take that road. All three doggedly proclaimed their complete innocence.

Why? On one side of the scales some very hard facts made of flesh and blood were in the balance: their lives, the future of their children, who, in the case of the Rosenbergs, would become orphans. On the other side were abstract concepts: devotion to Communism, loyalty to their fighting comrades. Had they confessed they wouldn't have betrayed anyone: both Yatskov and myself were beyond the reach of American authorities. They would have only limited the damage. Why didn't they do it? I have only one plausible explanation and I am sure it's correct.

I was in a fog at the time Julius was arrested. I constantly felt a deadly weight on my head and in my heart. I would imagine endless conversations with my dear old Libi, with Morty and Ethel whom I had never seen. I would try to persuade them to confess and I thought of only one thing when I listened to their reasons, the sincere enthusiasm Julius would display in describing the struggle of the partisans who were fighting the enemy anonymously, out of uniform, knowing full well what was in store for them should they be captured. I remembered seeing him tighten his lips and nod his head to avoid showing his happiness upon hearing me say that he and his comrades were real partisans who were not fighting in the forests but were taking just as many risks and bringing our common victory closer to becoming reality. Julius was an unreconstructed idealist. Resistance fighters do not betray, even under torture, even though they might know they would be executed. He was the New York partisan and would not betray his Russian comrades. Both Ethel and Morty didn't want to betray Julius' trust and they followed his lead.

In his summation the Rosenbergs' defense attorney tried to prove that the evidence introduced had no legal value, since they were copies of the drawings of the lenses or of the Jello box, for instance, or intended to prove the Rosenberg's Communist sympathies by producing the box with the inscription, "Save a Spanish republican child. We shall return," in which Julius kept his coin collection or the petition for a Communist candidate, which Ethel had signed in 1939. The prosecution's entire case was based on the testimony of three witnesses who were hostages of the FBI: David and Ruth Greenglass and Harry Gold. How credible could a man be if he chuckled and smiled while he pushed his own sister into the electric chair; or a woman who had memorized her testimony like a robot; or an inveterate liar? Emanuel Bloch gave his summation by appealing to the jury:

> ...if you will decide this case the way you would decide an ordinary problem that comes up in your life...you will either come to the conclusion that these defendants are completely innocent, or at the very, very least that you would have a reasonable doubt about their guilt.[*]

---

[*] Schneir, op.cit. p.154

The summation by the prosecutor, contrary to the defense attorney who appealed to the common sense of the jurors, was full of high-sounding language to gloss over the absence of any real evidence. Saypol insisted that Julius Rosenberg and his accomplices had stolen from the United States "the most important scientific secrets humanity has ever had" and that "there were no words to fully express the monstrous nature of their crime." He didn't hesitate to repeat the crazy inventions of David Greenglass. For example, that besides information on the A-bomb, the Rosenbergs had passed on to the USSR information on a "sky platform" and the use of atomic energy for aviation. I have no problem denying these wild exaggerations that have not been repeated since that time. Saypol drew a somber picture of Ethel at her typewriter: "Every key was a shot against her own country in the interests of the Soviet Union." I can vouch for the fact that the first notes given by David Greenglass to Julius in January 1945 were handwritten. The second batch was also handwritten, in July 1945, and Gold had immediately handed it to Yatskov. Neither Julius nor Ethel had seen it at all! "Never have the accused deserved less compassion than those three," was the prosecutor's conclusion.

In giving his instructions to the jury before they deliberated, Judge Kaufman stressed, "The government says that the accused were able to steal the secrets of the atomic bomb." He reminded them that during the period in question, the USSR was the ally of the United States. The verdict was therefore decided in advance, and yet the jury was unable to reach a decision after eight hours of deliberation. The twelve jurors slept in the courthouse and resumed the next morning. On March 29, 1951 at 11 a.m. the foreman read the verdict: Julius Rosenberg, Ethel Rosenberg, and Morton Sobell were guilty as charged by a unanimous jury. The formula Judge Kaufmann had used—"the accused were able to steal the secrets of the atomic bomb"—was not included in the verdict; apparently some of the jurors were not convinced of that fact. The trial was then adjourned for a week.

Those were among the eight most difficult days of my life. When we would meet in the cafeteria or in the lobbies, Kvasnikov, Yatskov, Rayna, and others who worked at the 10th Department and myself would avoid speaking or even making eye contact. Despite the threat of capital punishment that the press was brandishing since the beginning of the trial, that possibility appeared less likely. The espionage law of 1917 had a maximum penalty of twenty years in prison, except in wartime when the punishment could be thirty years or even death. Yet since the law had been enacted no such sentence had ever been handed down. I remembered that during the war the FBI had caught groups of about twenty or thirty American pro-Nazi saboteurs. During the war these agents of Hitler were convicted of committing espionage for the Third Reich (and not some allied power) and had been sentenced to only up to ten years in prison! And yet all our hopes were to be dashed.

April 5, 1951 was the day of the final touch on the greatest travesty ever perpetrated by American justice. Judge Kaufman rejected the points made by the defense attorneys seeking to show violations of due process. Afterwards it was the prosecution's turn to speak. Irving Saypol explained that the Rosenbergs deserved to die because their actions had endangered the life and liberty of an entire generation of men and women. The USSR had started the war in Korea because it felt strong enough thanks to its A-bomb, and the Rosenbergs were responsible for the deaths of thousands of American soldiers.

The hypocritical nature of these grandiose declarations appears even greater today when we know that President Truman was considering dropping a third atomic bomb on the Chinese volunteers in Korea and to enact plans for a nuclear attack on the USSR by using the American stockpile of 300 atomic warheads. So who was really threatening an entire generation of human beings? It is thanks to scientists such as Klaus Fuchs, Alan Nunn May and others— but never because of the drawings provided by David Greenglass— that Soviet scientists were able to produce the atomic bomb. The brave actions of these men allowed us to end the atomic monopoly of the United States, without which President Truman could have brought his deadly plans to fruition, starting a third world war that would have jeopardized the lives of future generations. It is to the credit of the "atomic spies" that all this was avoided. But neither

Julius Rosenberg nor Morton Sobell could take any of that credit, despite all the help they gave to the USSR.

The Rosenbergs' defense attorney, Emanuel Bloch, pointed out that it was impossible to judge the accused according to the situation of the early 1950s rather than the one when the alleged crimes actually took place and the United States and the Soviet Union were allies. His clients could not be judged for the deaths of American soldiers in Korea. The only crime his clients were guilty of was having been sympathetic to the USSR during the war. As he handed down the sentence, Judge Kaufman said how painful this had been for him. He had even gone to synagogue to ask God for guidance. The truth was, as we were to discover later on, that he and Irving Saypol had taken advantage of the adjournment to consult with the highest authorities in the country and with President Truman himself. They would all ultimately demand the death penalty.[82]

Judge Kaufman tied the crimes the Rosenbergs were being accused of to their ideas and the fact that they were sympathetic to the Soviet Union. He stated that they had given the atomic bomb to the Russians, which had triggered Communist aggression in Korea resulting in over 50,000 American casualties. He added that, because of their treason, the Soviet Union was threatening America with an atomic attack and this made it necessary for the United States to spend enormous amounts of money to build underground bomb shelters. Judge Kaufman sentenced Julius and Ethel Rosenberg to the death penalty and Morton Sobell to thirty years in prison.[80] The execution was to take place during the week of May 21, 1951. The sentence drew horrified cries from the audience. We found out some time later that FBI director J. Edgar Hoover was against the death penalty for Ethel, reaching the conclusion that there was no proof against her, but Judge Kaufman followed the suggestions of much higher authorities.[81]

The fact that the trial had been a travesty became clear the very next day when David Greenglass was in court, under the same Judge Kaufman and prosecutor Saypol. There was no further talk of 50,000 American casualties in Korea, nor of billions of dollars in taxpayer money spent on civil defense by the United States. David Greenglass went from being the devil's advocate to the role of fallen angel. He had sinned but his contrition had made possible the dismantling of an espionage network and the punishment of those responsible. Therefore, Saypol had decided not to prosecute Ruth Greenglass and asked for only 15 years for her husband. Greenglass' defense attorney, O. John Rogge, didn't agree. He used the same arguments that had been indignantly rejected just a few days before in the same courtroom. The accused had committed his crime at a time when the American people felt deep respect for the brave Russians against Nazi Germany. The lawyer recalled that General Douglas MacArthur had sent a cable to congratulate the Red Army, that President Roosevelt in his speeches had nothing but praise for the USSR, and even the fact that the Bronx City Council had proclaimed February 23 "Red Army Day," a holiday! At that time people smarter than David Greenglass had not been content with just admiring the courage of Russians but had also seriously considered helping them. At that point Judge Kaufman lost his patience and replied that individuals couldn't decide the kind of help they should extend to Russia. Rogge then made another point: David Greenglass had been promised immunity if he cooperated with the court and three years in jail seemed like a reasonable price to pay.

It all looked like a bad joke. Liaison agents were to be executed, the recruiter would remain free and the main provider of secrets would only spend three years in jail? Even if the trial was a sham, there had to be limits! Judge Kaufman sentenced Greenglass to fifteen years in jail. Unhappy and feeling wronged, agent Kalibr stopped smiling. Ruth was crying. They had dishonored themselves, they had lied, and they did everything they could to send the sister and brother-in-law to the electric chair. That was how they were rewarded!

Even though I may be repeating myself or saying what appears obvious, I wish to sum up my impressions of the Rosenberg trial. The analysis by progressive thinking people all over the world of the legal farce—if a farce may indeed end with the hero's death—was based on the premise of the complete innocence of the Rosenbergs. In this book I am telling the truth because I consider that Julius Rosenberg's collaboration with Soviet intelligence was not something shameful or a crime that had to be hidden, but a heroic act. I had a close relationship with Julius and I know how the PGU viewed the matter. I have also spent much time reading documents and books about this case and thinking about all its elements. I feel this allows me to express my viewpoint, even though no one should feel obligated to accept it.

First of all, the entire trial had nothing to do with the law. It was a political trial. The real protagonists never appeared in court and, in fact, the Rosenbergs and Sobell were only scapegoats. The entire case could also have been called "Senator McCarthy vs. Communism."

The two sides in question were extremely uneven: on one side all the power of American institutions, the government, the courts, the Attorney General, the FBI, the official American information agency, the press and even President Truman himself, against three lone individuals on the other side, who sympathized with an ailing Communist Party. The case was also "The Powers That Be vs. Three Individuals."

The accused were singled out as evil incarnate, as though their punishment would stop the deaths of American soldiers in Korea, the threat of nuclear war with the USSR, the outlandish expenses for civil defense and other worries of that period of fear and instability. The jury, made up of simple Americans who were asked to decide the case, was subjected to those pressures. So the entire matter was also "Society vs. Three Renegades."

One must not forget how badly flawed the case was. From the start the accused were thought to be guilty and the trial was only to satisfy a sort of ritual. Instead of three equal parties, the defense, the prosecution and the judge, there was, de facto, an alliance between the judge and the prosecutor against the defense. No one can win by fighting a referee who is able to change the rules of the game at any time. Therefore, it was really "The Judiciary vs. Three Individuals Deprived of Their Right to Due Process."

On a different level which changes nothing to what was just stated, the guilt of the Rosenbergs and Sobell was never really proved: not the fact of having transmitted secret information to a foreign power, nor having stolen the secrets of the atomic bomb.

The most outrageous and tragic part was that, along with two men who had helped us out of idealism at a difficult time for all the inhabitants of this planet, there was also an innocent woman who was the mother of two children.

I offer the words of Andrei Sakharov, one of the fathers of the Soviet H-bomb, whose development benefited so much from the work of Soviet intelligence, who correctly characterized the irrational motivations of those who organized the trial: "The death penalty handed down to Julius Rosenberg was nothing but vengeance, a form of retribution by U.S. counterespionage following the Klaus Fuchs case."[82] Just like the Stalinist purge trials of the 1930s and so many other legal travesties the world over, the Rosenberg-Sobell case will remain a stain against a type of justice abused by the State that places public welfare ahead of any individual rights.

36

I t was the first time the death penalty had been applied according to the espionage law of 1917, and was not at all the inescap-
able punishment for any traitor as American propaganda was repeating, a form of outright blackmail. The only way to reverse
the trend in a case where U.S. justice had demonstrated its own
inconsistencies was the admission of guilt by the accused. By placing the Rosenbergs in front of a single choice, "Confess or die!",
the government thought it would win in any case. The Rosenbergs
would confess to their espionage activities and America could then
prove to an outraged world that it was in the right. The most unprecedented abuses of the trial would be instantly forgotten; the
prosecution would have only preached falsely to get the truth by
catching the criminals. The FBI could then embark on other investigations, solve new cases and better understand the adversary's
methods. But no one could have foreseen that the Rosenbergs
would continue to proclaim their innocence. This miscalculation
turned out to be disastrous, pushing American justice into a dead
end.

The Rosenberg defense, refusing to give up, filed no less than
twenty-six appeals in just two years, but the entire American judicial system seemed united in a conspiracy against the couple. Higher

courts kept on rejecting appeal requests. On February 25, 1952 the court of appeals admitted that procedural violations had taken place during the trial but did not recommend a new trial. "None of the accused has followed the path set by David Greenglass and Harry Gold," said Judge Kaufman. "Their lips remained sealed." It was a new message to the accused: if you confess, your lives shall be spared! But the Rosenbergs remained silent. On October 13, 1952, by an 8 to 1 vote, the Supreme Court refused to hear the case "because of insufficient cause to hear arguments." A few days later Judge Kaufman set the date of execution for the first week of January 1953. Meanwhile, Morton Sobell was transferred to Alcatraz to begin his 30-year sentence. Besides the final appeals entered by the defense, only protests from public opinion could stop the executioner.

A wave of indignation swept the world like a nuclear chain reaction when news of the Rosenbergs' death sentence was made public. The young American couple's tragedy upset millions of people throughout the world. In Rome, Paris, Geneva, Brussels, and Rio de Janeiro hundreds of thousands of progressive thinking people and honest citizens, outraged by the injustice being perpetrated, took to the streets to demonstrate and organize picket lines in front of American embassies. Protest movements were created in many countries with the active participation and support of eminent politicians, scientists, artists, and the clergy.

A flood of letters and cables reached the White House. The great physicists Albert Einstein and Harold Urey asked President Truman to pardon the couple. "After reading the account of the Rosenberg trial proceedings," wrote Harold Urey in *The New York Times*, "I can't overcome my doubts about the verdict." Pope Pius XII and ten cardinals also sent requests for a pardon to the White House, all to no avail! On January 20, 1953, as he left the presidency, Harry Truman passed the problem on to his successor, General Dwight D. Eisenhower, the supreme allied commander in World War II. Eisenhower's position on the matter repeated almost word for word what Judge Kaufman had said when he sentenced the Rosenbergs:

> The nature of the crime [committed by the Rosenbergs] in-
> volves the deliberate betrayal of the entire nation and could
> very well result in the deaths of many thousands of innocent
> citizens.[*]

The President couldn't be so naïve as to believe that the
Rosenbergs had passed on the secrets of the atomic bomb to the
Soviet Union. His refusal to grant a pardon was the final blow in
the dramatic battle waged by the American judicial system against
the condemned couple. Eisenhower would later admit in his memoirs that the main purpose was to get the Rosenbergs to confess. As
the time for execution drew nearer, the defense attorneys submitted a new petition to the court of appeals, providing new evidence
of violations of procedural rules and of the rights of the accused,
which took place during the trial. The court decided to grant a stay
of execution over the objections of the Department of Justice.
The Rosenberg defense was then able to take its case to the Supreme Court. On May 25, 1953, by a vote of 7 to 2, the Supreme
Court rejected a stay and the execution was set for 11 p.m. on June
17, 1953.

The blackmail of American justice and the failure of the defense lawyers didn't break the couple's will as they were being held
at the infamous Sing Sing penitentiary. "No one will be able to
separate us from one another, not separation nor the threat of
death," wrote Julius to his wife. "Our enemies shall not break us
and whatever the final result may be they shall see our victory."

The Rosenberg defense attorneys fought until the very end. On
June 6, eleven days before the date set for the execution, Emanuel
Bloch submitted new evidence to Judge Kaufman proving that
David Greenglass had lied. "The guilt of the accused has been
proven and new testimony will not reduce the strength of the proof
introduced by the prosecution," answered the judge. On June 11,
the district court of appeals confirmed that decision. The defense
also requested the Supreme Court grant a stay of execution to have
the time to submit a request for a new trial. On June 13, the highest
court rejected the request by a vote of 5 to 4 and went into recess

---

[*] Schneir, op. cit., p. 192.

until October. Once again every judicial angle had been attempted unsuccessfully. Only President Eisenhower could stop what was really legalized murder. Many American personalities, Nobel Prize winner Harold Urey among them, requested a meeting with the new man in the White House to try to convince him. Eisenhower agreed to meet with three protestant ministers and a rabbi representing the 23,000 members of religious orders who had signed petitions requesting a pardon. The innocence or guilt of the couple was no longer in question; all that was being asked was a simple act of clemency. But the President spoke of American casualties in the Korean War and the fact that the Rosenbergs had "done it for money."

In the meantime two legal experts, Fyke Farmer and Daniel Marshall, had decided to help Emanuel Bloch. On their own initiative they met with Supreme Court Justice William O. Douglas to make a legal point that could change the sentencing. The law of 1917 was in contradiction with the law on atomic secrets of 1946, stating that capital punishment had to be decided by the jury and not the judge. Justice Douglas was about to go on vacation and asked the two lawyers to quickly prepare a brief on the matter. The next day, June 17, Justice Douglas announced his decision to grant a stay of execution, concluding that "the Rosenbergs should be given the opportunity to raise this point in court." The defense attorneys would have three months to prepare a new appeal before the Supreme Court reconvened.

But they had not taken into account political decisions within the administration. On that same day Attorney General Herbert Brownell objected to Justice Douglas' ruling. In an unprecedented move, Chief Justice Fred Vinson called a special session of the Supreme Court to consider the Attorney General's request. Douglas found out about this on the radio; his colleagues, who had already left on vacation, had to return to Washington and one even had to come out of the hospital, where he was supposed to have minor surgery, in order to attend. During those terrible hours when he didn't know whether he would be executed or not, Julius wrote to his friend and lawyer Emanuel Bloch: "I'm not inclined to say good-bye because I think good deeds last forever. But I can say this: my love for life has never been greater because I have seen how beautiful the future could be. Because I feel that, in some small way, we have made a contribution in that direction, I think of my own sons and the millions of others who will benefit from it."

These words prove that after three years in jail, after having endured the inhuman torment of waiting for execution, Julius had remained fully in control of himself and was convinced he had acted correctly. I also see a veiled reference to the fact that, having helped the USSR fight the Nazis, he had built a peaceful future for his children and the generations to come. There was somewhat of a panic at the White House generated by the Supreme Court battle. Early in the morning the following day, President Eisenhower called a special cabinet meeting. Brownell used all his powers of persuasion to convince the President that a stay of execution was not called for. The prosecution, he said, "has proof of the guilt of the Rosenbergs but it can't be introduced in court."[83] The President of the United States did not take the trouble to check if the "proof" involved Ethel and atomic espionage.

"I am in a kind of half dreamy state," wrote Julius as he awaited the final decision of the Supreme Court. "Everything seems unreal and out of focus. It seems that we are not really here but very far away and that we see everything from there without being able to act in any way."

At noon on the 19th, by a vote of 6 to 3, the Court vacated the stay of execution. The sentence was to be carried out that same evening at 11 p.m. Emanuel Bloch, arguing that it was Friday and that the Sabbath began at sundown, asked the court to pick a different date. The court simply changed the hour to that same evening at 8 p.m. Once again only a Presidential pardon could save the Rosenbergs. Eisenhower had received over 200,000 pieces of mail and cables asking him to stop the execution. Yet one hour after the Supreme Court decision he rejected the plea for clemency. Julius and Ethel were allowed some time together. A phone was installed in their cell; if the couple chose to talk all they had to do was pick up the receiver. But the Rosenbergs had no intention of giving in. They were together and saw only their love.

A few minutes before the execution Ethel wrote a short note to Emanuel Bloch: "I leave my heart to all those who are dear to me—

I'm not alone—and I die 'with honor and dignity.' I know my husband and I will be vindicated by history."

At 7:32 p.m. the White House announced the rejection of the final plea for clemency on behalf of Ethel Rosenberg and 13 minutes later Judge Kaufman rejected a last request for a stay of execution filed by Daniel Marshall. At 8 p.m. exactly, Julius Rosenberg was taken to the execution chamber. Serious and concentrated like a man about to accomplish something important, he sat down on the electric chair by himself. At 8:06 p.m., without saying a single word or making a sound, he was dead. A few minutes later Ethel entered the same room, from which her husband's body had already been taken away. There was neither fear nor anxiety on her face; she looked calm and sweet. She kissed one of the matrons before sitting down on the electric chair. It was a kiss she was sending to her children, to her loved ones, and to life on earth. Ten minutes later she joined her husband in death. The Manhattan partisan and his faithful bride had held up until their final breath.

37

In January 1953, in the thick of the struggle to save the Rosenbergs, Nobel Prize laureate Harold Urey wrote to *The New York Times* to protest the verdict. He asked what men of goodwill the world over would think of the United States "if after executing the Rosenbergs it was proved that two innocents had been put to death while one guilty person went free," meaning Ruth Greenglass. The scientist continued, "Somewhere there is a representative of the USSR who knows the whole truth."

Yes, he was right! I am that "representative of the USSR." I am the last case officer of Julius Rosenberg still living and I know first-hand the truth that Russian authorities still persist in denying, and that is what keeps me from remaining silent. Long before I decided to speak, I have often asked myself whether Soviet intelligence did everything in its power to save its agent and his innocent wife, as well as lighten the burden for Morton Sobell. Unfortunately, the answer is by far not a positive one.

The fall of Klaus Fuchs, followed by the breakup of the Rosenberg network and the tragic death of our agent and his wife, created a traumatic shock inside Soviet intelligence. An internal investigation lasting several months began when Harry Gold was arrested on May 23, 1950. Agent Guss was to play a role in three different trials. In November 1950 he testified against Abraham

Brothman and Miriam Moskowitz; one month later he was put on trial himself; and in March 1951 he helped send the Rosenbergs to the electric chair. All the newsmen who covered these cases have noted the chemist's strange demeanor and behavior as well as his extraordinary submissiveness to the court. Some didn't hesitate to call him an "inveterate liar," others, like the lawyer for Brothman and Miriam Moskowitz, spoke of a "twisted and degenerate mind." After six months in jail and having lost forty pounds Gold looked like "a shrunken, underprivileged cat."* In my opinion that was the result of the treatment the FBI had subjected him to in addition to other "special methods." Judge Kaufman, who thought of himself as a specialist in Soviet espionage, was full of praise for the FBI: "Their work is truly surprising, especially on Mr. Gold. I think Mr. Hoover and the Bureau ought to be congratulated."

During his own trial on December 7, 1950, Gold was just as cooperative with the prosecution: he was pleading guilty and all his answers were invariably in the affirmative. His attorney, John Hamilton, even suggested a psychiatric examination, but Judge McGranery said that Gold had already been examined and that he was of sound mind. The accused showed no emotion when he heard the heavy 30-year sentence and it seems obvious that he knew in advance what it would be. The FBI had certainly threatened him with much worse for his part as the liaison agent for Klaus Fuchs, the greatest atomic spy of all. Gold didn't enter an appeal. His sentence was probably part of the deal worked out with counterespionage in order to save his own life in exchange for his unlimited cooperation at the Rosenberg trial. Gold carried out very carefully and obediently whatever his new masters at the FBI asked of him.

Harry Gold, I must reiterate, became associated with the Rosenberg network against the most elementary rule of compartmentalization. The instructions, which authorized this unacceptable infringement of procedure, along with the fateful password "I come from Julius," were ordered by the Center. Actually the word "Center" sounds much too impersonal, as though there was an anonymous office imparting orders, reprimands and congratula-

---

* *Time* magazine, quoted in Schneir, op. cit., p. 96.

tions. But that is only for appearance purposes; there were real people behind the unfortunate decision regarding Gold.

Many years later, when I was working in the PGU archives, I was able to look at Harry Gold's file. I had rarely seen such high praise for an agent. From Gaik Ovakimyan, who had recruited Gold in 1935 and had continued to be his case officer until he was declared persona non grata in 1941, to Semyon Semyonov, Gold's case officer from 1940 to 1943, both couldn't speak highly enough about the Philadelphia chemist. They were, in fact, so confident in their agent that they signed off on the instructions to send Gold to Albuquerque and on how he was to make contact with David Greenglass. Better still, at their recommendation, Harry Gold, who had transmitted the extremely valuable information he received from Klaus Fuchs to us between February 1944 and September 1945, had been decorated with the Red Star, a combat medal that very few intelligence officers were awarded at that time.

In my line of work, when someone says, "He's a guy you can count on," he's making a deeply held value judgment, good or bad as it may be. In the spring of 1953, because of mistakes having far-reaching consequences, Major-General Gaik Ovakimyan, deputy director of the intelligence service, and division head Semyon Semyonov were both fired and deprived of their pensions.

As far as I am concerned, I feel that the person who executes orders is also responsible for them. Kvasnikov, Yatskov and I discussed the demise of the Rosenberg network innumerable times! I could not believe that my colleagues could have made such gross mistakes.

"Those were the Center's instructions," said Kvasnikov defensively. "Even the password came from Moscow."

Yatskov was more inclined to agree with me. Every time we delved into the subject the furrows on his face would grow deeper and he would have a sorrowful look in his eyes.

"I'll never forgive myself," he would say. "It was so stupid! We should have objected and tried to change the Center's mind. It was so obvious! We lost the Rosenbergs and the others!"

We would fall silent for a while, each one of us trying to accept what had gone wrong. Anatoly died, feeling personally at fault.

I ask myself another, equally painful, question. Beyond the mistakes that had been committed, did we react properly once the damage had been done? Did the PGU and the Soviet Union take the necessary steps to save the Rosenbergs after their arrest? My answer remains negative. First of all, the service should have properly organized the couple's defense. Emanuel Bloch, as devoted as he may have been, didn't have the experience or the caliber required to take on the American judicial system. There was at the time an International Association of Democratic Jurists that included some of the best progressive legal minds, like its former President, Dennis Pritt, whom I had met in London, and was also President of the Association for Cultural Relations with the USSR. Pritt was an independent Member of Parliament and a member of the Royal Council of Lawyers. He had defended Georgy Dimitrov when he had been indicted for the Reichstag fire and would not have refused to defend the Rosenbergs, who were being accused of crimes they had never committed. His colleagues in many other countries—who spoke up for the couple on their own—would have done the same.

I am also convinced that my country should have taken a bold step, unprecedented but honest, which offered the only possibility of improving the chances of the accused. Toward the end of the trial, the USSR should have openly declared that Julius Rosenberg and Morton Sobell had passed on electronic secrets that were used in the struggle against Nazi Germany. The USSR should have divulged the kind information it received from David Greenglass through Harry Gold while rejecting vigorously the accusation that Julius Rosenberg was the head of the atomic espionage network in the United States. The truth is much stronger than the best-woven lie. Despite the damage that would have followed, by recognizing the collaboration of Rosenberg and Sobell and pointing out its true nature, the Soviet Union would have destroyed the scenario set up by the American justice system. It would have become impossible to say that Rosenberg and Sobell were the main culprits in America's loss of the atomic monopoly. For all men of goodwill, these two anti-fascists, who had helped Russia break the Nazi military machine which was threatening the entire world, could not appear as criminals opposed to the U.S. government.

Had the USSR, whose international prestige at that time was very high, taken such a position, it would have had the support of the People's Republic of China, the Socialist bloc, and the liberated former colonies, of innumerable left-wing parties and progressive organizations, such as the World Peace Congress, the World Trade Union Organization, the World Democratic Youth Organization, the Women's International Democratic Federation, etc. This broad international front, with the assistance of a world-renowned legal team, would have prevented the travesty of justice of the sentencing not of Communist spies but of anti-fascist activists. Even if such a campaign had yielded nothing more, the statement of the truth would certainly have prompted the accused to confess: the Rosenbergs would have saved their own lives and Sobell would have received a lighter sentence.

I am convinced that if Julius, Ethel and Morty decided to plead not guilty it was not just out of idealism and admiration for the resistance fighters who died under torture rather than betray their comrades. As faithful sympathizers of the Soviet cause, they understood that American reactionaries would have used their confession to strengthen anti-Soviet attacks and whip up anti-Communist hysteria. Had the USSR admitted that they had collaborated, they would have understood the message: "you are freed from your obligation to silence and secrecy." In the final analysis American justice was not seeking anything more.

Many readers may find these ideas unrealistic, but that is not the case. In Moscow the capture of Klaus Fuchs and the fall of the Rosenberg network had gone far beyond the internal worries of the PGU. Following the internal investigation that began in May 1950, the Politburo created a special commission in the summer of 1951 under the leadership of Lavrenti Beria. Its mission was to discover the reasons for this awful fiasco, find those responsible, and limit the damage. If Soviet intelligence had submitted such a suggestion to the commission, as outlandish as it may have appeared, it would certainly have been examined. Stalin was very appreciative of the contribution made by intelligence in the victory over the

Third Reich and towards the production of the atomic bomb. He would have relished this suggestion as a way of tripping up our American rivals. But, crushed by their own sense of guilt, feeling that the damage was irreparable and expecting the fulminations of the Kremlin, the intelligence leaders kept a low profile. Their attitude was one of subordination and ironclad discipline. The higher-ups would know what to do! Rather than offer advice, it was best to improve the quality of the work. As for Yatskov and myself, we were simply operatives whose advice was not sought in political matters.

In such a paralyzing atmosphere, the only thing left to do following the arrest of Rosenberg and Sobell was to find reasons for doing absolutely nothing. After all, American justice had always been true to the letter as well as the spirit of the law. Ethel's complete innocence would therefore stand out. If a man like Klaus Fuchs, who could be considered as someone who had really stolen atomic secrets, had only been sentenced to 14 years in prison, what should the sentence be for Julius Rosenberg, who had done practically nothing? It's always easy to be intelligent after the fact. If I'm telling this story it is for the benefit of those intelligence officers who are operating in the field today, so that they may draw a lesson from the Rosenberg tragedy. One should pull out all the stops to help our friends in danger. Fear, inertia, and that typically Russian fatalism just contributed to increasing the damage done.

At the end of the summer of 1996, I spent eight days in New York to take part in a documentary on the Rosenbergs. Manhattan had changed a lot. The three-story building on West 89th Street where I lived with Zina and little Natasha was still there but in a completely changed environment. A beautiful residential building has taken the place of the Consulate General of the USSR at 7 East 61st Street. I was unable to find any of the cafeterias Julius and I used to meet in. The cheap Childs restaurant chain has disappeared and a bank is now at the location once occupied by the Horn & Hardart cafeteria at the corner of Broadway and 38th Street where we exchanged our Christmas presents in 1944. The building where the Golden Fiddle restaurant used to be, at the corner of 77th Street and Broadway, where we had our final good-bye dinner, now houses a youth organization.

On a beautiful morning at the end of August, feeling quite emotional, I walked up to the Rosenbergs' building at 10 Monroe Street, near the Brooklyn Bridge. Some older women were sitting in the sun on the benches near the plants that were being watered by a handyman. We asked them if they had known the Rosenbergs.

"We sure did!" answered two rather old women. "That was their entrance. Ethel would come down every day to take her boys out. We would talk very often, nothing special, just conversation among neighbors. We saw the FBI agents take her away the day she was arrested."

They were asked to describe her further.

"Don't ask me any more," said one of the women. "I'm going to cry."

She got up, holding on to a cane, and walked back into the building. Her neighbor told us in low, emotional voice:

"Ethel was a good mother and a very friendly, simple woman. They never stole any atomic bombs. They were killed for nothing. They were innocent."

Since I was retired and had nothing to hide, I was able to go and pay my respects at the cemetery where my friend and his wife were buried. On Labor Day, September 2, we went to Pine Lawn, near Farmingdale on Long Island. Since it was a holiday, the office of the Jewish cemetery of Wellwood was closed. We looked for a long time; the grave seemed exactly like all the others around it, covered only by a square stone and the name "Rosenberg" in a black frame. A little bush was sculpted in a rectangular shape in the center and it had two small inscriptions:

Ethel	Julius
Born: September 25, 1915	Born: May 12, 1918
Died: June 19, 1953	Died: June 19, 1953

I sat there for about a half hour or more. I remembered the many warm meetings with my dear Libi, how he laughed, and his lively sparkling eyes, full of intelligence. The Russian custom is to drop some earth taken from the front of your house on the grave of loved ones who are buried far away from where you live. Before coming to New York, I took two handfuls from under an apple tree on my dacha. I spread the earth in front of the two inscriptions with the names of my friends, then placed some red and white carnations, and bowed three times. I could have left, since my friends were waiting for me, but I felt something was missing, and I finally understood that there was a final ritual I had to go through. As a soldier honoring other soldiers, I stood at attention and said out loud, at the risk of sounding exaggerated:

"Julius and Ethel, here I am at your graves to pay my respects. You have helped us faithfully with devotion and bravery during the bloody war against our enemy, Nazi Germany. We shall be eternally grateful to you! Forgive us for not having known how to save your lives. May glory and peace be with you always!"

I hope they have found peace where they are now. Glory is something that exists on earth, and it is to give them their glory that I decided to awaken their memory.

38

What became of the survivors of this ordeal? Two of them, Joel Barr and Alfred Sarant, still had a full life ahead of them. As of June 22, 1950 Barr was safe in Czechoslovakia. He remained on the FBI's wanted list and even though he was out of reach, he was better off remaining anonymous. With the help of Czech intelligence, Barr acquired a new identity, he changed his name to Johan Burgh and became a citizen of the Union of South Africa. It was not just a distant country but a British dominion as well, without diplomatic representatives behind the "iron curtain," let alone an embassy. Barr was as unlikely to run into a real South African in the streets of Prague as meeting a Papuan native wearing traditional garb. His origins explained his European appearance, his knowledge of English and the fact that he didn't speak any Czech. The Afrikaans name in Czech became Josef Berg, which sounded very natural in Prague. As a final precaution, Joel took 18 months off his age by using his younger brother Arthur's birth date of October 7, 1917.

Berg was suddenly summoned to Moscow, without an explanation, at the beginning of 1951; he barely had time to throw some clothes and toiletries into a small suitcase. Once he checked into the Hotel Moskva, facing the Kremlin, he was greeted by a beaming Alfred Sarant and his girlfriend, Dorothy Carol Dayton. The

KGB had decided that it was best for the two friends to live and work at the same location. Since Barr already had a job in Prague, Sarant and Carol also went to Czechoslovakia.

It was not too hard to create a "legend" for Sarant, who was in the habit of changing names. His father had immigrated to the United States during the last century as Sarantopoulos, which was much too long and difficult for American ears; he became Sarant. Alfred had traveled to Moscow with a new identity: he was now Philip Staros, which sounded Greek enough to fit his looks and nothing like the name on the wanted lists. Staros was supposed to have been born in Greece and to have lived in Canada, which explained his excellent mastery of the English language.

The two Bach fans were to live in Czechoslovakia for five years. They were naturally very talented and after a few months they had mastered the Czech language well enough. Barr adapted and married a pretty Czech woman, Vera Bergova, who found out only some twenty years later that her husband was really an American from New York City. Barr and Sarant became the directors of a secret laboratory to develop military applications. They invented a machine that today we would call an analog computer, used to calculate the coordinates of enemy aircraft, their speed and direction and also made corrections according to wind direction changes. The computer allowed guidance of surface-to-air missiles by adjusting to the targets' flight patterns. The invention was very revolutionary for the time but had a rather important flaw; it was as big as a hotel room. For the system to operate usefully, its size had to be reduced many hundreds of times.

The Czechs were just as enthusiastic about this idea as its inventors, but the miniaturization of the components required enormous investments, the creation of new research centers and new production units. A whole new industry had to be created and Czechoslovakia was a small country without the resources to do it. In the summer of 1955 Barr and Sarant wrote to their Soviet comrades, and I was given the task of hearing out my excellent duo of the 1940s. I had been stationed in Prague for two years as the PGU representative to help our Czech comrades set up their foreign espionage department. I remember that we all met during a Western radio campaign. Voice of America, Radio Free Europe, the Deutsche Welle, were all calling on the populations of the Socialist countries to rise against the regime; the atmosphere was not conducive to feelings of joy and happiness.

I invited my former agents to a good restaurant. Barr came alone but Carol accompanied Sarant. It was the first time I was meeting the latter because in New York all his work came to me through Barr. He was a handsome southern European type, with black hair slicked back, bushy eyebrows, small mustache and swarthy complexion. His dark eyes were set very deep. I had seen pictures of him smiling and now he appeared dark and unhappy, just like Barr. They both gazed at me intensely. They were, in fact, very different types as I could observe during the meal. Alfred was not so tall, about five feet eight, well built, with broad shoulders full of Mediterranean exuberance. Joel Barr looked like an intellectual, over six feet tall, very thin and round-shouldered. He was losing his hair and this made his face look even longer, with his gray eyes behind his thin-rimmed glasses.

The conversation languished somewhat. I began with a toast to the memory of Julius and Ethel, saying that for Soviet intelligence and myself it was a great personal tragedy. We drank in silence and remained silent for some moments longer. Then we began eating. I attempted to cheer them up by asking questions. Sarant was the one answering. They liked their life in Prague and had no material problems; their Czech colleagues were friendly but they felt professionally stifled. The objectives they had set for themselves—which they could reasonably achieve—were very promising but were far beyond the capabilities of Czechoslovakia as a country. They wanted to build compact computers for military purposes but only the Soviet Union could provide the necessary funds to make headway in this area. Barr and Sarant wanted to work in the USSR.

It would be the last time I was to see my agents but I did my best to help them out. A few months later, toward the end of 1955, the Bergs and the Staros' moved to Moscow. Alfred and Carol already had two children; Joel and Vera had the first of the four children they were to have together. Their new life required a new legend. From now on they were to be Czech citizens! In Russia they needed to add a patronymic to their regular names. The words for Mr. and Mrs.—*gospodin* (Mr.) and *gospoja* (Mrs.)—had not been used since the Revolution, and to name someone by his or her family name proceeded by "comrade"—comrade Staros or comrade Berg—would sound much too official.[84] The father's name was used; Barr's father was Benjamin so he became Iosif Veniaminovich Berg. Sarant became Philip Georgiyevich Staros and Carol was now Anna Petrovna. Unlike her husband, she never managed to speak Russian properly. However, according to Joel Barr and many other people who had dealings with him, Sarant was a genius. Not only did he learn to speak the language of his new country, he mastered it better than most native Russians. In the lab the Russians would ask him to check the spelling of a word or the punctuation of a sentence. Barr also spoke excellent Russian, but with a slight Brooklyn accent.

At first the two engineers were to undertake research for aircraft equipment and were part of the civil ministry responsible for aircraft creation and construction. Their superiors did not believe Barr and Sarant when they said that all the parts of their massive computer could be reduced hundreds of times. Those misunderstandings were full of potential conflicts and it became obvious that the two talented inventors would soon be working on their own. They were given their own lab whose name, LKB, was completely unknown outside the Soviet military-industrial complex. The abbreviation simply meant Leningrad Study Group. Since most military expenditures in the USSR were hidden within civilian budgets, the LKB officially came under the State Committee for Electronic Technology. Sarant, who was always the leader of the duo, was named head engineer of LKB with Barr as his deputy. They had few scientists working with them but the funding was large enough and, above all, they had complete freedom of action. Both couples were very happy to be in the more European city of Leningrad where there was a greater feeling of freedom in the air than in the capital.

Even the LKB was an exception. Like all "post office boxes," a euphemism for secret companies, personnel were under extremely stringent security measures, there were no contacts with foreigners, and clearance for secret documents was required. The two "Czechs" were given special exemptions. They didn't even have to sign a declaration not to divulge state secrets. Sometimes they would take part in international conferences using their new names. While having lunch with their families on Sundays at the Astoria Hotel they could even talk with tourists and American businessmen. These exceptions to the tough counterespionage regulations set by the KGB would astonish those who were not in the know. But how could we humiliate these aces of covert operations by being too suspicious?

Sarant and Barr were to have glamorous careers and be given the means to make their dreams come true. The Soviet personnel working with them were just as enthusiastic as they were. The first LKB computer turned out ten times smaller than similar Soviet machines, using less electrical power and functioning flawlessly. The miniaturization work continued and the expertise in the field of my two former agents continued to grow. Important persons, such as the President of the Academy of Sciences of the USSR, Mstislav Keldysh, or Dmitri Ustinov, First Vice Prime Minister for military industry, were regularly present in this cutting-edge laboratory for computer research. The lab's requests for space and personnel were immediately fulfilled without any problems and the results were spectacular. Even salaries were higher at LKB than at similar facilities. LKB's prestige reached its high point very quickly as the first lab in the USSR to manufacture transistors and integrated circuits. The laboratory, with its 2,000 employees, was under the direct supervision of Alexander Shokin, President of the State Committee for Electronic Technology. Rather than having multiple bureaucratic offices, there was a single channel between the decision maker and the researchers.

At the end of the 1950s, when electronic chips didn't yet exist, Sarant and Barr invented the first computer to network technological procedures, the UM-1.[85] They were awarded the State prize for creating the first networking computer and their pictures were on the front page of *Pravda*, which could seem foolish. Apparently the FBI was no longer interested in Barr and Sarant, even though since the Rosenberg trial it knew that the two fugitives had gone to Eastern Europe. I am proud of the fact that my two agents almost started a technological revolution in the USSR. My country could have become the first world power in information technology. Sarant already knew at that time that the future belonged to computers, and they were just waiting to propose a project that was extremely important to them. They got the opportunity when the First Secretary of the Communist Party, Nikita Khrushchev, paid a visit to the LKB. The two friends decided to ask the Soviet leader to authorize the creation of a vast center to create and produce computers, a sort of Silicon Valley before its time. They wrote a detailed plan to hand to Khrushchev directly and Shokin approved of their idea.

Khrushchev arrived at LKB at 10 a.m. with an entourage of 30 people, including Dmitri Ustinov and military leaders, Minister of Defense Rodion Malinovsky, and the heads of the army, air force, and navy. Sarant showed them the old bulky computers and the LKB products built with transistors and the first generation of electronic chips. He closed his remarks with these words:

"Nikita Sergeyevich, we are on the threshold of an intellectual revolution that will not only change our way of life but our way of thinking."

The two-hour visit to LKB was enough to prove how correct this statement was.

"You have just seen," continued Sarant, once the visitors were in the conference room, "that in the manufacturing of computers we are practically at the same level as the United States. But we want to pull ahead of America! We need your support. We can make the USSR the first technological power in the world."

Pull ahead of the Americans? It was just what Khrushchev wanted to hear! And what he had just seen proved that it could be done. Furthermore, Staros and Berg had the brilliant public relations idea to give the First Secretary, as soon as he arrived, a radio that was no larger than a pea. Khrushchev immediately fit it into his ear and when he was about to leave the device was still piping music. Very much impressed, he put all his prestige behind the operation.

"Do you see these fellows," said Khrushchev to the LKB directors as he pointed to the many uniforms with gold braid in his entourage. "Don't you trust them: they can swindle you. This is my assistant Shuyski, he will give you the necessary phone numbers. If you need anything call him…or call me."

Three days later the government decided to build a microelectronic center near Moscow. Three months later the city of Zelenograd[86] was being built thirty miles outside Moscow. The capital was surrounded by satellite cities, each one with a different specialty in nuclear physics, missiles, and space travel. Now there would be a new one dedicated to high tech computers. Sarant and Barr recruited the necessary personnel and directed the operation. They had imagined a fifty-story skyscraper but Khrushchev preferred a vast complex of laboratories and private dwellings. Staros was named director of the center and Barr, as usual, became his deputy.

To be the director of any kind of establishment in the USSR, one had to be a Party member. On express orders from Khrushchev, Staros was immediately admitted. Barr had to go through the normal procedure: recommendations, interviews at the district committee, approvals, and confirmations… The future seemed as rosy for the two friends as it did for most Soviet citizens at the time. Alas! They had aroused too much jealousy around them; their great energy made them succeed at everything they worked on; they were heading a huge project in a revolutionary area; they attended conferences, met with foreigners and earned a good living: up to 1,000 rubles a month when an engineer's average monthly salary was 120 rubles; and they had talent, something for which they would not be forgiven.

Staros and Berg were quickly engulfed in a thick web of intrigue. The main idea was simple: foreigners couldn't be heading a pilot complex making cutting-edge technology. The fact that they had been naturalized many years before made no difference. Six months after being named director, Staros was fired as head of the center. Khrushchev's premonition was coming to pass. Staros and Berg wrote him a letter, asking his assistant, Shuyski, to deliver it to the First Secretary when he returned from vacation. This was in

October 1964, and once Khrushchev returned from the Crimea he was just another retiree. The Brezhnev team, now in power, was cleaning up in every direction. Staros and Berg were accused of having squandered the people's money and were dismissed. They were sent to the Svetlana factory in Leningrad. It was a laboratory with a computer production unit, but the limit on production was 100 computers per month, and they couldn't make more than 30. Berg was the first to understand what had happened and asked to be demoted from head engineer to head of the laboratory. He wished to remain in Leningrad.

Staros was more ambitious and independent and could only accept a leading role. A new laboratory for artificial intelligence was to be started from scratch in Vladivostok. The director would have to be as much a creative person as a manager, and my former agent appeared to be the ideal candidate. He didn't hesitate and in 1974 he and his family left for the Soviet Far East. Even his wife Anna Petrovna found an interesting job, giving English lessons on local television. Once again Sarant turned his laboratory into one of the best research institutes in the country. On March 16, 1979 he was proposed as a candidate for corresponding member of the Academy of Sciences of the USSR and traveled to Moscow to be present when his name came up for a vote. Even though he was living in exile, 5,000 miles away from the capital, he always maintained that aura of success and his jealous colleagues rejected his candidacy. He became ill in the car taking him back to the Moskva Hotel and a few minutes later Alfred Sarant died of a heart attack.

Carol Dayton, alias Anna Petrovna, his wife, informed his family in the United States and began writing to them. Since neither she nor Sarant had ever been divorced from their previous marriages, they had never been officially married in Eastern Europe. Had they been happy in exile? They were certainly in love when they fled together, but each one had left two children and a spouse behind in Ithaca. Alfred never saw his loved ones again. Anna Petrovna returned to being Carol Dayton and resumed her U.S. nationality, which she had never renounced. In 1991 she returned to the United States with her youngest daughter.

Barr was still living in Leningrad and his career was waning after his friend had left for Vladivostok. On top of 250 patented inventions, Barr was also an artist. He had never lost his love of music and his four children had graduated from the Leningrad Academy of Music. But he was unhappily married. He liked women and Vera ended up leaving him to return to Prague with the children. Two of them fled Czechoslovakia when it was still a Socialist country and established themselves in the United States as musicians. Barr remarried an old Soviet friend and had two daughters. One daughter also left for the United States while the other one remained with her father. In spite of his age, Barr was still the bohemian he had been when he was younger. His house was always full of artists and musicians while he would be telling jokes, playing the piano, singing and dancing as much as the younger generation.

The true identity of Philip Staros and Josef Berg was established only at the beginning of perestroika. Exchanges between researchers in both countries increased and an American physicist published an article telling the whole story. This didn't stop Berg-Barr from getting an American visa to visit the United States in 1990 with a delegation of Soviet scientists. With the disintegration of the USSR and the beginning of Russia's painful period of reforms, science had become a secondary issue in the national budget. Berg retired on only the equivalent of about $55 per month. In the United States Barr met with his two brothers, his sister Iris, and his nephews, but the welcome was not very warm. He was still suspected of having spied in the United States, though as far as the law was concerned he'd never been charged. In interviews with American newspapers he denied any collaboration with the INO. Barr, who had never given up his U.S. citizenship, took advantage of a trip to New York to request a passport. He was given a new one in two weeks' time and even received Social Security benefits of $244 per month. This money, like his Russian pension, wasn't enough for him to survive. Though he lived in New York for some time, sharing a large apartment with some old retired friends, where they took turns cooking, his life in St. Petersburg was more comfortable. There he had his own apartment, his friends, and a much better status in society. If only the Russian government could make his old age more comfortable after such valuable service to the country.

Barr remained an optimist in spite of everything, thinking that his invention for the fast production of electronic chips would make him rich! But the project never came to fruition; his family and his old friends in America hesitated to help him openly because they were afraid of having problems with the authorities. He was caught between a rock and a hard place. In 1996, when I began revealing the truth about the Rosenbergs, I wrote to Joel Barr to ask him to help me in defending the memory of our friends. I was hoping he would issue a statement to the press. He had nothing more to worry about: his collaboration with Soviet intelligence was an old story from 50 years ago and the statute of limitations had expired a long time before.

In March 1997 Barr gave a long interview to *Komsomolskaya Pravda*, but instead of telling the whole truth about the functioning of the Rosenberg network he denied that Julius was involved and denied his own participation as well.[87] He even spoke of heading a Russian-American committee to rehabilitate the Rosenbergs. Soon after, he took part in a Russian television program called "Strictly Confidential," where he stated that he had never met Alexander Feklisov. I was flabbergasted and yet I felt no resentment towards him. On the contrary, I wrote a personal letter to Vyacheslav Trubnikov, the new head of the SVR. After all, I had been Barr's case officer and I had a stake in the welfare of my former agent. I expressed my indignation in that letter, saying that it was shameful to have forgotten someone who had once been such an important source. The SVR had the moral duty to give him a decent life. I know that one of Trubnikov's deputies invited Barr to Moscow to discuss his material needs and improve his life.

I also told Trubnikov that I supported Barr's idea to start a rehabilitation effort for the Rosenbergs. In my view the only way to proceed was to tell the whole story, the truth. Legal experts from both countries should get together, open certain archives, hear witnesses who were still alive... That idea was not acknowledged. Barr continued to divide his time between St Petersburg and New York.

He remained active and full of new inventions. Every month he would organize a musical soirée in his St Petersburg apartment. He died suddenly in a Moscow hospital on August 1, 1998, while still full of new projects and only 83 years old.

I don't know what happened to William Perl. Michael and Ann Sidorovich walked away with few problems. They remained under FBI surveillance for many years. Michael had some problems at work during the Rosenberg trial, but his employer didn't fire him because even Ruth Greenglass testified that he couldn't have known of his wife's espionage activities. However, an FBI van was parked in front of their house for a long time. All their neighbors were questioned, and they lost many friends and acquaintances. Michael died in 1962.

Morton Sobell served eighteen years of his thirty-year sentence. In jail he became friends with some Italians and Austrians. After he was released he took a trip to Europe with his wife to see his old friends and naturally he wanted to visit Moscow. The Service welcomed him and the couple was accommodated in a PGU apartment for visiting foreigners who wished to remain incognito. They had a maid, a chauffeur, and even a cook at their disposal. Mrs. Sobell had come dressed too lightly for the Russian winter and was given a beautiful fur coat. The Sobells were amazed, not expecting such royal treatment. In Italy they had shared a tiny apartment with their friends. Morty insisted on having a reunion with his old case officer. We met at the National Hotel opposite the Kremlin. The American millionaire Armand Hammer, one of the first businessmen to have had dealings with Bolshevik Russia under Lenin, would rent several luxurious suites all year long, even in his absence; it was one of the most private places in all of Moscow.

I didn't recognize my old friend: he had let his beard grow and we were both 25 years older. Yet our reunion was a happy one. Sobell hadn't changed a bit and even wanted to be of use to the cause he had fought for during his youth, and even though no one would give him any secrets in the West he could still work as a liaison agent or as an illegal. He was touching in his sincerity.

"No, Morty," I said to him. "Drop that idea. You have suffered enough for us."

As I write these lines Sobell is still alive. In public he is keeping to the line he always had since his arrest in Mexico: he never had anything to do with Soviet intelligence. He doesn't stop drawing attention to the mistakes of the Venona decipherers who had identified him as "Rest" or "Serbe," and then to say that Serbe was another pseudonym used for Rest and, finally, that Rest had an artificial leg, which Sobell doesn't have. Just like Barr, he says he doesn't know who I am. I am not about to condemn him. My intent in naming him is to rehabilitate the name of the Rosenbergs as well as his own. How can one do that without telling the truth? This antifascist who supported the main country in its struggle in the war against Hitler has nothing to be ashamed of. To me Morton Sobell is a hero, as much as Julius Rosenberg, Joel Barr, Alfred Sarant, William Perl, the Sidoroviches, Klaus Fuchs, and so many other agents of mine. And it is to him, among others, that this book is dedicated.

I still have some more things to say about the two traitors. Harry Gold, who escaped being sent to the electric chair in exchange for his cooperation with the FBI, was sentenced to thirty years in prison. After fifteen years he had the right to ask for an early release for good behavior but was careful not to do so. In the mid-1960s Miriam Moskowitz came to Moscow. Even though she had never worked with Soviet intelligence, she had been the mistress of Abraham Brothman, one of our agents, who had been betrayed by Harry Gold. Together with Brothman in November 1950, she had been sentenced to two years in prison and each one had been fined $10,000 for espionage. Moskowitz used her trip to request a meeting with the KGB. I was retired from operations at the time but still worked for the PGU as a civilian employee and I was teaching at the intelligence school, the future Andropov Institute. Because of this and also because I knew our American agents of that period very well, I was asked to meet with her.

Miriam Moskowitz simply wanted to inform us of a fact that she thought strange: Harry Gold didn't want to be released from prison. His treatment had improved and he had a job, but he did not wish to be out of jail. The simple explanation was that Gold was afraid. He had betrayed Klaus Fuchs and the Rosenberg network, and the couple's death was on his conscience. He was afraid of being assassinated by the KGB as soon as he got out of prison, but he really had nothing to worry about because that kind of operation was no longer practiced since Khrushchev. He finally appeared to understand this and was released in 1966 after sixteen years in jail. He died of a heart attack in Philadelphia in 1972. To my knowledge David Greenglass is still alive, he is living under an assumed name in the United States. I think that for him, just as for Morton Sobell and myself, this whole story will end with his death.

PART SEVEN

The Clash of the Titans

39

The administrative shuffling within the Soviet intelligence service continued after the short-lived Committee for Information was dissolved. In January 1952 we became once again the First Chief Directorate of the Ministry for State Security (MGB) but only for a short time. In March 1953 the Intelligence Service changed its identity yet again, becoming a section of the Ministry of the Interior for one year. The abbreviation changed from NKVD to MVD when the People's Commissariats were turned into Ministries. With every new change, a new boss would surround himself with his own men and many excellent professionals were demoted or forced to leave.

There was a climate of uncertainty everywhere, especially following Stalin's death on March 5, 1953. Beria, the Minister of the Interior, was determined to have the secret services under his control. With the help of his deputy, Bogdan Kobulov, he reorganized the leadership of the PGU once again. A few days later, on March 14, Czech President Klement Gottwald died suddenly, leaving a vacancy for General Secretary of the Communist Party. During this time of instability for Czechoslovakia and some other Eastern European countries, Western radios such as Radio Free Europe,

Deutsche Welle, and Voice of America, were openly calling on the populations of the Socialist countries and the Soviet Union to rise up against their governments. I remembered the plans drawn up by the secret committee of the British-American high command, which the London Rezidentura had obtained in 1949, recommending that 1952 and 1953 would be the best time to start a war against the Socialist bloc, and now that Stalin was dead...

The leadership of the Socialist countries asked the Soviet government to provide experienced officers to organize their own intelligence and counterespionage services. On June 25, 1953 I was summoned by Kobulov and immediately ordered to go to Prague to become deputy to the head counselor of intelligence. Since my opinion was of no interest to the Deputy Minister of the Interior, I answered, "Yes sir." I was to be stationed in Czechoslovakia for two and a half years. My mission was to help our comrades set up an efficient intelligence service. Most of the people I worked with were new to this activity but they were dedicated and motivated, and a real pleasure to work with. Starting practically from scratch, my Czechoslovak colleagues took only three or four years to penetrate innumerable organizations in West Germany and Austria. I was proud of my students but I can say nothing more about that period of my life.

When I returned to Moscow in December 1955 I was shifted to another department. The PGU had been attached to the Committee for State Security, the KGB,[88] the new name given to the MGB. It was therefore within the First General Directorate of the KGB that I became head of the American division. I was in charge of supervising political intelligence for the entire western hemisphere under official cover. For us the United States remained the "main enemy," but that didn't mean that I was leading an army of spies. In Moscow I had only 80 people reporting to me, including a typist and a technical secretary. At the end of the 1950s the department was split into two divisions, the United States and Canada on one side, and Latin America on the other, I remained as head of North America.

The Cold War seemed to have reached its apex some time before. With Nikita Khrushchev in power and his famous speech on

Stalin's crimes at the XXth Congress of the Soviet Communist Party, the execution of Beria and the purge of the Stalinist hawks, Molotov, Malenkov and Kaganovich,[89] the biggest obstacles for a better understanding between the Soviet Union and the West were quickly disappearing. The Geneva summit of the heads of government of Britain, France, the United States and the Soviet Union from July 18-23, 1955 would inaugurate the "spirit of Geneva" and put an end to the real animosity that existed in East-West relations. Khrushchev's "thaw" coincided with spectacular space travel. The first Sputnik, launched on October 4, 1957, demonstrated that, with the balance established in nuclear weapons, the USSR was taking the lead in the conquest of space. The idea of negotiating with the Soviets not only at the great power level, but also in a spirit of cooperation and understanding, took hold slowly but surely within the halls of the American power structure.

The rapprochement of the two blocs was crowned by an exceptional event. In September 1959 Khrushchev became the first head of a Soviet government to pay an official visit to the United States. As head of the American department, I was part of the team of experts within the KGB in charge of the Soviet leader's security during his trip. I not only knew the political ramifications but also the operational situation. KGB President Alexander Shelepin held meetings with the group three to four times per week. He was constantly telling us that the success of this visit and Khrushchev's personal security were the most important task ever given to the special services. Intelligence service veterans who had lived through the struggle against the Third Reich, had secured the secrets of the atomic bomb, the Korean War and so many other real or simply averted conflicts, exchanged knowing glances around the table.

Our main working tool was the detailed program of the Khrushchev visit showing all the movements that would take place by the hour. We were to guard the First Secretary as well as his entourage very closely around the clock, no matter what unforeseeable circumstances could occur, such as car or plane accidents, breakdowns, anti-Soviet demonstrations, terrorist attacks and so on. These sessions were to produce a security plan. At first we discussed the possibility of writing the plan ourselves inside the KGB and then handing it to the Americans. Some of my colleagues were proposing to place a double line of U.S. soldiers to protect the Soviet leader from the crowd. Others answered that all it would take was a single crazy person among the armed troops to create a disaster. We finally decided to rely on the great experience of the U.S. Secret Service.[90] After all, the Americans were on their own turf and knew the kind of dangers they could expect better than us. Naturally, our counterparts would have to tell us what they intended to do and answer our questions.

The plan for the "most important operation in all the KGB's history" was ready just one week before departure. Instead of presenting the plan to Khrushchev himself, Shelepin delegated Lieutenant General Nikolai Zakharov, director of the 9th Directorate of the KGB in charge of government protection. The First Secretary was at his dacha with his advisors, preparing his trip and Zakharov had to wait until midnight to get into his office. Khrushchev looked tired.

"It's your job to see to my personal safety. Do you have a plan? Good, use it! I don't want to know anything; I have other things to worry about."

Zakharov was speechless. Khrushchev, who knew him well, shook his hand and nudged him toward the door:

"Nikolai Stepanovich, it's late, let's get some sleep."

The fruit of the KGB's administrative genius was not to receive the top man's approval.

General Zakharov didn't get much sleep that night. The next morning the core KGB group, which included Zakharov and his deputy, Colonel Vladimir Burdin, a few other officers and myself, flew to Washington D.C. I was officially listed as deputy to Fyodor Molochkov, chief of protocol for the MID. My real job was to head an intelligence team for the protection of the head of the Soviet government. We also were to find out, as broadly as possible, any information concerning potential terrorist attacks, sabotage, or provocations. My duties were to coordinate all these activities with our officers and their deputies. During the few days preceding the arrival of the First Secretary, we organized our work with the help of our ambassador, Mikhail Menshikov, and our various American counterparts. Zakharov and Burdin, who spoke English well, set up the action plan with the U.S. Secret Service. Molochkov and I met with the chief of protocol from the State Department. Finally, the schedule of the visit was printed, and was fresh off the press when I read it. I experienced a strange feeling: after the incredible antagonism we had been through with the Americans during my time in New York, we were suddenly on the same side of the fence, though not for long, but in any case my feelings during that moment made the entire trip worthwhile.

On September 15, 1959 I woke up at 6 a.m. and turned on the TV. A preacher began his sermon on NBC. I can still remember his words: "The Bible tells us that today is the day of the six sorrows. But this year we will have a seventh one: today, Nikita Khrushchev, the Antichrist, is arriving in our country." The good word ended in a prayer: may God save America from the perfidious Communist temptation. Khrushchev's Tupolev 114 landed, with about ninety people on board, including his wife and son, physicist Sergei Khrushchev (who took advantage of the trip to complete his collection of butterflies), his two daughters with their husbands, writer Mikhail Sholokhov and his wife, and advisors, experts, newspapermen, and bodyguards.

The official position of the guest of the U.S. government was a problem for protocol. Khrushchev combined two functions: First Secretary of the Communist Party of the Soviet Union and President of the Council of Ministers. He was the Soviet "number one" because he was head of the Party, but that function had no official status within the structure of the state and was not recognized overseas. The head of the Soviet State, as far as other countries were concerned, was the President of the Presidium of the Supreme Soviet of the USSR, as provided by the constitution. But that function was purely honorary in the Soviet system. Klement Voroshilov, who held that position, simply signed off on the decisions made by the Party. We agreed that for this visit to the United States and, in spite of the fact that he was only head of the government, Khrushchev would be welcomed as a head of state.[91] President Eisenhower was waiting to welcome him as soon as he stepped off the plane and the sound of 21 cannon shots could be heard. The visitor was driven off to Blair House, which would be his official residence.

All along the way, a vehicle with a large sign which preceded the official cars saying "No greetings, no applause. Be quiet and polite." Nevertheless, there were some 300,000 Americans along the route taken by the officials. Some signs were favorable to the Soviet leader; others asked him to go back home. Khrushchev had a very heavy schedule in Washington: a helicopter flight over the city, a meeting with President Eisenhower, lunch at the White House, a meeting with newsmen at the National Press Club, meetings with leaders of Congress, a dinner at the Soviet embassy to honor the U.S. President. When he spoke Khrushchev often ad-libbed and digressed from the printed text. He was not afraid to take what were sometimes bothersome questions.

He would behave as the realistic and cool statesman facing a polite and respectful audience, but once he was under attack he would lose his patience completely. American newsmen were well prepared for the National Press Club meeting. Khrushchev had their questions in advance. Among them were some real "tough" ones on the Stalin years or the armed intervention in Hungary in 1956. But those that were asked more often concerned a *faux pas* committed by the Soviet Premier. In a speech he made some time before, Khrushchev had said, in a moment of rhetorical excitement, "We will bury you all!"—a poor paraphrase of Marx's words, "The proletariat is the gravedigger of capitalism." Yet the sentence was taken to mean the threat of physical extermination of the population of the Western countries. Some newsmen, by their questions, used this to point out the duplicity of the Communists as they were preaching peaceful coexistence. Khrushchev exploded each time, raising his voice, clenching his fists, and spouting phrases such as: "That dead rat again? If you keep on talking like that I'll throw you a dead cat!" Sometimes people laughed, but rarely because it was a good joke.

After two crazy days in Washington, the First Secretary, with a long entourage of newsmen, cameras, microphones and notepads, was off on a cross-country tour: New York, Los Angeles, San Francisco, Des Moines, Iowa, Pittsburgh, and back to Washington. Everywhere there were official receptions, visits to businesses, research facilities, universities, high schools, and farms. Khrushchev had exceptional stamina and unlimited curiosity. Despite a full schedule, exhausting even for the younger members of the group, he would constantly add more stops on the way.

One day we were driving along country roads to reach a farm and the Soviet leader stopped his car four or five times to stroke some ears of corn or wheat. The whole convoy would stop every two or three miles and a crowd of reporters and cameramen would run over to Khrushchev, crushing the beautiful fields like a score of elephants. I would also jump out at top speed and run over to my boss: an accident can happen very quickly! Then the First Secretary would climb back into his car and the crowd of newsmen would run in the opposite direction. At one point a rather heavy-set cameraman, carrying his camera and equipment, complained as he walked past me:

"Are you Russian? Please tell Khrushchev not to stop. I can't take this anymore!"

In Los Angeles, after a meeting with movie stars in Hollywood and the traditional city tour, the official guest went to a reception at the Ambassador Hotel. In his welcoming speech Mayor Norris Poulson made a *faux pas*:

"You won't succeed in burying us, Mr. Khrushchev, so don't even try; we'll fight to the death!"

Khrushchev kept his temper and read his own prepared speech where he advocated disarmament, peace and friendship. Then after a while he brushed his pages aside and, looking at Poulson, he cried out:

"Why do you persist in going over that misunderstanding, which I clarified when I came to Washington? We hold out our hand in friendship. If you don't want it, say so openly. If you're not ready to disarm and prefer to keep up the armaments race, we can only go ahead and build more and more missiles."

Taking things one step further, Khrushchev said that if the Americans were not ready for a serious and orderly exchange of ideas, he could also end his trip and go back home. The following day the newspapers criticized the speech by the mayor of Los Angeles as impolite, unfriendly and destructive. We traveled to San Francisco by train, where the population as well as the authorities made an effort to erase the bad impression created in California. Yet one could see that the altercation with Poulson had made its mark on the First Secretary. During a sightseeing trip on a Coast Guard vessel around the beautiful San Francisco Bay, newsmen surrounded Khrushchev when he was with Henry Cabot Lodge, the U.S. ambassador to the UN, and the ship captain. The reporters with long microphones were able to catch every word that was said. Khrushchev, trying to be funny, pointed to an aircraft carrier and said:

"It's time to chop those big things up to use the metal."

"And what will you do with your submarines, Mr. Khrushchev?" asked a reporter.

"We're starting to switch them over to fish for herring!"

Encouraged by the laughter, the Soviet leader began giving an ironic explanation of fishing techniques. Then, turning serious once again, he announced that he had to tell Mr. Cabot Lodge some important secret information. The bodyguards pushed the newsmen back. A heavy silence overcame everyone and Khrushchev whispered something to his interpreter who then translated back to the ambassador. They all looked serious until they began laughing. The newsmen became restless:

"What's going on? Can you translate for us too!"

Khrushchev said that none of this information could be made public, which was true since nothing leaked to the press until the end of his trip. I found out that evening from General Zakharov that the First Secretary had told Henry Cabot Lodge:

"That Poulson is really not such a bad fellow. He just wanted to fart a bit but his enthusiasm took him too far and he did it in his pants!"

During those two weeks I got to know Khrushchev better. At the time I was rather pleased to be able to observe at close range the man who was leading my country and among the very few who really made a difference in the world, whose name was always in the news everywhere. I could not foresee at the time that my personal knowledge of the Soviet leader's impulsive but never vindictive temperament and the sway his emotions had on his behavior, would become so useful to me. Three years later, during the Cuban Missile Crisis, without my even realizing it, that experience would lead me to bluffing in a manner that was closely related to Khrushchev's temperament. Americans didn't trust the Soviet leader, who made everyone feel uncomfortable. After being Stalin's right-hand man, he had revealed and condemned his former boss's crimes. Following the forceful policies of Vyacheslav Molotov, "Mr. Nyet," Moscow was now preaching peaceful coexistence, an end to the arms race and global cooperation between the two countries. Could that be some new trick? Many American politicians were saying that if the USSR wanted peace so much it must be because it expected to benefit more from peace than the United States. One must remain vigilant! That was no doubt the reason the visit did not produce any important agreements.

During my travels overseas I was able to observe and listen to four U.S. Presidents—Roosevelt, Truman, Eisenhower, and Kennedy—and two British Prime Ministers—Churchill and Attlee. Khrushchev was nothing like a Western statesman. He lacked self-control, the ability to keep cool, and had no patience whatsoever. He lacked sound judgment and was incapable of announcing a decision with just a few choice words that would be as forceful as an entire speech. He was stubborn, capricious, and quick to anger, very talkative and often displayed a total lack of good manners and elementary courtesy. At official receptions he would take large portions of food and drink even when he was supposed to make a speech, which would then be affected by his drinking.

When the issue of Soviet-American rivalry came up Khrushchev would lose all sense of proportion. Like a mountebank at a country fair, he would start boasting and promoting Soviet progress. We launched the first Sputnik! We built the first nuclear ice breaking ship! We planted the Soviet flag on the moon! Khrushchev had even answered President Eisenhower, admitting with a wry smile that Americans lived better than Soviet citizens, but said that twenty years from now, the USSR would leave the United States behind and build Communism. It is understandable that his Western counterparts could not take such a braggart seriously.

One of Khrushchev's main faults was that he loved to attract attention and it was impossible to listen to anyone else if he was present. In his desire to please and make people laugh, with his proverbs, jokes (most of them off-color), and Russian peasant sayings, he'd forget he was the leader of a great power. He had been Stalin's court jester for years, forced to sing Ukrainian songs and dance the gopak, and somehow he was unable to shed this second nature once he followed in Stalin's footsteps. Yet Khrushchev did not tolerate any attack on his self-respect, probably reacting to the many humiliations he'd endured as part of Stalin's entourage. In such situations he would completely lose control.

I shall never forget a meeting with American trade union leaders in San Francisco. Under attack by his audience, Khrushchev forgot about establishing any kind of relations with American workers. During the three hours of constant invective, he hurled insults that not even the worst scandal sheets would print. He often said words just to see what effect they would have. Once, in a limousine with Menshikov, Cabot Lodge and the U.S. ambassador to Moscow, Foy Kohler, Khrushchev told the Americans:

"Your CIA director Allen Dulles thinks he's a superspy. But his backwoods mentality,"[92] Khrushchev said pointing to his temple, "has some problems. He gives away lots of dollars and radio stations to Arab organizations, but in the end we cash in on all that!"

Not knowing how to react, Cabot Lodge and Kohler attempted a forced smile.

As for the intelligence service, Khrushchev made an even more extreme statement. I went to his official residence at Blair House on the morning of the next to last day of his trip with my GRU colleague. Khrushchev was having breakfast. As we did every day, we made our report to General Zakharov who would then decide what information to give to his boss. We warned him that the Americans were expected to make an unfriendly gesture while Khrushchev was still in the United States. The CIA was about to schedule a reconnaissance flight in the international airway along the Black Sea coast of the Caucasus. The mission was designed to trigger the radar systems of the anti-aircraft guns to allow American tracking stations in Turkey and Iran to pinpoint their locations.

Fifteen minutes later Khrushchev walked into the hallway where the international press corps was in waiting and stated dryly:

"I have just been told that the United States intends to send a spy plane along the coast of the Black Sea near the Caucasus. I have issued the order to shoot the plane down."

We were stunned. Apart from any other consideration, such a statement could very well expose our source! Actually the trip that everyone had placed their hopes in justified the nickname the American press had given Khrushchev: "Unpredictable." Having failed to make a good impression on the American people and its leaders, the Soviet leader made no progress whatsoever in bilateral relations. Once he left, the Eisenhower administration stated that it would not change its policies of superior force and the arms race. At the beginning of 1960 Washington resumed nuclear testing.

In expectation of the Soviet-American summit in Paris scheduled for May 15, the U.S. prepared many proposals which were obviously unacceptable to the Soviet Union. The U2 spy planes continued their high-altitude overflights above Soviet territory. One of the American pilots, Francis Gary Powers, was shot down on May 1, 1960 over Sverdlovsk—thanks to the proximity fuse that Julius Rosenberg had given us as a prototype. The day before the conference, Washington placed its forces on alert in the United States and overseas. Once he arrived in Paris, Khrushchev stated that he would attend the meetings only if President Eisenhower apologized to the Soviet Union and promised to end U2 flights over Soviet territory. The summit was cancelled. After a short thaw we were back into the cold war once again.

40

I n the spring of 1960 my superiors asked me if would agree to
become Rezident in a major country. I had no objection but did
not wish to return to the United States and I thought they had
noted my request. But in June General Alexander Sakharovsky, the
director of the PGU, called me to his office.

"I understand that you're not too keen on working in Washington. It's no sinecure, the FBI is very active, but we have no one else
who can handle the job."

He was right. To manage the Rezidentura in the main enemy's
country was a real challenge. Since I was the head of the American
department and knew the problems of that job better than anyone
else; it was now my turn to go to the grind. I reluctantly accepted.
At the end of August, less than one year after Khrushchev's state
visit, I stepped into the imposing offices of the Soviet embassy in
Washington on 16th Street. Officially, I was counselor for U.S. internal politics, specializing in trade unions. I was also to head the
embassy's consular section, which was located in a different building. My trip with Khrushchev had done me no harm. After the
delegation left, some newspapers had written that Vladimir
Burdin[93] headed the American department of the KGB, so it didn't

look like I had been "burned," or rather that the newspapers hadn't discovered my true line of work. There was nothing to prevent my entry into the Washington diplomatic circuit.

Ambassador Mikhail Menshikov greeted me warmly. He informed me of the latest developments in Soviet-American relations, along with advice on how to make some useful acquaintances, and asked the minister and counselor Mikhail Smirnovski to introduce me to the Soviet desk of the State Department. I was to make the rounds for two months exchanging courtesy visits with my counterparts in various American departments as well as other diplomatic colleagues. Out of curiosity, I also paid a visit to the editors of *The Washington Post*. They were our neighbors and took two full hours to show me how they made their newspaper. My address book was soon full of names of American officials, foreign diplomats, and newspapermen; in short, people who had information that could be of interest to Moscow.

I arrived in Washington just a few months before the Presidential election of 1960, while the campaign was in full swing. According to the Constitution, President Eisenhower had to step down after two terms. The Republican candidate was Vice President Richard M. Nixon, a shrewd politician, and—according to the Soviet press—a "flaming reactionary" who had the support of the military-industrial complex. His running mate and vice presidential candidate was none other than Henry Cabot Lodge, whom I had met during the Khrushchev visit. Senator John F. Kennedy, the Democratic candidate, with Lyndon Johnson as his running mate, had a different base of support: the Kennedy clan, headed by his father, Joseph Kennedy, as well as powerful industrial and banking groups. Some people added the Mafia to his base. The Boston Catholic also had the support of intellectuals, youth, labor and ethnic minorities. His younger brother Robert was running the campaign.

Following the U2 incident, relations between Khrushchev and the Republican administration had seriously deteriorated. Nixon, as the former Vice President, meant that there would be continuity of administration policies. The Democratic candidate, even though he was a millionaire, appeared friendlier and closer to us. The Soviet Union wanted Kennedy to win.

Besides its normal workload concerning the election, the Rezidentura was also required to provide diplomatic, propaganda, and other suggestions to Moscow that could help secure a Kennedy victory. A single operation was to fulfill that request. Intelligence is not just following people, covert meetings with secret agents, dead letter boxes, and secret radio transmissions. Many important pieces of information can be obtained legally and publicly. In fact, a decrypted message with information secured at enormous risk and huge expense can be sitting on an analyst's desk next to an article in a scholarly journal that had precisely the same information. Conversely, an official's answer to a question can be as valuable as the report provided by the best-hidden mole. In this case that is exactly what happened.

Yuri Barsukov, the *Izvestia* correspondent, had a good relationship with an American newsman close to Robert Kennedy. I asked him to use that excellent contact to request an interview for his newspaper with the Kennedy campaign manager. Barsukov accepted the task—which was perfectly aboveboard—and was quickly granted the interview. The meeting with Robert Kennedy took place at the future President's campaign headquarters. The newsman said straightaway that the Kremlin was following his bother Jack's run for the White House with the greatest interest. Moscow wanted to gauge the true chances of the Democratic Party and was ready to use the media if it could be of any assistance.

"It's a tough fight but my brother hopes to win," said Robert Kennedy.

He got up and parted a curtain that hid a huge map of the United States. Each state had estimates of the number of votes both candidates could gain. These projections were based on studies and forecasts made by the Democratic Party, and were a piece of information we could only dream about. Seeing the keen interest displayed by the Soviet newsman, Robert Kennedy told him to take all the notes he wanted, and Barsukov duly wrote down all the numbers on the map in his diary.

"As for the Kremlin," the candidate's brother added, "the most positive thing for them is to do nothing in favor of John Kennedy. The only result of any open support would mean defeat for Democratic candidates. If Moscow really wants to see Jack in the White House, the best would be to take a neutral attitude. If we do win I hope we will have normal and mutually favorable relations."

The text of the "interview" was sent to Sakharovsky. From that point on, the Center didn't bother us until the election, which goes to prove that gathering information is the same for the press as it is for an intelligence service. I quickly found out that my report had reached the highest level of the government and had been helpful. During an official reception in Moscow a few days later, an American newspaperman asked Khrushchev:

"Which one of the two candidates do you want to see win?"

The Soviet leader used his particular style to answer, keeping our recommendations in mind:

"Nixon and Kennedy are tweedledee and tweedledum. The Soviet government has no preference."

That statement prompted many humorous commentaries in U.S. newspapers, but Khrushchev's secret wish and Robert Kennedy's forecast came to pass. On November 8, JFK won the election by a narrow margin of 118,574 votes, or 0.2% more than Nixon. At 43, he became the youngest President elected in U.S. history.

Khrushchev's hopes were to be dashed. Kennedy didn't intend to give up world leadership or the struggle against the Socialist countries. As he proclaimed his intention of improving relations with the USSR, the new administration continued the policy of strength and a buildup of the arms race. Relations between the two countries were still characterized by suspicion and the fear of being overtaken by one another. They progressed in waves; periods of relative calm were interrupted by violent crises. Khrushchev did show some goodwill. On January 25, 1961 the USSR freed two American pilots of an R47 shot down over Soviet territory in the summer of 1960, a gesture that could be interpreted as an inaugural gift for the incoming President, who had just been sworn in five days earlier.

Kennedy, however, was following his own agenda. On April 17, an invasion attempt took place at the Bay of Pigs in Cuba by counterrevolutionaries supported by the CIA, which was seeking to overthrow Fidel Castro's regime. That failure was a first major foreign policy fiasco for the new President and in the ensuing months

Khrushchev sought to benefit from the loss of prestige by the United States. On June 3 and 4 in Vienna, Kennedy and Khrushchev met for the first and only time. They were able to find a common language with regard to Laos, but their positions on West Berlin were diametrically opposed. The USSR demanded that the American, British, and French sectors be demilitarized. Kennedy replied that if Western troops left, the western sector of the city would be completely surrounded and defenseless inside East Germany, and therefore rejected the idea. Having used all means at his disposal, Khrushchev threatened to sign a separate peace treaty with the GDR and cease to recognize the West's rights over West Berlin. Kennedy, who viewed the Vienna summit as a way of getting to know the Soviet leader personally, didn't give an inch. As he left Vienna he commented, "Yes, it's going to be a cold winter!"

On July 25 Kennedy announced on television that the United States was ready to go to war to defend West Berlin. He ordered that draftees be tripled, that 250,000 reserves be called into service and the military budget be increased by 6 billion dollars. A head of state doesn't take such measures unless he's preparing for war. Moscow's answer came on August 13. In one night Berlin was to be cut in half by a wall. The underground trains that allowed free passage without identity checks between the two parts of the city, but also between the two enemy camps, were also shut down. On September 1, 1961 after a three-year moratorium, the USSR resumed its nuclear tests in the Novaya Zemlya archipelago with a series of thermonuclear bomb drops of over 50 megatons.[94] A Norwegian diplomat told me on that occasion:

"With every explosion, the new tenants of the White House have blurred vision for a long while."

The Americans answered by testing nuclear devices as well on September 12. It was during the Berlin crisis that a secret back channel was set up between the USSR and the United States, which was to play a crucial role in the Cuban Missile Crisis a year later. Khrushchev was very much aware of the fact that increased tension between the two camps could lead to a sudden armed conflict. Sometimes, despite his own impulsive temperament, he could be clever and take action that diplomats have used for centuries.

During the Vienna summit, Mikhail Kharlamov, President of Gosteleradio, the USSR's state committee for broadcasting, had established contact with Pierre Salinger, President Kennedy's press secretary. The initiative came at the right time. At the beginning of September, Khrushchev sent Kharlamov with the Soviet delegation to the UN General Assembly, led by our Minister for Foreign Affairs, Andrei Gromyko. On September 22, JFK came to New York to speak at the General Assembly. The same day a counselor at the Soviet embassy, Georgy Bolshakov, who was really a colonel in the GRU, requested an urgent meeting with Salinger, who, when told Kharlamov would also be coming, immediately agreed. Kharlamov started by saying, "The storm over West Berlin has passed!" Then he said that the First Secretary was in favor of a settlement. Khrushchev was ready to meet with Kennedy once again but understood that, due to the political exigencies of the moment, it would difficult for the U.S. President. In any case, he hoped that the speech at the General Assembly would be less aggressive than the one of July 25.

Kennedy, after consulting with Secretary of State Dean Rusk, wrote a polite answer that Salinger read to Kharlamov. The President said that he was pleased that the Soviet leader was taking a new step to solve the West Berlin crisis. He also reminded Khrushchev that both parties should enforce their Vienna agreement and end hostilities in Laos with the creation of a neutral government. This back channel set up by Bolshakov and Salinger (who was sometimes replaced by Robert Kennedy) became quite productive.[95] It was used in November to get JFK to agree to an interview with Khrushchev's son-in-law, Alexei Adzhubei, editor-in-chief of *Izvestia*. Salinger went to the USSR in June 1962, after being invited by Adzhubei. He met with Khrushchev about West Berlin and the German problem, while Adzhubei was meeting Kennedy again in Washington. The Americans used this channel to suggest the end to nuclear testing in the atmosphere, in space, and underwater.

The success of these unofficial contacts provoked the jealousy of some rare people in the know. Just like the White House, our Washington embassy had changed heads, since Foreign Minister

Gromyko and Ambassador Mikhail Menshikov were not on the best of terms. The Minister took advantage of Kennedy's election to name a new ambassador, Anatoly Dobrynin. While Menshikov was close to sixty, the new man was forty-one, about the same age as the U.S. President. Dobrynin was a career diplomat, specialized in Soviet-American relations and who had spent several years in the United States and had established good contacts in Washington. He also had another important asset: he was "gromykoed," as we said at the time. In other words, he was part of the Minister's personal team. Dobrynin knew of the Bolshakov-Salinger channel and the type of information that filtered through it, which was not to his liking: he wanted to be the sole channel of communication for all contacts between the Soviet government and the U.S. administration.

41

Soviet-American relations stabilized once the storm over Berlin had passed, but the fighting between the intelligence services did not slow down. I knew that before sending me off to America, the PGU had obtained my file at MI5 and the FBI. I was listed as a diplomat, nothing more. There was nothing that could be interpreted as suspicious about me and yet... In Washington we lived in a large building that included a hotel with furnished apartments. There were doormen and guards at the entrance day and night, and despite my lily-white résumé, the FBI was watching me around the clock. One morning when I was to travel to New York, I left my apartment at 5 a.m., only to find my new blue Chevrolet Impala completely sandwiched between two parked cars, front and back; it could not be moved an inch. What could I do? I looked around and saw that "they," three crumpled-looking men who spent the entire night watching and waiting in a nondescript Dodge, were right there. They were young, muscular types, so I went up to them and asked:

"Could you help me please, sir?"

The one in the driver's seat looked over his shoulder to another man sitting in the back with a fedora lowered over his eyes. The man in the back nodded. The driver wiggled my Chevy out of the squeeze in a dozen or so moves, like a good professional, then the Dodge followed me all the way for about 250 miles.

The surveillance couldn't be characterized as being very discreet. One day my younger daughter, Ira, who was only 10 years old, came up from the courtyard where she had been playing with some other girls.

"Daddy," she said, "there's a strange car in the courtyard with three men in it. They have a walkie-talkie, a phone, a camera, and even a hot plate to make tea. I went over with my friends to get a closer look but the men waved us away. Who are they?"

Obviously, I had no idea.

As always in every country in the world, the fellows who were doing the tailing were simple, often friendly, people. All you had to do with them was to make sure you followed the rules: don't make them feel you have noticed them, don't try to shake them, don't trick them unless it was absolutely necessary. If you broke that unwritten code, they could get nasty and cross your ignition cables or poke a hole in one of your tires, or both, according to the seriousness of what you had done to them. But it was all fair play.

The FBI loved to set us up with "bait," meaning men or women who would come and offer us their services, generally for money in order to appear genuine. It is difficult to separate these from the real "walk-ins,"[96] but generally we were on the lookout for that kind of subversive operation. Sometimes, obviously, there were blunders: two of my colleagues were arrested during my three and a half years in Washington, while taking documents from "bait." They were declared persona non grata and expelled. Yet we did have many interesting agents among citizens of the Third World who were opposed to American policies, as well as American citizens, even in very sensitive positions.

The most glaring example was the case of William Martin and Bernon Mitchell, two walk-ins who made it possible for the PGU to effect a spectacular penetration of the holy of holies of American secret services, the infamous National Security Agency (NSA) also known as "No Such Agency." To this day the National Security Agency remains the most important special department of United States intelligence, gathering electronic intercepts, ELINT,[97] of radio or telephone communications throughout the world. Thanks to its "big ears," the NSA can eavesdrop on an encrypted phone conversation between, for example, the Premier of Thailand in his Bangkok palace and his foreign minister in Paris; or listen in on a radio conversation between two tank crews during an exercise in the steppes of the Volga. In 1990 the NSA had 13,000 employees at its headquarters at Fort Meade, 25 miles outside Washington, and some 130,000 personnel at interception stations throughout the world. With an annual budget of over 15 billion dollars, it is the best-equipped intelligence agency in the United States.

Our two agents, Martin and Mitchell, offered us their services in 1960 when I was still in Moscow. Bernon Mitchell was only 31 and he was the older of the two. They both came from well-to-do families and had shown early on an excellent aptitude for mathematics. Martin had started graduate studies in Washington State and Mitchell in California. During military service in the navy they were assigned to decrypting secret messages sent and received by the Soviet Union and the People's Republic of China. Martin began his tour in Alaska, before being stationed on a secret base in Japan where he became friendly with Mitchell. After military service, both young men went back to their graduate studies, and in 1957, having obtained their doctorates, they both accepted job offers at NSA. They were good recruits and excellent mathematicians, who had been vetted for secret work ever since their time in the military. Yet they slowly came to the conclusion that the policy of the Eisenhower administration was aggressive and a threat to world peace. At the beginning of 1960 they contacted a Soviet intelligence officer stationed in Washington.

The meetings took place in the suburbs of the capital and our informers were fully aware that they were taking terrible risks. Soon they told us that they preferred to defect to the USSR so that they could hand over everything they knew to us in a secure environment. They also wished to explain their motivations to their fellow Americans and to the world. The Center set up a rather classic exfiltration plan; during their vacation Martin and Mitchell were to go to Mexico and then take a roundabout itinerary to Moscow. They left a letter in a safety deposit box in Laurel, Maryland, with a statement for publication explaining their motivations. NSA security broke into the safety deposit box at the beginning of August, after noticing that their employees had disappeared. Naturally the authorities didn't publish the letter, and limited its statement to the fact that two NSA employees had not returned from vacation and had probably defected "behind the iron curtain." However, Martin and Mitchell held a press conference in Moscow, organized by the MID on September 6, 1960.

They explained that during the 1950s American spy planes would regularly patrol along the borders of the Soviet Union to gather information on secret facilities. In September 1958, a C130 took off from Turkey, crossed into Soviet airspace in Armenia, and was shot down. The U.S. government claimed that the plane, with a team of scientists aboard, had made a navigational error, when it was really carrying NSA experts attempting to intercept Soviet radar signals at close range. Martin and Mitchell were convinced that this violation of the Soviet border could have led to war. The two Americans also revealed that the NSA had broken the codes of about 50 countries, including allies of the United States, and was reading their secret communications. Martin cited, among others, France, Italy, Turkey, Uruguay, Indonesia, Egypt, and Yugoslavia. The press conference was like a bomb prompting a three-month investigation of the NSA by the U.S. Congress.

Naturally, during their debriefings at the PGU, our agents told us much more about their former agency. We found out new information about the Venona operation and its success in decoding cables between our New York Rezidentura and the Center during the war. That piece of information, among a thousand others, allowed us to fix the failures in our encryption system. Thanks to the two defectors, who were granted asylum in the Soviet Union, NSA activities became much less secret to us. Martin and Mitchell had defected out of ideological conviction, and at that time such agents were quickly becoming rare. Our budget would not allow us to compete with our CIA opponents, who, as our sources had confirmed, had successfully recruited an entire army of paid informers among officials in foreign countries.

At the time the CIA had opened a special listening post on Wall Street in Manhattan, for the purpose of identifying and checking foreign visitors, government officials, politicians and bankers who came to the world's greatest financial district to negotiate loans. At some point in the discussions someone willing to help would approach them. In exchange for their cooperation and willingness to provide information on their country's policies, the "Company," for starters, would help them secure the loans they were seeking at extremely favorable rates, which also reflected favorably upon them at home, allowing them to successfully pursue their careers. They were also given some very attractive gifts, sometimes as much as hundreds of thousands, even millions, of dollars transferred every year into a numbered bank account.

That type of operation was way beyond our means. We would much rather recruit "lower level employees," such as typists, secretaries, translators, code clerks and guards who also had access to the same top secret documents. Persons at that level often have low-paying salaries and larger needs: a new car, a house needing repair, debts to repay, surgery or college tuition for their children and so on. We had an entire arsenal to approach such potential recruits and sometimes fate played its part.

At the Rezidentura I had one particularly clever officer on my team who shall be named Bukharov.[98] One Saturday he drove to the country to relax with his wife and son who were vacationing at a lake. The road was close to a military area where we knew there was a missile base. Bukharov stopped when he noticed a young sergeant hitchhiking near the entrance. The young soldier, whom I shall name Chris, was friendly and gregarious.

"Are you stationed on the base?" asked Bukharov suddenly.

"Yeah, there are lots of secrets and not much money."

Bukharov answered him jokingly:

"I've got lots of money and very few secrets."

Chris looked at him:

"So let's make a deal: my secrets for your money!"

It seemed too good to be true.

"Aren't you thirsty?" asked Bukharov. "I'd like to have a beer...."

"Why not?"

"OK, my treat."

As they drank, Bukharov learned that Chris was the son of a miner in Virginia, came from a large family and could only count on himself. Many of his fellow soldiers got help from their middle-class families and could take their girlfriends out on a date dancing or go to the movies, while Chris spent his Saturdays making a few extra dollars working at a gas station or at a supermarket.

Bukharov tried some simple jokes:

"Yeah, better rich and in good health than poor and sick."

Then they got down to serious business as he started asking the sergeant questions that were apparently harmless enough. He found out that Chris was part of security, and his job was to record and check secret documents. He also had to destroy manuals on SAM missiles or manuals for electronic guidance devices when they were replaced by a new system. Bukharov had to make his move; there was the risk of running into "bait," but he didn't have the time to go back to his superiors and the man looked sincere.

"Okay," he said, chuckling, "the trade of money for secrets sounds exciting, but there must be some risk attached to it?"

"None at all," answered Chris, who was a quick study. "No danger at all. Instead of destroying a manual I could easily slip it into my bag and take it off base. I know most of the guards personally, they're buddies of mine, they'd never even dream of frisking me."

The deal was on and Bukharov couldn't hold back any longer. He and Chris agreed on the time and place where he'd be hitchhiking with his bag next time. Naturally my officer could always decide not to keep the rendezvous should his plan be rejected. After all, nothing illegal had yet taken place.

I liked Bukharov because he was often bold, and we were made of the same stuff. As a pupil of Vasily Zarubin, my New York Rezident, my motto was always "he who risks nothing gets nothing," which had worked for me, especially during my contacts with the French agent Antelope.[99] So I had no hesitation in agreeing with Bukharov's arrangements, but a formal recruitment had to be approved by the Center. This was not just a bureaucratic requirement; the archives of the Lubyanka were filled with the most detailed information on unexpected people. After making a check, the Center gave its approval. We now had to take some precautions locally.

On the day of the meeting, Bukharov took a very complicated security itinerary with the help of several officers from the Rezidentura. A red pickup truck parked in front of a McDonald's outside Washington indicated to him that the coast was clear. If not, he would just have a Big Mac and turn around. Once out of town, and on country roads, Bukharov was safe; he could have spotted any kind of tail. Chris was on schedule and climbed into the car with his gym bag. They immediately made the exchange: one manual for $300. Then the sergeant got out of the car and Bukharov quickly followed him. They made a new appointment for four weeks hence, and he asked Chris to come without anything valuable on him. The first try had been positive, but before getting into a long relationship an instructional meeting was required. In a few months Bukharov taught Chris the ABCs of konspiratsya: do nothing to attract attention, and, above all, no extraordinary spending, shake a tail without appearing to do so, and a thousand other tricks. A year later Chris followed his handler's advice and passed the exam and training for military counterespionage, becoming an even more valuable source to us.

42

I n the early 1960s, in a matter of just a few months, relations between the USSR and the United States took a serious turn for
the worse because of a little island with a population half the size
of New York City. Americans were used to considering Cuba as
their private domain. In 1898, after a war with Spain, they had helped
Cuba shake off colonial rule. At the turn of the 20th century Cuba
agreed to submit to Washington's approval any military or diplomatic treaty. In 1903, in return for an agreement to purchase Cuban
sugar at a favorable price, the United States obtained an unlimited
lease to a naval base at Guantanamo Bay, as well as the right to
intervene militarily to ensure peace and security on the island. Washington was to use that prerogative five times until General Fulgencio
Batista established his dictatorship in 1940.

On December 2, 1956, a young Cuban lawyer named Fidel
Castro, who was opposed to Batista and exiled in Mexico, landed in
Cuba with 82 of his followers to begin a guerrilla war against the
dictator. During this whole period of their struggle, public opinion
in North America was favorable to the young democratic revolutionaries. After they seized power on January 1, 1959 and Fidel
Castro became Prime Minister, the United States immediately recognized the new regime on January 7, even before the USSR. But

relations between the island and its big neighbor soured quickly. In May agrarian reform was achieved by, among other things, nationalizing foreign sugar companies. In February 1960 a commercial agreement was signed with the USSR and on July 7 the United States refused to purchase the balance of its quota of sugar. The Soviet Union immediately agreed to exchange this product for oil at very favorable rates. The Standard Oil and Texaco facilities in Cuba refused to refine the oil and were nationalized as well. One month later, on August 6, 1960, all North American businesses were also nationalized and Washington announced a commercial embargo, breaking diplomatic relations with Cuba on January 3, 1961.

At the end of 1960, during the final days of the Eisenhower administration, the United States decided to overthrow the Castro regime. The new President, John F. Kennedy, continued the previous administration's policy of support for the anti-Castro refugees. On April 15, 1961, American planes flying Cuban flags raided Havana and Santiago airports. Two days later, on the 17th, 1,500 counterrevolutionary forces, equipped by the CIA, landed at Playa Girón in the Bay of Pigs, where, to their surprise, they were expected. After three days of heavy fighting the operation turned into a colossal fiasco. Fearing military escalation, Kennedy refused to extend air cover requested by the "contras," and on April 25 he ordered the economic blockade of the island. Castro's reply came swiftly, on May Day (May 1): he announced that the Cuban revolution was a Socialist revolution.

The USSR had already been considering the revolutionary Cuban regime as its ally in the western hemisphere prior to that date. Besides providing economic support, beginning in September 1960 the Soviet Union began sending arms and military advisors to Havana. That same year the Rezidentura in Washington was ordered to obtain accurate information regarding American intentions toward Cuba. We therefore directed our efforts toward the acquisition of new sources and the reactivation of older ones among Latin American diplomats and journalists as well as various organizations handling Latin America. We also had sources inside the Organization of American States, the OAS, which eventually excluded the Cuban government in 1962. We knew a landing of contras was to take place at the Bay of Pigs and we had even transmitted the exact date to the Center. Nevertheless, I found out later that Cuban intelligence had even better sources and was well informed without our help.

Despite this disaster, Kennedy saw no other solution to the Cuban problem than the overthrow of the Castro regime. Latin America was a giant powder keg and Cuba was the detonator for the spread of Communist ideas in every direction within the hemisphere from whence they had been banished. The CIA and the Pentagon hurried with new plans, which included, beyond economic blockade, acts of sabotage and the assassination of Cuban leaders.

The responsibility for the Bay of Pigs fiasco was placed at the doorstep of the CIA, forcing Director Allen Dulles to resign. Henceforth, secret operations would be under the control of the Attorney General, Robert Kennedy, who approved "Operation Mongoose" under the command of General Edward Lansdale, a specialist in counterinsurgency fighting. Two CIA operational groups of 700 men were set up in Florida to carry out actions against Castro. Cuban émigrés, with the support of American commandos, were to infiltrate the island to destroy the harvests, ruin overseas sugar shipments, begin new guerrilla groups and recruit informers. In the early spring of 1962, two American fishermen from south Florida walked into the consular section of the Soviet embassy in Washington. They felt responsible for the aggressive operations of their government against Cuba and were full of remorse. The CIA was paying them well for their services, along with many other fishermen on the Keys, to ferry the commandos into Cuba by night with weapons and explosives.

On a map of the Florida straits the two men pinpointed to our personnel in the Consulate the itineraries and landing points which had increased in the last few weeks. They thought the U.S. government was preparing a new attack to overthrow the Castro regime.

"It's shameful!" they said. "How can a rich and powerful country try to crush a little island? They talk about freedom and democracy but they refuse to let the Cubans live the way they want to."

The two fishermen asked us to give the map and their information to the Cubans, which we did. At the same time with the Center's approval, we began a disinformation operation: we organized a leak of information in favor of the State Department. Relations between the diplomats and the intelligence services were tense, as is often the case in America and elsewhere. A station chief overseas finds things out faster than the ambassador, and the head of intelligence is almost always ahead of the Minister of Foreign Affairs. All this causes friction and dissension but at the time those rivalries took on monstrous proportions in the United States. Through my press contacts I knew that bulletin boards at the State Department were regularly full of appeals to expel all CIA agents operating inside the embassies. The problem had even been submitted to the President of the United States, but intelligence clearly needed diplomatic cover.

Using a rather complicated trick to make it appear real, the State Department found out that Castro's counterespionage was controlling the itineraries for the transportation of commandos and weapons in Cuba. Part of this equipment was used by the regime against the United States. Castro's intelligence had also succeeded in turning some commandos and was trying to get even more supplies and funds out of the CIA to hand them over to the Cuban government. The disinformation operation succeeded. Since the information came from the State Department, the cabinet was informed even before the CIA could act. We quickly found out that subversive operations against Cuba had been greatly reduced. However, we were also told that the United States was preparing a new, armed intervention against Cuba.

There was even a dress rehearsal: at the beginning of 1962 U.S. armed forces practiced a simulated invasion of the island to overthrow a dictator named Ortsac, Castro written backwards! In Cuba itself things had changed dramatically. In December 1961 the regime formally adopted Marxism-Leninism and the Cuban people were now building a Socialist society on their island. The United Party of the Socialist Revolution was founded and Cuba was now firmly in the Socialist camp so that its defense became a matter of principle for the USSR. To help its ally resist another American aggression, Moscow increased its military and economic aid and, in April 1962, Khrushchev decided to install midrange nuclear missiles on the island to discourage any foreign intervention.

In doing so he was killing two birds with one stone: on the one hand it was a response to American Jupiter missiles that were 150 miles away from the Soviet border in Turkey and about the same distance from Cuba to the United States. Should the U.S. attack the Soviet Union with nuclear weapons, their own territory would also be attacked within a few minutes. During the era of deterrence, reestablishing strategic balance was extremely important. On the other hand, the missiles would also deter Washington from attacking Cuba.

The KGB Rezident in Havana, Alexander Alexeyev, who had been promoted to the rank of ambassador at the beginning of the crisis, was entrusted to negotiate with Castro. The "lider maximo" was hesitating because the island would become a prime target in the event of a nuclear conflict, but the threat of U.S. invasion was so strong that he chose the lesser of two evils. By mid-July 1962, a Soviet military mission began construction of missile launch pads. The increase in deliveries to Cuba by sea attracted American attention. On August 10, the new CIA director, John McCone, told President Kennedy he suspected that the Russians were installing midrange nuclear ballistic missiles. On August 29, a U2 spy plane revealed that Soviet SA2 missiles were present in Cuba. These were anti-aircraft weapons and Kennedy preferred to take the initiative since there were rumors in the press and in Congress. On September 4, JFK announced the presence of those weapons in Cuba but carefully stated that they were not offensive missiles. The Soviet ambassador on the same day was reassuring Robert Kennedy that no offensive weapons would be introduced in Cuba. Dobrynin was speaking in good faith but as far as Soviet officials were concerned, it was only a device to gain time. A first shipment of SS4 missiles with offensive nuclear capability arrived on the island eleven days later.

At first it appeared as though the White House was satisfied with the Kremlin's assurances, but under pressure from the CIA, the military and Congress, Kennedy authorized another overflight over Cuba by a U2 on October 14, 1962. The photographs identified six SS4 missiles, in addition to the SA2s. The SS4s had a range of 1,200 miles and could hit most of the large cities on the east coast, including Washington, Philadelphia, and New York. Once this was ascertained, October 15, 1962, became the starting point for the crisis that took the world to the brink of nuclear catastrophe. The White House reacted instantly, and Kennedy created an Executive Committee of the National Security Council—Ex-Comm—on Tuesday, October 16, which included Vice President Lyndon Johnson, Secretary of State Dean Rusk, Defense Secretary Robert McNamara, Attorney General Robert Kennedy, CIA Director John McCone, and the Chairman of the Joint Chiefs of Staff, General Maxwell Taylor, with the participation of other Cabinet members, the NSC, and Soviet experts. The Committee's mission was to effect measures to get rid of the threat of nuclear attack coming from Cuba.

During that opening meeting the Pentagon and the CIA were clearly advocating tough initiatives. They proposed massive bombing of Cuba, followed by a landing to overthrow the Castro regime. This plan had the backing of McGeorge Bundy, special assistant to the President for national security affairs, and of other participants. Defense Secretary McNamara was, ironically, the first to speak up against such a scenario, stating that bombing the missile ramps would cause the death of Soviet military personnel and the certainty that Moscow would retaliate, in which case the conflict could escalate into a world war. Furthermore, any missiles that had not been destroyed could be launched against American cities.

Security around Ex-Comm was incredible; Moscow didn't know that Washington was aware of the missiles. Committee members were convinced that, should the Soviets find out, they could hide or even launch the missiles. The U.S. population had to be kept in the dark to avoid any panic. To keep the press off the story, Committee meetings were not always held at the White House but in other government buildings and the information was made public only on October 22. During the night of the 17th new photographs from reconnaissance flights identified midrange SS5 missiles as well, making all U.S. territory except Washington State and Oregon vulnerable to Soviet nuclear warheads. President Kennedy met with Andrei Gromyko at the White House on October 18. Kennedy didn't know whether the Soviet foreign minister knew about the missiles or whether he knew that the Americans knew. My feeling is that Gromyko had to know, even though he was not part of the Politburo. He joined its ranks only in 1973, but he already had enormous influence there. On the other hand, he probably didn't think that the Americans had found out.

In his book *Thirteen Days*,[100] Robert Kennedy wrote about that tedious meeting. Gromyko read a declaration stating that the Soviet government only intended to increase the defensive capabilities of Cuba and help the development of its peaceful democracy. Kennedy, in reply, reiterated his statement of September 4: the United States would not tolerate offensive weapons in Cuba. But as he told his brother, he was tempted to shove an enlarged photo of a missile site under his guest's nose and ask him: "And this? What's this supposed to be?" During a ball in Gromyko's honor at the State Department, Ex-Comm was working just one floor below on two scenarios: naval blockade or bombing raid. The President was hesitating; he asked his speechwriter, Theodore Sorensen, to prepare two different speeches for his October 22 nationwide address.

Kennedy flew to Chicago the next day to help the campaigns of democratic candidates during midterm elections, since the press would have reacted to a cancellation of the trip. Robert Kennedy presided over Ex-Comm in his brother's absence. At that session most participants agreed on the naval blockade, but the military felt that it should only be the prelude to the bombing and invasion of Cuba. The Pentagon concentrated a force of 100,000 men in various bases in the southeast. On Saturday, October 20, the Committee discussed the two Presidential speeches. Since there was no consensus, Robert Kennedy called his brother and asked him to return to Washington. The last aerial photographs indicated that Soviet and Cuban specialists were completing the launching pads as fast as they could. The President grudgingly agreed to fly back to Washington, the official reason being a "respiratory infection." At 1:30 p.m. John Kennedy chaired a meeting of the committee. Five options were presented: invasion, bombing of the missile sites, blockade, secret negotiations with Khrushchev through diplomatic channels, and bringing the matter to the UN Security Council. The Committee backed a solution that was firm and moderate: the blockade of the island. Kennedy took one more day to make up his mind.

The President spoke with the military on Sunday, October 21. A bombing raid couldn't guarantee the complete destruction of the missiles. Those that remained operational could be launched in retaliation, and casualties could range to 10,000 civilians and 20,000 military personnel. Faced with such results, Kennedy excluded a bombing raid. What was left was the blockade. Undersecretary of State George Ball made an important suggestion: according to international law a blockade was an act of war. He proposed the "quarantine" formula and the President liked the idea. There was one final problem, the press had found out about the presence of offensive missiles in Cuba. Kennedy called the editors of *The Washington Post* and *The New York Times* and asked them to keep silent on the issue. His message had to have a surprise effect or otherwise, as he told them, "I don't know what the Soviets might do." The last photographs over Cuba indicated the feverish assembly of IL28 midrange bombers and MIG fighter planes, as well as more launching pads being built on the northern coast of the island.

43

A ll this excitement affected only the highest councils of power. None of our American agents in the State Department or elsewhere had noticed anything out of the ordinary. I had no way of knowing what was going on since I was not aware of the presence of Soviet missiles in Cuba. By Sunday, October 21, I knew that there was a crisis. At noon a Soviet newsman told me that there were many reporters outside the White House where the Cabinet and the Joint Chiefs of Staff were in session. Everyone was expecting an important announcement but nobody knew what it was about. I asked my newsman friend to try and get more information, then I sent a short message to the Center. During the afternoon Ambassador Dobrynin called an urgent meeting. The military attaché told us that in the southern part of the United States the armed forces had been placed on DEFCON 3, the advanced state of alert.[101] The meeting was drifting into speculation. Neither the military attaché, nor the ambassador—that, at least, was what they were to say later on—knew of the presence of our missiles in Cuba. The American press gave no clue that a conflict was in the offing and we didn't even know of the Ex-Comm meetings.

On October 22 I was in my office at the embassy, trying to find an American contact who could help me in my mission. Who would know what was going on in the Oval Office? My thoughts were interrupted by a phone call from John Scali. He was inviting me to lunch at the Occidental restaurant. I immediately accepted; it was an excellent coincidence since his name was high on my contact list.

"Is 1 p.m. good for you?" asked Scali.

I could wait until then.

"Fine."

"Very good, see you later then."

I had known Scali for about 18 months. He was a foreign news commentator on ABC, where he also had a popular weekly show called *Questions and Answers.* Many politicians in the news were eager to be on his show. Scali was from Boston, with entrée to the Kennedy clan, and he knew the President personally. He was also a personal friend of Secretary of State Dean Rusk, who took him along on almost every official trip.

I had met Scali at a party and knew who he was, having seen him on television. Mikhail Sagatelian, a TASS correspondent who also worked for us and knew everyone in Washington, called me over and introduced us. We chatted for about a half hour. Scali's "beat" as a newsman was the White House, the State Department, the Pentagon and the intelligence community. He was just as interested as I was in getting together and we exchanged addresses. Since then we had been meeting regularly and to our mutual benefit. I was his direct connection at the Soviet embassy. I would explain some aspects of Soviet foreign policy that were not well known or could give rise to misunderstandings while he kept me informed on what was happening inside the administration. John was an exuberant type and it was not too hard to squeeze information out of him. All I had to do was broach a topic I wanted to know more about and say at a certain point:

"No, it can't be!"

He would immediately react:

"What do you mean it can't be? I can even tell you I got it firsthand. The meeting took place last Tuesday at 4 p.m. and I can even tell you it was on the 11th floor!"

Our relationship had become friendlier with time. We called each other at home and were on a first-name basis, yet we both kept a certain distance. Obviously Scali knew who I was. Although

I had come to Washington as an inconspicuous embassy counselor, I was unaware of the fact that the FBI already knew all about me. I also suspected that John had excellent contacts at U.S. intelligence but probably not at CIA. Scali often alluded to the State Department's own intelligence section and that was where our conversations ended up.

The Occidental restaurant was on Pennsylvania Avenue, next door to the Willard Hotel. Not an overly luxurious place, it had style and its clientele consisted of government officials, businessmen, lawyers, and journalists. If a tablecloth is the dividing line between a restaurant and a fast food place, then the Occidental had white, cotton tablecloths, no less.

Scali was already waiting for me when I walked in and he looked very nervous. He was of medium height, slightly balding, a few years younger than me, with intelligent eyes and an extroverted Italian personality. He immediately sounded off with a tirade against Khrushchev's aggressive behavior. In Vienna, rather than negotiating, the Soviet leader had tried to impose his views on Kennedy concerning the problem of West Berlin. And now he was threatening the United States with a nuclear attack coming from Cuba. I answered that Washington was attempting to surround the USSR with a web of military bases, sending spy planes over our territory and was now trying to overthrow our ally, Fidel Castro. We had every right to defend ourselves and ensure the security of the Cubans. It was a nervous exchange and Scali appeared to be in a hurry. Before leaving the restaurant, he told me that at 7 p.m. President Kennedy would address an important message to the country to announce measures that the administration had decided to take against the Soviet Union and Cuba.

Before his speech President Kennedy had made all the necessary moves: Washington's allies had been informed of his decision; Congressional leaders had been briefed at a special meeting; over 300 U.S. Navy ships were at sea but hadn't yet been issued their "quarantine" orders; three Marine battalions had been sent as reinforcements to the U.S. base at Guantanamo and the alert had gone to DEFCON 3 for all the armed forces. Just minutes after the President's address, a nuclear force could hit the Soviet Union with missiles and twenty strategic bombers. At precisely 7 p.m., while the President was speaking to the country, U.S. Air Force planes took off toward the Gulf of Mexico to be near Cuba should Castro opt for a military response.

Everyone in America was glued to the television screen during the 17 minutes of JFK's speech. Kennedy announced that it had been clearly established that offensive missiles, capable of delivering nuclear attacks on the entire western hemisphere, were being set up in Cuba. In order to stop these offensive preparations the President had ordered a stringent quarantine of all military equipment being delivered to Cuban ports. U.S. warships would stop any ship sailing towards the island. Should any weapons be found on board, the ship would not be allowed to proceed. The surveillance of Cuban military preparations was greatly increased. Finally, a nuclear missile launched from Cuba on any other country within the western hemisphere would be considered an act of aggression against the United States and would trigger an appropriate response against the USSR. The U.S. armed forces were on the alert and a resolution had been introduced at the UN Security Council requiring the withdrawal of Soviet missiles and the dismantling of the launching pads. Kennedy pointed out that quarantine was just the first step and that he had told the Pentagon to continue military preparations. The Secretary of Defense had been ordered to create a strike force of 250,000 Infantrymen, 90,000 Marines and Paratroopers.

Moscow had received the text of the speech before it was given. Khrushchev didn't know until then that the Americans knew everything and he became extremely angry. It wasn't only against the quarantine, which he interpreted as an act of war: he was furious at the Soviet generals for failing to hide the missiles properly. Khrushchev's initial reaction was to order the ships on their way to Cuba not to stop and to send a very terse message to Kennedy:

> I honestly must say that the measures announced in your speech are a serious threat to peace and to the security of the people of the world. We reiterate that the weapons that are in Cuba, whatever they may be, are only there for defensive rea-

sons. I hope that the United States will show its wisdom and withdraw the measures you have begun that could have catastrophic consequences for world peace.

Khrushchev's reaction had no impact on the measures that had been decided. On October 23, the Organization of American States approved Kennedy's decision. That same evening 90 U.S. Navy ships encircled Cuba at a distance of 80 nautical miles from its coasts. The quarantine would begin at 10 a.m. the next morning. We didn't know it with certainty at the time, but 42 missiles with nuclear warheads had already been set up in Cuba. Aerial photographs showed that work was proceeding night and day and the launching pads could be operational at any moment. U2 planes were such a vital source of information concerning military preparations that Ex-Comm decided that the island would be immediately bombed if the Cubans shot down one of their planes. On Friday, October 24, for the first time in American history, the alert was increased to DEFCON 2, the highest before a state of war. The notification was sent to all American military installations without being encrypted to make sure that the Soviets would take American intentions seriously. An attack on Cuba or the USSR could now occur at any moment.

A new message from Khrushchev reached the White House that evening. Its language was hard:

> Mr. President, it is not a quarantine but an ultimatum that you are announcing and you threaten the use of force if we don't agree to your demands. No, Mr. President, I cannot accept it and I believe that, at the bottom of your heart, you know that I am right. I am convinced that in my place you would react the same way. Naturally we shall not remain as passive observers in the face of acts of piracy committed by American ships in the high seas. We will be obliged to take measures that we consider necessary and adequate to protect our rights. We have everything we need to do this.

The correspondence between the two leaders became so intensive that they quickly decided to use plain text. The atmosphere was so tense that any type of incident on the sea or in the air could trigger the irreparable. Why then waste time encrypting and decrypting messages? The members of Ex-Comm knew they were racing against the clock: as soon as the launching pads were ready, the threat of nuclear attack on U.S. targets would be real and the Soviet position would be reinforced. Washington had to stop the deployment of nuclear launch capabilities at any cost. Many close advisors to President Kennedy were pushing for an immediate landing in Cuba. Some even thought that the Kremlin was purposely delaying its answers to the White House to gain time to deploy its missiles. John Kennedy continued his search for a peaceful solution.

There was a second moderate member of Ex-Comm: Robert Kennedy. He spoke of the Japanese attack on Pearl Harbor and thought that the world would never forgive the United States if it invaded a small island. He thought the American people would also regret such a decision. The President's brother, as I mentioned, often used the back channel created by Salinger and Bolshakov. He was all the more disappointed. On October 23 Robert Kennedy came to the Soviet embassy at 9:30 p.m. He couldn't help complaining to Dobrynin, who, he thought, had lied about missiles being installed in Cuba. The Ambassador protested; to his knowledge, he said, there were no offensive weapons, but Robert Kennedy's confidence in his Soviet counterparts was greatly diminished.

The international community attempted to separate the two opponents. On October 23, UN Secretary General U Thant proposed a cooling-off period of two to three weeks, during which time the Soviets would stop making weapons deliveries to Cuba and the Americans would lift the quarantine. This didn't solve the problem of the missiles already deployed. President Kennedy rejected the offer on October 25 and that same day ordered Adlai Stevenson, the U.S. representative to the United Nations, to publicly demand an explanation from his Soviet counterpart, Valerian Zorin, who refused to answer. Stevenson then produced the enlarged aerial reconnaissance photographs; there could now be no doubt in anyone's mind. That afternoon the tension was further heightened when CIA Director McCone informed Ex-Comm that some missiles deployed in Cuba were now operational.

The Cubans were ready to resist aggression and their army of 1 million volunteers was being given military training. Soviet military commanders of units stationed on the island declared that their 43,000 men would take active part in its defense. Beginning on October 26, Kennedy increased the pressure. Fighter planes were flying over the island at low altitude every two hours; B-52 strategic bombers in the southeastern United States were in the air around the clock. As soon as one landed, another would take off. Americans were stocking up on food and necessities and many were looking for safe places to stay inside the country.

44

S oviet embassy personnel were working around the clock. Since
Sunday, October 21, there was barely enough time to go home
and sleep for a few hours. My family was in Moscow and I was
spending all my time at the embassy. The Americans were working
just as hard. Every evening some of my men would drive past the
White House, the Pentagon, the State Department, the CIA, or the
FBI: the lights were blazing in the offices of the Latin American
and Soviet sections. Hundreds of cars were in parking lots that
were normally empty at night. On Friday morning, October 26,
seeing that the situation was deteriorating by the hour, I called John
Scali to invite him to lunch. I was hoping to gather some firsthand
information and Scali immediately accepted. We would meet at the
Occidental at 1:30 p.m. I found out later that as soon as I got off
the phone, Scali had called Dean Rusk. The Secretary of State
thought it necessary to inform President Kennedy of the meeting
between the newsman and the KGB Rezident in Washington. It
was obvious that this Mr. Fomin would report the conversation to
his superiors, who would then relay the information higher up, and
there was a good chance that it might quickly reach Khrushchev.
Kennedy asked Rusk to send a simple message to the Russians:
"Time is of the essence." In other words, Khrushchev had to accept unconditionally to pull out the missiles.

I have gone over that lunch with Scali so many times in every detail that it is fixed in my memory as though it had happened yesterday. We ordered two martinis, the only hard liquor we'd have at our meetings. Usually we would only have the ice water the waiter brought us. I always had soup at lunch, true to old Russian habits. That day I had Manhattan clam chowder. Scali had a vegetable salad that he would drown in a sauce hot enough to stop you from breathing. I tried it only once. As a main course we shared the same tastes of steak and potatoes. Scali sipped his cocktail before rubbing his hands with a smile:

"So, how is Khrushchev doing?"

The question was unexpected but I didn't react.

"I don't know. I don't know him personally. And then he's so far away! You're the one with access to the White House."

Scali chuckled and looked satisfied. He asked:

"Khrushchev is wrong to think of Kennedy as some kind of young upstart. He's going to regret it."

Without giving me any time to answer, Scali went on:

"The Ex-Comm members are more and more inclined to accept the military option and invade Cuba without further delay. The Pentagon is telling the President that if he agrees, he can be free of both the missiles and the Castro regime in 48 hours."

"First of all," I answered very calmly, "as far as I know, our leaders consider President Kennedy to be an insightful and clever statesman. I think he's a reasonable man who will know how to stop some of your more warmongering generals. He will not let himself be dragged into a catastrophic adventure. Furthermore, the Cubans will defend their freedom no matter what it takes and American casualties will be very high."

I then added something I had no intention of saying. It was certainly not a message I had been asked to pass along so that it would reach Kennedy. I was simply talking, just like the street fighter of the 12th Worker's Street I had been and who couldn't accept being shoved into the mud.

"John," I said, leaning over toward him, "you should know that your President must realize a landing in Cuba would untie Khrushchev's hands completely. If you attack, the Soviet Union would be free to retaliate in another part of the world, at a sensitive point for you, having great political and military importance."

Had I been seeking to make an impression I couldn't have done any better. Scali looked at me straight in the eyes.

"You're thinking about West Berlin?"

I was still following my train of thought.

"As a countermove, it's highly probable," I responded.

"But West Berlin will be defended with everything we have," answered Scali, "by our own troops and by our allies."

"Listen, John, there would be an avalanche of armored tanks! There would be thousands of tanks and hundreds of low-flying fighter planes. We would also have the GDR's army with us. The resistance of the American, British, and French garrisons would be overwhelmed and we would end up occupying West Berlin."

That vision of Dante's inferno ended any discussion. We finished the steak and pondered the meaning of my statement.

"So war is around the corner," said Scali. "What do you think can make it start?"

"Fear," I answered. "Cuba is afraid of invasion, you're afraid of being attacked by missiles."

It was not our job to find a solution to the crisis; we were simply trying to imagine a phase of its possible development. We parted and hoped that our leaders would prevent a world catastrophe. I could imagine where Scali was headed. I went to report to Ambassador Dobrynin. I had clearly gone beyond my mission. A diplomat would never have spoken for his country without having been authorized to do so. It was up to the leaders to analyze each aspect to make threats or choose compromises. Yet it was not just a bluff on my part. I firmly believed it, and I knew that, should the situation worsen, it was one way events might evolve. I knew I was acting at my own risk and that more than my career was at stake, but I was never afraid of accepting my responsibilities. By saying that West Berlin would be invaded within 24 hours, I was somewhat short of our own plans. I subsequently learned that there really was an ultrasecret plan, known to very few people inside the Soviet and East German high commands, and that West Berlin was to be taken in 6 to 8 hours.

I knew Scali would inform higher authorities about our conversation, but I couldn't imagine the importance that our exchange over steak and potatoes was to have. My words quickly reached the man in the White House. Kennedy was not bluffing when he announced his intention to invade Cuba. That very morning he asked Dean Rusk to set up a government-in-exile among the anti-Castro émigrés and create a civilian administration once the island had been occupied. Yet the President was still seeking a peaceful solution and he seized the opportunity to use a new channel when the usual ones were not working. The intelligence services had often been very efficient in apparently hopeless situations. He therefore decided to bet on the "KGB line."

I had to wait until 4 p.m. before being able to discuss my lunch with Dobrynin, who had a meeting outside the building. As soon as he returned I went to his office to make my report. I had just begun when the ambassador's assistant, Oleg Sokolov, opened the door: John Scali was on the phone and wanted to talk to me urgently. I grabbed the phone. Scali wanted to see me right away.

"Go," said Dobrynin. "You'll tell me the whole story later."

We met at the Statler Hotel, a symbolic location, halfway between the White House and our embassy. We were actually very close to one another, our offices on 16th Street were a few hundred feet from the White House. That hotel and the headquarters of the AFL-CIO, were the only buildings separating the White House from the Soviet embassy. Five minutes after hanging up we both reached the lobby together. We went to the bar on the first floor, which was practically empty during the afternoon. We sat at a table in the back; I took the couch and Scali an armchair facing me. The waiter brought us two coffees and Scali got right to the point:

"Okay Al, the highest authority has asked me to give you the conditions to solve this crisis. One: the USSR dismantles and ships back its missiles under United Nations control. Two: the United States lifts the quarantine. Three: the United States will officially agree not to invade Cuba. This agreement could be reached within the United Nations."

I had taken out my notebook and took it down very quickly. Once Scali had finished I read my notes back to him.

"That's it," he approved.

"What does 'the highest authority' mean?"

He looked at me straight in the eyes and said, marking each word:

"John Fitzgerald Kennedy, President of the United States of America."

I told Scali that I would transmit that proposal immediately to my ambassador, who would send it on to Moscow. I also pointed out that the conditions were not fair. If withdrawing missiles was to take place under UN supervision, the UN should then also ascertain the return of U.S. troops to their barracks in Florida and the southeastern United States. Scali answered that any additional element could complicate and delay reaching an agreement while time was of the essence. In an emotional voice he added:

"The military is pressing the President to let them go ahead. Kennedy doesn't want to be a second Hideki Tojo[102] and he's trying to find a peaceful solution to the crisis."

I assured Scali once again that the proposal would go to Moscow immediately. I couldn't imagine that this would be a problem when we were facing the threat of nuclear conflict.

I went as fast as I could. I composed a cable of my two meetings with Scali and handed them to Dobrynin for his signature. Naturally, I could have signed them myself, but in this case I could only send the message to the head of intelligence, General Sakharovsky, or at best to the President of the KGB, Vladimir Semichastny. The ambassador could go to his minister but also to the Politburo and even to the First Secretary of the Party himself. Since every minute counted, the sooner the message reached Khrushchev's desk the better the chances to stop the mechanism that controlled the detonator. There was also a question of precedence: the most important documents were sent to Moscow with the ambassador's signature, unless he was not on good terms with the Rezident, which was not the case with us. Dobrynin trusted me, he often delegated security and intelligence problems to me and asked for my advice on difficult matters. During this crisis he had sent a car over at 3 a.m. just to know if I thought we should immediately inform Moscow of a new bombing threat.

Had Gromyko found out that such a crucial message had gone directly to the Politburo, without going through the Ministry of Foreign Affairs, he would certainly ask Dobrynin some very unpleasant questions. I didn't want to go behind the ambassador's back by sending my report on my own. Dobrynin, who knew administrative games very well, would understand this perfectly. Yet to my surprise he didn't sign my cable right away; he said he would study it and call me back once he was done. I returned to my office. In my usual phlegmatic way I began working on other files without thinking that from one minute to the next all these efforts could appear ridiculous. One hour, then two, went by. I had completely forgotten about the cable when finally the phone rang, Dobrynin wished to see me. I looked at my watch. It had taken him three hours to read the text.

Dobrynin was with three other assistants; Georgy Kornienko, Alexander Zinchuk, and Igor Kolossovsky were sitting on both sides of the long conference table. Kornienko looking serious and concentrated, staring at me intently from behind his glasses. The other two were averting their eyes. The ambassador got up and approached me.

"I cannot send this cable," he said calmly, as if to excuse himself. "The MID has not authorized the embassy to conduct this type of negotiation."

There was nothing to say. I took the cable back and left the room. At the Rezidentura I signed it and gave it to the code clerk. The message was to go urgently to Lieutenant General Alexander Sakharovsky, head of the PGU. Still, in spite of its urgency, my boss would only be able to read it several hours later. The document had to be encrypted, which would take some time, then typed as an ordinary cable but with groups of five digits rather than words, then placed in an envelope. In the secretariat the person at the desk would press the button connecting the embassy to the nearest Western Union office, and the messenger would arrive fifteen minutes to half an hour later. It would take time to bring the message to the telegraph office, transmit it to Moscow and decrypt it over there. It would be noon in Moscow when Sakharovsky could take the special phone where the dial had been replaced with the coat of arms of the USSR, and hear on the line the voice that had become so familiar since Khrushchev's visit to the United States—on the condition, of course, that my initiative did not cause an inextricable bureaucratic problem inside the PGU.

As for the answer, by the time it was written and took the same path in reverse it would not reach me before noon Washington time, the next day. It was midnight when the cable was finally sent; one day of crisis in one capital was ending while a new day was starting in the other capital. But those divisions were purely conventional. For the Russians, Cubans, and the Americans who lived through the crisis from the inside, it was one endless day that lasted a whole week. I took my jacket, which was hanging on the back of my chair, and went home.

45

While I was waiting for the ambassador's decision that evening, a new letter from Khrushchev reached the White House. The Soviet leader felt that the two parties facing each other in this crisis were only tying the knot tighter, making it impossible to unravel and that in the end it would have to be cut. He was proposing to withdraw the missiles against Kennedy's promise to never attempt to invade Cuba. After refusing to sign my cable late in the evening, Dobrynin met with Robert Kennedy. Not only was this an unofficial visit, it had also been decided without Ex-Comm's knowledge. The Attorney General didn't expect Dobrynin to introduce a new element into the negotiation: the issue of U.S. missiles in Turkey. After all, in deploying nuclear weapons in Cuba, Moscow was only reestablishing a certain balance. Now Washington could appreciate how uncomfortable it felt to be a target for a nuclear missile only a few minutes away. If America wanted such a threat to disappear, it was only fair that the same should take place for the Soviet Union.

The issue was bothersome for the Americans. The Jupiters were obsolete missiles that Kennedy wanted to remove from Turkey anyway, but the crisis had not allowed him to do so and now it had become virtually impossible. Walter Lippmann, the famous American political writer, had mentioned the possibility on Monday, October 22, along with Austrian Chancellor Alfons Gorbach, who promoted the concept of equal security. The United States had rejected the idea out of hand. Under different circumstances the trade-off of withdrawing old equipment out of Turkey against the dismantling of new missiles in Cuba would have been a good deal for Washington. In the midst of a crisis though it would look like a concession to a stronger opponent. Many Americans would interpret this as a sign of weakness and it might harm Kennedy's chances for reelection to a second term.

Dobrynin's reasoning was persuasive however and Robert Kennedy left the conference room to call his brother. The President was truly intent on avoiding war. When he came back, the Attorney General told the Ambassador:

"The President is willing to consider the question relating to Turkey."

Once Robert Kennedy left, Dobrynin sent an encrypted report to Khrushchev. In Cuba that same evening of April 26, the tension reached its zenith. Fidel Castro went to the Soviet embassy in Havana but refused to have a conversation in Ambassador Alexander Alexeyev's office, so they both went down to the air raid shelter to talk. The Cuban leader, who was usually calm and smiling, was extremely nervous. He was convinced that the Americans were about to bomb his island. Alexeyev and Castro composed a message to Khrushchev where they feared that the launching pads would be bombed within the next few hours. Alexeyev, with whom I was friendly, told me later he was convinced that this alarming message persuaded Khrushchev to accept a compromise solution.

Saturday, October 27, was the most anguishing day of all. Robert McNamara would say later: "I thought I wouldn't see another Saturday night." That morning the Ex-Comm members were to find out that an incident far away from Cuba had almost triggered the conflict. A U2 stationed in Alaska had penetrated Soviet air space by mistake. Realizing what had happened, the pilot immediately requested assistance. A few F-102 fighters immediately took off to give the U2 cover. In the meantime Soviet radar had detected the spy plane and a MiG patrol had taken off to intercept it. The two combat groups, all of them equipped with air-to-air missiles, were flying toward each other at full speed. Fortunately, the

U2 had been able to fly out of Soviet air space before our planes were within firing range. Some Ex-Comm members like McNamara feared that the Soviets might think this intrusion was a reconnaissance mission as a prelude to nuclear attack. Fortunately, Moscow did not give too much importance to this minor incident while much more crucial matters were in the balance.

At 11 a.m., a second letter from Khrushchev reached the White House. It had been sent by radio, as it had become customary, to save time. The language in that message was much harder than the preceding ones: it placed the Jupiter issue in Turkey on the table and proposed that both parties withdraw missiles placed on each other's border under United Nations Security Council supervision. This new proposal surprised the Ex-Comm members. Fearing leaks, the Kennedy brothers hadn't yet informed anyone about the late evening conversation between Robert and Dobrynin at the Soviet embassy. The Attorney General voiced the opinion, which was immediately accepted, to ignore the second letter and answer the first one, which proposed the withdrawal of Soviet missiles against guarantees of non-aggression against Cuba. Yet the Kennedy family secret couldn't be kept for long, and the President shared it with five of his closest advisors: Robert McNamara, McGeorge Bundy, Dean Rusk, Llewellyn Thompson, former and future U.S. ambassador to the USSR, and Theodore Sorensen. A "Turkey for Cuba" agreement offered a real possibility to resolve the crisis. The major inconvenience was the negative effect it would have on John F. Kennedy's image with the American people. Dean Rusk then proposed a separate secret agreement regarding the withdrawal of Jupiter missiles from Turkey. It was agreed that Robert Kennedy would meet with Dobrynin to confirm American agreement in principle and request that the Soviets keep the Jupiter withdrawal secret.

If Moscow showed self-control when confronting the U2 incident over the Bering Straits it was to be the Americans' turn to face a difficult choice. A SAM missile shot down a U2 piloted by Major Rudolph Anderson over Cuba around noon that day. The United States had previously announced that it would retaliate against anti-aircraft batteries should the Cubans shoot down one of its reconnaissance planes. McNamara and General Taylor felt that, without a firm response, the Russians would multiply such actions. The Joint Chiefs of Staff were insisting on an invasion of Cuba by Monday, October 29, at the latest. President Kennedy decided to wait for another plane to be shot down before ordering the site responsible be bombed.

On that same day, four Crusader F8U-1P reconnaissance planes were fired upon by Cuban anti-aircraft and automatic weapons fire. One plane was hit but managed to return to its base. In spite of this, Kennedy didn't order any retaliation. He was convinced that these attacks were based on false premises: Khrushchev hadn't had the time to study his proposals as transmitted by Scali and Fomin. The Soviet leader had to be given the time to show what his true intentions were. If there was no change in the Cuban attitude, then he would have enough time to order a counterattack. Just like all the big and small actors in the unfolding drama, Scali was on call all the time. He immediately phoned for an urgent meeting at about 12:30 p.m.

Moscow's response to my cable had arrived faster than I expected. At 9 a.m. a code clerk brought me Sakharovsky's confirmation requesting that I retransmit through the MID channel with the ambassador's signature. My worse fears were being confirmed. I had not stated in my message that Dobrynin had already refused his confirmation and now I could no longer cover for him. I answered that the ambassador had refused to sign because he had not received instructions from Moscow to negotiate with the White House.

I was in my office when Scali called. We met in the street five minutes later and went into a bar. I had nothing to give him. Already very animated under normal circumstances, John was a bundle of nerves. He accused me of the worse things without mincing his words: he was acting in good faith and wanted to avoid the irreparable while I was trying to trick him by being underhanded, to try to gain time by dragging out the negotiations; I was attempting to lull the Americans while the launching pads were being completed in Cuba, and he, Scali, who had successfully obtained a new initiative to seek a compromise, was looking silly in front his country's leaders. I tried to calm him down as best I could by saying that I was sincere. I explained how all lines of communication with Moscow were saturated and that Khrushchev must have been buckling under the flood of urgent messages that were directed at him.

"John, believe me, we are just as impatient as you are. Just like you, we are waiting for the answer any minute."

Scali believed me but that didn't solve the problem and we were both troubled when we parted company. He went directly to the White House and reported our conversation to President Kennedy. I was not the only Soviet official trying to do something, naturally. Dobrynin had two meetings with Robert Kennedy that day and I was present at the first meeting at the embassy. When I returned from my meeting with Scali at 2 p.m., the ambassador called me in. I went to the second floor. In front of the staircase there were two large rooms used for official receptions that could each easily hold 300 people. If they were meeting there it was only because in the larger the room the harder it would be to place any bugs.

The position of the two persons is always very important. A rectangular table in between generally looks like a front line separating two belligerents. If they are both lounging in armchairs facing each other, it's a much less formal situation. Anatoly Dobrynin and Robert Kennedy were both sitting on the same sofa and yet the tone of their discussion was far from being that of a friendly conversation. When I entered, Dobrynin got up and spoke to me in Russian. I didn't understand what he wanted. I was supposed to draft a memorandum but the subject was unclear. The ambassador, who was generally very clear and precise, was now fumbling, searching for words. I understood that it was not he who wished to see me but Robert Kennedy, who had remained seated on the edge of the sofa, and was looking at me intently. I had the impression that he had come to the embassy just to make sure that counselor Fomin, on whom his brother had placed such a large bet, did in fact exist and had given the President's message to the Soviet ambassador.

The situation worsened as the hours went by. At 7:15 p.m., there was still no answer from Khrushchev. The President asked his brother to meet with Dobrynin once again. The second meeting took place in the Attorney General's office. The war of nerves was getting some results: Robert Kennedy handed Dobrynin a copy of the answer to Khrushchev's first letter. At the same time he proposed a secret transaction that could be boiled down to two points. First: the Jupiter missiles would only be dismantled three to five months after Soviet missiles had been taken out of Cuba. Second: this condition would remain strictly confidential and would not be included in the official text of the agreement on the resolution of the crisis. As justification, Robert Kennedy spoke of the complicated domestic situation in the United States, the need to negotiate with Turkey and other NATO members. Soviet missiles, however, must be withdrawn without delay.

"If you don't dismantle those bases we'll do it ourselves," said Robert Kennedy.

The Americans wanted a positive answer from Khrushchev by the next day. At 8 p.m. while this meeting was taking place, John Kennedy answered Khrushchev's previous message. To avoid any delays the text was handed out to the press immediately: if under UN supervision, the USSR took its missiles out of Cuba and guaranteed not to provide Castro with any more, the United States would end the quarantine and pledge not to invade the island. Late in the evening, Robert Kennedy also used the second channel with Bolshakov. He repeated to this shadowy figure the same conditions he had given to Dobrynin and stressed that should Moscow not agree within 24 hours, the President could no longer restrain the military from attacking Cuba. During that crucial day the White House took four separate initiatives to elicit the Kremlin's response to the proposals given by Scali. JFK was seriously intent on a peaceful solution to the crisis and avoiding an armed conflict that would produce an incalculable number of victims. The ball was in our court. Another night of anguish was beginning.

I was right to think that in Moscow, just as in Washington, all relevant offices had been working around the clock since October 22. Politburo members were sleeping at the Kremlin to be ready for discussions at any time. I found out later that Khrushchev was no longer able to hide how worried he really was. He kept on nodding his head as he repeated:

"Cuba is done for!"

Early in the morning of October 28, the First Secretary summoned his advisors to his residence outside Moscow. He had received all our reports, mine included, and was aware that peace was hanging by a thread. An alarming bit of news was announced at the beginning of the meeting: President Kennedy would address the American people at 5 p.m. It could be the announcement of an attack on the island. It was now up to the Soviets to show that they didn't want war.

The decision came immediately. Despite the time difference, under normal circumstances Khrushchev's letter would reach the White House *after* 5 p.m. The fastest way was to read it over the radio. The message also said:

> Mr. President,
>
> I have received your message of October 27, 1962. I express my satisfaction and my gratitude for the understanding and common sense that you show in exercising your responsibilities to maintain world peace.
>
> In order to quickly resolve this conflict, besides previous instructions stopping construction at the sites, the Soviet government has ordered that those weapons and their ramps, which you have characterized as offensive, be dismantled, as well as their launching pads.

Washington received the message at 9 a.m. on Sunday, October 28, and was able to draw a sigh of relief. Some Ex-Comm members still feared some Kremlin trick to gain time, but President Kennedy was confident. He wrote an immediate answer and since every minute was of the essence, it was first read over Voice of America radio.

> I think that you and I who bear the heavy responsibility to maintain peace are aware that developments in this crisis were reaching a point beyond which events would have become unmanageable.

The crisis was over. At 11 p.m. Dobrynin went to the Department of Justice to congratulate Robert Kennedy and the President.

Ex-Comm had already cancelled flights over Cuba and the rest was just routine work. Following that week's anxieties came a sense of relief. Now that the worst had passed we all felt that nothing was important anymore, as though the future was promising us just a long string of vacations.

I was in such a state of mind on October 29, when Scali called me. He wanted to celebrate the happy ending. Later he would write that on November 3 he invited me to dinner a second time. It's possible but I remember only one meal and I remember it perfectly well: it was at Rive Gauche, famous for its cuisine. Scali told me that he was inviting me at President Kennedy's request because he considered our back channel as very important to the resolution of the crisis and wished to express his thanks. As he ordered the best dishes on the menu and some rare wines, Scali repeated with a smile:

"We deserve it!"

I was all the more inclined to agree, since the Rezidentura wasn't footing the bill. Our personalities, Scali's and mine, couldn't have been more different. His Italian ancestry made him very joyful: he wouldn't stop laughing, rubbing his hands and talking loudly. I, who by nature am slow and phlegmatic even under ordinary circumstances, just felt exhausted, empty and drained after having used up all my nervous energy for eight days. My host apologized for having accused me of double-talk and betrayal two days before, but I didn't bear a grudge. I could well imagine how tense and anguished the atmosphere was at the White House. We drank to the good health and wisdom of our leaders who had been able to find a compromise, even though it came at the last minute. The conversation then drifted to other subjects, on America and Russia, their shared responsibilities for world peace and the need to agree. I remembered a thousand details from our previous meetings, words, looks, and gestures, but what I remember of that meal was the atmosphere. I can see John's smiling face as he told a new joke that I cannot remember. It's true that I was relaxed after so much excitement, possibly the highest in my entire, rather exciting career.

46

Robert McNamara would say later on that the world was only one step away from nuclear war. But even though the two leaders had succeeded in preventing the hawks on each side from using nuclear weapons, an American invasion of Cuba would nevertheless have turned into a terrible war. The Americans had seriously underestimated the military forces on the island. Castro had mobilized not 100,000 but 270,000 men and women. The Soviet forces were not 10,000, as the White House had estimated, but 42,000 officers and men. The Americans also didn't know about the presence of tactical nuclear weapons on the island. Had the Soviet generals in Cuba been unable to reach the highest echelons of the Kremlin in case of invasion, they were authorized to use those weapons as they saw fit. Unquestionably the losses would have been much higher than the 10,000 civilians and 20,000 military personnel the Pentagon had projected.

Only one participant was to feel cheated. Castro found out about the deal on the radio because Khrushchev hadn't had the time to consult his ally. The Cuban leader was furious. He said that a true solution to the crisis required five additional points: the end of the economic blockade of Cuba; the end of all American subversion; the end of attacks coming from bases in Puerto Rico; forbidding reconnaissance from both the air and within the island's territorial waters; return of the military base at Guantanamo to Cuba. He even attempted to oppose the dismantling of the missile launch pads but in the end he had to go along with the agreement. The missiles were loaded on the decks of ships so that reconnaissance planes could verify that they had really been shipped back to the Soviet Union. A few months later Kennedy kept his promise and the Jupiter missiles were withdrawn from both Turkey and Italy.

Most of the participants in the crisis—Robert Kennedy, McGeorge Bundy, Arthur Schlesinger, and Pierre Salinger—have written their memoirs. All of them speak of the two meetings between John Scali and myself on October 26, 1962. I have kept silent for over some thirty years. The reason is simple: when there's a snafu, the high and mighty always manage to find a fall guy. But when the underling does something good, the credit always goes to the high and mighty. Furthermore, my goal was never to change the world, yet since I am retired and look at my life and the events I was involved in, I have decided to speak up. My contribution has been recognized and accepted by many participants. Even Gromyko, when he traveled to Washington—which he did once a year for the UN General Assembly—would always take some time for a private meeting with me.

Since 1990 I have come out of hiding, but looking back on that busy week I have often asked myself a few questions. I think I have found an answer to at least three of them.

The first question is why didn't Ambassador Dobrynin sign the cable with Kennedy's proposals? The excuse he used, the MID not having the authority to conduct such negotiations, was clearly only a decoy. Diplomats are not simple subordinates and their initiatives can turn out to be very valuable, especially in a crisis where every hour counts. My conclusion is rather harsh: I feel the ambassador answered out of bureaucratic habit, laced with some egotistical considerations. I'm convinced that had Scali handed the conditions for the resolution of the crisis to a real diplomat or even to Dobrynin himself, the latter would have jumped at the opportunity to communicate them to his Moscow superiors. Furthermore, I think the ambassador felt that I would not have the nerve to send such an important message to Moscow under my own signature. Therefore, the White House could only turn to him. I found out the next day that Dobrynin had sent someone to check if I had actually sent the cable. The code clerk at the Rezidentura was located in a room in a specially equipped part of the embassy. His MID colleagues were in the other rooms. That evening a diplomat, acting as supervisor, asked my code clerk to lend him a hand. Naturally our codes were different but the procedure was the same, so much so that he could actually do things faster. My man refused but the diplomat was able to verify that the cable was in fact going out.

Was it possible that Kennedy chose to go through me because he wanted his message to come from the KGB rather than the ambassador? I don't think so. I actually feel the President wanted to send a simple message to Khrushchev: "Make your decision quickly before we attack Cuba!" He calculated that the head of the intelligence station would do his utmost to make sure that the message reached its destination, outside Soviet bureaucratic protocol, which Americans could very well not be acquainted with.

Second question: why did the White House not use the Salinger-Bolshakov channel or go directly in the messages from Kennedy to Khrushchev? The answer is obvious in this case: it was impossible to make an agreement between leaders simply because they were corresponding in plain text when it was not, as in the final day of the crisis, through communiqués broadcast on radio. Neither one could be the first to agree without harming his public image. Therefore, this channel only made the bidding go higher because it was a contest as to who would be the toughest. What about the Bolshakov channel? As we have shown, it was used only at the very last moment, perhaps because the Soviet journalist had the reputation of being a party boy, and not too trustworthy. When Alexei Adzhubei, chief editor of *Izvestia* and Khrushchev's son-in-law, came to Washington, he would organize some unforgettable soirées both for the participants and the neighbors. I knew about them even though I never went.

As for the embassy, it seems to me that Kennedy didn't trust Soviet diplomacy that much. One week before, on October 18, Andrei Gromyko had told him that the USSR would only make deliveries of civilian or defensive materials that were no threat to the United States' security and that the Soviet Union would take no steps to undermine Soviet-American relations before the midterm elections took place. As for Dobrynin, who was ordinarily a Gromyko man, he had also seconded his minister's statements. Kennedy, who already had aerial photographs, could only see in the assurances given by Gromyko and Dobrynin a deliberate set of lies. Dobrynin himself recognized it:

> Immediately following the Cuban crisis, the White House even considered asking Moscow for my replacement as ambassador to Washington because of "having deliberately misinformed the administration of the United States."[103]

In January 1989, during a roundtable conference about the Caribbean Crisis, in Moscow, McGeorge Bundy and Theodore Sorensen roundly accused Gromyko of having lied.

"But Mr. Dobrynin also knew," answered the former minister, pointing to his subordinate.

"Not at all! Not at all!" protested the interested party.

The twenty-odd people in the audience, where I was sitting, burst out laughing.

Finally, the third issue. The Americans tried to promote the idea that the proposals that were to end the conflict didn't come from President Kennedy, but from the Soviet side, through embassy counselor Fomin. This is the position taken by all the American sources I was able to consult, starting with the books by Pierre Salinger and Arthur Schlesinger who, as assistants to Kennedy, were aware of the truth. I can understand that people may not believe what I am saying. But it is more difficult to reject logical explanations indicating that Kennedy was the first one to open his hand to Khrushchev. Clearly, neither Scali nor I had the necessary stature to submit our own proposals to the heads of state, especially while facing a nuclear threat. I only drew the attention of my counterpart to a possible scenario as to how events might unfold in case of aggression against Cuba. The mistake the Americans made was to overestimate my own authority: I was speaking as a mere analyst while they saw me as a Kremlin spokesman.

If it was impossible for me to offer proposals in my own name, I also couldn't be a non-official emissary of the Soviet Premier. If one considers the improbable scenario that Khrushchev had proposed identical conditions to resolve the crisis, he would have transmitted them, either directly or through Ambassador Dobrynin, to the President of the United States. Yet there is no such documentary evidence in the correspondence between the two leaders. Only one possibility remains: the man in the White House reacted once he was informed of my first meeting with Scali on October 26. Scali, the President's advisors and JFK himself took my scenario as a warning from the Soviet leader: should you attack Cuba, we will invade West Berlin. There are two possible attitudes in any negotiation when facing a higher bid. One, increase your own bid, as in a poker game, and keep up the pressure until one of the players breaks. But in such cases any kind of incident, a plane shot down, a damaged ship, can start a war. Two, put a reasonable compromise on the table. That is what John F. Kennedy did by having John Scali transmit the proposal made by "the highest authority."

Kennedy may have preferred to switch things around by saying that the Soviet side had suggested the compromise, which is understandable. The President wished to exclude from the official deal his pledge to withdraw Jupiter missiles from Turkey for the same reason. Midterm elections were only ten days away. In a country convinced that its system of government is the best and should be the model for other countries, to seek a compromise in a struggle with evil incarnate would have been suicidal for the President and his party. But it's also hard to understand why Americans hang on to this fantasy.

I took part in the roundtable on the Caribbean Crisis held in Moscow on January 26-30, 1989, with the authorization of the KGB. There was a reception on the opening day at the Continental restaurant. Scali was genuinely surprised to see me among the guests. We were very happy to meet again to air our differences and we had a few drinks while talking about our lives. Scali had been international affairs advisor to President Richard Nixon, and U.S. ambassador to the UN from 1973 to 1975. After leaving public service he returned to his profession as a newsman and advisor to ABC television.

But suddenly he felt sick and couldn't breathe. We left the room. His wife gave him some pills and a waiter brought a glass of water. Then the couple left and I wished him well for the discussions the next day as we shook hands.

The morning of the first day was set aside for the celebrities: Gromyko, McNamara, Dobrynin, and Bundy, to name just a few. During the noon break, Soviet television wanted to film a short conversation between Scali and me. On camera Scali said that I, Alexander Fomin, had proposed the famous compromise and not President Kennedy. I interrupted him to make my point, we had an argument, and the filming was cancelled. That afternoon I had to insist several times to be able to make a point myself. Finally Professor Joseph Nye, who chaired the meeting, allowed me to speak. I recounted my two meetings with Scali and left out only one fact: Dobrynin's refusal to sign my cable. I expected Scali to object but nothing happened and the Americans didn't react.

The MID had organized a dogged defense and when Gromyko and Dobrynin saw me in the hall they looked somber and avoided conversation. Vice Foreign Minister Viktor Komplektov had the task of expressing their displeasure. He attacked me indirectly and complained that I had revealed my conversations with Scali to Fyodor Burlasky, editor-in-chief of *Literaturnaya Gazeta*, who was also participating in the roundtable. Until then, the credit for having solved the crisis had been attributed to the Ministry of Foreign Affairs. Could intelligence not also get some credit? Many people, even at the conference, were convinced of this because Burlasky had told the story to other Soviet participants like Georgy Shakhnazarov, one of Mikhail Gorbachev's foreign policy advisors, and to well-known academics such as Georgy Arbatov, Director of the Institute for the United States and Canada, and Evgeny Primakov, who at the time was Director of the Institute for World Economics and International Relations, known as IMEMO. (Primakov later was to become Director of the PGU renamed SVR in democratic Russia, then Minister of Foreign Affairs and Prime Minister under Boris Yeltsin.)

My answer to Komplektov was that Burlasky had known of my meetings with Scali for a long time. In 1982 he'd even written a play concerning the Cuban crisis in which one of the characters was named Fokin, a Soviet intelligence officer. The entire matter was no secret long before this conference.

"On the other hand," I attacked him, "wouldn't it be interesting to find out about the real mystery of why Dobrynin refused to sign my cable?"

"I will not answer that question," was Komplektov's curt answer as he walked away.

I met Scali in the hotel lobby the next day. He didn't look good and was obviously ill. I asked him if he was going to speak and he shook his head. But a day later, on January 29, Scali opened the proceedings with a short statement where he said, and I quote verbatim:

"I have listened carefully to the statement made by Alexander Fomin regarding the content of our conversations in October 1962. I think highly of Mr. Fomin and agree that we both played a significant role on that occasion. Yet I must say that some facts he mentioned do not match those that, as an experienced and professional newsman, I remember perfectly well. I don't wish to start an argument with him but, for the record, I wish to say that my recollections differ from those of Mr. Fomin."

My sense is that this statement was the collective product of the American delegation. There were no further comments, yet it was abundantly clear that, had I really changed the facts around, the U.S. delegates would have cut me down to size.

Another colorful detail is even more revealing about the strange American attitude toward this story. A small commemorative plaque was placed just above the table where Scali and I sat at the Occidental restaurant during that memorable lunch. The text reads: "At a tense moment of the Cuban crisis (October 1962), a mysterious Russian, Mr. X, advanced a proposal here to John Scali, a newsman at ABC News. That meeting averted the threat of nuclear war." I knew this plaque existed for a long time but didn't find out its exact wording until the conference regarding the crisis. I asked Scali why the text didn't reflect the facts. He answered that he didn't know who had decided to commemorate our meeting that way and had not been told in advance.

A year later I wrote to him regarding the idea of a Soviet film-maker, Andrei Stapran, to produce a Soviet-American documentary on the thirtieth anniversary of the crisis. I also wished to reestablish the truth and correct the inscription on the plaque. Scali didn't address the issue in his answer.

I arrived in Washington in September 1992 with Stapran to shoot the American scenes of the film. The director wanted to reconstruct the two meetings with Scali at the Occidental restaurant and the bar at the Statler Hotel. We went to see Scali at his office at ABC, but John was not enthusiastic at the idea of being filmed with me. On October 22, one month later, ABC was going to broadcast a two-part documentary for the 30th anniversary of the crisis. Since he had participated in that film, he couldn't be in another production, so Stapran offered to have an ABC team on the set to make its own documentary. The advantage of having both participants on screen was obvious and Scali agreed to discuss it with his bosses. We were to return two days later. On September 4 the answer was "no" to both questions. The ABC film was 80% edited and the network didn't want to add last minute changes. The management didn't see the point in meeting with the Russian director and had expressly forbidden that Scali participate in his documentary. I could only express regret and that was where things stood.

Since I didn't want that rejection to cloud our relationship, we spent some time chatting and reminiscing about things from thirty years before that had drawn us together. Scali spoke of the parts of the ABC film where he appeared and said that he had made no negative statements about me. He was relaxed and joked all the time. Neither he nor any of his colleagues could imagine the changes that had taken place in the Soviet Union. I asked for one of his photos and he gave me two with his autograph, asking me to return to see him before I left. We filmed the Occidental scene with me in it, alone. The restaurant had moved to the ground floor of a modern building and had become more expensive. Yet the table from my lunch of October 26, 1962 with Scali was still there. At least that is what was written on the metal plaque with its specious message. Joan Danoff, the manager, told me that without Scali the plaque could never have been placed there. As agreed, I called him on the morning of September 10. The man was in a bad mood, and asked:

"What do you want?"

"Nothing special. We agreed to meet before I left."

Scali asked me to stop by his office early in the afternoon. When I arrived he was standing in the middle of the room, holding his head and visibly in pain. He told me he had a terrible migraine and pointed toward the ceiling. I didn't understand.

"I just got out of a rough meeting with my boss."

He was nervous and was speaking quickly, not his usual happy self. I expressed regret that we couldn't appear together on film or in an article to tell the truth about what happened behind the scenes.

"I have no intention of writing anything at all," he said. "You are the one refusing to admit that you handed me a compromise proposal!"

Until then Scali had avoided the question because he hadn't forgotten the truth but would not or could not say so. There, for the first time, he dared lie to me. I almost exploded but held my temper.

"It's nonsense and you know it as well as I!"

He completely lost his cool, beginning a ranting sentence in a high-pitched voice. His face was beet red and he looked furious. It was useless under those circumstances to keep the conversation going.

"All right," I said. "Keep your opinion. I can sleep nights, my conscience is clear."

He didn't answer and walked me to the elevator. I wished him and his family all the best and we exchanged a cold handshake. I was never to see him again. Scali died in October 1995. One of the obituaries said "Scali was unanimously praised for his eminent role as White House representative during the back channel negotiations to help prevent a nuclear war in 1962 during the Caribbean crisis. Following President Kennedy's request, Scali remained silent about the part he played. His contribution to the settlement of the Caribbean crisis was revealed only recently by a high level State Department official."

I think Victor Hugo said something about history being at the threshold of legend. Strangely enough, no one claims credit for the famous proposals that brought about a solution to the crisis. John Kennedy, who deserves the credit, didn't want it because it could have been interpreted as a sign of weakness in facing the harshness of a Khrushchev. To maintain that image, and perhaps to avoid being seen as JFK's letter carrier, Scali doggedly refused to tell the truth, even thirty years later. I have no right to take the credit they want to force on me. Too bad! Had I really carried the proposals of the head of the Soviet government, I would certainly have asked for my reward.

I am the only one who knows the truth today. No commitments or censorship can stop me from telling that truth, now that the old battles are only of an historical interest. I feel that, more than forty years later, we must put aside ridiculous national pride and salute the brave and insightful initiative by John Kennedy during the dramatic events of October 1962. Who knows how Soviet-American relations would have evolved had the President not been assassinated? Twenty-five years before Gorbachev, John Kennedy, in his famous speech at American University on June 10, 1963, laid the foundations of a new way of thinking:

> Today, should total war ever break out again—no matter how—our two countries would become the primary targets. It is an ironic but accurate fact that the two strongest powers are the two in the most danger of devastation. All we have built, all we have worked for, would be destroyed in the first 24 hours. And even in the cold war, which brings burdens and dangers to so many nations, including this nation's closest allies—our two countries bear the heaviest burdens. For we are both devoting massive sums of money to weapons that could be better devoted to combating ignorance, poverty, and disease. We are both caught up in a vicious and dangerous cycle in which suspicion on one side breeds suspicion on the other, and new weapons beget counterweapons.

Kennedy asked Americans to stop viewing the Russians as their enemies and began a number of initiatives towards an understanding. During the crisis the leaders appreciated the importance of communications, and a direct telex was set up between the Kremlin and the White House. The dramatic trials they had gone through brought the two leaders together and reinforced their desire to cooperate. Less than one month later, on August 5, 1963, they signed, together with Great Britain, a treaty banning nuclear testing in the atmosphere, in space, and underwater. Kennedy was promoting an end to the arms race and a reduction of military budgets that were detrimental to both superpowers. What follows is well known. The President's new policy could only alarm the American military-industrial complex whose prosperity was jeopardized.[104] On a sunny November day in 1963, John F. Kennedy was assassinated in Dallas. One year later Nikita Khrushchev was overthrown by his rivals in the Politburo. The clash between the superpowers continued for several more decades.

47

"Khrushchev was right to avoid a war during the Caribbean crisis. He could not risk losing what had cost so much to build in the USSR and Cuba."

Despite being 73 years of age, the man was alert and forceful. His rugged face showed strength and determination. Such an ordinary statement took on special significance because it came from him. Pitirim Sorokin was known for his infallible vision, which saw through not just current events but also the future contained in the present. I was fortunate to have several conversations with the father of modern sociology and, despite our ideological differences, he always impressed me with his observations and good judgment which I can confirm. I met him during my first American tour in the fall of 1942. I went to Boston to speak at a meeting of the local Russian War Relief committee. A few political workers and Professor Pitirim Sorokin came to greet me at the station. He introduced himself and expressed his sympathy for Russia in the face of Nazi aggression.

"I've wiped my resentment away and I'm doing whatever I can to lighten the sufferings of my fellow citizens," he told me as we walked to a waiting car. "You are the first Soviet citizen I've spoken to in the United States."

I thanked him for his support and his compassion toward the USSR. We did not speak to each other after that. Sorokin was on the dais but made no speeches during the rally and I took the train back to New York the same evening. We established real contact some twenty years later, just after the missile crisis, at the beginning of December 1962. I was asked to address the students at Harvard University. I called Pitirim Sorokin before flying to Boston. He immediately remembered the first Soviet citizen he had spoken to in exile and was delighted to see me again. He invited me to dinner at his home. After the lecture I traveled to Winchester, a small town near Boston. A few ranch-style houses surrounded by trees and bushes were lined up on both sides of a narrow street. Sorokin was waiting for me on the small paved pathway that crossed his lawn. He was wearing an old-fashioned double-breasted coat and broad brimmed fedora from years before.

"Welcome to my shack," he said as he invited me up the path. "This is where my wife and I are spending our old age."

Elena Petrovna was slim for her age and had maintained all of her feminine charm. She had a pleasant face and her hair was carefully pinned up in a bun. I brought some Russian specialties with me: a box of caviar, a bottle of Stolichnaya vodka, and some chocolates. The lady of the house showed me around: the parlor, a large living room, a kitchen downstairs, two bedrooms, a study, and a library upstairs. We sat in comfortable armchairs up in the study as we reminisced about the war years.

"I was afraid the Red Army would buckle under the assault of Hitler's war machine," said the professor. "The Wehrmacht had conquered practically all of Europe without too much effort and I feared that Moscow and Leningrad would fall."

I noted that the Reich would have been defeated much sooner had the Western Allies opened the second front at the right time.

"The plans agreed to by Churchill and the American interest groups were as much centered on defeating Germany as on the complete exhaustion of the Soviet Union in the course of this war. In point of fact, since Peter the Great, England has done everything it could to keep Russia down. Now it's the United States' turn to fear that Russia could become a powerful country."

Elena Petrovna announced that lunch was served and my hosts asked me to talk about myself. I began with my childhood hardships.

"Well, I think my origins are even more proletarian than yours." said Sorokin, once I had finished.

The sociologist was born in 1889 in the village of Turia in the current Republic of Komis.[105] His parents were poor illiterate peasants. His father was a hired hand, a carpenter and painter, and Pitirim began helping him when he was 8 years old. He was only ten when both his parents died and he had to struggle alone to survive. He traveled the country working as a farm boy, an itinerant artisan, a maintenance man, a worker and even as leader of a chorus. Yet he had a hunger for learning and, "by accident" he learned how to read and write, attending a parochial school and then a high school. As a brilliant student he was admitted to St Petersburg University where he defended his doctoral thesis in criminal law in 1916. In 1922 he received a Ph.D. in sociology. Sorokin joined the Socialist Revolutionary Party at the university and was arrested three times and sent to jail by the Tsarist government. After the revolution of February 1917, he was among the founders of the Soviet of Russian Farmers and editor of *Narodnaya Volya* [The People's Will]. He even became Alexander Kerensky's secretary for two months while Kerensky was Prime Minister of the Provisional Government. At that time and continuing after the Bolshevik takeover, Sorokin never stopped the ideological struggle against Lenin.

"Lenin and I knew each other well," he said.

I reminded Sorokin of a rather favorable article that Lenin published in *Pravda* on November 21, 1917 entitled "The Valuable Confession of Pitirim Sorokin," where he commented on an open letter written by the scientist who announced that he was leaving the Socialist Revolutionary Party and the Duma. The Bolshevik leader analyzed the reasons for these resignations and spelled out his strategy to attract the petit-bourgeois and the intelligentsia to Bolshevism.

"Why did you leave the Socialist Revolutionaries?" I asked Sorokin.

He adjusted his thick-rimmed glasses.

"Lenin explains the reason quite well. I noticed that the peasants had not supported the Socialist Revolutionaries in the power struggle in the countryside where the poorest and middle-income peasants were favorable to the Bolsheviks. Without core support among the people, there is no way you can win, and I was also opposed to the terrorist attacks my party engaged in."

The sociologist's relations with the Soviets were not good at all and Sorokin was a relentless critic of the Bolshevik leaders: Lenin, Trotsky, Kamenev. The Cheka[106] arrested him in January 1918 and he was taken to the infamous St. Peter and St. Paul fortress in Petrograd, the dungeon of the Russian Empire. He was released after four months and went to Archangel to prepare the overthrow of the Bolsheviks. He was arrested again in October 1918 and jailed at Vologda. The court sentenced him to death and he was to be executed within ten days. Sorokin wrote to Lenin, Anatoly Lunacharsky, and Lev Karakhan,[107] who had been his classmate at the university, pointing out that his was an ideological struggle against the Bolsheviks and not a violent one. During such troubled times his letters didn't have much of chance of reaching their destination and Sorokin expected to be executed any day. Ten days went by, then ten more, and another ten.

After forty days a group of Chekists came into his cell and told him to get dressed. He was prepared for the worst, but instead of shooting him they took him to Moscow. After a short interrogation at the Lubyanka, he was brought to Lunacharsky, who announced that his sentence had been cancelled on Lenin's orders. He was free to go. Lunacharsky, who knew Sorokin's worth as a scientist, offered him a job to represent his ministry in the northern part of the country but Sorokin refused. He was then offered the position of head of the history department at Petrograd University, which he accepted, and taught there until the end of 1922. Then, along with other intellectuals opposed to the Bolsheviks, he was arrested for the third time and deported from Russia.[108] He taught sociology at the University of Prague and in 1923 he was offered a position at the Universities of Illinois and Wisconsin and came to the United States. He became a U.S. citizen in 1930 and was appointed chairman of the philosophy department at Harvard University that same year, a position he kept until his retirement in 1955. Many students who were planning a political career, including Dean Rusk and John

F. Kennedy, took sociology with the world's eminent authority on the subject.

At one point in our conversation we discussed the problem of the cult of personality. At the time I was convinced that it was an accident and would not be repeated; the principle of collective leadership adopted by the 20th Congress of the Communist Party and the development of Socialist democracy would keep it that way. Sorokin sighed.

"You are making a mistake, young man. You have not lived long enough, not seen enough and, apparently, not read enough. My life has been longer and more eventful than yours and I have studied this problem, which has existed from the earliest times. The cult of personality derives from a very human tendency, the thirst for power, and develops best within a limited democracy. Power lust is the most dangerous defect, more than drunkenness or debauchery; it inhibits creativity and leads to the extermination of millions of people. The cult of personality is the cause of immeasurable harm to society." Then he added:

"Unless a true democracy appears and its leaders are elected directly by the people, succeeding each other according to the law, the cult of personality will not disappear from Russia."

I had to admit that he was correct in his assessment with every new leader. We discussed those who emigrated from Russia and were a gift to the United States, a whole list of extraordinary talent: Vladimir Zworykin, who invented television; Igor Sikorsky, the father of the helicopter; Georgy Kistiakowski and Georgy Gamow, who worked on the atomic bomb; Vladimir Ipatyev, who invented high octane gasoline; Stepan Timoshenko, author of the theory of stability of moving matter; and all the great artists and thinkers. Sorokin felt that most Russian émigrés were homesick: if Soviet representatives contacted them and invited them to the USSR, many would accept and some might even return to live in their homeland. When we parted I was convinced that he was still a Russian patriot who wanted to see his country of origin prosper and above all didn't wish to see the United States and the USSR on opposite sides of an armed conflict. Once I left I thought of proposing that he write a scientific study on the Soviet Union.

I returned to Boston only in July 1963 and called the Sorokins ahead of time; they were both happy to see me again. The professor and I went upstairs to his office, and we talked about modern music while a stereo was playing a string quartet.

"All these twists and rocks are noise fit for dogs. I like classical music. I don't have a favorite composer; I just follow the mood I'm in. Right now I'm under the influence of Mozart."

I looked at the books on his shelf: Hegel, Marx, and Lenin, the historians Soloviov and Kliuchevsky, some recent scientific works.

"Do you read our journals?" I asked him.

"I only read interesting things and articles that attack either me or my ideas! Here."

Sorokin opened a Soviet journal at a spot he had marked.

"Here is an author who has copied verbatim one of my papers from twenty years ago and is trying to pass them for his own work!"

He took one of his books in English and asked me to compare the two texts, which were identical. He tracked everything that was happening in the Soviet Union. At the 22nd Party Congress, Khrushchev had said that before 1970 the USSR would have higher per capita production than the United States and that by 1980 Communism would be a reality. Sorokin felt that such bragging was unworthy of a world leader.

"Even the building of Socialism is not for tomorrow. You will ask me for when? It depends on many things and on your leaders. You know how it is: each priest makes a different parish and if he steals from the charity box, drinks and chases women, his parishioners will behave the same way. And then you are wrong to want to do everything yourselves. One must not be fearful of borrowing what can be useful from the West."

Sorokin went on as he shifted in his armchair.

"What I don't understand is why your theoreticians don't stop criticizing my theory of convergence; it's merely my version of your policy of peaceful coexistence."

I answered that the theory of convergence perpetuates capitalism, which doesn't coincide with Communist doctrine.

"How silly! Nothing is forever; no one can tell what will happen to the Soviet Union and to the United States in one hundred years or even in fifty years! Convergence is already taking place: capitalism is becoming more socially minded; Socialism is worrying about productivity, and cost effectiveness. They will converge; it's inevitable."

Elena Petrovna came in.

"Aren't you two tired of arguing? Dinner is served."

A bottle of red wine from Soviet Georgia was on the table.

"You can have your red wine!" said the professor in a mock rough tone of voice. "The men will have vodka!" Turning to me, he said, "Ordinarily I don't drink, but I'd rather have vodka if I do drink, just as I did in Russia in my youth."

The conversation drifted to more worldly topics with his wife but soon we were discussing politics once again.

"It's true that the Soviet Union enjoys a lot of prestige right now, but don't expect too much from the fact that so many former colonies have followed the Socialist model. Why run after short-lived political victories in Africa or Asia? Economic assistance weakens the USSR. If you want to build Socialism it must grow like a bloc of granite and shine from every facet like a giant diamond."

I felt it was the right moment to place my secret idea.

"Pitirim Alexandrovich, when will you finally write a book on your own country?"

I didn't expect his reaction; he got up walked around the table and stopped in front of me.

"You won't let me!" he cried waving his arms. "I've been wanting to for years! But I can't do it using what others are describing. I must go to Russia myself!"

His wife got up as well.

"Calm down, Pitirim," she said, taking him back to his chair. "Sit down and have some tea. You must not get so excited."

Seeing that he was calm, I asked:

"What do you need to write this book?"

"I have to be invited by the Academy of Sciences or Leningrad University. Every civilized country has invited me to lecture except my own! I want to go to Russia and see everything for myself, but I will not go back as a tourist!"

He told me how many times he tried to contact his Soviet colleagues; he had often sent his books and books by American authors to the Academy of Sciences and to Leningrad University without ever getting an acknowledgement! What could I answer? I said diplomatically that I hoped relations between the two countries would improve enough to allow him to fulfill his dream. Back in Washington I wrote a report on my conversation with the sociologist and sent it on to Moscow. I recommended that he be invited to the USSR with his wife. Shortly after in August, I took advantage of a vacation in Moscow to discuss this problem with the head of intelligence. General Sakharovsky told me that the international department of the Party's Central Committee was considering my proposal and that Boris Ponomarev, its chairman, was hesitating. How could they invite a scientist whose sociological theories had been systematically attacked in over twenty doctoral dissertations in the USSR? I knew that there was another reason: there were even more dissertations that had been plagiarized from the scientist's work.[109] Before returning to Washington I found out that a decision had been reached: be patient one or two more years. I was about to call Sorokin to inform him, but he preceded me because he was in Washington with his wife and I immediately invited them to lunch.

We had just given the waiter our order when he asked for a taxi: they had to be at the airport two hours later and they both looked somber and downcast. I told them that their wish to visit the USSR had met with a positive reaction but that the trip would have to wait until 1964. Sorokin wasn't paying too much attention. Then he talked about their vacation in Canada, but he was jumping from one subject to another and I could see that something was bothering him and asked if he was having problems.

"You're right, I do have a problem."

He told me that morning he had met one of his former students who held an important position at the State Department. He asked how U.S. authorities would view his wish to travel to the Soviet Union. The diplomat had tried to talk him out of the idea: Moscow would certainly use the trip for propaganda purposes. Sorokin answered that he only intended to speak of the need for a better understanding between the two countries, but his former student still tried to dissuade him.

"It's the second time they tell me not to go to Russia," said Sorokin bitterly. "The first time was last year, when the President of the Congress for World Peace invited me to the meeting that was to take place in Moscow. I didn't go because Dean Rusk asked me officially to turn down the invitation and now I can see that I must forget about what I was hoping for until things change."

We parted on that sad note but remained on good terms. The Sorokins asked me to visit them when I was in Boston. I was unable to because in March 1964 I returned to Moscow and four years later Pitirim Sorokin died without ever setting foot in his homeland.

I pursued my career in the KGB. I participated in other secret operations that are still too recent to be told. I trained intelligence officers at the Andropov Institute and gave a course of my own. At the same time I have done research on intelligence matters and defended a doctoral dissertation in history. I retired permanently from the KGB in 1986.

I have witnessed events that changed the world. The cold war has ended, the Socialist bloc doesn't exist anymore, the Soviet Union has exploded and Communist ideology is banished. In spite of it all, I don't have the feeling that I worked for the wrong cause. As Pitirim Sorokin predicted, both social systems converged—or tend to converge, my country still being neither fish nor fowl—but Russia had to travel part of the way.

Notes

1. Throwing hand grenades was part of the tests of the GTO (Russian initials for "Loans for work and defense") for young people. This was considered a sport at the time.
2. NKVD—People's Commissariat for the Interior, at the time State Security—the secret services—belonged to that ministry.
3. Nickname for Alexander.
4. Pavel Sudoplatov (1907-1996) had been one of the major NKVD operatives from the 1930s to the 1950s. He was the organizer of the assassination of Leon Trotsky in 1940, the coordinator of partisans during the Second World War, and one of the main officials involved in atomic espionage at the end of the 1940s. In 1953, after the execution of Lavrenti Beria, the head of Stalin's secret services and his immediate superior for over twenty years, Sudoplatov was sentenced to fifteen years in a penitentiary as a "Stalinist executioner."
5. INO—*Inostrannyi Otdel*, or Foreign Department, the official name of Soviet intelligence from its founding on December 20, 1920 to July 10, 1934, when it became part of the NKVD. The insiders were still using the original name for many years.
6. Covert agent operating without official cover and using false foreign documents.
7. Akhmerov was also known as Bill Greinke, Michael Green, and Michael Adamec and was the main INO agent in the United States. He married Earl Browder's niece, Helen Lowry. Browder was Secretary of the Communist Party of the United States. Akhmerov returned to the U.S. in the 1940s to head an important illegal intelligence network. See Christopher Andrew and Oleg Gordievsky, *KGB The Inside Story*, Harper Collins (New York), 1990, pp. 287-292.
8. Lenin, who didn't like Molotov, had nicknamed him "iron ass." Yet, the little party bureaucrat would later be Lenin's successor as head of the Soviet government. Vyacheslav Molotov became President of the Council of People's Commissars from 1930 to May 1941 when Stalin, who was running the country as General Secretary of the Party, replaced him. Molotov was Vice-Prime Minister from 1941 to 1957 and Foreign Minister from 1939 to 1949 and from 1953 to 1956.
9. Border troops were under NKVD control.
10. The Office of Strategic Services, which preceded the CIA.
11. Besides the fact that Soviet economic data was notoriously falsified, the author forgets that the United States was fighting on two fronts and making their main effort in the Pacific. The USSR waited until August 8, 1945,

two days after Hiroshima, to declare war on Japan, which allowed the creation of a Communist North Korea. Germany and Italy declared war on the United States on December 11, 1941, three days after Pearl Harbor.

12. This Soviet view of America's attitude during the Second World War was repeated for decades. Allied operations in the Pacific, South East Asia, North Africa, the Middle East, Sicily, and Italy were not mentioned, nor were the war in the Atlantic and the bombing of Germany. The Soviets were also careful to omit that France and Great Britain had been fighting Fascism since 1939 while the USSR was supplying Germany and occupying parts of Eastern Europe, thanks to the Nazi-Soviet Non-Aggression Pact.

13. Lithuania, independent since 1920, had been annexed by the Soviet Union in 1940 following the Nazi-Soviet Pact. The same applies to Latvia and Estonia, the other two Baltic States.

14. Amtorg was a Soviet-American company founded in 1924, through which all import and export operations between the two countries were channeled.

15. See *Veterany vneshnei razvedki Rossii* (Veterans of Russian foreign intelligence), Publications of the Foreign Intelligence Services, Moscow, 1995, pp. 108-110.

16. Nickname for Pyotr.

17. Nikolai Yezhov, People's Commissar for Internal Affairs of the USSR, the NKVD, directed the bloodiest purges from 1936 to December 1938; he was given that nickname because of his diminutive height.

18. This Russian word describes the rules of security that are required for covert operations.

19. Passing of secret material from hand-to-hand (documents, film, money, etc.) between an agent and his case officer, both of whom walk past each other without apparent acknowledgment.

20. Pejorative nickname, meaning "hairpiece," that Russians give to Ukrainians.

21. Pejorative nickname Ukrainians give to Russians: katsap means "goat," and describes the thin goatee many Russians grow.

22. GRU—*Glavnoye Razvedovatelnoye Upravlenye*—or Chief Directorate for Intelligence in the Red Army High Command, renamed Soviet Army in 1946.

23. SVR—*Sluzhba Vneshnei Razvedki*—is the Foreign Intelligence Service of Russia since it replaced the KGB's PGU department in 1991. The SVR is pursuing the policy of the KGB in denying that the Rosenbergs and Morton Sobell were Soviet agents.

24. Soviet intelligence jargon indicating sensitive information from a source that doesn't suspect it is giving state secrets to a foreign power.

25. Special hiding places where an agent leaves documents to be picked up by the case officer to be microfilmed and returned to the same location. The agent will pick them up at a specific time. The system allows both parties to avoid dangerous physical contact.

26. Lavrenti Pavlovich Beria was the all-powerful head of Soviet intelligence services from 1938 to 1953. He also supervised the Soviet atomic development project and was executed shortly after Stalin's death in 1953.

27. Fictitious code name; this agent's identity was never discovered.

28. The Walther PPK was a pistol widely used in the 1940s.

29. The predecessor of the National Security Agency, the NSA, which is involved in decrypting foreign coded messages and ensuring the security of U.S. electronic communications.

30. See Chapter 14.

31. Cut out—an intermediary who allows the case officer to communicate without having physical contact with a source.

32. His real name was Theodore Hall. See Joseph Albright and Marcia Kunstel. *Bombshell, the Secret Story of America's Unknown Atomic Spy Conspiracy,* Random House, NY 1997; Vladimir Chikov and Gary Kern *Comment Staline a volé la bombe atomique aux américains. Dossier KGB No. 13676,* Robert Laffont, Paris 1996.

33. Nikita Khrushchev in his memoirs, *Khrushchev Remembers* (Little Brown, Boston 1970), mentioned the Rosenberg case. Pavel Sudoplatov also mentions it in his book *Special Tasks,* Little Brown, Boston 1995.

34. *Za okeanom i na ostrovye,* DEM, Moscow, 1994.

35. Nickname for Alexander.

36. See Walter and Miriam Schneir, *Invitation to an Inquest. A New look at the Rosenberg-Sobell Case,* Penguin Books, Baltimore 1973.

37. After being sentenced for espionage, Francis Gary Powers was exchanged for Colonel Rudolf Ivanovich Abel, a famous illegal KGB agent operating in New York.

38. Joel Barr died in Moscow in August 1998 at the age of 83.

39. See Schneir, page 293.

40. See Chapter 5.

41. *Ministerstvo Gosudarstvennoy Bezopasnosti,* Ministry of State Security. The People's Commissariats changed their names into ministries in 1946. The NKGB—which included the intelligence services, counterespionage and the political police—had been separated from the NKVD (Internal Affairs) in 1941.

42. Not to be confused with Vasily Zarubin, my former boss in New York.

43. It would later become the Union of Friendship Associations and Cultural Relations Overseas (SSOD).

44. In his Fulton speech, Winston Churchill, who was no longer Prime Minister, said that an "Iron Curtain" had descended upon Europe.

45. Andrei Vyshinsky, as Chief Prosecutor, had managed the infamous Stalinist show trials of the 1930s. In 1940 he became Deputy Foreign Minister before replacing Molotov as Foreign Minister in 1949. After Stalin's death he was Soviet representative to the United Nations.

46. Hidden microphones in intelligence jargon.

47. It is strange that, despite U.S. nuclear superiority, most of the crises of those years, such as the blockade of West Berlin in 1948, originated with the Soviets. Soviet archives confirm that Stalin waited to have nuclear weapons before he encouraged North Korea's leader Kim Il-Sung to launch an invasion of South Korea in 1950 with Mao Zedong's support, which almost started the Third World War.

48. Fuchs means "fox" in German.

49. R.C. Williams, *Klaus Fuchs Atom Spy,* Harvard University Press, London, 1987, p.184

50. Kuczynsky was the representative of the underground KPD in Great Britain and in constant contact with Walter Ulbricht who, with Wilhelm Pieck, headed the Party in exile in Moscow.

51. Under the pseudonym "Ruth Werner," she wrote her memoirs, *Sonya's Report*, Chatto & Windus, London, 1991, and died in Berlin in the summer of 2000, at the age of 93. A real virtuoso of covert action, she served the GRU under various identities in China, Poland, Switzerland and ended her career as a colonel in the Soviet Army.

52. See Chapter 10.

53. The word means "goose" and is used in Russian in such expressions as "he's a funny kind of guy" or "it slides over him like water over goose feathers." I still wonder whether that code name was given to Harry Gold as a coincidence or if the signs that would justify these derogatory names later on were already apparent in his attitude and character.

54. In May 1944, their pseudonyms were changed: Guss became "Arno" and Rest became "Charles."

55. Fuchs may have attended the dinner in Los Alamos where General Groves made a statement that shocked Joseph Rotblat, another physicist, so much: "You understand, naturally, that the reason for being of the project is to subdue the Russians." See Vladimir Chikov and Gary Kern pages 176 and 177.

56. He was to become an important personality in the GDR, Chairman of Political Economy at Berlin University and Director of the Economic Institute of the Academy of Sciences.

57. After the defection of one of the members of Sandor Rado's Swiss network, Ursula Kuczynsky was kept dormant. She was living at Great Rollright near Oxford under the name of Ruth Beurton. Even though MI5 had a thick file on her, she was never questioned. Following the Fuchs trial in

1950 she was allowed to leave the United Kingdom and moved to the GDR.

58. Despite its one thousand or so members, including Thomas and Heinrich Mann, it was a cover for the underground KPD.

59. PGU—*Pervoye Glavnoye Upravlenye*—First Chief Directorate of the MGB, later to become the KGB, in charge of foreign intelligence. That name would remain operational until the dissolution of the KGB in 1991 and the creation of the SVR as an independent Foreign Intelligence Service, after the disappearance of the USSR.

60. Vasily Tyorkin is the hero of a popular poem by Alexander Tvardovsky: a smart soldier, always in good spirits, he knows how to see the positive side of things.

61. This is the date that appears in the archives but I have my doubts. Out of superstition I don't think I would have made an appointment on such a day. For the same reason I never would see my agents on Mondays, when in my day ships would never sail. The dates I preferred were the 2nd, 9th, and 27th. I also wanted to make sure the calendar of meetings was easy to remember. If it was too complicated it could discourage my informers. If my memory serves me, I would meet Fuchs on Saturdays, which allowed him to leave Harwell easily enough. That's why I think our final meeting was on Saturday, April 2, 1949.

62. This episode will be discussed further in Chapter 31.

63. Procedure to be followed in case of loss of contact for an extended period: a meeting place is agreed to in advance where the case officer and the agent will appear every month, on the same day and at the same time.

64. Quoted in Robert C. Williams, *Klaus Fuchs Atom Spy,* Harvard University Press, London, 1987, page 85. Another Manhattan Project scientist, British physicist Alan Nunn May, had collaborated with the USSR. Betrayed by Igor Guzenko, he was sentenced to ten years in prison in 1946. When he was freed in 1952, he stated that he had "acted correctly" and had no regrets.

65. This statement, along with Harry Gold's confession to the FBI of July 10, 1950, can be found in R.C. Williams, pp. 196-220.

66. SED, East German Socialist Unity Party, the equivalent of the Communist Parties in other Eastern European countries.

67. It is possible, but I cannot be certain, that our service was able to obtain the complete confession of Klaus Fuchs through one of our British agents—this would then prove that the version given to the FBI and published in 1980 did not contain operational information.

68. She died on January 5, 1999 at the age of 92.

69. Under FBI questioning and in the course of his trial, Harry Gold said the opposite. According to him he not only worked for Soviet intelli-

gence without compensation but also had to dip into his own pocket to pay for his trips.

70. Yet the plan was a good one and future events would prove it. Once he returned to Great Britain, Fuchs traveled extensively within Europe from 1946 to 1949. To avoid suspicion when he wasn't traveling for work-related purposes, he made sure he traveled with his friend and supervisor Herbert Skinner or with Henry Arnold, who was also his friend and the head of security at Harwell. Nevertheless Moscow felt the situation was critical: time was marching on and contact with the best source of atomic secrets hadn't yet been reestablished. Since the physicist had taken the initiative, the Center decided to handle him from London.

71. See Chapter 25.

72. Random House, NY, 1968, page 3.

73. See W. and M. Schneir, page 115.

74. I found most of what follows in the Gold file, which is still classified, at the PGU.

75. See Chapter 16.

76. David Greenglass named Joe Barr as a member of the Rosenberg network.

77. See Chapter 16.

78. An international pacifist organization under Soviet control that included people from different countries.

79. Most sources agree that the prosecution wanted to use the charges brought against Ethel as "leverage" to get Julius to confess.

80. The atomic bomb wasn't part of Morton Sobell's espionage activities, a fact that saved his life.

81. Western sources do not indicate direct contact between Judge Irving Kaufman and President Harry Truman. The judge, according to these sources, consulted some of his colleagues and asked prosecutor Irving Saypol to discuss the matter with the Justice Department. Any contact with the executive branch would have gone through the prosecutor.

82. See his interview in *Moskovskiye Novosti* of November 8, 1986, page 14.

83. It concerned the Venona transcripts that were still classified at the time.

84. To address someone politely it is customary to use the first name and patronymic, meaning the father's name followed by "ovich" for men or "ovna" for women: Ivan Petrovich (son of Piotr), Anna Petrovna (daughter of Piotr). These forms of address are the equivalent in English of Mr. or Mrs. so and so.

85. Abbreviation of "Upravlayushchaya mashina" or directing machine. In Russian the word "um" means "mind."

86. Means "Green City" in Russian.

87. We have borrowed some facts and conclusions from the issues of March 16, 17 and 18, 1997 containing statements made to Nikolai Dolgopolov.

88. The KGB, *Komitet Gosudarstvennoy Bezopasnosty* Committee for State Security, was to keep its name until the failed putsch of August 1991.
89. Beria's execution and Nikita Khrushchev's rise to power took place shortly after Stalin's death in 1953. The 20th Congress took place in 1956. As for Molotov and the other members of the "anti-party" group who were seeking to replace Khrushchev, they were all removed from their positions in 1957.
90. Bodyguards of the President of the United States and the U.S. Administration.
91. Leonid Brezhnev would use the same reasons when, in 1977, he combined the functions of Party leader and President of the Presidium of the Supreme Soviet. Yuri Andropov, Konstantin Chernenko, and Mikhail Gorbachev would do the same.
92. A synonym for intelligence in the colorful vocabulary of popular Russians.
93. He was actually in charge of cooperation with the secret services of other Socialist countries.
94. By comparison the bomb dropped on Hiroshima was less than 20 kilotons.
95. It was operating until JFK's assassination in November 1963.
96. Agents who spontaneously propose their services as opposed to those who are recruited.
97. "Elint" also means "electronic intelligence" as opposed to "Humint" or "human intelligence," the traditional form of intelligence gathering through human sources.
98. This is an alias; the agent is still operational.
99. See Chapter 9.
100. Robert F. Kennedy, *Thirteen Days, A Memoir of the Cuban Missile Crisis*, W.W. Norton, NY 1969.
101. DEFCON—Defense Condition—has 5 numbered alert stages from 1 to 5, number 1 being the highest level.
102. General Hideki Tojo was Prime Minister of Japan from 1941 to 1944 and ordered the attack on Pearl Harbor. He was executed for war crimes in 1948.
103. *Mezhdunarodnaya Zhizn* magazine, November 1992, page 55.
104. The "military-industrial complex" conspiracy theory that is dear to filmmaker Oliver Stone is just one the many theories regarding the Dallas assassination.
105. The Komis are a Finno-Ugric ethnic group living in northern European Russia.
106. Cheka—Extraordinary Commission for the Struggle Against Counter-Revolution and Sabotage (1917-1922), the precursor of the KGB.

107.   Anatoly Lunacharsky (1875-1933) was People's Commissar for Education at the time and helped intellectuals. Lev Karakhan (1889-1937) was Deputy People's Commissar for Foreign Affairs.

108.   On the famous "philosopher's ship," which took the major figures of the Russian intelligentsia into exile on Lenin's orders.

109.   Since Sorokin's books were banned, only members of the nomenklatura and their friends could read them. Many didn't hesitate to plagiarize the famous sociologists' works in the knowledge they would not be prosecuted.

Index

Acknowledgments

The publisher of Enigma Books wishes to thank the following:

Jean-Pierre Bertrand and Sylvie Guéric-Bertrand of Editions du Rocher de Monaco; Pierre Lorrain, author and publicist; Robert Stewart, Editorial Director of Enigma Books; John Earl Haynes of the Library of Congress; Sam Roberts of *The New York Times*; Gary Kern; Roland Winter; Todd Bleudeau; Jay Wynshaw; Asya Kunik; Charles P. Miller; Catherine Dop; and Woody Batzer.

Photographs

The sources for the photographs used in this book are the following: *author's collection, SVR, FBI, Sovfoto, Corbis, Wide World, and other private collections.*